CLARENDON A

General Editors

J. L. ACKRILL AND LINDSAY JUDSON

Also published in this series

Categories and *De Interpretatione*
J. L. ACKRILL

De Anima Books II and III
D. W. HAMLYN
New impression with supplementary material by Christopher Shields

De Generatione et Corruptione
C. J. F. WILLIAMS

De Partibus Animalium I and *De Generatione Animalium* I
D. M. BALME
New impression with supplementary material by Allan Gotthelf

Eudemian Ethics Books I, II, and VIII
MICHAEL WOODS
Second edition

Metaphysics Books Γ, Δ, and E
CHRISTOPHER KIRWAN
Second edition

Metaphysics Books M and N
JULIA ANNAS

Physics Books I and II
WILLIAM CHARLTON
New impression with supplementary material

Physics Books III and IV
EDWARD HUSSEY
New impression with supplementary material

Posterior Analytics
JONATHAN BARNES
Second edition

Other volumes are in preparation

ARISTOTLE

Metaphysics

BOOKS *Z* AND *H*

Translated
with a Commentary
by

DAVID BOSTOCK

CLARENDON PRESS · OXFORD

This book has been printed digitally and produced in a standard specification in order to ensure its continuing availability

OXFORD
UNIVERSITY PRESS

Great Clarendon Street, Oxford OX2 6DP

Oxford University Press is a department of the University of Oxford.
It furthers the University's objective of excellence in research, scholarship,
and education by publishing worldwide in

Oxford New York

Auckland Bangkok Buenos Aires Cape Town Chennai
Dar es Salaam Delhi Hong Kong Istanbul Karachi Kolkata
Kuala Lumpur Madrid Melbourne Mexico City Mumbai Nairobi
São Paulo Shanghai Taipei Tokyo Toronto

Oxford is a registered trade mark of Oxford University Press
in the UK and in certain other countries

Published in the United States
by Oxford University Press Inc., New York

Reprinted 2003

ISBN 0-19-823947-5

ACKNOWLEDGEMENT

It is now some thirty years since I first took part in serious discussions of these central books of Aristotle's *Metaphysics*. From that time onwards I have learnt so much on the topic, from so many friends and colleagues, that now I cannot say what in this book should really be credited to others. So I here offer a general 'thank you' to all who have helped me to form my views. But I must make special mention of the two editors of this series. John Ackrill is responsible for many improvements to the translation, and both he and Lindsay Judson have done their best to save the Commentary from its more obvious faults. I am very grateful for the time and effort that they have given to this task. I have gained much from it, and so will everyone who reads the book.

DAVID BOSTOCK

Merton College, Oxford
January 1993

CONTENTS

INTRODUCTION

The books of Aristotle's *Metaphysics* are standardly referred to by their Greek numbering, i.e. by the letters of the Greek alphabet, because of the anomaly that after book I there comes a short book labelled, as it were, not 'I' but 'i'. Translators have often called this 'book II', so that the following book is then called 'book III' in English, though in the Greek it is unambiguously entitled '*B*', which means 'II'. This creates confusion, which is avoided by using the Greek numbering throughout. For those unfamiliar with the Greek alphabet, here are the relevant letters, and the confusing 'translation' of them into Roman numerals, which is found in translations of the *Metaphysics* but nowhere else:

A	*α*	*B*	*Γ*	*Δ*	*E*	*Z*	*H*	*Θ*	*I*	*K*	*Λ*	*M*	*N*
I	II	III	IV	V	VI	VII	VIII	IX	X	XI	XII	XIII	XIV

This peculiar numbering reflects a more important fact about the books themselves, namely that they do not form a single and well-organized whole, and one should not think of them as intended for publication as they stand. Aristotle clearly did mean there to be a connected series of books which we could call his 'Metaphysics', but the writings that have come down to us under that title contain much that would have been either abandoned or re-formed in a final version. For example, book *α*, which is an alternative introduction, would surely have found no place at all; book *A* would certainly have been pruned of the material in the first half of chapter 9 (which reappears almost unchanged in chapters 4–5 of book *M*), and probably of other material in consequence. There is no book of the existing *Metaphysics* of which one can confidently say that it would have figured in the final version just as it now is. This is especially true of the two books *Z* and *H* (pronounced 'zēta' and 'ēta') that are the subject of this volume. The two books go closely together, and between them they contain Aristotle's main treatment of the topic of perceptible substance. But one should think of them as being, in effect, a collection of papers on this topic, probably of different dates, and perhaps for that reason not entirely consistent with one another. There are plenty of signs that Aristotle intended there to be one continuous discussion of perceptible substance that would evolve from these papers, but there are also some quite clear signs that the evolution is not completed.

This naturally makes some difference to the interpretation of these texts. If we make the assumption that in every passage we are dealing with a finished work, then there will be a strong pressure to find ingenious lines of interpretation which minimize conflict between one passage and another, and such conflicts as remain must simply be put down to inadvertence on Aristotle's part. But if we assume instead that what we are dealing with is more like a record of 'work in progress', then it will not be too surprising if we find Aristotle pursuing a line of thought in one place that does not harmonize very well with a different line pursued elsewhere, or if what has been clearly asserted at one stage seems later to be superseded by a fresh approach. In my opinion (which will be argued in the Commentary), the conflicts that are to be found in our text demand something more like the second assumption. But even so there are many serious problems of interpretation that remain.

On such problems I hope that the translation is neutral enough not to prejudge any important issue, but no translation can preserve a complete neutrality. This is partly because the Greek of Aristotle's day was in some ways not well adapted to the thoughts that he was trying to express. A conspicuous example is that it lacks the indefinite article 'a', and consequently its definite article 'the' has a wider range of uses than the English 'the'. A translator is constantly faced with the question whether Aristotle's thought is better represented in English by using 'a' or 'the' or no article at all, and on several occasions one choice rather than another would suggest a somewhat different message. But a more important feature of Aristotle's own usage is that many of his sentences are quite remarkably elliptical, and the ellipsis must somehow be filled if an English rendering is to be comprehensible. For the most part I have simply supplied the filling that seems to me to be required, leaving no sign to the reader of what I have done. But on a few occasions, where the right supplement is genuinely in doubt, I have indicated this by the use of square brackets, and discussed the point in the Commentary.

There are other ways in which a translation of Aristotle will inevitably embody an interpretation. The original text will have contained no punctuation of any kind, and (we presume) not even any division into books and chapters. Such divisions are due to early editors, and the manuscripts that have come down to us have already imposed their own punctuation. By and large one does not wish to quarrel with this. But any translator will feel free to choose between a comma and a full stop, and to decide where to begin a new paragraph, since these features of a modern text do not represent anything in the original. I have taken this freedom yet further, by not attempting to reproduce Aristotle's own sentence-structure. On the contrary, he will often write long and convoluted sentences which are not too easy to follow, whereas in my translation I have broken these up into several shorter and simpler sentences. So I do not claim that this translation is especially literal, but I do hope that it is much more comprehensible than any truly literal translation could possibly be.

Despite my attempt to smooth out Aristotle's elliptical and often convoluted style, there are some barbarisms of his that I have felt must be retained. These are more or less literal renderings of expressions of his own invention, corresponding to nothing in ordinary Greek, and evidently used by him as technical terms. The principal instances are:

(i)	*to ti ēn hekastōi einai*	what being is for a thing
	to ti ēn einai	a what-being-is
(ii)	*to ti estin hekaston*	what a thing is
	to ti esti	a what-it-is
(iii)	*tode ti*	a this
(iv)	*to hupokeimenon*	an underlying thing

In the first two cases (both conventionally rendered as 'essence'), something like Aristotle's own phrase must be retained in order to indicate the way that it connects with other related locutions of his. In the third case, the meaning that Aristotle attaches to the expression is wholly obscure. In the fourth case (conventionally rendered as 'subject' or 'substrate'), Aristotle's word harbours an ambiguity that no simple English word will reproduce. For my treatment of other technical terms of Aristotle's, see the Glossary at the end of the book.

The two most important modern editions of the text of Aristotle's *Metaphysics* are those by Sir David Ross (*Aristotle's Metaphysics, Text and Commentary*, Oxford University Press, 1924, corrected 1953) and by Werner Jaeger (Oxford Classical Texts, 1957). Comparing these two, I have come to the conclusion that for books *Z* and *H* Ross's text is preferable overall, and that is therefore the text translated here. For book *Z*, but not book *H*, we also have a recent text by Michael Frede and Gunther Patzig (*Aristoteles, Metaphysik Z*, Munich, 1988), which I have taken into account. There are several places where I would have preferred not Ross's reading but another, but the question is really of no importance, and here I have stuck to Ross without comment. Where I do depart from his text the divergence is footnoted, and the footnotes also signal the agreement or disagreement of Jaeger and of Frede & Patzig. The footnote references are to the three texts cited here, with 'Frede & Patzig' abbreviated to 'F & P'.

The numbers in the margin of the translation give the page number, the column (^{a} or ^{b}), and the line number of Bekker's edition of the Greek text (Berlin, 1831), which is always used when referring to Aristotle's writings. The line numbers mark the breaks between sentences, so that the sentence that begins in the line marked *n* in this translation corresponds to a passage that begins in the nth line of the Greek text.

All those who study Aristotle owe an incalculable debt to Ross's edition of the *Metaphysics* (and to his editions of other works of Aristotle), and to his excellent translation of the *Metaphysics* in the series The Oxford Translation of Aristotle, which he edited. In preparing my own translation I have frequently made use of this. Otherwise I think I have profited most from the translation of books *ZHΘI* of the *Metaphysics* by Montgomery Furth (Hackett Publishing Company, Indianapolis, 1985), subtitled 'A Translation from Greek into Eek'.

TRANSLATION

BOOK ZETA

CHAPTER 1

1028
We speak in many ways of what is, i.e. the ways distinguished a10
earlier in our work on the several ways in which things are
spoken of. On the one hand it signifies what a thing is and a this,
and on the other of what quality or quantity or any of the other
things thus predicated. But while what is is spoken of in these
various ways, it is clear that the primary thing that is is what a
thing is, which signifies [its?] substance. (For when we say of a15
what quality a thing is we say that it is good or bad, but not that
it is three feet long or a man; but when we say what it is we do
not say that it is pale or hot or three feet long, but that it is a man
or a god.) And other things are said to be by being either
quantities of what is in this way, or qualities, or affections, or
something else of this sort.

That is why one might indeed be puzzled as to whether walking a20
and being healthy and sitting down do signify each of these things
as beings, and similarly for any other thing of this sort; for none
of them either is of a nature to be in its own right, or is capable
of being separated from substance. If anything, it is the walking a24
thing and the sitting thing and the healthy thing that is. These
things more clearly are, because there is some determinate thing
that underlies them—namely the substance and the particular—
which is apparent in such a predication; for one cannot speak of a
good thing or a sitting thing apart from this. Evidently, then, it is a29
on account of this, i.e. substance, that each of those is also; and
therefore what primarily is—not is something but is without
qualification—will be substance.

Now we speak of what is primary in many ways, but substance a31
is primary in every way—in definition, in knowledge, and in
time. For none of the other predicates is separable but this alone;
and in definition too this is primary, since in the definition of
everything there must occur the definition of a substance; and a36
we think we know a thing most fully when we know what the
man is, or the fire, rather than when we know its quality or
quantity or place—since it is also true that each of these them-

selves we know only when we know what that quantity or quality is.

b2 Indeed the question that was, is, and always will be asked, and always will cause difficulty—that is, the question 'What is being?'—*is* the question 'What is substance?' This it is that some say is one, some more than one; that some say is finite in number,
b6 some infinite. And so we too must consider chiefly and primarily and (so to say) exclusively what it is that is in this way.

CHAPTER 2

b8 Substance seems most clearly to belong to bodies. That is why we say that animals and plants and their parts are substances, also natural bodies such as fire and water and earth and anything of this kind, together with all their parts and all things composed from some or all of them, such as the universe and its parts—sun,
b13 moon, and stars. But we shall have to consider whether these are the only substances, or whether there are others; or whether only some of these are substances, or some of these and some others; or whether none of these are substances but only certain others.

b16 Some think that the limits of a body—i.e. surfaces, lines, points, and units—are substances, and more so than the body and the solid. Again, some think that there are none but perceptible substances, while others think that there are more substances that are not perceptible, and that they are substances
b19 to a higher degree, because eternal. Thus Plato held that the forms and the objects of mathematics were two kinds of substance, perceptible bodies being the third kind. Speusippus held that there were even more kinds of substance, starting from the one, and that there were different principles for each kind—one for
b24 numbers, another for magnitudes, another for the soul. He spun out the substances in this way. Some, however, say that forms and numbers have the same nature, but that there are other substances following upon these—lines and planes and eventually the substance of the universe and the perceptible things.

b27 We must consider which of these views is right and which wrong; and what substances there are; and whether there are or are not any substances beside those that are perceptible, and in what way these latter are; and whether there is or is not any separable substance, apart from the perceptible ones, and if so why and in what way. First, however, we must say in outline what substance is.

CHAPTER 3

Of the several ways in which substance is spoken of, there are at b33
any rate four which are the most important: the substance of a thing seems to be (*a*) what being is for that thing, and (*b*) its universal and (*c*) its genus, and fourthly (*d*) what underlies.

What underlies is that of which other things are predicated b36
while it itself is predicated of nothing further, and we must
therefore distinguish this first. For what most seems to be substance 1029
is what primarily underlies. In one way matter is said to be a a2
thing of this sort, in another way shape, and in a third the compound of these. (By matter I mean, for instance, the bronze; by shape, the figure of its perceptible form; and by the compound of these, the statue as a whole.) So if form is prior to matter, and more a being than matter is, it will also be prior to the compound
of both, for the same reason. This has explained in outline what a7
substance is, namely that it is that of which other things are predicated while it itself is predicated of no underlying thing. But it is not enough to say only this. It is itself unclear, and moreover on this view matter becomes a substance.

If matter is not a substance, it is hard to see what else could be; a10
for when all else is taken off, nothing apparent remains. For while other things are attributes, products, and capacities of bodies, length, breadth, and depth are quantities and not substances (for a quantity is not a substance). Rather, the substance
is that primary thing to which these quantities belong. And yet a16
when length, breadth, and depth are taken away, we see nothing remaining unless there be something which is determined by these. So on this view it must appear that matter alone is substance.
(By matter I mean what is not said to be in its own right any a20
thing, or any quantity, or anything else by which being is determined. For there is something of which each of these is predicated, and which itself has a being different from that of each of the predicates—for while others are predicated of substance, substance is predicated of matter—and so the last thing will not be in its own right either a something, or of any quantity, or anything else at all. Nor will it be in its own right the negations of these, for they too will belong to it only coincidentally.)

If, then, we proceed on this basis, matter turns out to be a a26

substance. But this is impossible, for separability and thisness seem to belong chiefly to substance; and for this reason the form and the compound would seem to be substance more than matter
a30 is. However, the substance compounded from both, I mean from both matter and shape, we may disregard; for it is posterior and clear. Matter also is in a way evident. But we must investigate the third kind of substance, i.e. form, for this is the most puzzling.

a33 It is agreed that some perceptible things are substances, so we will search for it among these first, for it is of advantage to
b3 proceed by stages towards that which is more intelligible. All learning comes about in this way, proceeding by means of what is by nature less intelligible towards what is more intelligible. Just as the task in conduct is to start from what is good for us and to make what is entirely good also good for us, so here the task is to start from what is more intelligible to us and to make what is by
b8 nature intelligible also intelligible to us. What is intelligible to a man at first will often be only slightly intelligible, and will have in it little or nothing of reality. Nevertheless we must start from what we do understand, though we only understand it badly, and try (as I have said) to advance by means of this to an understanding of what is entirely intelligible.

CHAPTER 4

b1 At the beginning we distinguished the several ways in which substance is determined, and one of these appeared to be what being is for a thing. Accordingly we must now investigate this. And first let us make some logical remarks about it.

b13 The what-being-is of each thing is what the thing is said to be in its own right. Thus being for you is not the same as being for an artistic thing, since you are not in your own right artistic. So what being is for you is what you are in your own right. But not everything that a thing is in its own right is what being is for it.
b16 For in one way pallor applies to a surface in its own right, but it is not this sort of 'in its own right' that is relevant here, since being for a pale thing is not the same as being for a surface. Nor again is it what being is for the compound, i.e. the pale surface, for
b19 here it itself is being added on. Wherever, then, the formula expressing a thing does not include that thing itself, this is the formula of what being is for the thing. (Thus, if being for a pale surface is the same as being for a smooth surface, then being for a pale thing and being for a smooth thing will be one and the same.)

Now there are compounds from the other categories too, since b22
there is something which underlies each of them—e.g. quality, quantity, time, place, and motion. We must see, therefore, whether there is a formula of what being is for each of these compounds, and whether these too have a what-being-is, e.g. a pale man. Suppose 'cloak' to be a name for this; what, then, is
being for a cloak? It may be said that this is still not one of the b28
things we speak of in its own right. But we may reply that a thing may fail to be expressed in its own right in two ways, one of them
being from an addition and the other not. In the one case what is b31
being defined is expressed by being added to something else, as for instance would happen if in defining being for a pale thing one were to give the formula of a pale man; in the other case the reverse occurs, as for instance would happen if 'cloak' were to signify a pale man but someone defined it as a pale thing. (In fact
a pale man is a pale thing, but what being is for a pale man is not **1030**
being for a pale thing.) But is being for a cloak a what-being-is at a2
all? Presumably not, for a what-being-is is just what is a this,[1] but when one thing is predicated of another we do not have just what is some this. Thus a pale man is not just what is some this, if indeed thisness belongs only to substances.

Therefore there will be a what-being-is only for those things a6
whose formula is a definition. And we do not have a definition wherever we have a name and a formula which mean the same, otherwise every formula would be a definition (for there will be a name to any formula whatever, so that even the *Iliad* would be a
definition). Rather, we have a definition only where it is of a10
something primary, i.e. of something which is expressed without predicating one thing of another. A what-being-is, then, will belong to nothing but what is a form of a genus. Only these will have a what-being-is, for these seem not to be expressed by predicating one thing of another by way of participation or as an
attribute, or coincidentally. Everything else as well will have a a14
formula stating what it signifies, e.g. stating—if it be a name—that this belongs to that; or instead of a simple formula it may have a more exact one. But it will not have a definition or a what-being-is.

Or is it that we speak of definition too in many ways, like what a17
a thing is? For indeed what a thing is signifies in one way the substance of the thing and the this, and in another way each of the predicates—predicates of quantity, quality, and so on. For just as 'is' belongs to everything, but not in the same way—to

[1] I read *ὅπερ γὰρ <τόδε> τι* in a3, as Jaeger.

one in a primary way and after that to the others—so also what a
thing is belongs without qualification to a substance, but in a way
a23 to other things as well. For indeed we can ask what a quality is,
and so a quality is something with a what-it-is, but not without
qualification. Just as in the case of what is not, some people make
the logical point that what is not is—not that it is without qualification, but that it is a thing that is not—so too with a quality.

a27 Now one should ascertain how to express oneself on each
point, but not more than how things are. And so, since the
present point is quite clear, what-being-is too will belong in a
similar way primarily and without qualification to substance, and
after that to other things, as does what-it-is. In these cases it will
not be what-being-is without qualification, but what being is for a
a32 quality or for a quantity. For it must either be by an equivocation
that we say these things are, or by adding something and subtracting something, as when the unknown is said to be known [sc.
known to be unknown]. And in fact we speak neither equivocally
nor univocally, but, as with 'medical', with reference to one and
the same thing—not meaning one and the same thing, nor yet
equivocally. For a patient and an operation and an instrument
are all called medical, not equivocally, nor in virtue of one thing,
b3 but with reference to one thing. But it makes no difference which
way one prefers to put the point. At least this is clear, that
the primary and unqualified sort of definition and what-being-is
applies to substances. Admittedly it will similarly apply to other
things as well, but not primarily.

b7 It does not follow from this that there will be a definition of
anything which means the same as some formula. The formula
must be of a certain sort, in fact a formula of a unity—and
not a unity by being continuous like the *Iliad*, or what is bound
together, but a unity in one of the ways in which we speak of
b10 unity. These correspond to the ways in which we speak of being,
and being signifies in one way a this, in another of what quantity,
in another of what quality. So there will be a formula and a
definition even of a pale man, but not in the same way as there is
of pallor or of a substance.

CHAPTER 5

b14 If one says that a formula constructed from an addition is not a
definition, it will be a problem to say which of the things that
are coupled and not simple have definitions. For these must be

explained from an addition. I mean that we have, for instance, a nose and concavity, and snubness which is expressed by coupling the two, as the one in the other. And it is not coincidentally that b18
concavity or snubness is an attribute of the nose, but in its own right; it is not in the way that pallor is an attribute of Callias, or of man—i.e. because Callias, who is in fact a man, is pale—but rather in the way that masculinity is an attribute of an animal, and equality of a quantity, and generally in the way in which anything may be said to belong to a thing in its own right. These b23
are those attributes in which there occurs either the name or the formula of that of which they are attributes, and it is not possible to explain such things without reference to this. Thus pallor may be explained without reference to men, but femininity cannot be explained without reference to animals. Hence either none of these things have a what-being-is and a definition, or—if they do—it must be in another way, as we have said.

There is a further difficulty concerning these things. If a snub b28
nose is the same as a concave nose, then snubness will be the same as concavity. But if we reject this, on the ground that it is not possible to express snubness without reference to that of which it is an attribute in its own right (snubness being concavity in a nose), then it must either be impossible to speak of a snub nose, or the same thing will be said twice, i.e. concave nose nose. (For a snub nose will be a concave nose nose.) And therefore it b34
would be absurd if such things had a what-being-is. If they did, there would be an infinite regress; for in snub nose nose there will be yet a further nose. 1031

It is evident, then, that only a substance will have a definition. a1
For if the other predicates also had definitions, they would have to be constructed from an addition, as is the definition of oddness,[2] which involves reference to numbers, and of femininity, which involves reference to animals. (By 'constructed from an addition' I mean those definitions in which—as in these cases—it turns out that the same thing is said twice.) If this is true, then a5
things that are coupled, e.g. odd number, will not have a definition either, though this is not noticed because our formulae are not precisely expressed. But if they do have a definition, then either it must be in another way, or definition and what being is must be spoken of in many ways, as was said before. Thus on the one alternative there will not be a definition or what-being-is of anything but substances, and on the other there will.

[2] I read *οἷον τοῦ* [*ποιοῦ καὶ*] *περιττοῦ* in a3, as Jaeger and F & P.

a11 It is now clear that a definition is the formula stating what being is for a thing, and that what-being-is belongs either to substances alone, or to substances chiefly and primarily and without qualification.

CHAPTER 6

a15 We must consider whether a thing is the same as, or different from, what being is for it. This is relevant to our investigation of substance, for a thing is thought to be no different from its own substance, and what being is for a thing is said to be the substance of the thing.

a19 In the case of things which are spoken of coincidentally, the two would seem to be different. Thus a pale man seems to be different from what being is for a pale man. If they were the same, then being for a man and being for a pale man would also be the same; for a man and a pale man are the same, as they say, and so therefore would be being for a man and being for a pale
a24 man. Or is there no necessity that things that are coincidentally [the same] should be the same? For it is not in this same way [namely, coincidentally] that the extreme terms become the same. However, it would perhaps seem to follow that the extreme terms would be the same coincidentally,[3] e.g. being for a pale thing and being for an artistic thing. But this seems not to be the case.

a28 In the case of things which are spoken of in their own right, is it necessary that they should be the same as what being is for them?—for instance, if there are substances such that no other substance is their substance, and no other nature is prior to them,
a31 as some say holds of the Forms? For if goodness-itself and what being is for a good thing are different, and similarly animality-itself and what being is for an animal, being-itself and what being is for a being, then there will be other substance and natures and Forms over and above those mentioned, and these other sub-
b3 stances will be prior, if what-being-is is substance. And if on the one hand the two are divorced from one another, then the form will be unknowable, and the what-being-is will not be a being. (By 'divorced from one another' I mean that being for a good thing does not belong to goodness-itself, and being good does not
b6 belong to being for a good thing.) For first, we know a thing when we know what being is for it; and second, the case of

[3] I read *ταὐτὰ [τὰ] κατὰ συμβεβηκός* in a27, as F & P.

goodness is no different from any other, so that if being for a good thing is not good, nor will being for a being be a being, nor being for a unity be a unity. But all cases of what-being-is are or are not equally, so that if not even being for a being is a being, nor will being for anything else be a being. Further, that to which being for a good thing does not belong is not good.

It must be, then, that goodness and being for a good thing are b11
the same, and similarly beauty and being for a beautiful thing. Generally, the same result will hold for anything that is primary and spoken of in its own right, and not in virtue of something else. Indeed this is itself sufficient even if they are not forms—or, perhaps one should say, even if they are forms. (At the same b15
time it is also clear that if the Forms are as some people say, what underlies will not be substance. For the Forms must certainly be substances, but not because something underlies them; if that were so, they would exist only by being participated in.)

These are some arguments to show that what being is for a b18
thing and the thing itself are one and the same, and not coincidentally. Another is that to know a thing just is to know what being is for it, so that even by exhibition of cases it must follow that the two are one and the same.

In the case of what is spoken of coincidentally, e.g. the artistic b22
or the pale, it is not true to say that the thing itself is the same as what being is for it, because of its double meaning. For that to which the coincidental attribute attaches and the attribute itself are both pale. In one way, then, the thing and what being is for it are the same, and in another way they are not. For what being is for a pale thing is not the same as the man or the pale man, but it is the same as the attribute.

An absurdity in the view that the two are not the same would b28
be evident if one merely gave a name to each what-being-is. For beside the original what-being-is there will also be another; for instance, there will be another what-being-is for what being is for a horse. But even as things are, what prevents some things from b31
being at once the same as their what-being-is, if what-being-is is substance? Moreover, it is not only that they are one and the same, but their formulae are also the same, as is evident just from what has been said. For it is not coincidentally that unity **1032**
and being for a unity are one. Further, if they are different, we a2
shall have an infinite regress. On the one hand we have the what-being-is of unity, and on the other hand unity, and so the same argument can be repeated for these too.

It is clear, then, that in the case of things that are primary and a4

spoken of in their own right, the thing and what being is for it are one and the same. Sophistical objections to this position are evidently solved in the same way as is the problem of whether
a9 Socrates and being for Socrates are the same. There is no difference in the points one would use to raise one's questions, or in those one would use to answer them successfully. It has been explained, then, in what way a thing is and in what way it is not the same as what being is for it.

CHAPTER 7

a12 Things which come to be do so either by nature or by skill or spontaneously; and they all come to be *something*, and come *from something*, and are brought to be *by something*. (When I say that they come to be *something*, I mean the 'something' to apply in any category; they may come to be a this, or to be somehow quantified or qualified or placed.)

a15 Natural generation applies to those things whose generation is due to nature. What they come *from* is what we call matter; what they are brought into being *by* is something which exists naturally; and what they come to *be* is a man or a plant or something else of
a20 this sort, which we most strongly affirm to be substances. (It is in fact common to all things that are generated, whether by nature or by skill, that they have matter. For each of them is capable both of being and of not being, and this is due to the matter in
a22 them.) But, to speak more generally, that from which they come is a nature, and so too is that in accordance with which they come to be—since what comes into being has a nature, e.g. a plant or an animal—and so also is that by which they are brought into being. For this is the nature that is spoken of in accordance with form, the nature of the same form, but in another; for man begets man. This, then, is how things come to be by nature.

a26 The other cases of generation are called productions, and all productions are effected either by skill or by some capacity or by thought. (Some of them may also be effected by spontaneity and by chance, in much the same way as may also happen in natural generations; there too the same things may sometimes be generated from seed and sometimes without it. But we will consider
a32 this later.) The things produced by skill are those whose form is in the soul of the producer (and by the form I mean what being is for each thing and its primary substance). For in fact opposites have in a way the same form, since the substance of a privation is

the opposite substance. Thus health is the substance of disease,
since disease is the absence of health, and health is the formula in
the soul and the knowledge of it. Health is produced when one b6
thinks thus: since health is of such a kind, if the subject is to be
healthy he must have so-and-so (e.g. an equable state of body),
and if he is to have that he must have warmth, and so on. One
continues to think in this way until the case is finally reduced to
something which one can oneself produce, and then from this
point on the process towards health is called production. Thus it b11
turns out that in a way health is produced from health, and a
house from a house, the one that has matter from the one that
does not; for the skill of curing is the form of health, and the skill
of building is the form of a house; and by the substance without
matter I mean the what-being-is.

Of the processes of generation, then, the one [part] is called b15
thinking, namely that which proceeds from the originating form,
and the other is called production, namely that which follows
upon the completion of the thinking. The intermediate steps
come about in the same way. For example, one thinks: if the
subject is to be healthy, he must be made equable. But what is
being equable? It is such-and-such; and that will come about if he
is warmed. But what is being warmed? It is such-and-such; and
this he is capable of becoming. That is already in one's power.
Thus the thing that produces health, and is what the process b21
towards health begins from, is the form in the soul—that is, if it
is brought about by skill. But if it is spontaneous, it begins from
what would on other occasions be the beginning of production for
one who produces by skill, e.g. in the case of health it might
begin from the warming (which he would produce by rubbing).

Consequently the warmth in the body either is a part of health b26
or is followed, more or less directly, by something which is a part
of health; and this last thing which produces health, and produces
it in this way, is a part of health[4] (and similarly of a house—e.g.
the stones—or of anything else). So, as is said, a thing could not
come into being if nothing were present beforehand. Indeed it is b31
clear that some part must necessarily be present, since the matter
of a thing is a part of it (as it is present in it), and it is this which
comes to be the thing. But must there also be present a part that 1033
occurs in the formula? Well, in fact we speak in both ways when
we say what a bronzen circle is, saying that the matter is bronze

[4] I read (after EJΓ) *τοῦτο δ' ἔσχατον τὸ ποιοῦν, καί τὸ οὕτως <ποιοῦν>, μέρος ἐστι τῆς ὑγιείας*. Given this punctuation, perhaps *ποιοῦν* need be supplied only in thought.

and the form is such-and-such a shape (that being the genus
under which it first falls). So a bronzen circle has its matter in its
formula.

a5 Some things, when they have come into being from a certain
matter, are said to be, not *that* from which they came, but rather
of that, or *that-en*; for instance, a statue is not said to be [some]
stone, but rather *of* stone. By contrast, a healthy man is not said
a8 to be that from which he came to be healthy. The reason is that
although what he comes from is in fact what underlies (which we
call the matter) no less than the privation—for not only does the
sick become healthy but so also does the man—nevertheless we
most often say that he comes from the privation. We say that he
came to be healthy from being sick, rather than from being a
a12 man. (That is why the healthy is not said to be sick, but is said to
be a man, and the man is said to be healthy.) On the other hand,
where the privation is nameless and obscure, as for instance the
privation of any shape in bronze, or of a house in bricks and
timber, the thing appears to come *from* these materials as in the
a16 previous case the healthy came *from* the sick. This explains why,
as we do not in that case say that the thing is what it has come
from, nor do we say in these cases that the statue is [some] wood,
but with a change of ending that it is wood*en* (or of wood), and
not that it is [some] bronze but that it is bronzen (or of bronze),
not that it is [some] stone but that it is of stone; and similarly we
do not say that the house is bricks, but that it is of bricks.
a19 (Though indeed, if we considered the question closely, we would
not say without qualification that a statue comes into being *from*
wood, or a house *from* bricks, since what a thing comes into
being from should change, and not remain.) That is the reason
for this way of speaking.

CHAPTER 8

a24 Now whatever comes into being is brought into being by something, by which I mean what the generation starts from; and
it comes from something, by which let us understand not the
privation but the matter (for we have already discussed our way
of speaking on this point); and it comes to be something, namely
a28 a sphere, circle, or whatever. But just as the bronze which
underlies is not itself produced, so neither is the sphere (except
coincidentally, in that the bronzen sphere is produced, and the
bronzen sphere is a sphere). For to make a this is to make a this

from what in general underlies. I mean that to make the bronze a32
round is not to make the round or the sphere, but something
else: it is to produce this form in some other thing. For if one
makes anything, it will be made *from* something else, as we have
premissed. Thus one makes a bronzen sphere, but in such a way b1
that from this, which is bronze, one makes this, which is a
sphere. If then this itself were also made, it would evidently have
to be in the same way, and the productions would go on to
infinity.

It is clear, then, that neither does the form—or whatever one b5
should call the shape of a perceptible thing—itself come into
being or undergo generation, nor does the what-being-is. (Rather,
this is what comes to be in something else, either by nature or by
skill or by some capacity.) There being a bronzen sphere is
something that is produced; it is produced from bronze and
sphere, by introducing the form into the bronze so that the result
is a bronzen sphere. But if being for a sphere in general could be b11
generated, it would have to be one thing made from another,
since what comes into being must always be divisible into two
components, one matter and the other form. Since, then, a
sphere is a shape equidistant everywhere from its centre, one part
of this would have to be that in which the other part is produced,
the whole thing being what is generated (as in the case of the
bronzen sphere). It is thus clear from what has been said that the b16
one part which is expressed as form or substance does not come
into being, but the combined whole that is called after it does
come into being, and that in every created thing there is matter—
it consists of this part and of that.

Is there, then, any sphere apart from these particulars, or any b19
house apart from the bricks? No, for nothing else could ever have
come into being if it were in this way a this.[5] Rather, it signifies
such a kind of thing, and is not a determinate this; from a this
one makes and creates such a kind of thing, and when it is
created it is a this of such a kind. The complete this, e.g. Callias b24
or Socrates, is like this bronzen sphere here, while man and
animal are like bronzen sphere in general.

It is clear, then, that the causality of the forms—if there are b26
such forms apart from the particulars as some maintain—is of no
use so far as concerns coming into being and substances; they
need not be substances in their own right just on this account. In b29

[5] In b21–2, Ab has *ἀλλὰ τὸ τοιόνδε*, EJΓ have *ἄλλο τι τοιόνδε* (or *ἀλλ᾽ ὅτι τοιόνδε*). I read *ἄλλο τι, ἀλλὰ τοιόνδε* (or alternatively *ἄλλο τι, τοιόνδε* <*δὲ*>).

some cases, indeed, it is perfectly clear that the creator is such as the created (not the same, or numerically one, but one in form), for man begets man, and the same is true of natural things generally—unless what is generated is contrary to nature, as
b33 when a horse begets a mule. (Yet even here the case is similar; for the nearest genus of horse and ass, what is common to both,
1034 is nameless, but it would presumably be both, like the mule.)
a2 Consequently we evidently do not need to set up forms as paradigms, for this is the area where we should most have looked for paradigms, since these substances are most assuredly substances. But here it is sufficient that the begetter is the producer, and is
a5 the cause of the form being in the matter. The complete result, such a kind of form in this flesh and bones, is Callias or Socrates. What makes them different is their matter, which is different; but they are the same in form, since their form is indivisible.

CHAPTER 9

a9 One might be puzzled over why it is that some things, such as health, are produced both by skill and spontaneously, while others, such as a house, are not. The reason is that the matter which begins the process of producing and generating something made by skill, and in which some part of the object is already present, is in some cases capable of being set in motion by itself,
a14 and in others not. And in the former case, it can sometimes initiate motion in the required way, and sometimes not. For many things can be set in motion by themselves, but not in a particular manner, e.g. so as to dance. Things which have matter of this sort, then, such as stones (or fire), cannot be set to move in the relevant way except by the agency of another, though they
a18 can move in other ways. That is why some things cannot exist without someone who possesses the relevant skill, while others can. It is because they are set in motion by things which do not possess the skill, and which can themselves be set in motion by others which do not possess the skill [, or from a part].[6]

a21 It is also clear from what has been said that in a way everything comes to be either from something of the same name, just as in the case of natural generation[7] (for example a house comes from a house, in so far as it is brought into being by thought; for the skill is its form), or from a part of itself,[7] or from something

[6] It is probable that ἢ ἐκ μέρους should be deleted from a21, as Ross suggests.

[7] I delete ἢ ἐκ μέρους ὁμωνύμου from a23 and retain ἢ ἐκ μέρους at a24.

which possesses a part of it—that is, unless it comes to be
coincidentally. For the primary cause of the production, the cause a25
in its own right, is a part of what is produced. Thus the warmth in
the movement produced warmth in the body, and this either is
health, or is a part of health, or is followed by health itself or
some part of health. That is why it is said to produce the health, a29
namely because it produces that on which health follows and to
which it belongs. (Thus, as in reasoning, substance is the start of
everything; for reasoning proceeds from the what-it-is, and so too
does generation.)

Things which are formed by nature are in a similar situation. In a33
the one case they are produced from seed, and this resembles the
products of skill, for the seed has the form potentially, and the
parent from whom it came has the same name in a way (except
where there is an abnormality—that is why a mule is not generated from a mule—but we must not expect everything to be like
a human coming from a human; indeed a woman comes from a
man). And the case of spontaneous generation is similar, for it b4
occurs where the matter is capable of being set in motion both by
itself and by the seed, in just the same way. Where this is not so,
the things cannot come into being in any other way than from
their own kind.

The proof that a form does not come into being applies not b7
only to substance but equally to whatever is primary, such as a
quality, a quantity, or any other predicate. Just as the bronzen b10
sphere is generated, though the bronze and the sphere are not—
and just as, if the bronze itself is generated, its matter and its
form must be present beforehand—so also in the case of what a
thing is, and of its quality, quantity, and the other predicates
similarly. It is not the quality that comes into being, but wood of
that quality, not the quantity, but wood or an animal of that
quantity. But we can see from this discussion that it is peculiar to b16
substances that for their generation there must already be present
another substance, actually existing, which produces them: if an
animal is to be produced, an animal must already be present. But
if a thing comes to be somehow qualified or quantified, this is not
necessary: the quality or quantity need only pre-exist potentially.

CHAPTER 10

Now a definition is a formula, and every formula has parts; b20
further, as the formula stands to the object, so do the parts of the

formula stand to the parts of the object; so we are already involved in the problem of whether the formula of the parts
b24 should or should not occur in the formula of the whole. In some cases it is clear that the formula of the parts is present in that of the whole, while in others it is clear that it is not. Thus the formula of the circle does not contain that of its segments, whereas the formula of a syllable does contain that of its letters. Yet a circle is divided into its segments just as a syllable is
b28 divided into its letters. Further, if the parts are prior to the whole, then since an acute angle is part of a right angle, and since a finger is part of a man, the acute angle will be prior to the right angle, and the finger to the man. But the reverse appears to be the case; for the former are defined in terms of the latter, and are posterior also in independent existence.

b32 Perhaps it is that a part is spoken of in many ways. (In one sense a part is a measure of quantity, but this may be disregarded. We need consider only the parts of which a substance is com-
1035 pounded.) If, then, there is both matter, and form, and the compound of these, and if each of them is a substance, then there is one way in which even the matter of a thing could be called a part of it, but in another way only the constituents of the formula
a4 of its form are parts of the thing. For instance, flesh is not a part of concavity, for it is the matter in which concavity occurs; but it is a part of snubness. Similarly, the bronze is a part of the statue as a combined whole, but not of the statue spoken of as form. (Each thing may be said to be the form, or the thing *qua* having the form; but it cannot be said to be in its own right the material part.)

a9 It is for this reason that the formula of a circle does not contain that of its segments, while the formula of a syllable does contain that of its letters. For the letters are parts of the formula of the form, and are not the matter of the syllable, whereas the two segments are parts only in the way that the matter on which the form supervenes is a part—though they are closer to the form
a14 than is the bronze that has circularity in it. (Yet in a sense the formula of the syllable will not contain *all* its letters; for example it will not contain these on the paper here or those in the air. For they too are parts of the syllable only by being its perceptible
a17 matter.) Indeed, even though a line is destroyed when it is divided into halves, or a man when he is dispersed into bones, sinews, and flesh, it does not follow from this that they are composed of these parts as parts of their substance. These are rather their matter, and are parts of the combined whole, but not parts of the

form or of what has the formula. Hence they do not occur in the formula.

So the formula of some things does contain the formula of such a22
parts, but the formula of others must not, if it is not to be a formula of the thing taken together with matter. For this reason some things have as their principles the things they are made from and destroyed into, while others do not. Things which are a25
both matter and form taken together, e.g. a snub nose or a bronze circle, have matter as a part and are destroyed into their parts; however, things which are not taken together with matter but are without matter, things whose formula is a formula of the form alone, are not destroyed at all—or at any rate not in this way. So material constituents are both parts and principles of the former, but they are neither parts nor principles of the latter. And this is why a clay statue is destroyed into clay, or a bronze a31
sphere into bronze, or Callias into flesh and bones, and even a circle into its segments. (For there is one sort of circle which is taken together with matter, since the same word is used both for what is without qualification a circle and for particular circles, there being no name peculiar to the particulars.)

The truth has now indeed been stated, but let us take up the b3
question again and state it yet more clearly. The parts of the formula, into which the formula is divided, are prior—some of them or all of them. And the formula of an acute angle is not b6
part of the formula of a right angle, but conversely, since an acute angle is defined as an angle that is less than a right angle; the same is true of the circle and the semicircle, since a semicircle is defined by reference to a circle; and similarly a finger is defined by reference to its whole, as such-and-such a part of a man. Thus b11
those parts that are material, and into which the thing is divided as into its matter, are posterior; but those that are parts of the formula, and of the substance given by the formula, are prior—some or all of them.

Now in animals the soul—which is the substance of any living b14
thing—is the substance given by the formula, i.e. the form and what being is for bodies of this sort. (At least, no part of such a body can be properly defined without reference to its function, which it could not have in the absence of perception.) Accordingly b18
the parts of the soul—some or all of them—will be prior to the animal as a combined whole, and similarly in particular cases, whereas the body and its parts will be posterior to this substance; and it is not this substance but the combined whole that is divided into these bodily parts as into its matter. So the bodily parts are

prior to the combined whole in one way, but in another way they
b23 are not; for they cannot exist separated from it. (It is not a finger
in any and every state that is the finger of an animal; a dead
finger is a finger only in name.) But some bodily parts are neither
prior nor posterior to the combined whole, namely the most
important parts and that part that is the first thing that the
formula and the substance is in—whether this be the heart or the
brain, for it makes no difference here.

b27 But man and horse and things thus universally predicated of
particulars are not substances but combined wholes of a certain
kind, namely combined of such-and-such a formula in such-
and-such a matter taken as universal; but in the particular case
Socrates is compounded immediately from the ultimate matter,
and similarly for the others.

b31 Now there are parts of the form, i.e. the what-being-is, and of
the whole combined from form and matter, and of the matter
itself. But only the parts of the form are parts of the formula, and
1036 this is a formula of what is universal. (For being for a circle is the
same as the circle, and being for a soul the same as the soul.) But
there is no definition of what is already a combined whole, for
instance of this circle, or of any other perceptible or intelligible
particular. (By intelligible circles I mean, e.g., the mathematical
circles; and by perceptible circles I mean those made of bronze or
a5 wood.) These are known by thought or by perception, and when
they depart from this actuality it is not clear whether they still
exist. They are always known and spoken of by means of the
a9 universal formula, for matter is in itself unknowable. (Some
matter is perceptible, e.g. bronze, wood, and all changeable
matter, while some is intelligible, namely that which is present in
perceptible things but not *qua* perceptible. Such is the matter of
the objects of mathematics.)

a12 We have now explained how matters stand concerning the
whole and its parts, and their priority and posteriority. And if
anyone asks whether the right angle, the circle, and the animal
are prior or posterior to the parts of which they are composed
and into which they are divided, we must reply that the question
a16 cannot be answered simply. If the animal or living thing is also
the soul, or if each thing is its soul, and if the circle is being
for a circle, and the right angle being for a right angle (i.e. the
substance of a right angle), then we should say that the thing
taken in one way is posterior to certain of its parts, namely to the
parts in its formula and to the parts of the particular right angle.
a20 This is so if we take the thing as combined with matter, either the

bronze right angle or that formed by particular lines. But the thing which is without matter, though it is still posterior to the parts in its formula, is prior to the parts in the particulars. So the answer is not simple. If on the other hand the soul and the animal are not the same, then again we must say that some parts are and some are not prior, as has been explained.

CHAPTER 11

It is also natural to raise the problem: what sort of parts are parts a26
of the form, and what sort of parts are parts of the whole taken together? If we are not clear on this, we shall not be able to define each thing; for definition is of the form and the universal, so unless it is clearly seen which sort of parts are parts as matter, and which not, the formula of the object will not be clearly seen either.

Now where a thing can be seen to supervene on others that a31
differ in form amongst themselves—as for instance a circle may be found in bronze or in stone or in wood—in such cases it seems clear that the bronze and the stone can be no part of the substance of the circle, since it may be found separated from them. And where a thing is never seen separated from certain
materials, the case may be no different. Thus even if all the b1
circles we ever saw were bronze, none the less the bronze would still be no part of the form; though it would be difficult to abstract it in thought. For example, the form of a man is found always in flesh and bone and parts of this sort. Are these, then, also parts of the form and the formula? Or are they rather matter, which we cannot separate from the form because it never supervenes on anything else?

Since this situation seems possible, but it is not clear how often b7
it occurs, some have raised the problem even in the case of the circle and the triangle. They suggest that the circle and the triangle should not be defined by reference to lines and continuity, but that these too should rather be understood in the same way as the flesh and bones of a man, or the bronze or wood of a statue. Thus they reduce everything to numbers, and say that the
formula of a line is simply the formula of two. (And of those who b13
believe in the Forms, some say that duality *is* the line-itself, while others say that duality is the form of the line, maintaining that although in some cases the form and that of which it is the form are the same—e.g. duality and the form of duality are the

b17 same—yet this does not hold in the case of the line.) But from this position it follows both that there will be one form of many things which evidently differ in form (a consequence which also confronted the Pythagoreans), and that it will be possible to set up just one form-itself for everything, the rest not being forms. But this has the result that everything is one.

b21 Now we have explained that the question of definitions contains some difficulty, and why this is so. It is therefore useless to reduce everything [to form?] in this way, and to eliminate the matter. For some things presumably are one thing in another,
b24 or certain things in a certain state. And the comparison which Socrates the Younger used to draw between an animal and a circle is not sound; it misleads one into supposing that there might be a man without his parts, as there can be a circle without
b28 bronze. But the cases are not the same. For an animal is a perceptible object, and cannot be defined without reference to change, nor therefore without reference to the state of its parts. (For it is not a hand in any and every state that is a part of a man, but only a living hand, which can fulfil its function. A hand which is not living is not a part of a man.)

b32 (Yet the objects of mathematics are not perceptible objects. So why is it that here the formulae of the parts (e.g. the semicircles) are not parts of the formula of the whole (e.g. the circle)? But in fact there is no difference, for some non-perceptible objects also
1037 have matter. Indeed everything has matter of some sort unless it is not a this but a what-being-is and a form itself in its own right. Accordingly the semicircles will not be parts of the universal circle, but they will be parts of particular circles, as was said before. For matter may be either perceptible or intelligible.)

a5 It is also clear that the soul is the primary substance, that the body is matter, and that man or animal is the compound of the two taken universally. But Socrates and Coriscus are twofold if Socrates is also his soul (since some regard him as a soul, and some as a combined whole), whereas if Socrates is simply this soul and that body, then the particulars correspond to the universal.

a10 We must consider later whether there is any other matter than that of such substances as these, and whether we should enquire after some other kind of substance, for instance numbers or the like. (It is in fact for this purpose that we are attempting to analyse perceptible substances too, since the study of perceptible substances is in a way the task of physics or second philosophy.
a16 For a physicist must have knowledge not only of the matter of

things but also, and more especially, of the substance given
by the formula.) We must also consider later in what way the
elements of the formula are parts of the definition, and what it is
that makes the definition a unitary formula. (Evidently the object
is a unity; but what makes it so? For clearly it has parts.)

We have now said, universally and for all cases, what a what- a21
being-is is, and in what way it is itself in its own right. And we
have said why it is that the formula of what being is for a thing
sometimes contains the parts of the thing being defined, and
sometimes does not. For we have said that the formula of the
substance will not contain those parts that are parts as matter—
which indeed are not parts of *that* substance at all, but of the
substance which is the combined whole. And this latter in a way a26
does not have a formula, though in another way it does; when
taken together with its matter it does not have a formula, since
matter is indeterminate, but it does have a formula in accordance
with its primary substance. (Thus a man has the formula of the
soul.) For the substance is the form that is in the thing, and the
whole combined from this and the matter is called a substance
from this. Thus concavity is the substance, and from this and the a30
nose there is formed a snub nose and snubness [for in these the
nose will occur twice].[8] But the substance which is the combined
whole, e.g. a snub nose or Callias, has matter in it as well. We a33
have also said that what being is for a thing is the same as the
thing itself in certain cases, as when the thing is a primary substance. Thus crookedness and being for crookedness will be the
same, if crookedness is primary. (By 'primary' I mean what is not
expressed by one thing being in another which underlies it as
matter.) But things that are as matter, or as taken together with b4
matter, are not the same as what being is for them; indeed they
are not even one coincidentally,[9] in the way that Socrates and the
artistic thing may, for instance, be the same coincidentally.

CHAPTER 12

Now let us first discuss what was omitted in the treatment of b8
definition in the *Analytics*, for the problem there raised is of
some relevance to the discussion of substance. The problem I
mean is why a thing whose formula we call a definition is a unity.

[8] Ross deletes the words *δὶς γὰρ ἐν τούτοις ὑπάρξει ἡ ῥίς*.

[9] I read *οὐδὲ κατὰ συμβεβηκὸς ἕν* in b5, as F & P.

For instance, let the definition of man be 'two-footed animal'; then why is it that this is a unity and not a plurality consisting of 'two-footed' and 'animal'?

b14 Now 'man' and 'pale' form a unity when what underlies, namely the man, has pallor as an attribute, so that the one belongs to the other (for in that case they become one thing, and we have a pale man); but otherwise they are a plurality. In the present case, however, the one does not participate in the other. For the genus seems not to participate in its differentiae, since if it did the same thing would participate in opposites at the same time (for the differentiae which differentiate the genus are op-
b21 posites). And even if it does participate in its differentiae, the same problem would again arise when there is more than one differentia, e.g. 'going on foot' and 'two-footed' and 'wingless'. For why are *these* a unity rather than a plurality? It is not because they are all present in the one genus, for at that rate *all* the
b24 differentiae would form a unity. But the things in a definition must in fact be a unity, for a definition is a unitary formula, and must be a formula of some unitary thing since it is a formula of a substance; for a substance is a unitary thing, and signifies a this, as we say.

b27 We must first consider definitions obtained by division, for here the definition consists only of what is called the primary genus and the differentiae, the other genera being the primary genus taken with certain differentiae. For example, the primary genus may be 'animal', the next 'two-footed animal', and after that 'wingless two-footed animal'; and similarly if yet more con-
1038 stituents are involved. But in general it makes no difference whether the constituents are many or few, nor therefore whether they are few or just two; of these two one will be the genus and one the differentia, as 'animal' and 'two-footed' are genus and
a5 differentia respectively in 'two-footed animal'. If, then, the genus does not, in an unqualified sense, exist apart from the forms of the genus, or if it exists but only as matter—for voiced sound is the genus and the matter, and the differentiae make from this the forms of sound and the phonetic elements—then it is clear that the definition is just the formula composed of the differentiae.

a9 But moreover, the division should be continued by taking the differentia of the differentia. Thus footed is a differentia of animal, and the differentia of footed animal must again be a differentia of it *qua* footed. So one should not properly say that of footed things some are winged and some wingless—though we do say this, because of our inability—but only that some are

cloven-footed and some uncloven. For these are differentiae of a14
foot, since cloven-footedness is a kind of footedness. And one should try to proceed always in this way until one reaches things with no further differentiae. Then there will be as many forms of foot as there are differentiae, and the footed animals will be equal in number to the differentiae.

Now, if this is so, it is clear that the last differentia will be the a18
substance and the definition of the object (assuming, of course, that a definition should not be needlessly repetitious. Though this does happen; when one speaks of a two-footed footed animal one has simply said 'an animal with feet, with two feet'. And if this in turn is divided by a proper division, the same thing will be said
once more, in fact as many times as there are differentiae.) So a25
then, if each new differentia is a differentia of the previous one, there will be one last differentia and it will be the form and the substance. But if one divides coincidentally—for instance if one divides footed things into those that are pale and those that are dark—then the differentiae will be as many as there are cuts. Thus it is clear that the definition is the formula composed of the differentiae, and—if it is correctly performed—just of the last
differentia. This would become evident if one were to change the a30
order of such definitions, saying for instance that a man is an animal with two feet with feet. For 'with feet' is superfluous once 'with two feet' has been said. But there is no order in the substance, for how in this case could one understand one thing being earlier and another later?

So much, then, as a first statement of the nature of those a34
definitions that are obtained by division.

CHAPTER 13

Let us return to the subject of our investigation, which is sub- b1
stance. Now what underlies is said to be substance, and what being is, and the compound of these; but it is also said that what is universal is substance. Two of these we have already treated of. We have treated of what being is and what underlies, explaining that it underlies in two ways, either by being a this (as the animal
underlies its attributes), or as matter underlies the actuality. But b6
some people think that it is the universal which is in the highest degree a cause, and that the universal is a principle. So we must come to consider this too.

It seems impossible for any of the things predicated universally b8

to be a substance. For, first, the substance of a thing is peculiar to it,[10] in that it does not belong to anything else; but a universal is common to many things, for it is precisely what is of a nature to
b12 belong to many things that is called a universal. Of which of these things, then, will this be the substance? It must be the substance of all or of none, and it cannot be the substance of all. But if it is the substance of one, then all the others will be this one; for things whose substance is one have the same what-being-is, and are themselves one. Further, a substance is said to be what is not predicated of any underlying thing; but a universal is always predicated of some underlying thing.

b16 But perhaps the universal, though it cannot be substance in the same way as the what-being-is, can yet be present in the what-
b18 being-is, as for instance animal is present in man and horse? In that case there is evidently some formula of it. And [or: But] it makes no difference even if it is not [or: there is not] a formula of everything in the substance, for this will none the less be the substance of something, as man is the substance of the man in whom it is present. So the same thing will happen again. For it (e.g. animal) will be the substance of that thing in which it is
b23 present as something peculiar to it. Further, it is absurd and impossible that a this and a substance, if it is composed of anything, should be composed not of substances, nor of a this, but of a quality. For then the quality, which is not a substance, will be prior to the substance and the this. And this is impossible; for attributes cannot be prior to substance either in formula or in time or in generation, since if they were they would also be separable. Further, it will be present in Socrates, a substance in a
b30 substance, so that it will be the substance of two things. In general it follows, if man and other things spoken of in the same way are substances, that nothing in the formula of such things can be the substance of anything; nor can it exist apart from them, or in anything else. I mean that there is not, for instance, any animal apart from the particular [species of?] animals; and the same holds for anything else that is in a formula.

b34 From these considerations it is clear that none of the things
1039 that belong universally is a substance, and also because none of the things predicated in common signifies a this, but rather such a kind of thing. If this is denied, the difficulty of the third man will arise, and many others.

[10] I retain *οὐσία ἡ ἑκάστου* in b10, as F & P, rather than Ross's conjecture *οὐσία ἑκάστου ἡ*. Consequently I read *ᾗ* for *ἥ* later in the line.

The issue can also be made clear in this way. It is impossible a3
for a substance to be composed of substances present in it in actuality. For what is in actuality two things cannot also be in actuality one thing, though a thing may be one and at the same time potentially two. (For instance, a line that is double another line is composed of two halves, but only potentially; for the actuality of the two halves separates them from each other [sc.
and so destroys the line].) Therefore, if a substance is one thing, a7
it cannot be composed of substances present in it for this reason also, as Democritus rightly says. For he claims that it is impossible for one atom to come from two, or two from one, and he makes atoms his substances. (Evidently the same will also hold for number, if a number is a combination of units, as some say. For either the number two is not one, or there is no unit present in it in actuality.)

This result, however, involves a problem. For if no substance a14
can be composed of universals (since a universal signifies such a kind of thing, and not a this), and if also no substance can be composed of substances present in it in actuality, then every
substance must be incomposite and so indefinable. Yet everyone a19
thinks—and we have long ago asserted—that it is only or chiefly substances that can be defined. Now it appears that not even these can be, and so nothing can be. But perhaps in a way it can, while in a way it cannot. What is meant by this will become clearer from what follows.

CHAPTER 14

From these same considerations we can see what consequence a24
also results for those who believe in the Forms as separable substances, and at the same time hold that the form is composed of the genus and the differentiae. For if there are forms, and if animality is present in man and in horse, we may ask whether it is one and the same animality in each, or a different one. (I mean, of course, numerically the same. It is clear that they are the same in formula, for one would state the same formula in either case.)

Now if there is such a thing as man-itself in its own right, which a30
is separate and a this, then what it is composed of—e.g. animality and two-footedness—must also each signify a this and be separable substances. So this will apply to animality too. If then it is one and the same animality in man and in horse (the same in the way that you are the same as yourself), how will that one

thing, present in two separate things, be *one* thing? How will it
b2 avoid being separated from itself? Then again, this animality will not participate in both two-footedness and many-footedness without the impossible result that opposites will both belong at the same time to one and the same thing, and to something which is a this. But if this is not how it is, what is one saying when one says that an animal is two-footed, or has feet? (Possibly that the two things are placed together and in contact, or intermixed? But all this is absurd.)

b7 We must say, then, that the animality in each is different. In that case there will be practically an infinite number of things with animality as their substance. (For it is not coincidentally that man is composed of animality.) And further, there will be many
b9 things which are animality-itself. For first, the animality in each thing is its substance (since man, for example, is not called an animal by virtue of anything other than its animality; if it were, that other thing would be the genus of man and what man is composed of). Second, everything that man is composed of is a form. In that case it will not be the form of one thing and the substance of another (that is impossible), so each one of the animalities in the various animals must be animality-itself.
b14 Further, what are these animalities composed of, and in what way are they composed of animality-itself? And how can these animalities, whose substance is precisely animality, exist apart from animality-itself?

b16 Further, in the case of perceptible objects we find not only these consequences but others yet more absurd. Since this situation is impossible, they evidently do not have forms in the way that some suppose.

CHAPTER 15

b20 The combined whole and the formula are different substances, the one being a substance in that it is the formula taken together with the matter, while the other is the formula on its own.[11] Accordingly the combined whole may cease to be (since it may also come to be), but there is no ceasing to be of the formula, in
b24 the sense that it is ever in the process of ceasing to be. (For it cannot come to be either. Being for a house cannot come to be; only being for this particular house. Rather, such substances exist

[11] I read ἁπλῶς for ὅλως in b22, as Jaeger.

or do not exist without coming to be or ceasing to be, for we have
shown that one cannot create or produce them.) For this reason b27
also, particular perceptible substances cannot be defined, or be
the subject of demonstration, because they contain matter, whose
nature it is to be capable both of being and of not being. That is
why all of them that are particular are destructible.

Now demonstration pertains only to necessary truths, and defi- b31
nition is also a scientific matter. That is, just as knowledge cannot
be knowledge at one time and ignorance at another, such a state
being opinion and not knowledge, so also demonstration and
definition cannot apply at one time but not at another, and there
can only be opinion of what is capable of being otherwise. From **1040**
this it is clear that there can be no definition or demonstration of
such a thing. For destructible things are not evident to those who
have knowledge when they are no longer perceived, and even
though the same formula be retained in the soul there is no
longer any definition or demonstration of them. That is why, a5
when one who is concerned with definition defines any particular,
we must realize that it is always possible to refute it; for particulars cannot be defined.

Nor indeed can any of the Forms be defined. For a Form is a a8
particular and is separable, as they say. But its formula would
necessarily consist of names, and one cannot define by coining a
new name (which would not be understood), but must employ
the names already existing in common usage. And these will
necessarily apply to more than what is being defined. For instance, a12
one who tried to define you would say that you are an animal
which is lean, or pale, or something else of the sort, which
applies to others besides you. If it be objected that there is
nothing to prevent each name separately applying to several
things, while together they apply to this one thing alone, we
should reply in this way. First, the set of names together will
apply in addition to both its elements, for instance 'two-footed
animal' will apply to 'animal' and to 'two-footed'. (This in fact a17
must be the case where eternal things are concerned, since they
are prior to the compound, and parts of it, and moreover separable (assuming man to be separable). For unless both are separable, neither is; but if neither is separable then the genus will not
exist apart from its forms, and if the genus is separable then so is
the differentia. And further [they are both separable] because
they are prior in being to the compound and would survive its
destruction.) Second, if the components of the Forms, being a21
simpler than their compounds, are themselves Forms, then these

components of the Form, e.g. 'animal' and 'two-footed', must also be predicated of many things. For how else could the Form be known? It would simply be some Form which cannot be predicated of more than one thing. However, it seems in fact that every Form may be participated in.

a27 As has been said, the impossibility of defining particulars is not noticed in the case of eternal things, especially those that are unique, like the sun and the moon. People err in including attributes which could be removed without preventing it still being the sun, for instance 'going round the earth' or 'hidden
a31 at night'. (They thus imply that if it stood still, or was visible at night, it would no longer be the sun. But this is absurd, for the sun signifies a certain substance.) And they also err in including attributes that might apply to something else, implying that if there came to be some other thing of the same sort it too would be a sun. A formula, then, is common to many things, but the sun was supposed to be a particular like Cleon
b2 or Socrates. For why does no one produce a definition of them?[12] If one tried it, the truth of what I am here saying would be clear.

CHAPTER 16

b5 It is clear that even of the things that are commonly thought to be substances the majority are potentialities. This applies both to the parts of animals, since none of them exists when separated (and when they are separated then too they are all as matter), and to earth and fire and air. For none of these is a unity, but as it were a heap, until they are concocted and some unity is formed from them.
b10 One might most readily suppose that the parts of living things, and the closely related parts of the soul, turn out to be both, i.e. to exist both potentially and in actuality, on the ground that they have principles of movement deriving from something in the joints. (That is why some animals still live when divided.) But in fact they all are only potentially—that is, when they form a continuous unity by nature; when they are unified by force or by growing together that is simply an abnormality.

b16 Since unity is predicated in the same way as being, and the substance of [a?] unity is one, and things whose substance is numerically one are themselves numerically one, it is clear that

[12] I delete ἰδέας from b3.

neither unity nor being can be the substance of things, for the same reason as being for an element and being for a principle cannot be. (Rather, we ask *what* the principle is, so as to reduce it to something
more intelligible.) In fact being and unity have a better claim to be b21
substance than do principle or element or cause, and yet not even these are substances, since nothing else either that is common to many things is a substance. For a substance belongs to nothing but to itself and to that which has it, i.e. that of which it is the substance.
Further, a unity could not be in many places at once, though what is b25
common to many things is present in many places at once, so it is clear that no universal exists separately from the particulars.

Those who believe in the forms are right in making them b27
separate, if indeed they are substances, but are wrong in supposing that the one over many is a form. They make this mistake because they cannot say which substances are thus indestructible, existing
over and above the particular perceptible ones. So they make them b32
the same in form as the destructible ones which we know, simply adding the word 'itself' to perceptible substances, as in 'man-itself' and 'horse-itself'. Yet even if we had never seen the stars they would
none the less, I presume, have been eternal substances other than **1041**
those we knew. And so now, though we may not know what they a2
are, still it is perhaps necessary that there must be some.

It is now clear that nothing at all that is predicated universally a3
is a substance, and that no substance whatever is composed of substances.

CHAPTER 17

Let us now take a fresh starting-point and say what, and what a6
kind of thing, substance should be said to be. For these considerations will perhaps also make clear the nature of that substance that is separated from the perceptible substances. Let us start, then, from the fact that substance is a principle and a cause of some sort.

When one asks why, one is always asking why one thing belongs a10
to another. For to ask why an artistic man is an artistic man is either, as we have just said, to ask why a man is artistic, or it is something else. But to ask why a thing is itself is to ask nothing at
all. For before we can ask why, it must be clear *that* the thing is a15
so—I mean, for instance, that the moon is eclipsed—but there is just one explanation and one cause for all cases of why a thing is itself, e.g. why a man is a man, or why an artistic thing is artistic.

a18 (Unless perhaps someone will say that a thing cannot be divided from itself, and this is what it is for it to be one thing. But this explanation applies to everything alike, and is too brief.) However, one could ask why a man is such a kind of animal. It is clear
a23 that this is not to ask why one who is a man is a man. So what one asks is why it is that one thing belongs to another. (It must be evident that it does belong, otherwise nothing is being asked at all.) Thus one may ask why it thunders, for this is to ask why a noise is produced in the clouds, and in this way what is sought is one thing predicated of another. And one may ask why these things here (e.g. bricks and stones) are a house.

a27 It is clear, then, that what is sought is the cause—and this is the what-being-is, to speak logically—which in some cases is that for the sake of which the thing exists (as presumably in the case of a house or a bed), while in some cases it is that which first began the change; for this latter is also a cause. But such a cause is sought in cases of coming to be and ceasing to be, while the former is sought also in cases of being.

a32 One is particularly liable not to recognize what is being sought in things not predicated one of another, as when it is asked what a man is, because the question is simply put and does not
b2 distinguish these things as being that. But we must articulate our question before we ask it, otherwise we shall have a case of asking both something and nothing. And since the existence of the thing must already be given, it is clear that the question must
b5 be why the matter is so-and-so. For instance, the question may be 'Why are these things here a house?' (and the answer is 'Because what being is for a house belongs to them'), or it may be 'Why is this thing here a man?', or 'Why is this body in this state[13] a man?' So what is sought is the cause by which the matter is so-and-so, i.e. the form. And that is the substance.

b9 Now it is clear that no enquiry or instruction is possible in the case of simple things, and some method other than enquiry has to be adopted here. However, things that are compounded in such a way that the whole is a unity, not like a heap but like a syllable—

b12 And the syllable is not just its elements—BA is not the same as B and A—nor is flesh just fire and earth. For on dissolution the flesh and the syllable no longer exist, but the letters exist, and
b16 so do the fire and the earth. So the syllable, then, is not only its elements (vowel and consonant) but something else besides; and flesh is not only fire and earth, or the hot and the cold, but

[13] I read *ὡδί* for the second *τοδί* in b7, as F & P.

something else besides. And this something else cannot itself be
an element or composed of elements. For if it is an element, the b20
same argument will apply again (since flesh will be composed of this element and fire and earth and something else besides), and so we have an infinite regress; and if it is composed of elements, then it must be composed of more than one element (otherwise it would be that one element) and so we shall apply to it the same
argument as to the flesh and the syllable. It would seem, then, b25
that this something else does exist, and that it is not an element, and that it is the cause of this thing here being flesh and that thing there being a syllable. And similarly in other cases. And this is the substance of each thing, because it is the primary cause of its being.

But since not all objects are substances, but only those that are b28
formed naturally and in accordance with their nature, it would appear that this nature is their substance. And it is not an element of them, but it is their principle; an element is rather what is present in the thing as its matter, and into which it may be divided, as for instance A and B are the elements of the syllable.

BOOK ETA

CHAPTER I

1042
a3 Now we must bring together what has been said, draw our conclusions, and so bring the enquiry to its completion.
We have said that the object of our search is the causes,
a6 principles, and elements of substances. And some substances are
agreed by all, while some have been put forward by certain
people only. Natural substances, such as fire, earth, water, air,
and other simple bodies are agreed by all; so are plants and their
parts, animals and their parts, and finally the universe and its
parts. On the other hand, only some say that the forms and
a12 the objects of mathematics are substances. But other substances
result from arguments, namely what being is and what underlies,
and in another way it is argued that the genus is more a substance
than its forms, and the universal more than the particulars. Closely
connected with the universal and the genus there are also the
Forms, for it is for the same reason that they are thought to
a17 be substances. And since what being is is substance, while a
definition is a formula of what being is, we discussed definition
and being in one's own right. Also, since a definition is a formula,
and a formula has parts, it was necessary to consider the parts of
a thing, to discern which parts are parts of the substance and
which are not, and whether these parts are parts of the definition
too. Moreover, neither the universal nor the genus is a substance.
a22 We must consider later the Forms and the objects of mathematics,
which some say are substances over and above the perceptible
substances. But now we must proceed to the agreed substances,
which are those that are perceptible; and all perceptible substances have matter.
a26 What underlies is a substance, and in one way this is the matter
(by which I mean that which is not a this in actuality, but is a this
potentially), though in another way it is the formula and the
shape (which is a this and is separable in formula), and in
a third way it is what is compounded from these (and this
alone can come to be and cease to be, and is separable without
qualification—for of those substances which are given by a formula some are separable and some are not).
a32 It is evident that matter too is a substance, since in all changes
from one opposite to the other there is something which underlies
the change. Thus in a change of place there is that which is now

here and later there; in a change of size there is that which is now
of such a size and later larger or smaller; in a change of quality
there is that which is now healthy and later sick. Similarly in a b1
change of substance there is that which is now coming into being
and later perishing, and which now underlies as a this and later
underlies by way of privation. This last kind of change implies all
the others, but they—one or two of them—do not imply it. For a b5
thing which has matter for change of place need not necessarily
have matter for generation and destruction. (The difference between generation in a qualified sense and unqualified generation
has been explained in the *Physics*.)

CHAPTER 2

That which is substance as what underlies and as matter is gener- b9
ally accepted; and this is that which is potentially. It remains,
then, to explain the nature of that which is the substance of
perceptible things as actuality.

Democritus seems to have thought that there were three dif- b11
ferentiae, for he held that the underlying body—the matter—was
one and the same, but was differentiated by 'rhythm' (i.e. shape),
or 'inclination' (i.e. position), or 'contact' (i.e. arrangement). But
it is clear that there are in fact many differentiae. Thus some b15
things are defined by the way their matter is combined, whether
by being blended, tied, glued, or nailed (as honey-water, a faggot,
a book, a box, respectively), or in more than one of these ways;
others by their position (as a threshold or a lintel, which differ by
their situation); others by their time (as dinner and breakfast); b20
others by their place (as the winds); others by their perceptible
attributes, such as hardness and softness, density and rarity,
dryness and wetness—sometimes by some of these and sometimes by all of them—and in general some by excess and some by
defect.

So it is clear that 'is' is said in just as many ways. A threshold is b25
because it is situated so, and [in this case] being signifies its being
so situated; and [there?] being ice signifies [its?] being solidified
so. (The being of some things is defined by all of these at once,
i.e. by their being partly mixed, partly blended, partly tied, partly
solidified, and so on. Examples would be a hand or a foot.)

We should, then, grasp the genera of differentiae, as these b31
differentiae will be principles of being. For instance, there are
things differentiated by more and less, or by dense and rare, or

others of this sort, and all these are cases of excess and defect; and things differentiated by shape or smoothness or roughness are all differentiated by straight and crooked; and for other
1043 things being is being mixed, and the opposite of this is not being.
a2 From this it is clear that, since the substance of a thing is a cause of its being, it is among these that we must look to determine
a4 what is the cause of the being of each of these things. (In fact none of these differentiae just mentioned is a substance, not even when it is coupled with matter; nevertheless it is in each case what is analogous to substance. Just as in substances what is predicated of the matter is the actuality itself, so in other defi-
a7 nitions it is what is closest to actuality.) For instance, if we have to define a threshold, we shall say that it is wood or stone in such a position; and similarly a house is bricks and timbers in such a position (or in some cases there may also be a purpose to consider); and to define ice we shall say that it is water congealed or solidified in such a way; and a harmony is such-and-such a
a12 mixture of high and low; and similarly in other cases. So from this it is clear that where the matter is different the actuality and formula is also different. For some things it is the combination, for some the mixture, and for some another of the things we have mentioned.

a14 That is why some who define a house say that it is stones, bricks, and timbers, and so give what is potentially a house, i.e. the matter; some say that it is a receptacle to shelter people and property, or propose something else of this sort, and they give the actuality; and some combine both, giving the third substance
a19 compounded from these. (For it seems that the formula constructed from the differentiae is a formula of the form and the actuality, while the formula composed of the constituents is rather
a21 a formula of the matter.) The definitions which Archytas used to approve are of this last sort, since they are of both combined. For instance, 'What is windlessness? Stillness in a large expanse of air'—here the air is the matter and the stillness is the actuality and substance. Or again, 'What is a calm? Smoothness of the sea'—here the sea is what underlies as matter, and the smoothness is the actuality and shape.

a26 From what has been said it is clear what perceptible substance is, and how it is—either as matter, or as shape and actuality, or thirdly as the compound of these two.

CHAPTER 3

One must bear in mind that sometimes it is not clear whether a a29
word signifies the compound substance or the actuality and shape; for instance, whether 'a house' means a shelter made from bricks and stones placed thus (the compound) or just a shelter (the actuality and form), and similarly whether 'a line' means duality in length or just duality, whether 'an animal' means a soul in a body or just a soul (for the soul is the substance and actuality of a
certain kind of body). 'Animal' might indeed be applied to both, a36
if it is not expressed by a single formula but with reference to a single thing. However, this is not important for our enquiry into perceptible substance (though it is elsewhere), since the what-
being-is belongs to the form and the actuality. For soul is the b2
same as being for a soul, but man is not the same as being for a man (unless the soul too is to be called man; and in that case in one way they are the same and in another way not).

Now, on investigation it is evident that a syllable is not com- b4
posed of the letters *and* their combination, and a house is not bricks *and* combination. And this is correct, for the combination and the mixture are not themselves composed of the things that are mixed or combined, and the same holds of all other cases.
For instance, if a threshold is defined by its position, the position b9
is not composed of the threshold; it would be better to say that the threshold is composed of it. Nor, then, is man an animal *and*
two-footed. If these are matter, then there must also be some- b11
thing over and above them, something which is not an element and not composed of elements but is the substance; and this they eliminate when they state only the matter. So if this is the cause of man's being, and this is the substance, they will be failing to state the substance itself!

(This substance must either be eternal or come to be and cease b14
to be without ever being in the process of coming to be and ceasing to be. It has been shown and demonstrated elsewhere that no one produces or creates the form; rather, one makes something be this,[14] and what is composed of these comes to be.
On whether the substances of destructible things are separable b18
nothing is yet clear, though it is clear that some cannot be. Substances such as a house or an implement cannot exist apart from the particular houses and implements. Perhaps indeed these are not even substances, and nor is anything which is not formed

[14] I read ποιεῖ τι for ποιεῖται in b17.

by nature; one might well hold that the only substance to be found in destructible things is their nature.)

b23 Consequently the puzzle raised by the followers of Antisthenes and similar uneducated persons has some point here. They said that one cannot define what a thing is, since a definition is a long formula. (However one can explain[15] what it is like; for instance, one cannot say what silver is, but one can say that it is like tin.)
b28 So some substances, namely those that are composite, may have a definition and a formula (whether they be perceptible or intelligible), but what they are primarily composed of cannot, since a defining formula must predicate one thing of another, one of these playing the part of matter and one of form.

b32 It is also clear that, if substances are in some way numbers, they are so in this way and not—as some maintain—as numbers of units. For a definition is a sort of number, since it is divisible into indivisibles (every definition being finite) and the same is
b36 true of a number. And just as, if you add or subtract anything—however small—from the things of which a number is composed, the result is no longer the same number but a different one, so
1044 also a definition or what-being-is will not survive if anything is
a2 added or subtracted. Further, a number must be something in virtue of which it is a unity, though people cannot now say what it is that makes it so, if indeed it is. (For either it is not, but is like a heap, or it is, and then it should be explained what it is that makes it one out of many.) Similarly a definition is a unity, and
a6 again people cannot explain this either. Nor is this surprising, for the explanation is in each case the same; substances are one in this way, not by being a kind of unit or point, as some say, but because each substance is an actuality and a certain nature. (Also, just as no number admits of being more or less, so neither does the substance taken as form; if any does, it is the substance with matter.)

a11 Let this suffice for an account of the ways in which it is and is not possible for what are commonly called substances to come to be and to cease to be, and of the reduction of substances to numbers.

CHAPTER 4

a15 On the topic of material substance, we must notice that even if everything does come from the same primary stuff, or stuffs, and

[15] I delete *καὶ* from b26, as Jaeger.

even if it is the same matter that functions as a principle of the things that come into being, nevertheless there is a different matter appropriate to each. Thus the matter appropriate to phlegm is sweet or fatty stuffs, while that appropriate to bile is stuff which is bitter or something else; but these latter perhaps come
from the same stuff. The same thing will come to have several a20
matters when one is the matter of the next; thus phlegm may come from what is fat and from what is sweet, if fat itself comes from what is sweet. But it comes from bile by the resolution of the bile into its primary matter. For one thing may come from another in two ways, either because the one is reached via the other, or by the other being resolved into its principle.

It is possible for different things to come from the same matter a25
if the cause which effects the change is different; thus both a box and a bed may come from wood. (Nevertheless in some cases different things must have different matter. Thus a saw cannot be made from wood, and this does not depend on the effecting cause; one just cannot make a saw from wood, or from wool.)
But if it is possible to make the same thing from different matter, a29
it is clear that the skill and the effecting principle must be the same. For if both it and the matter were different, the product would be different too.

When one is seeking the cause, then, since causes are spoken a32
of in many ways, one must mention all of the possible causes. For instance, what is the cause of a man as matter? The menstrual fluid, perhaps. And what is the cause which sets it in motion? The seed, perhaps. And what is the form? The what-being-is.
And what is the purpose? The goal. (These last are perhaps b1
identical.) And one must give the nearest causes. It will not do to say that the matter is fire or earth; one must give the matter peculiar to the thing in question.

This is the correct procedure with natural substances that are b3
subject to generation, if indeed the causes are these and of this number, and it is the causes that must be known. But a different account applies to substances that are natural but eternal. For some things perhaps do not have matter, or do not have matter of this sort but only matter capable of spatial movement.

Things which are by nature, but are not substances, also do not b8
have matter; what underlies them is the substance. For instance, what is the cause of an eclipse? What is its matter? It has none. Rather, the moon is what undergoes the change. And what is the cause which effects the eclipse and extinguishes the light? The
earth. There is perhaps nothing that is its purpose. The cause as b12

form is the formula, but this is not clear if it does not include the [effecting] cause. (Thus, what is an eclipse? A deprivation of light. But if one adds 'due to the earth coming between' this is now the formula that includes the cause.)

b15 In the case of sleep it is not clear what it is that is primarily affected. Is it the animal? Yes, but in virtue of what primarily? The heart, or something else? Next, by what is sleep effected? Next, what is the affection—not of the whole animal, but of that which is primarily affected? Is it a certain sort of stillness? No doubt, but to what affection of the primary subject is this due?

CHAPTER 5

b21 Some things are or are not without coming to be or ceasing to be, for instance points (if they exist) and forms generally. For it is not pallor that comes to be, but wood that comes to be pale (if, that is, everything that comes to be comes from something and
b24 comes to be something). Hence not all opposites come to be from one another; a pale man comes from a dark man and pale from dark in different ways. Nor does everything have matter, but only those things that come to be and change into one another. Things which are or are not without changing have no matter.

b29 There is a problem over the relation of the opposites to a thing's matter. Thus if the body is potentially healthy, and disease is the opposite to health, must the body be potentially both? And is water potentially both wine and vinegar? Or is it rather that it is the matter of the one in virtue of its state and form, but of the other in virtue of the privation of that state and a decay that is contrary to its nature?

b34 There is also a certain problem over why it is that wine is not the matter of vinegar, nor is it potentially vinegar, even though vinegar comes from it; and similarly a living thing is not potentially a corpse. Perhaps the reason is that the decay is coincidental. It is not the animal but the matter of the animal that is also, by decay,
1045 the matter and potentiality of the corpse; and it is not the wine
a2 but the water that is the matter of the vinegar. They come to be from the animal and the wine only as night comes from day. All things that change into one another in this way must revert to their matter. For instance, if an animal comes from a corpse, the corpse first reverts to its matter and from there becomes an animal, and vinegar first turns to water and from there becomes wine.

CHAPTER 6

Let us now consider the problem we have already mentioned a7
concerning both definitions and numbers, namely: what is the
cause of their unity?

Whenever anything which has several parts is such that the a8
whole is something over and above its parts, and not just the sum
of them all, like a heap, then it always has some cause. Indeed,
even in the case of bodies there is a cause of their unity—
sometimes contact, sometimes stickiness, or some other attribute
of this sort. A definition, however, is a unitary formula, not by a12
being bound together (as the *Iliad* is) but because it is the formula
of a unity. What is it, then, that makes man a unity rather than a
plurality—for instance animal and two-footed? This problem is a15
especially acute if, as some say, there is an animal-itself and a
two-footed-itself. For then why is man not these two things, so
that men exist not by participation in the one thing man but in
the two things animal and two-footed? In short, on this view man
is not one thing at all, but two, namely animal and two-footed.

So it is clear that those who proceed with definitions and a20
explanations in this way, as they usually do, cannot give an
account which solves the problem. However if, as we say, there is
on the one hand matter and on the other hand shape, and the
one is potentially while the other is actually, the question will no
longer seem a difficulty. For this problem is the same as would a25
arise if the definition of a cloak were a round bronze. The word
would then be a sign of the formula, and the question would be:
what is the cause of the roundness and the bronze being one?
The difficulty has thus disappeared, since the one is matter and
the other form. What, then, is the cause of what is potentially a30
being in actuality (discounting, in the case of a created thing,
whatever produces it)? There is no further cause of the potential
sphere being actually a sphere; this is precisely what being is for
each of them.

There is intelligible matter as well as perceptible matter, and a a33
formula always consists part of matter and part of actuality. (For
instance, a circle is a plane figure.) But things that have no
matter, either perceptible or intelligible—a this, a quality, a
quantity—are each at once just what is some unity, as too they
are at once just what is some being. (That is also why neither b2
being nor unity occurs in a definition.) Also a what-being-is is at
once some unity, as too it is at oncc some being. That is also why
there is no further cause for any of these things of their being a

unity, or of their being a being. Each is at once a being and a unity (and not because being or unity is their genus, nor because they are separable from particulars).

b7 This difficulty has led some to talk of participation though they cannot say what it is or what its cause is; others talk of communion, for instance Lycophron, who says that knowledge is the communion of knowing and the soul; others say that life is the
b12 composition or tying together of soul with body. But in fact the same account applies in all cases. Being healthy will be the communion, tying together, or composition of a soul and health; the bronze being a triangle will be the composition of bronze and a triangle; being pale will be the composition of pallor and a
b16 surface. The reason for their difficulty is that they are seeking both a unifying formula and a differentia for potentiality and actuality. But in fact, as has been said, the final matter and the shape are one and the same thing, one potentially and the other actually, so that it is as if they were asking what was the cause of
b20 unity and of being one. For each thing is one, and the potential and the actual are in a way one, and so there is no other cause unless there be something which effects the change from potentiality to actuality. But things which have no matter are all unqualifiedly just what is some unity.

COMMENTARY

PRELIMINARIES

The titles of Aristotle's works are abbreviated as follows:

Logical Works

Cat	*Categories*
Int	*De Interpretatione*
An. Pri	*Prior Analytics*
An. Post	*Posterior Analytics*
Top	*Topics*
SE	*Sophistici Elenchi*

Physical Works

Phys	*Physics*
Cael	*De Caelo*
GC	*De Generatione et Corruptione*
Meteor	*Meteorologica*
Anim	*De Anima*
PN	*Parva Naturalia*
PA	*De Partibus Animalium*
IA	*De Incessu Animalium*
GA	*De Generatione Animalium*

Others

EN	*Nicomachean Ethics*
EE	*Eudemian Ethics*
Rhet	*Rhetoric*
Poet	*Poetics*

References to passages in these works are given in full, with the book numbers in Roman numerals, where relevant. References to passages in the *Metaphysics* are abbreviated by omitting '*Metaphysics*' throughout, and giving just the book number in Greek, and the chapter number. References to passages of books *Z* and *H* in particular are further abbreviated by omitting the first two digits of the page number, i.e. '10'. Thus a reference to the first line of book *Z* of the *Metaphysics* would be given in the form '*Z*1, 28^a10'; and a reference to what is said on that line in the Commentary would be given as 'Z1, 28^a10 n.'. The line references are always references to the Greek text, and not to the lines of any translations.

Where I have quoted passages from other works of Aristotle, I have borrowed the translations of other volumes in this series, wherever they exist. But I have silently adapted them to the terminology used in the present volume. Citations of modern authors are explained in the Bibliography. Please note that references to 'Ross' and to 'Frede & Patzig' are references to the comments on the passage under discussion in the commentaries by Ross and by Frede & Patzig respectively.

INTRODUCTORY NOTE

Early in book *Γ* of the *Metaphysics* it was argued that the philosopher should study substance (1003^a33-^b19). Books *Z* and *H* take up that task, and apparently they complete the discussion of perceptible substance. Imperceptible substance is the main topic of books *Λ*, *M*, *N* (though *Λ* also contains a discussion of perceptible substance in its first five chapters).

'Substance' is a conventional, and somewhat misleading, translation of the Greek word '*ousia*', which is etymologically a noun formed from the present participle '*ousa*' of the verb 'to be'. Latin translators, attempting to mirror this derivation, coined for it the words '*essentia*' and '*entitas*'. If we attempt a similar coinage in English, we might come up with 'be-ence' or 'be-ity'. Of these, the second would perhaps be preferable, since it is a little better adapted to the two quite different uses which Aristotle gives to this word. On the one hand he uses it as an abstract noun, speaking of the *ousia* of a thing, and often equating this with what being is for that thing. Here we could perhaps speak either of the 'be-ence' or of the 'be-ity' of the thing. But he also uses it as a concrete noun, naturally taking a plural, and in this use he will claim that men, horses, and trees are all *ousiai*. Here 'be-ity' would seem a little less harsh. For example, the claim 'men are be-ities' could be construed on the model of 'men are realities'. Indeed, though it lacks the etymological connection with the verb 'to be', the word 'reality' would serve well as a translation. For it has both the grammatical uses just mentioned, and at the same time reflects another facet of Aristotle's word: the *ousiai* are the things that really, genuinely, or fundamentally are. Hence 'reality' is sometimes used as a translation (e.g. in the present series by Charlton [1970], Barnes [1975], Annas [1976]). But I have nevertheless retained the conventional translation 'substance'.

Aristotle introduces us to the concept of substance in his short work the *Categories*. There we are told that every simple thing that is falls under one of these ten headings: substance, quantity, quality, relation, place, time, position, state, action, or affection (1^b25-2^a4). This list of ten is elsewhere reduced to eight (e.g. *Δ*7, 1017^a24-7); more often it is simply left open-ended, in some such form as 'substance, quality, quantity, and the rest' (e.g. *Z*1, 28^a11-13). It is a list of what are elsewhere called the categories. Now the word 'category' is just a transliteration of Aristotle's own word '*katēgoria*' and it means 'predication' or 'predicate'. So if everything is in some category, it would appear to follow that everything is a thing predicated. But this is not actually Aristotle's view in the *Categories*. The members of the categories other than substance are indeed things predicated, and they are all predicated of substances. But in the category of substance we find two kinds of item. There are the primary substances, which are defined as things which are always subjects and never predicates—examples are particular men, horses, and trees—and there are the secondary substances, which are the species and genera of primary substances. These play an intermediate role, since they are predicated of primary substances, but can also figure as subjects of which non-substances are predicated. (Partly because primary substances are not predicated, Frede [1981] has argued that Aristotle did not originally call the substances a 'category'. But at any rate he soon came to do so, e.g. at *Phys* V, 225^{b}5; *GC* I, 317^{b}9.)

Thus the first thing to note about the concept of substance is that the category of substance includes both primary and secondary substances, though the first are particulars and the second universals. The second thing to note is that the same word 'substance' in its other use characterizes the relation between them, for the species or genus is said to be *the substance of* the various particulars that fall under it (and the genus is also *the substance of* the species). In this other use, where the word is often translated 'essence', it is not officially confined to the category of substance, for one can give the substance *of* an item in any category. On the other hand, Aristotle quite often does seem to confine his attention in just this way, i.e. to the substance of what is itself a primary substance. For example, in the very brief discussion of substance in Δ8 of the *Metaphysics* he says that there are just two kinds of things called substances, namely (i) the primary substances, and (ii) the 'cause of being' of what is a primary substance (1017^{b}13–16). Here one might naturally suppose that he means to equate 'the cause of being of *x*' with 'the substance of *x*' (cf. *Z*17). (In fact his own discussion in Δ8 does not quite say this, but it does go on (in ^{b}21–6) to identify both 'the cause of being of *x*' and 'what being is for *x*' with 'the form of *x*' (cf. *Z*3).)

At several places in Aristotle's discussion of substance in the *Metaphysics* one can be puzzled by the question: is he thinking of primary substances, or of secondary substances, or of being the substance of something (in particular, the substance of a primary substance)? The very first chapter of book *Z* is a notorious example of this problem.

BOOK ZETA

CHAPTER 1

Aristotle has already argued that philosophy studies beings as such (*Γ*1), and that this study reduces to the study of substances, because although 'being' has many senses the primary sense is that in which it applies to substances (*Γ*2, $1003^{a}33$–$^{b}19$). Book *Z* begins with the same claim about the primary sense of 'being', and goes on to support this by what appear to be rather different arguments. It concludes that substance is the topic to be considered from now on, and thereby it introduces all the rest of books *Z* and *H*.

The main problem in the interpretation of the chapter is to determine what kind of substance Aristotle is talking of when he claims that it is substance that has being in the primary sense. Before we consider this, however, we should ask what he means by his opening claim that 'being' has a variety of senses—or, as he puts it, that 'we speak in many ways of what is'—since he gives no elucidation here. I therefore begin with a prologue on this question. But since the question is in fact rather complex, readers may prefer to postpone all but the first three paragraphs of this prologue until after they have studied the rest of the chapter.

Prologue to *Z*1: The Senses of 'is'

The somewhat awkward locution 'we speak of *X* in many ways' ('*X legetai pollakhōs*') is Aristotle's standard way of saying that the word (or phrase) '*X*' has several senses. One has only to read a few lines of this, or any other, book of Aristotle's to see that he is utterly careless of our distinction between *using* a word in the normal way, to speak of whatever that word stands for, and *mentioning* the word itself. Though he does occasionally employ the Greek equivalent of quotation marks, we much more often find that he appears on the surface to be speaking of what the word stands for, whereas his thought can only be understood if we see that it is directed at the word itself. The present idiom is a case in point. At first sight it seems to say that there is a single thing, *X*, for which we have many words, but in fact it is quite clear that it should be understood in the opposite way, as claiming that there is a single word, '*X*', which does not mean any one thing. So here Aristotle's claim is that the word 'is', or the phrase 'what is', has several meanings. Now we are familiar with the view that 'is' has three meanings: it can mean 'exists' (rare in English, but very common in Greek), or it can mean 'is the same as', or it can function as the copula in an ordinary predication. But it is clear that it is not this triple distinction that Aristotle is thinking of.

He refers us back to his account in book *Δ* (that being his work 'on the several ways in which things are spoken of'), where the topic is indeed expounded in chapter 7. That chapter distinguishes four main kinds of being, labelled 'coincidentally', 'in one's own right', 'truth', and 'potentially or actually'. Of these we can certainly set aside being as truth (discussed in *E*4 and in *Θ*10), and the distinction between being potentially and being actually (discussed in *Θ*1–9). It would appear that we can also set aside being coincidentally, which has been discussed and dismissed in *E*2–4, and that the being with which *Z*1 is concerned should be what is called in *Δ*7 'being in one's own right'. For *Z*1 immediately connects the multiplicity of being that it mentions with the multiplicity of the categories, and so too does the description of 'being in one's own right' in *Δ*7 (1017^{a}22–7). (The same connection is found in many other places where the multiplicity of being is mentioned, e.g. *Phys* 185^{a}21, *Anim* 410^{a}13, *EN* 1096^{a}24.) Since the categories classify 'the things that are', evidently meaning by this 'the things that exist', one naturally supposes that it is 'is' in the sense of 'exists' that Aristotle is speaking of.

Now the doctrine of the *Categories* can easily be seen as implying that there are *two* different senses of 'exists'. For Aristotle claims that all the other items concerned are predicated of primary substances, and infers from this that if the primary substances did not exist then nothing else would exist either (2^{b}5–6). For other things, then, to exist is to be (truly) predicated of some primary substance, but this cannot be how primary substances themselves exist. So there is one sense of 'exist' in which it applies to primary substances, and this is the basic or primary sense, since the other sense makes reference to it. For example, to say that a colour exists (in the sense of 'exists' that is appropriate to colours) is to say that there exists some primary substance (in the different sense of 'exists' that is appropriate in this case) which has that colour. And generally, where *X* is not a primary substance, to say that *X* exists is to say that there exists some primary substance which is *X*, where this last 'is' is an 'is' of predication. However, if this theory is to be extended to obtain the result that there are as many senses of 'is' (i.e. 'exists') as there are categories, then more needs to be said. We must apparently go on to claim that the 'is' of predication *also* has a variety of senses, and in particular that the sense of the 'is' in 'some substance is *X*' will vary according to the category of *X*. (This problem is noted, but not further explored, in the careful account in Ferejohn [1980], 117–24.)

Aristotle never directly asserts this. But in his idiom 'some substance is *X*' may also be phrased '*X* belongs to some substance', and in one brief passage of the *Prior Analytics* he does appear to say that 'belongs to' has a different sense for each category (49^{a}6–10). Owen [1965*c*], 82 n., has offered this explanation: '*X* belongs to *Y*' will be paraphrased differently in the different cases, either as '*X* is a quality of *Y*' or as '*X* is a quantity of *Y*' or as '*X* is the place of *Y*', and so on, as appropriate. (Similarly Kirwan [1971], 142.) In fact, the argument suggested is quite inadequate, since the whole force of the phrase 'belongs to' reappears in this supposed paraphrase in the little word 'of'. That is, '*X* is a quality of *Y*' is simply short for '*X* is a quality *and X* belongs to *Y*', so it merely *adds* something to '*X* belongs to *Y*' and does not paraphrase it at all. But of course Aristotle might not have seen this point. However, it is more important to notice that in any case the interpretation of the *Prior Analytics* passage is far from clear. Considered out of context, the passage *could* be taken as saying that the meaning of '*X* belongs to *Y*' differs according to the category of *X*, but equally it could be taken just as saying that the same locution applies whatever the category of *X*. And when the context is considered, the latter is much more probable, for the former would be quite irrelevant to Aristotle's purposes in this part of the *Prior Analytics*. (Compare 48^b2–4, considered with and without the examples that follow it.) Finally, even if Aristotle did mean to say in that passage that 'belongs to' differs in meaning from one category to another, there is clear evidence from Δ7 itself that it is not *this* point that he has in mind when he claims that being is spoken of in as many ways as there are categories.

To see this, we must note first that he did believe that 'is', as a copula, has *two* different senses. Even in the *Categories* we find a distinction between two different kinds of predication: in one of them the thing predicated is *said of* the subject; in the other it is (claimed to be) *present in* the subject. This particular terminology is not found elsewhere—indeed it is not really very appropriate—but the distinction that it introduces is constantly adverted to, in varying terminology, throughout the Logical Works. To use what is perhaps the most favoured vocabulary, in the one kind of predication the predicate says *what the subject is*, and this occurs when the predicate is the species or the genus (or possibly the differentia) of the subject. As is clearly explained at *Topics* 103^b27–39, the subject of such a predication may be an item in any category, and the predicate will then be in the same category. This is traditionally called essential predication, and I shall follow the traditional usage, though I shall not regard the word 'essential' as translating any particular expression of Aristotle's. It is contrasted with what is traditionally called accidental predication, though in my version I follow Kirwan ([1971], 76–7) in preferring *coincidental*; both words are intended as a translation of Aristotle's phrase '*kata sumbebēkos*'. All the other predications that Aristotle recognizes in the Logical Works are called coincidental, and he claims that they all reduce to the one primary case in which the subject is in the category of substance and the predicate is in any other category. Thus in simple cases either the subject is a substance and the predicate is a non-substance (which is a coincidental predication), or subject and predicate are both in the same category (which is an essential predication). All other predications are in some way complex, and may be analysed into some combination of predications of one or other of these simple kinds.

As I have said, Aristotle characterizes this distinction in different ways in different places. For example, we have observed that he often describes an essential predication as one in which the predicate gives *the substance of* the subject. But another equally common description of an essential predication is that it is one in which the predicate says what the subject is 'in its own right' ('*kath' hauto*'; for more on this expression, see Z4, 19^b13–22 n.). It is thus extremely natural to suppose that the distinction with which Δ7 opens, between what is coincidentally and what is in its own right (1017^a7–8), is intended to introduce just this distinction between the two different kinds of predication that Aristotle recognizes. But then, where *X* is a non-substance, the claim 'some substance is *X*' is a coincidental predication, and in Δ7 it is coincidental predications that are discussed first, at 1017^a8–22. Yet in that discussion there is no suggestion whatever that the relevant 'is' has a different sense for each category of predicate. On the contrary, it is the *second* kind of being discussed, i.e. being in one's own right, that is said to be divided as the categories are.

We must conclude that this way of trying to elucidate the multiplicity of being does not work out too well. Our initial suggestion provides a perfectly good explanation of why 'exists' should apply, in its primary sense, to primary substances and to them alone. For this reason I shall not abandon the account; indeed, one cannot ignore it when considering the interpretation of Z1. But it is quite difficult to see how to extend that initial suggestion to an explanation of why, in Aristotle's view, being must be supposed to be different for each different category. So I turn now to a different account, which is based more closely on the very puzzling structure of the discussion in Δ7.

As I have observed, Δ7 opens with the distinction between being coincidentally and being in one's own right, which is in the first place a distinction between different kinds of predication. It then proceeds to discuss being coincidentally, and certainly that appears to be a discussion of coincidental predications. So when it turns to consider being in one's own right we naturally expect a discussion of essential predications. But what we actually find is this:

> The things that signify the figures of predication are those that are said to be in their own right. For 'to be' signifies in the same number of ways as they [i.e. the figures of predication] are spoken of. Since, therefore, among things predicated some signify what a thing is, some a qualification, some a quantity, some a relative, some doing or being affected, some where, some when, 'to be' signifies the same as each of these. (1017^a22–7)

The things 'that signify the figures of predication'—or possibly, the things 'that the figures of predication signify' (the Greek is ambiguous)—are the simple items that are the members of the various categories. These, Aristotle says, are said to be in their own right, and in this phrase they are clearly introduced as *subjects* of the verb 'to be', with no complement indicated. So apparently 'to be' must here mean 'to exist', and there is after all no concern with the 'is' that appears in an essential predication. But in that case there is no proper contrast between the 'coincidental being' discussed just before and the 'being in one's own right' that figures here.

The problem may be partially resolved in this way. As we shall see in *Z*6, Aristotle does not confine his contrast between 'coincidentally' and 'in one's own right' to the two different kinds of predication, but is also prepared to speak of what he regards as a compound item, e.g. an artistic man, as a thing that is expressed (or spoken of) coincidentally, and to contrast this with a simple item as one that is expressed (or spoken of) in its own right. Bearing this in mind, we can view the discussion of coincidental being as concerned *both* with the 'is' of a coincidental predication *and* with the 'is' of existence, as applied to a coincidental item. The two locutions are in fact interchangeable, since an artistic man exists if and only if there exists a man who is (coincidentally) artistic. In fact Aristotle's examples clearly involve an 'is' of predication when they are first introduced (1017^a8–13), but his expression then becomes more elliptical, and at $^a18$ he has undoubtedly slipped into an 'is' of existence. His summing up at $^a19$–22 then begins with what seems again to be an existential use of the verb ('The things said to be coincidentally, then, are so described either because . . .'), though its continuation cannot be understood without recalling the associated predications. It is possible, as Kirwan has suggested ([1971], 145) that Aristotle did not notice that genuinely different grammatical constructions are involved, for some of his illustrations are in fact ambiguous between the two. For example '*ho mousikos anthrōpos estin*' can mean either 'the artistic man is [i.e. exists]' or 'the artistic [one] is a man'. But it is fair to say that even if he did see the difference still he did not regard it as having any philosophical significance, and that the first paragraph of *Δ*7 can reasonably be seen as concerned with either, or both, of these locutions.

This allows us to restore a tolerable contrast between the first paragraph and the second, for both may now be seen as concerned with the 'is' of existence, applied first to coincidental items (i.e. compounds) and next to items 'in their own right' (i.e. simples). Aristotle himself seems to view *Δ*7 in this way when at the opening of *E*2 he describes all four of the kinds of being discussed in *Δ*7 as cases of 'what is, said simply', i.e. without qualification (*haplōs*, 1026^a33–$^b2$). For the phrase 'to be simply' is standardly contrasted with 'to be something-or-other' in order to indicate that the verb needs no complement. Yet it would be extraordinary if Aristotle's account in *Δ*7 of the various uses of 'is' simply overlooked its use as a copula, and anyway we have said that the discussion of coincidental being does include an account of 'is' as a coincidental copula. In fact it treats this 'is', and the 'is' of coincidental existence, as interchangeable. What is missing, then, is some recognition of the 'is' that functions as a copula in an essential predication. One might naturally expect this to be the central case of 'being in one's own right', but apparently *Δ*7 never mentions it.

To meet this point, it is very tempting to offer a speculation (cf. Owen [1965*c*]). Just as Aristotle seems to equate the 'is' of coincidental predication with the 'is' of coincidental existence, so perhaps he *also* equates the 'is' of a predication in one's own right with the 'is' of existence in one's own right. Then, in mentioning the latter, he will think that he has mentioned the former too, so that no important kind of 'is' has been omitted. But how could one suppose that these two 'is's are the same? Well, the obvious suggestion is this. If we are to explain what being (existence) comes to, for this or that kind of non-coincidental item, we must do so by explaining what *kind* of thing it is, which just is to say what can be predicated of it in its own right. In fact it is to give part or all of the definition of the thing. For example, for a threshold to be (i.e. exist) is for it to be positioned in such-and-such a way, this being the definition of what a threshold is (*H*2, 42^b25–8). (There is, of course, a serious confusion here, but it is one that Aristotle may well have been capable of. See *Z*4, 30^a17–27 n.; *Z*15, 39^b21–40^a8 n.; *H*2, 42^b25–8 n.) In favour of this speculation are three considerations. One, which we will be exploring further as we proceed (from *Z*4 on) is the constant connection that Aristotle draws between what being is for a thing, or what it is for a thing to be, and what that thing is, or what it is to be that thing. For this apparently conflates an existential use of the verb 'to be' (in the first two cases) with its use as a copula in a predication 'in one's own right' (in the second two). The second consideration is what led me to advance the speculation, i.e. that it would explain what is otherwise a very puzzling feature of the structure of Aristotle's discussion of the senses of 'is' in *Δ*7. But the third consideration, which brings us back directly to our main question, is that it would make clear *why* Aristotle should have apparently taken it to be obvious that being (i.e. existence) was different for items in different categories. It is because when we say *what* these items are, we of course say something different in each case.

An obvious difficulty is that the suggestion seems to yield many *more* kinds of being than there are categories. For example, according to the *Categories* being in a position is itself a category. But the threshold differs from the lintel by the one being in one position (below the door) and the other in another (above it). This states what being is for each of them, and thus in each case their being is different, though still in the same category. But we can perhaps reply that what Aristotle is concerned with is the most general kinds of being that there are; and since the most general answer that one can give, in reply to the question 'What is it?', is a specification of the category of the thing, the most general kinds of being will correspond to the categories. Thus we still have a sense in which there are as many ways of being as there are categories, for any more specific way of being will be a further specification of the way of being given by the category in question. And there is no way of being that does not fall under one or other of the categories, for the categories are the ultimate genera. As Aristotle claims, it is a mistake to suppose that being is *itself* a genus, under which each of the categories will fall (e.g. *B*3, 998^b22; *An. Post* II, 92^b14. See Loux [1971] for a useful elucidation of the argument.)

It may be debated whether this is an adequate response to the difficulty. Aristotle's doctrine that there are as many kinds of being as there are categories is found in works that must be earlier than books *Z* and *H* of the *Metaphysics* (cf. Owen [1960]), but it is only in *H*2 that we find any explanation of what the many kinds of being are, and how they arise. Now in *H*2 they certainly arise because different things have different definitions, but *H*2 stresses not the *genus* given in the definition but the *differentia*. It is the genus that needs to be stressed if one aims to argue that the kinds of being are as many as the categories, using the point that the categories are the ultimate genera. But in fact *H*2 does not think of a definition as containing a genus at all, its account is not applied to items in any non-substantial categories, and it seems perfectly happy to conclude that there are very many kinds of being indeed. So the support which this speculation gains from *H*2 is actually very limited. While *H*2 does indeed show us an 'is' of definition and an 'is' of existence being (mistakenly) connected, the way in which the connection is drawn in that passage owes a great deal to points that have been made for the first time during the discussion of book *Z*. *Perhaps* Aristotle was making a *similar* connection between these two uses of 'is' when he first came to the conclusion that there are as many kinds of being as there are categories, but if so we have no record of it.

I have canvassed two suggestions as to what Aristotle had in mind when he claimed that 'we speak in many ways of what is'. It will be helpful to label them here as 'account A' and 'account B', and to summarize them for future reference.

Account A. Being (i.e. existence) applies to all kinds of things, but to primary substances in a primary way and to all other things in a derivative way. The sense in which being applies to substances is basic, and not further analysable (or at any rate, not yet further analysed). But to say of any non-substance that it exists is the same as to say that it is in some appropriate relation to a substance, which exists in the primary way. This appears to be the doctrine of *Γ*2:

> Some are called things that are because they are substances; some because they are affections of a substance; some because they are a route to substance, or destructions, or lacks, or qualities, or productive, or generative of a substance . . . (1003^b6–9)

All things that are, then, either are substances or are somehow related to substances, but they are related in different ways. That is why there are many kinds of being and not just two (i.e. one for substances and one for everything else); it is because the way that other things are related to substances is different in the different cases. But if we are to take this account in *Γ*2 as explicating the opening of *Z*1, then since *Z*1 explicitly connects the multiplicity of being with the multiplicity of the categories, we must suppose that the items in each different category are differently related to the substances to which they belong. But that is to say, in effect, that the 'is' which connects a substance as a subject with a non-substance as predicate, i.e. the 'is' of coincidental predication, introduces a different relation for each different category of predicate. However, there is no good evidence to show that Aristotle espoused this doctrine, and there is quite good evidence to show that he did not. For the discussion in Δ7, to which he refers in Z1, appears to see no such multiplicity in the 'is' of a coincidental predication. This suggests that we should look for an alternative account.

Account B. Being (i.e. existence) applies to all kinds of things. It applies to 'coincidental items', which are compound, but there it simply means that the one element of the compound belongs to the other, or that both elements belong to some other, where in each case the 'other' in question is a thing that has being in its own right. Thus, as just implied, being applies also to 'items in their own right', which are non-compound. But the being of such things is different in different cases, for what being is for a thing is given in full by its full definition, and this of course is different in different cases. Nevertheless, it is not unreasonable to say that two things which fall under the same genus will each have a being of the same kind, since that same genus will figure in the definition of each, and thus we may conclude that the ultimate kinds of being, not further resoluble, will correspond to the ultimate genera of things. But these are the categories. Hence there are as many (ultimate) kinds of being as there are categories.

Thus the (confused) line of thought in account B is at least in accord with the correspondence drawn in Z1, and many other passages, between the number of the (ultimate) kinds of being and the number of the categories. By contrast, no such correspondence emerges from account A. But on the other side the priority of substance is simply built into account A, whereas there is nothing in account B (as so far developed) that yields any privileged position for substance. So if substance is to be regarded as in some way primary among the things that are, a further argument will have to be given. Without trying to resolve this dispute between account A and account B, but bearing it in mind, let us therefore turn to consider the arguments that we actually find in Z1. I shall return to this dilemma in my epilogue to the chapter.

28ᵃ10–20

In this opening paragraph Aristotle first reminds us that there are many kinds of being, and then he states that it is clear that the primary kind is 'what a thing is'. This, he says, signifies substance—either the category of substance or the substance of the item in question—and the parenthesis that follows gives his reason for this *latter* claim. Finally he explains in what way other things may be said to be.

It appears not to matter which of the alternative translations we adopt, for in any case the phrase 'what a thing is'—or, more literally, 'what it is' (*ti esti*)—must be being used here to refer to the category of substance. The end of the paragraph makes this clear, for it says 'other things are said to be by being either quantities of what is in this way, or qualities, or . . .'. These 'other things', then, are evidently the things that are not substances, and so what they are contrasted with must be the things that are substances.

Although the point has recently been questioned by Frede [1981], it is usually held that Aristotle very frequently employs the phrase 'what a thing is' as a label for the category of substance, and that the idiom is found as early as *Top* I, $103^{b}23$. The idiom is highly misleading, as the same passage in the *Topics* goes on to point out ($^{b}27-37$), since in Aristotle's view one can ask and answer the question 'What is it?' of an item in *any* category, and not only of a substance. But we may perhaps explain it in this way. Aristotle seems to envisage his categories as generated by taking some particular item as subject and then raising different questions about it, the answers to the different questions yielding the members of the different categories. That is why many (though not all) of the labels that he uses for his categories are in Greek simple interrogatives, like 'where' and 'when'. Thus where we translate 'quantity' Aristotle simply writes 'how-much' ('*poson*') and where we translate 'quality' he again has a simple little word '*poion*' which equally functions as an interrogative. (The Latin equivalent is '*qualis*'; there is no simple English equivalent.) Accordingly he seems to have hit upon the interrogative 'What?' or 'What is it?' as the question that generates answers in the category of substance. But of course the question has to be understood in a specially loaded way if it is to do this, so that it generates as answers only the species or genus of the item asked about (*Cat* $2^{a}14-19$). Two points may be made about this.

First, we must assume that the item we are asking about is itself in the category of substance if the question 'What is it?' is to yield answers in that category. Indeed, this assumption must be built into the explanation that is given in the present paragraph, in the parenthesis at $^{a}15-18$. (For example, if the item in question were a quantity, then the answer 'It is three feet' *would* be a proper answer to the question 'What is it?', contrary to what is claimed at $^{a}17$.) But when we are thinking of our different questions as generating the different categories, this restriction is not as arbitrary as it may at first seem. For Aristotle holds, at least in the Logical Works, that the *other* questions apply *only* to substances. That is, he will not allow that there could be such a thing as a quality of a quality, a quality of a quantity, a quantity of a quality, and so on. Second, the answers to this question that Aristotle mainly has in mind are, as I have said, answers that give the species or genus of the subject, that is, what he calls *secondary* substances. (There is a problem over whether an answer that gives the differentia of the subject is also a proper answer to this question, but we may set that problem aside here.) He *never* seems to envisage an answer such as 'It's Socrates', i.e. one that names a *primary* substance. So this way of referring to the category of substance would seem to focus more on the *predicates* in that category than on the particular things of which they are predicates.

One might suggest that this is why our passage begins by conjoining the two phrases 'what a thing is and a this' (^{a}11–12). Perhaps Aristotle's thought is that secondary substances will fall under the first phrase, and primary substances under the second. At any rate, in the *Categories* he does appear to use the odd phrase 'a this' in just this way, claiming that primary substances do signify a this and that secondary substances do not (*Cat* 3^{b}10–23). However, we shall find that here in book *Z* the notion of 'a this' is used in a very puzzling way, and at least in some passages it is clearly not intended to pick out a particular rather than a universal. (See *Z*3, 29^{a}27n.) So one should, I think, remain agnostic about this suggestion.

This, then, introduces the main problem for the interpretation of *Z*1: is it primary substances, or secondary substances, or both, to which Aristotle wishes to attribute the primary kind of being? From the last sentence in this paragraph, it seems natural to infer that it is primary substances that he has in mind. The claim that 'other things are said to be by being quantities, etc., of what is in this way' very naturally suggests—as in account A of the prologue—that quantities and so on are (i.e. exist) by being truly predicated of *primary* substances, and that it is therefore primary substances that are (i.e. exist) in the primary way. On the other hand, although one might allow that primary substances may be included under the general heading 'what a thing is', in view of Aristotle's tendency to use this expression as a label for the category of substance as a whole, still we are offered a reason for saying that what a thing is 'signifies substance', and this reason very clearly focuses on the role of *secondary* substances. The point is that when we ask what a thing is we get an answer such as '(a) man' or '(a) god', and this is an answer which tells us what *kind* of thing our subject is, and not what *particular* thing it is. This makes it very difficult to maintain that Aristotle means to focus exclusively on primary substances. But one *could* suppose that he is thinking always of secondary substances. At any rate, at *Cat* 2^{b}37–3^{a}6 he says that non-substances all are predicated of *secondary* substances, in such predications as 'some men are pale', and he gives that as one of his reasons for saying that secondary substances do deserve to be called substances. So perhaps he now wishes to extend this line of thought, and to say that non-substances have being by being thus predicated.

28^{a}11: 'on the one hand it signifies . . .'. 'Signifies' is a deliberately vague translation of Aristotle's word '*Sēmainei*', which also is extremely vague. Aristotle's use of this word is quite unsystematic (*pace* Irwin [1982]). But the Greek verb, like the English, naturally takes as subject some mentioned expression, so we should understand the translation in this way: 'We speak in many ways of what is . . . on the one hand "what is" signifies . . .'. As remarked earlier (p. 45), one must constantly be prepared to switch between use and mention when reading Aristotle. The same remarks apply to subsequent uses of 'signifies' in this chapter (^{a}14, ^{a}21) and throughout.

28ᵃ19: 'affections'. I use 'affection' to translate '*pathos*'. In old-fashioned English there is a contrast between what one does and what one suffers, co-ordinate to the contrast between acting and being acted on, and in terms of this contrast a *pathos* is etymologically what one suffers, what happens to one when one is acted upon; it is, one might say, how one is affected by something. Considered in this way, Aristotle counts the 'affections' as constituting a category, contrasted with the category of doings, though he also considers that long-lasting affections may be counted as qualities (*Cat* 9ᵇ19–10ᵃ10). But often in the *Metaphysics* (and elsewhere) '*pathos*' is used in a very general way, covering any property of a thing other than those properties that form part of its essence. Where it seems clear that the word is being used in this more general way, I translate it 'attribute'.

28ᵃ20–31

In this paragraph Aristotle contrasts walking and so on with walking things. He says that one might well doubt whether walking is a being, whereas a walking thing appears 'more' to be a being, because the phrase implies that there is some definite particular substance which is walking. He infers that it is because of this, i.e. (the?) substance, that walking too may be said to be, and concludes that it is (the?) substance that primarily has being.

It is perfectly clear that 'being' in this paragraph means 'existence', and that the phrase 'the substance and the particular' in ᵃ27 indicates a particular, i.e. primary, substance. So one naturally supposes that the doctrine is that of account A, that primary substances exist in the primary way, and all other things—such as walking—exist by being truly predicated of primary substances. On this reading, one will include the definite article 'the' in the two places queried in my summary above, so that the text refers to a particular primary substance throughout. But in fact the Greek may just as well be translated without the definite article in these places, as in my translation. Reflection on this may suggest a slightly different interpretation.

Aristotle offers two reasons why one might doubt that walking exists: (i) that it is not the case that walking is (by its nature) in its own right, and (ii) that walking cannot be separated from substance. These two reasons seem to come to the same thing: both appear just to mean that walking exists only because there exist substances which walk, which apparently is just the same as to say that there are walking things. But it should be noted that Aristotle does *not* say that the substance (which is walking) *is the same thing as* the walking thing. On the contrary, he says that the substance *underlies* the walking thing. So his view apparently is that if we have a man who is walking, then the man is one thing and the walking thing another, and the first is a substance which underlies the second. From our point of view, this is absurd: since the man *is* the thing that is walking, it must be nonsense to suppose that the man is a substance and the walking thing is not, or that the man underlies the walking thing whereas the walking thing does not underlie the man. Nevertheless, we can see what is in Aristotle's mind by switching from use to mention, and speaking explicitly of the two different *expressions*, 'the man' and 'the walking thing'. In the situation imagined these two expressions do refer to the same object, but they describe it differently. In fact the first describes that object by giving its essence, by expressing what that thing essentially is, namely a man, whereas the second describes it only by a coincidental attribute that it happens to have. Moreover, a description such as 'the walking thing' can only describe what *also* has a description that reveals its essence, e.g. as a man, or a dog, or maybe a spider. This, roughly, is the theory of 'Aristotelian essentialism' as we would nowadays describe it. It relies on the idea that certain descriptions or characteristics of things do 'reveal their essence' or 'say *what* they are' in a way that others do not. (See Matthews [1990] for more detail on what Aristotle's theory is.) But whereas we put this theory by carefully distinguishing between things and their descriptions, Aristotle habitually adopts a way of talking which blurs or confounds this distinction. And this is not *just* a way of *talking*, for in several places one can see that it is confusing his thinking too. (There are useful general discussions in Matthews [1982] and Lewis [1982]. See also Z6, 31^a19–28 n.)

Thus in Aristotle's eyes there are at least three different kinds of entities being spoken of in this passage, namely particular substances (e.g. men), particular walking things, and walking itself. The first, he tells us, underlies the second. But in what relation do either of the first two stand to the third? Our text is hardly explicit on the point. One very natural suggestion (in accordance with account A) would be that the second underlies the third, and hence—by transitivity of underlying—the first underlies the third. But there is another *possible* suggestion, which would bring secondary substances back into the discussion, in the way envisaged at the end of the last note. Aristotle's thought may be that just as particular substances underlie particular walking things, so universal substances will underlie the universal walking. That is, this walking thing exists because it is true that Socrates (say) is walking, but walking exists because it is true that man (say) walks.

28^a20–1: 'whether walking and being healthy and sitting down do signify each of these things as beings'. This translation (which follows Ross) is to be understood by restoring a distinction between use and mention in this way: one might wonder whether 'walking' signifies walking as a being, whether 'being healthy' signifies being healthy as a being, and so on in each case. But the basic point is just that one might wonder whether walking *is* a being, i.e. exists.

28^a23: 'none of them is of a nature to be in its own right'. Contrast Δ7, cited above (p. 48), which claims that an item in *any* category 'is in its own right'.

28^a26: 'some thing which underlies them'. The phrase 'an underlying thing' (*to hupokeimenon*) is often translated simply as 'a subject', meaning a subject of predication. It is sometimes translated 'a substrate'. I have preferred, however, to retain a more literal rendering throughout. (See the prologue to Z3.)

28^a28: 'which is apparent in such a predication'. It may be noted that Aristotle calls the phrase 'the walking thing'—where 'walking thing' is all one word in Greek—a *predication*. This loose usage is evidently connected with his claim that there is something that underlies the walking thing, i.e. is the subject of which it is predicated.

28^a30–1: 'not is something but is without qualification'. As already noted (p. 49), this is Aristotle's standard way of distinguishing the 'is' of existence from 'is' as a copula. Presumably it should be understood here simply as a gloss on the way in which 'is', 'being', and so on have been used throughout this paragraph. It surely is *not* intended to suggest that the primary 'is' is the 'is' of existence, whereas 'is' as a copula is derivative. Rather, *both* the 'is' that is primary (as in 'Socrates is') *and* the 'is' that is derivative (as in 'walking is') are to be taken as 'is's of existence.

28^a31–$^b2$

Having claimed that substance is what is in the primary way, Aristotle proceeds to elaborate on the ways in which substance is primary. It is, he claims, primary in all the senses of 'primary', and he proceeds to list three such senses, namely in definition, in knowledge, and in time. It is not completely clear here whether he means (*a*) that there are *four* ways in which substance is primary, i.e. the three just enumerated *and* 'primary in being' (which we have already discussed); or whether he means (*b*) that the three ways just enumerated *are* each ways of being primary in being. I return to this point in my epilogue to the chapter. Here I consider the three kinds of priority enumerated and their relations to one another. Since it is priority in definition that is explained at $^a34$–6, and priority in knowledge at $^a36$–$^b2$, it must be priority 'in time' that is explained first at $^a33$–4.

28^a33–4: *Priority in time (separability)*. Presumably Aristotle does not mean to say that substance is literally 'earlier in time' than the other categories, so we look to his explanation to find out what he does mean. But the explanation is far too laconic: it tells us that no other predicate is 'separable', but only substance, yet it offers no gloss on what might be meant here by the metaphor of separation. Indeed, it is not even clear just what metaphor is being employed, for the word in question (*chōristos*) appears to be Aristotle's own coinage, and there is nothing in its formation to indicate whether he intended it to mean 'separable' or 'separate'. In fact I suspect that he sometimes means one and sometimes the other, though I have stuck to the translation 'separable' throughout. According to what may be called the orthodox interpretation of the present passage (found, e.g., in Ross, ad loc.), it is certainly 'separable', rather than 'separate' that is the correct translation here, for we are to understand the present claim as contrasting with ^{a}23–4 above, where it is said that walking, and similar items, are not 'capable of being separated' from substance (*dunaton chōrizesthai*). So the suggestion is that Aristotle means to say that items in other categories cannot be separated from substances, whereas substances can be separated from items in other categories. And since the first claim means that items in other categories cannot exist unless substances also exist, the new claim added here is that substances *can* exist without items in other categories existing. But the difficulty is to see how this claim could be at all a reasonable one. For surely, if a substance such as Socrates is to exist then he must be of *some* definite colour (quality), of *some* definite weight (quantity), and so on?

It has been suggested (e.g. in Burnyeat [1979], 4) that the required asymmetry can be defended if we confine our attention to the 'particulars' in the various categories, and construe 'particulars' in the non-substantial categories in a special way, as depending for their existence on the particular individual substances that they are 'in' (cf. *Cat* 1^{a}23–9. This way of reading the doctrine of the *Categories* is defended by Ackrill [1963], 74–5). The idea is that a 'particular weight', for example, should be understood as 'the weight that is in Socrates', and it is identified as the weight that it is precisely by the fact that it is Socrates who has it. Thus, as a matter of definition, *that* particular weight cannot be found in anything else, though no doubt there may be exactly *equal* weights in other things. Then that particular weight cannot exist unless Socrates does, whereas Socrates can exist without that particular weight, since Socrates could have been less heavy than he was. We may note two points about this proposal. The first is that the proposal only works if we suppose, rather unfairly, that whether a 'particular weight' continues to exist depends on *two* distinct criteria: first, it must remain the weight of the same particular substance, and second, it must *also* remain the same 'particular weight' in the *other*—and more usual—sense of that expression, i.e. it cannot change from being (say) a weight of 9½ stone to being a weight of 10 stone while still being the same particular, namely Socrates' weight. For if it were allowed to change in this latter way, then however heavy Socrates had been he would still have had the same 'particular weight', namely Socrates' weight, and he could not exist without it just as it could not exist without him. The second point is the obvious one: it is not clear why, in seeking to explain Aristotle's asymmetry of existence between substance and the other categories, we should be entitled to restrict attention to the particulars in those categories.

This second point, of course, has all the more force if we anyway reject Ackrill's reading of the *Categories*, on which the suggestion is based. For it is controversial whether Aristotle did recognize, in the

Categories, the 'particular' non-substantial items that it relies upon. (Ackrill's reading was challenged by Owen [1965*b*], and defended by Matthews and Cohen [1967], Allen [1969], and Duerlinger [1970]. But Owen's view has since been championed by Frede [1978]. There is a full discussion in Heinaman [1981].) If we turn our attention to the more familiar universals in the various non-substantial categories, then the best that we can say would appear to be this. There are many (fairly specific) non-substantial universals of each of which we can say that all the substances that there are could still exist without it existing. For example, no substance has to weigh exactly 10 stone, or be of just such-and-such a complexion, in order to exist. But we cannot say this of all. In particular we cannot say it of those non-substantial universals which either are part of, or are implied by, the definitions of the particular kinds of substances. For example, no animal can exist unless perception exists, for perception is (on Aristotle's view, *Anim* 413^b1-4) what distinguishes animals from other living things. No doubt there could still be some substances without there being perception; indeed there could be substances without anything having weight, or any other such perceptible property. For Aristotle's God is a substance that is in another sense 'separable', i.e. he is actually separate from anything perceptible, or anything material. But even God would not appear to be 'separable' from all the non-substantial categories: he could not exist without engaging in his own proper activity, which is thinking. In general, then, it would seem that no substance can exist without also exemplifying *some* non-substantial universals, though these of course will be different for substances of different kinds. So it is not true that substances are in this sense 'separable' from non-substances. But what other sense can be suggested? (Morrison [1985] proposes that Aristotle's point is that primary substances are separate *from one another*. No doubt that is supposed to be true of Aristotle's primary substances, but one cannot see how it could be thought to give them any such 'priority' over other categories as is claimed here.)

Well, an alternative suggestion is that Aristotle actually means what he says when he claims here that 'none of the other *predicates* are separable, but only substance.' These words evidently imply that it is *predicates* in the category of substance, i.e. secondary and not primary substances, that are being claimed to be 'separable' (cf. Patzig [1979], 43). If that is right, then the relevant kind of 'separability' will presumably be something along these lines: a predicate from the category of substance is complete in itself, since it itself reveals what the subject is, whereas a predicate from any other category does not reveal this, and hence requires supplementation. (This suggestion builds on Aristotle's point that 'nothing can be pale without being something *else* that is pale', e.g. a pale *man* or a pale *flower* or a pale *stone*. *An. Post* 73^b6, 83^a32, 83^b23; cf. Δ 11, 1018^b36-7.) One could, then, supply a way in which secondary substances may be regarded as 'separable', but it must be admitted that the suggestion is not convincing. In what follows 'separability' will be mentioned again as a criterion for being a genuine substance at Z3, 29^a28; Z16, 40^b28; *H*1, 42^a29-31; and possibly *H*3, 43^b19. In the second of these passages it appears to be implied that only particular substances can be 'separable', and in the third this implication is perfectly clear. So the probability must be that it is what the *Categories* counts as primary substances that Aristotle wishes to claim as separable, and not secondary substances, even if there is no satisfactory elucidation of this claim. For more on separability see Z3, 29^a28 n.

28^a34-6: *Priority in definition.* ('Definition' here translates '*logos*'. From Z4 on I shall reserve 'definition' for '*horismos*', and use 'formula' for '*logos*', because Z4 draws a distinction between the two. But evidently no such distinction is intended here.) In the definition of anything, Aristotle claims, there will occur 'the definition of a substance'. My translation of this phrase, '*ton tēs ousias logon*', reflects an ambiguity in the Greek: we might understand it as 'the definition of substance', or we might understand it as 'the definition of the appropriate substance'. In the first case the definition in question will be an explanation of the notion of substance, and in the second an explanation of this or that particular kind of substance, i.e. of some secondary substance, no doubt different kinds in different cases. Let us take the second case first.

It will be claimed in Z5 below that one cannot explain what snubness is without reference to noses, or femininity without reference to animals, or oddness without reference to numbers. Assuming for simplicity that noses, animals, and numbers may each be counted as substances, we may say that this claim implies that particular kinds of substance need to be mentioned in the definition of these non-substances. Hence, when the definitions are *fully* spelt out, the definition of these non-substances will include the definition of these particular kinds of substances, i.e. the so-called 'first recipients' of the non-substances in question. Moreover, in Z5 Aristotle generalizes this claim: just as femininity cannot be defined without reference to animals, so in the definition of *any* predicate from a non-substantial category there will be reference to something else, presumably the analogous 'first recipient' of that predicate (31^a1-11). If we may continue to assume that these 'first recipients' are particular kinds of *substance*, we therefore have a simple explanation of this claim in Z1 that substance is 'primary in definition'. (The assumption is an over-simplification, but one that does no harm in the present context. See Z5, 31^a1-11 n.) The main objection to it, as an interpretation, would seem to be this: it appears to presuppose that the audience of Z1 is already familiar with the doctrine of Z5, and this is an unreasonable presupposition.

Let us turn, then, to the alternative suggestion that Aristotle means to refer, not to the definition of this or that special kind of substance, but to the definition of 'substance' itself. The first problem here is evidently this: does Aristotle believe that there is such a thing as the *definition* of 'substance'? On the one hand, one might say that he himself *gives* a definition: in the *Categories* a primary substance is defined as what is a subject of predication and never a predicate, while a secondary substance is defined as what is either a species or a genus of some primary substance. But on the other hand, one must notice that here in *Z* he will apparently reject that definition (*Z*3), and although it is no doubt fair to say that the object of *Z* as a whole is to reach a more satisfying view of what substance is, still it surely does not issue in a revised *definition* of the notion. (It would be better to say that the discussion reveals that substance, like being, is something 'spoken of in many ways'.) But perhaps it is rash to rely on this objection. Just as Aristotle always assumes, without either illustration or argument, that any specific kind of substance will have a definition (e.g. *Z*4, 30^a11-14), so here he is perhaps assuming, without stopping to think, that there will also be a definition of substance itself. All he really means, one might suggest, is that in the definition of any non-substance there will be some *mention* either of substance or of substances. (For a similar carelessness on his part, see *Z*10, 34^b20-32 n.) But even if we reduce his claim in this way, it still is not clear why he should take its truth to be so obvious as to need no argument or explanation.

An explanation that may at first seem tempting is this. Aristotle holds (in the Logical Works) that anything that is not a primary substance is predicated of primary substances. Hence its definition may be held to involve what is, in our eyes, a universal quantification over primary substances. For example, to define the colour white one says 'any primary substance is white if and only if it . . .'. This, perhaps, is how substances get mentioned in *any* definition. But against this suggestion one must observe that it denies an implicit presupposition of the *Categories*, which claims that the word 'white', but *not* its definition, is predicated of the things that are white (*Cat* 2^a31-4). This doctrine clearly assumes that it is not the *adjective* 'white' that is defined, but the noun. Its point is that the definition runs 'white is a colour which . . .', and though one may say that Socrates is white, one cannot say that Socrates is a colour. If, however, the definition went 'to be white is to be coloured in such-and-such a way', then the definition *would* be predicated of whatever 'white' is predicated of. (By contrast, the *Categories* is also presupposing that one defines '(is a) man' rather than 'manhood', and '(is an) animal' rather than 'animality'. That is why it can offer it as a mark of secondary substances, distinguishing them from non-substantial predicates, that in *their* case both the name and the definition are predicated of the subject (*Cat* 2^a19-34).) It is thus an (unnoticed) presupposition of the *Categories* that the definitions of non-substances do *not* involve such a universal quantification over primary substances. This therefore creates a strong presumption against the present suggestion.

The only other interpretation that I can see is this. Initially it would appear that one defines white as a colour of a certain sort, and one may then go on to define colour in terms of something more general (e.g. as an 'affective quality', *Cat* 9^a28-^b33), and so on, until eventually one reaches the most general feature of whiteness, namely that it is a quality. And there, apparently, one must stop. For the titles of the categories are the most general classifying concepts, and hence cannot be defined further. (No doubt, the concept of a quality can be informally explained, as in *Categories* ch. 8, but such an explanation will not take the form of a definition.) But it may be that Aristotle now views the situation in this way. Instead of saying that the question 'What is it to be a quality?' has no answer, he equates this with the question 'What it is for a quality to be?', and supposes that this now *can* be answered, in view of his 'reduction' of the several kinds of being to one central case. Thus a quality is, i.e. exists, by being a quality of a substance, and that is how substance gets mentioned in the 'definition' of any non-substance, i.e. in the account of what being is for that thing. This, of course, is exactly the confused line of thought employed in account B of the prologue, and on this account the present claim that substance is 'primary in definition' is just the same as the claim, already argued in the first two paragraphs, that it is 'primary in being'. That is why it needs no further argument here.

Just because this last interpretation explains why Aristotle could take his claim to be so obvious as to need no defence, I am inclined to prefer it. But I shall leave both interpretations in play for the moment, noting that on the first, which involves *Z*5, it is clearly secondary substances that are here assigned priority in definition, while on the second we invoke account A to give the existence-conditions of non-substances, and the confusion characteristic of account B to represent this as part of their definitions. Thus the claim is that the definition of a non-substance will contain a general reference to (primary) substances (and so, when fully spelled out, a definition of what it is to be a primary substance, if there is such a definition).

28^a36-^b2: *Priority in knowledge*. This time at least Aristotle does offer an explanation, which is quite clear so far as it goes: we regard ourselves as knowing an object when we know *what* it is, rather than when we know its quantity, quality, or whatever. Clearly the relevant priority here is indeed to *predicates* in the category of substance, and the knowledge that one of these predicates applies to our subject is counted as in some way 'prior' to knowledge that a predicate from some other category applies. But one may still complain (*a*) that Aristotle does not really explain in what way this knowledge is 'prior' (on this see *Z*6, 31^b6-7 n.), and (*b*) that to obtain his conclusion one must again assume (as at 28^a15-18) that the subject we are talking about is itself a primary substance (e.g. a man, or fire). But the final observation of the paragraph acknowledges that we can ask 'what is it?' of quantities and qualities themselves, and seems to show that 'priority in knowledge' is really being assigned to predications which state what their subject is, i.e. to essential predications'. Yet *any* predicate can turn up as the predicate of such a predication, given a suitable subject.

As a further aid to the interpretation of this paragraph on 'priority', I add here a general note on the several kinds of priority that Aristotle standardly recognizes.

Kinds of priority. Although Aristotle often distinguishes various kinds of 'priority', his terminology is not consistent. If we may discount *Z*13, 38^b27 (which is no doubt influenced by *Z*1), we may say that elsewhere 'priority in time' seems always to be taken literally as indicating temporal precedence (e.g. *Cat* $14^a26–9$; *Phys* 260^b18, $^b29$ ff.; *Δ*11, $1018^b14–19$; *Θ*8, $1049^b11–12$, $^b17$ ff.). In the last passage it is also called 'priority in generation' (1050^a3), and often appears under this title elsewhere (e.g. *PA* 646^a26; *A*8, $989^a15–16$; *M*2, 1077^b19). It is standardly contrasted with what Aristotle calls 'priority in nature', or sometimes 'priority in substance', by which he means not the priority that attaches to the *first* stages of a development, but the priority that attaches to its *final* stage, the goal at which it aims, since it is this (in his view) that explains why the development proceeds as it does. ('Priority in nature': *Cat* $14^b3–8$; *Phys* $261^a13–14$; *PA* 646^a26; *A*8, $989^a15–16$. 'Priority in substance' (in this sense): *M*2, 1077^a19.) Neither of *these* kinds of priority seem to play any part in the discussion of *Z*1.

There are two other kinds of priority that often figure in Aristotle's distinctions. One is 'priority in definition', apparently always understood in the same way as here in *Z*1, but usually counted either as a variety of 'priority in knowledge' (*Δ*11, $1018^b30–7$) or simply identified with it (*Θ*8, $1049^b10–17$). Where the two are distinguished in *Δ*11, the other variety of 'priority in knowledge' is apparently 'priority in perception', and in this sense the particular is said to be prior to the universal. But although our paragraph in *Z*1 also distinguishes the two, it would not seem to be *this* contrast that it has in mind, for it evidently does not claim that *perceiving* what a thing is is somehow prior to *perceiving* anything else about it. Nevertheless we can perhaps see this connection between the two passages: priority in definition automatically yields a priority that applies to our knowledge *of universals* (i.e. if *X* occurs in the definition of *Y*, then one cannot know what *Y* is without first knowing what *X* is), and this may be contrasted with a priority that applies to our knowledge *of particulars*. In *Δ*11 the thought is just that knowledge (i.e. perception) of particulars is temporally prior to any knowledge of universals; in *Z*1 the thought is rather that one kind of knowledge of particulars (i.e. knowledge of what they are) is in some other way prior to other kinds of knowledge about them. But in each case it is the fact that there may be, in some sense, knowledge of particulars that is preventing Aristotle from simply identifying 'priority in knowledge' with 'priority in definition'.

The other kind of priority that often figures in Aristotle's discussion is usually called 'priority in being', or sometimes 'priority in substance', or occasionally 'priority in nature', and is the priority that *X* has to *Y* when *X* can exist without *Y* existing, but not conversely (*Cat* $14^a29–35$; *Phys* $260^b16–19$; *Δ*11, $1019^a2–4$; *Z*10, $35^b22–5$; *M*2, $1077^b2–11$). In the last two of these passages, this kind of priority is explicitly equated with the 'separability' of *X*. So it would be natural to infer that *this* is the kind of priority that is here called 'priority in time', and consequently that it is indeed *primary* substances that are here called 'prior in time'. Let us call this the priority of separable existence.

But there is also a further kind of priority, for which Aristotle appears to have no special name, although he illustrates it at some length in *Γ*2, and it would appear to be *the* crucial priority for our present purpose. This one might call a priority of meaning, and it occurs when the same word is said to have many meanings, but one of those is distinguished as the primary meaning, and the others as derivative from this, since they may be paraphrased in terms which relate them to the primary meaning. According to our account A of why it is that 'being' has many meanings, its primary meaning is that in which it applies to primary substances, for this meaning of 'being' turns up in the analysis of every other. According to our account B of why it is that 'being' has many meanings, namely that the meaning of 'being' is given in each case by the definition of the thing said to be, no reason was given in the prologue for saying that any of these meanings was primary. But now we can supply one. If indeed it is true that substance is prior in definition, in that the definition of any non-substance must contain a reference to (a?) substance, then all definitions do after all have a common element, and the kind of 'being' (definition) that applies to a substance will be primary, because it occurs in the analysis of the 'being' (definition) of all other kinds of thing. But notice here that if account B is to be kept *independent* of account A, then the reason for saying that the definition of anything will contain the definition of a substance must be that given by *Z*5, and not the alternative I suggested. For that alternative *did* rely on account A, as well as on the confusion characteristic of account B.

To sum up, then, we have four kinds of priority to consider in this chapter. First there is the priority of meaning which one sense of 'being' has over others; then there is the priority of separate existence (which appears to apply to primary substances), then priority in definition (which cannot apply to primary substances, since they have no definitions (*Z*15)), and finally the priority in knowledge that is distinguished from this last perhaps because it concerns knowledge of particulars. According to account A, the priority of meaning is assigned to the sense of 'being' (existence) in which it applies to primary substances, and from this it follows at once that only primary substances could have the priority of separate existence (for nothing else could exist unless primary substances did). According to account B, the priority of meaning is assigned to the sense of 'being' (definition) in which it applies to secondary substances, and this just is to say that secondary substances are prior in definition. On either account, the claim that substance is 'prior in knowledge', as expounded here, is a new point not directly implied by anything that precedes it. But the claim is in effect a claim for the priority of essential predication, though Aristotle seems to regard it as a claim for the priority of predicates in the category of substance, i.e. of secondary substances. At any rate, it surely cannot be taken as a claim for the priority of primary substances. What, then, are we to say of the structure of the chapter as a whole? I return to this in my epilogue to the chapter.

28^b2-7

Aristotle concludes that the question 'What is being?' simply *is* the question 'What is substance?', and that, therefore, is the question to be tackled from now on. (The question which I translate 'What is being?' would be more literally translated 'What is what is?') Presumably he is speaking somewhat loosely when he says that the one question simply *is* the other. More accurately, his position is that *part* of the answer to the question 'What is being?' has already been given, for we have explained how the being of non-substances is to be analysed in terms of the being of substances. Hence, one would have thought, what *remains* is to answer the question 'What is the being of substances?' But Aristotle prefers to put his question more generally, as 'What is substance?' The question, of course, could be taken in many ways, e.g. 'What things are substances?' or 'What conditions must things satisfy in order to be substances?' or indeed 'What is it to be the substance (i.e. essence) *of* a thing?' All these, and other, aspects of the question are considered in what follows.

The brief reference to the views that others have held on this question would appear to be a reference to the views of the older physicists on what basic stuff or materials the world is made from. Thus those who hold that 'substance is one' would be the Milesians (e.g. Thales, who opted for water, or Anaximenes, who opted for air); those who hold that it is more than one but a finite number would include Empedocles (earth, water, air, fire); those who espouse an infinite number would be Anaxagoras (who posited infinitely many stuffs) and the Atomists (who posited infinitely many atoms). But if this is right then the reference is somewhat misleading, for Aristotle discusses such views as these in his Physical Works, and they will not figure in what follows.

28^b3: 'always'. Following a point raised by Patzig [1979], 44, some have tried to understand the word 'always' here as meaning 'always so far', in order to avoid the apparently pessimistic prediction that no one will ever reach a satisfactory answer to 'What is being?' But while it may well be that Aristotle did not *mean* to sound pessimistic, still his words do inevitably carry just such an implication.

Epilogue to *Z*1

It is not possible to take the view that throughout this chapter whenever Aristotle refers to substances he means primary substances. It cannot be primary substances that 'signify substance' in the way illustrated at

^{a}14–18, and it cannot be primary substances that are said to be prior in definition or in knowledge at ^{a}34–^{b}2. It is *just* possible to take the view that he always means secondary substances, as my comments on each paragraph have indicated. Admittedly one cannot deny that primary substances are mentioned in ^{a}27 ('the substance and the particular'), but we may perhaps maintain that they are mentioned there only for the sake of an analogy. (Just as a particular substance—say Socrates—'underlies' a particular walking thing, so perhaps a secondary substance—say man—'underlies' walking in general.) But the chief difficulty here is clearly with the claim that substance is 'prior in time', i.e. 'separable'. Although one *can* make out a case for saying that *predicates* in the category of substance enjoy a certain kind of 'separability', it seems very doubtful that this is the claim Aristotle intends. It is much more likely that he means to claim that primary substances are capable of separate existence (even though we have not seen how this claim could decently be defended).

Given this point, the most coherent way of construing the whole chapter would appear to be this. We adopt account A of the way in which 'being' has many senses (despite the objections to that account raised in my prologue), and we note that it automatically yields a priority to primary substance, for it is this that has being in the primary sense of 'being'. We set ^{a}14–18 aside as not strictly relevant in its context, and apart from this we construe the first two paragraphs as concerned always with primary substances, and as intended to elucidate how it is they that have being in the primary sense. The elucidation is intended, we may suggest, merely to remind us of the rather fuller account of this doctrine already given in *Γ*2, since the general principles of how a word with many senses may have one that is primary, the others being derivative from this, are clearly explained and illustrated in *Γ*2, but are not mentioned here at all. Then in the third paragraph Aristotle notes that the fact that primary substances have being in the primary sense of 'being' carries with it a further kind of priority for primary substances: they and only they have the priority of separable existence. He then adds that substance also has two other kinds of priority (in definition, and in knowledge), but here it is actually secondary substance that has these priorities, so we treat this as a mere aside, of no importance to the main claim that the chapter is making.

This, it appears to me, is the most coherent way of reading the chapter. But it does not seem to be Aristotle's own way of reading it. At any rate the first sentence of book *Θ* refers back, presumably to *Z*1, in this way:

> We have discussed that which is primarily, and to which all other categories of being are referred, namely substance. For other beings—quantity, quality, and the others expressed in this way—are expressed in accordance with the definition of substance, since they all contain the definition of (a?) substance, as we said at the beginning. (1045^{b}27–32)

The plain implication of this passage is that it is the fact that substance is prior *in definition* that is actually the ground for the claim that substance has being in the primary sense of 'being'. We cannot, then, regard that priority as a mere aside, of no importance; it was, apparently, the central point. To explain this, one must invoke something along the lines of account B.

The being of a thing is given by its definition, and since different things have different definitions being must be spoken of in many ways. Originally Aristotle's thought was that we could regard two things as having the same kind of being if they fell under the same genus, since that genus would be a common element in the definitions of each, so that there will be as many ultimately different kinds of being as there are ultimate genera, i.e. categories. But two things from different categories will have no common element in their definitions, and therefore there can be no unified study of *all* the things there are. But now he has come to the view that there is after all a common element in all definitions, namely substance, and this notably alters the position. For it means that we are now entitled to take the being of substance as the central or primary case of being, regarding all other cases as derivative from this. The study of substance, then, is the study of the primary case of being, and 'universal because primary' (*E*1, 1026^{a}30–1; but note that I quote it out of context).

On this account, then, the things that have being in the primary way are the things that have definitions in the primary way, i.e. secondary substances (in the language of the *Categories*). Other things are said to be by being attributes *of these*, perhaps in this way: walking is in the sense that walking is such-and-such an action *of animals*, for the fact that it is only animals who walk must be built into the definition of walking. And generally, to obtain the most coherent reading of the chapter, given *this* starting-point, one tries to suppose that it is indeed secondary substances that we are concerned with throughout. But, as I have already said, this too presents several difficulties of detail, and besides, the whole endeavour seems perverse. Could Aristotle have simply *forgotten* that in the *Categories* he had given reasons for saying that these things were indeed *secondary* substances, and not primary ones?

I am driven to conclude that in his claim that substance has being in the primary way Aristotle is applying *both* account A *and* account B simultaneously. His point is that with non-substances

A. the fact that they are depends upon the fact that (primary) substances are,

and either

B^1. the question what they are depends upon the question what (secondary) substances are,

or, better

B^2. the question what they are depends upon the question what (primary) substance is.

Given that account A *is* being invoked, B^2 seems preferable to B^1. For in Z1 we rely upon account A to explain the first two paragraphs, and the claim that substance is prior 'in time' (i.e. is separable). Then, rather than having to anticipate Z5 (which is what is reflected in B^1), we may again rely upon account A, together with the confusion inherent in account B, to explain how substance is prior in definition (and this is what is reflected in B^2). It is legitimate to invoke this confusion because, as the opening of book *Θ* shows, B^2 (or possibly B^1) is *also* regarded as the ground for saying that substance has being in the primary way. Apparently Aristotle regards A and B^2 as equivalent to one another, and as each assigning to (primary) substance the same priority among things that are. Yet, given that account B *is* also in play, the being of a primary substance is given by what it is, i.e. by the secondary substance that is predicated of it essentially, so it is this that *is* the primary kind of being, i.e. the kind of being that a primary substance *has*. That is why Aristotle can open his discussion with the claim that the first sort of being 'is what a thing is, which signifies its substance' (^{a}14–15). It is also why he does not see his remarks on 'priority in knowledge' at ^{a}36–^{b}2 as irrelevant to his present topic.

In attempting to clarify Z1 I have thought it reasonable to use the *Categories*' distinction between primary and secondary substances, even though our text does not use that terminology. But presumably it will be a familiar terminology to many. However, we shall see that in the bulk of Z the distinction is drawn in quite a different way, and the notion of a primary substance is quite differently applied.

CHAPTER 2

In this brief chapter Aristotle sets out various opinions on what things are substances, and promises to investigate what truth there is in them.

28^b8–15

The view that 'substance seems most clearly to belong to bodies', and the subsequent elaboration of it, might fairly be said to be Aristotle's own view. At any rate, the list of substances that he proceeds to give is almost exactly the same as the list of substances at *De Caelo* III, 298^a29–32, which is given as his own list. The *De Caelo* makes explicit what is left implicit here, that it is intended as a list of substances that exist 'by nature' (as opposed to those, if any, that are man-made). The point is also made explicit in the recapitulation at *H*1, 42^a6–11, which adds that this list represents not just Aristotle's view, or even (as is implied here) a commonly held view, but in fact one that is universally agreed.

Living things, i.e. animals and plants, are clearly Aristotle's favourite examples of material substances. In *PA* II, 1, 646^a12–$^b12$, as a preface to his explanation of the parts of animals, he orders the relevant parts of the list in this way. First are the four primary or elemental stuffs—earth, water, air, and fire; next various inorganic stuffs compounded from these, e.g. bronze or coal, oil or smoke; next organic stuffs, also compounded from the four elemental stuffs, such as blood and flesh and bone; after them the shaped organs formed from these stuffs, e.g. the heart and the liver, the eye and the hand; and finally the whole animal. This ordering progresses from what is more in the nature of 'matter' to what is more in the nature of 'form'. (For more on this distinction, see the Commentary on *Z*3, *passim*.) A similar ordering would evidently apply to plants and their parts, and no doubt inorganic compounds would be formed first into the organic stuffs found in plants (wood, leaf, and so on), and from there into the organic stuffs found in animals. The universe (or more literally 'the heavens'), and the heavenly bodies counted as its parts, seem to stand outside this ordering, since the doctrine of the *De Caelo* is that the heavenly bodies are not made of earth, water, air, or fire, but of a fifth element whose nature is to move not to the centre or from the centre but round the centre. (No doubt the phrase 'fire and water and earth *and anything of this kind*' is intended to allow for this.)

Aristotle promises to investigate which, if any, of these alleged examples are actually substances. The promise is fulfilled mainly in *Z*16, 40^b5–16, where it turns out that most of them are not. (Cf. also *Z*17, 41^b28–30; *H*2, 43^a4–7; *H*3, 43^b21–3.)

28^b16–27

The views set out in this second paragraph are views that Aristotle does not agree with. Those who think that surfaces, lines, points, and units are substances, and more so than solid bodies, are probably some Pythagoreans. (The view is set out at greater length, and objections are raised to it, in chapter 5 of book *B*.) Those who think that there are none but perceptible substances are presumably other pre-Socratic thinkers, e.g. the Milesians. Of those who think that the more important substances are eternal and non-perceptible Aristotle mentions first Plato, then Speusippus, then a third view credited to 'some' which appears to be that of Xenocrates. (See Ross, ad loc.) These views are among the main topics of books *M* and *N*. Here in *Z* and *H* the discussion is largely confined to perceptible substances (as is made explicit at the end of the next chapter).

28^b27–32

The chapter ends by proposing to 'say in outline what substance is'. From the context which introduces this proposal one might have expected that it would lead to an attempt to formulate some very general criteria for being *a substance*, criteria that could be used to assess the various candidates for this title that have just been suggested. But this is not, at first sight, how the next chapter begins.

CHAPTER 3

This chapter apparently opens by distinguishing four candidates for being 'the substance of a thing', namely (*a*) 'what being is' (i.e. essence; see *Z*4, 29^b1–14n.), (*b*) 'the universal', (*c*) 'the genus', and (*d*) 'what underlies'. This fourfold distinction is reflected in the structure of the remainder of book *Z*. In rough outline, the present chapter discusses (*d*), chapters 4–6 and 10–11 discuss (*a*), and chapters 13–16 discuss (*b*). But this last discussion also includes the discussion of (*c*). As for the remaining chapters, chapters 7–9 form a digression on coming to be (which, however, is not irrelevant to the topic of essence, as I shall make clear in a moment); chapter 12 seems to me to be clearly misplaced, and best regarded as an editorial addition; chapter 17 explicitly announces itself as a 'new start'. None of these chapters are mentioned in the summaries at the end of *Z*11 and at the beginning of *H*1. It seems a probable hypothesis that there was once a version of book *Z* that did not include them. (For more on this hypothesis, see the introductory remarks to the chapters in question.)

The structure just outlined is, however, complicated in this way. The discussion of what underlies in this chapter says that this may be taken in three ways, either as matter, or as form, or as the compound of the two. But after some discussion it proceeds to dismiss the compound as 'posterior', remarks (rather surprisingly) that matter too is 'in a way evident', and promises a discussion of form. Since chapter 4 begins an apparently unrelated discussion of essence, this promise appears to be left in suspense, and we do not begin to hear very much about form until chapters 7–9. But then it becomes clear that Aristotle simply equates form and essence, so that the discussion of the one is at the same time the discussion of the other. The equation is made in passing in chapters 7–9 (32^b1–2, ^{b}12–14, 35^b5–8), and is everywhere evident throughout chapters 10–11 (most explicitly at 35^b14–16, ^{b}32, 37^a1–2; cf. also *Z*13, 38^b2–3). It was no doubt because what chapters 7–9 have to say about form is highly relevant to the discussion of essence begun in chapter 4 that Aristotle decided to incorporate these chapters where he did. Thus, with the text as we now have it, chapters 4–11 constitute both the discussion of form promised at the end of the present chapter and the discussion of essence implied by its opening.

The present chapter, then, begins by outlining the programme for the rest of book *Z*. It then discusses the claims of 'what underlies', which in one way is matter. Since the discussion is difficult to interpret, I shall not try to summarize it here. But a brief introduction to Aristotle's concept of matter will be useful.

Prologue to *Z3*: Matter

Aristotle's Logical Works show no awareness of the analysis of material things into matter and form, but this is a prominent feature of his Physical Works. The distinction is first introduced in connection with his account of change in *Physics* I. On this account, in every change there is something that persists throughout the change, and some characteristic that it acquires or loses during the change. In chapter 7 of *Physics* I, where this doctrine is expounded, the characteristic acquired or lost is called a form, and the thing that persists throughout is called what underlies. Thus if a man becomes pale, then the man is what underlies this change, and pallor is the form that he acquires. But the more interesting kind of change is that in which a new substance comes into being, as when someone makes a statue. Here the underlying thing will usually be a stuff of some sort, e.g. bronze, and the form acquired will be in this case a certain shape. So the resulting substance will be a 'compound' of that form in that material. Although occasionally Aristotle continues to use the word 'form' (i.e. '*eidos*') in a wide sense in which it covers *any* characteristic that may be acquired or lost in a change (e.g. *Z*9, $34^{b}8$), he more usually restricts it to the kind of form that is acquired in such a 'substantial change', and he frequently glosses 'form' as 'shape', no doubt because the statue is one of his favourite cases. He also introduces the word 'matter' ('*hulē*')for what underlies a change, and occasionally he uses this word too in a wide sense for what underlies *any* change, even such an ordinary change as a man becoming healthy (e.g. *Z*7, $33^{a}9$–10). But more usually he restricts this word as well to what underlies a substantial change (cf. *GC* I, 4, $320^{a}2$–5), so that it means much the same as 'stuff' or 'material', and the matter of a thing is what it is made from.

One should note here two departures from the standard terminology of the Logical Works. First, the word '*eidos*', which I always translate as 'form', is standardly rendered as 'species', in contrast to 'genus', in the Logical Works. Moreover, to give the *eidos* of a thing was to give the best possible answer to the question 'What is it?', and presumably, if one is faced with a statue, then the best answer to the question 'What is it?' will be 'It is a statue'; it will *not* be a description of its *shape*. Second, in the Logical Works the verb 'to underlie' was used simply for the relation of subject to predicate, so that 'what underlies *X*' meant simply 'the subject of which *X* is predicated'. But in the new vocabulary this phrase can also mean the same as 'the matter of *X*', which in turn is ambiguous between 'the matter that *X* was originally made from' and 'the matter that *X* is currently made of'. (These are the same where *X* is a statue, but not where *X* is a living thing.) This shift is obviously not irrelevant to the argument of the present chapter.

Finally, I introduce here a further aspect of Aristotle's views on matter, which would also appear to be not irrelevant. Ordinary kinds of stuff such as bronze or wood or bone are not eternal; they come to be and they cease to be. Applying Aristotle's general doctrine of change, they too must therefore be compounds of form in matter, for they are created when some pre-existing matter acquires a new form, and destroyed again when it loses that form, but the matter in question exists throughout. We are to understand it as underlying the bronze, and being what the bronze is made of, in analogy to the way in which bronze itself underlies the statue (*Physics* I, 7, 191^a7–12). In fact this matter is no doubt some mixture of the four elemental stuffs: earth, water, air, and fire. But even these elemental stuffs are not, in Aristotle's view, eternal, but come to be and cease to be out of one another. That is, air can change into water, water into air, and so on. So again there must be some further matter which underlies these changes, and this is what is called 'prime' matter—though 'ultimate' would perhaps be a better title—to distinguish it from the various specific kinds of matter. *This* genuinely is eternal, and cannot be created or destroyed (*Phys* I, 9, 192^a25–34); it is what all the four elemental stuffs are made of (*GC* II, 1, 329^a24–$^b1$), and so ultimately what all material things are made of (*H*4, 44^a15–25). There are some who have claimed that Aristotle was not committed to the existence of this ultimate matter, or anyway did not accept the commitment. Since it seems to me quite clear that he was committed to it and did accept it, I shall not discuss that issue here. (In modern times doubts have been raised by King [1956]; Charlton [1970], appendix; Jones [1974]; and answered respectively by Solmsen [1958]; Robinson [1974]; Code [1976]. Since then the case for doubt has been presented again by Stahl [1981]; Furth [1988], 221–7; Gill [1989], ch. 2 and appendix; and the case for orthodoxy by Williams [1982], appendix; Cohen [1984*a*]; Graham [1987].)

A given lump of matter, then, may persist first in one form and then in another; there is *no* form that it must always preserve. That is to say, it is not 'in its own right' any particular thing, or of any specified quantity, or anything else 'by which being is determined' (29^a20–1). It is something 'indeterminate' (*Z*11, 37^a27), and in a sense a mere 'potentiality' (*H*2, 42^b10), in so far as it is capable of taking on any form, but need have none in particular. To clarify this, a given lump of matter, at a given time, certainly will have some definite position, some definite shape, size, weight, and so on. But it can change its position, and its shape, and its size, and its weight, without ceasing to exist. So no particular position, shape, size, or weight is essential to it. If one wishes to insist that it has essentially the determinable properties of always possessing *some* position, etc., then no doubt that is acceptable. Equally, it has essentially the property of being matter, and I think we can confidently add (though Aristotle never mentions the point) that its path through space and time must be spatio-temporally continuous. From *our* point of view we can add that there is in fact a certain *quantity* that it must always preserve, namely its mass (or, in the light of the theory of relativity, its 'rest mass'); *we* do not believe that the same matter can be now of one mass and now of another. But that is our view and not Aristotle's. So one can see why, from his point of view, he should say that there is *nothing* that matter is 'in its own right', i.e. that it has *no* essential properties.

28^b33–36

The programme with which chapter 3 begins is not quite what we expect. Chapter 2 has prepared us for a discussion of the question 'What things are substances?' (cf. 28^b27–32 n.), whereas here the question at issue appears to be 'What is the substance of a thing?' What is the relation between these questions?

A very natural suggestion would be this. To determine what things are substances we need to know what it is about a thing that makes it a substance, and this perhaps is the substance *of* that thing. So the relation between the two is this: X is a substance if and only if there exists some Y such that Y is the substance of X. But there is clearly an alternative hypothesis, that the relation is rather the other way round: X is a substance if and only if there exists some Y such that X is the substance of Y. Moreover, it seems to be this alternative hypothesis that is needed to explain how Aristotle argues. For in the present chapter he may be taken to be reasoning thus: if we say that the substance of a thing is what underlies it, then (in one way) it will follow that the substance of a thing is its matter, from which he infers that 'matter will be a substance' (29^a10, $^a26$). Similarly in chapter 13 when he turns to consider the universal: the first argument that he gives is that a universal is not the substance of anything, from which he infers that it is not itself a substance (38^b8–15). If this is right, then the connection that Aristotle is assuming—without stating it—is that the substances are just those things that are the substance *of* something-or-other.

This conclusion depends, however, on two somewhat doubtful assumptions, (*a*) that Aristotle means what he says in this programmatic paragraph, and (*b*) that the last two words are elliptical for 'what underlies *it*', which is needed if the fourth candidate is to be co-ordinate to the first three. But against (*a*), while a given thing may be said to have its own essence (i.e. 'what being is'), and its own genus, it is very distinctly odd to speak of *its* universal; there appears to be nothing that would count as *the* universal that pertains to it. And against (*b*) the doctrine of the *Categories* is that what underlies is *a* substance, not that it is the substance *of* the thing that it underlies, and it certainly does appear to be the doctrine of the *Categories* that is cited in the next sentence. It is therefore very tempting to speculate that Aristotle has not quite said what he meant. He had meant to say simply that there were four candidates for being substances, namely essences and universals and genera and things that underlie. Then, since an essence is always an essence *of* something, and is the substance *of* that same thing, he carelessly wrote as if the same applied to all his other candidates too, thus giving a quite misleading impression. This speculation certainly fits very much better with the coming discussion of what underlies than the account that I gave first. Moreover, it seems to be confirmed by the summary in *H*1, 42^a12–16, which incidentally adds the information that the four candidates listed here, unlike the candidates reviewed in chapter 2, are each supported by arguments. It also tells us that the arguments in favour of the universal and the genus are comparative arguments; they aim to show that the genus is *more* a substance than the species, and that the universal is *more* a substance than the particulars. But concerning both the essence and what underlies the arguments in question simply aim to show *that they are substances*.

28^b36–29^a10

The initial description of what underlies is that it is a subject of predicates and never a predicate. This is precisely the definition of a 'primary substance' that is given in the *Categories* (2^a11–14). Some things (e.g. secondary substances) will be the subjects of some predications and the predicates of others, but a primary substance is never a predicate; it is an ultimate subject. ('Primarily' (*prōton*) in $^a2$ is to be understood as 'ultimately'.) But the *Categories* gives as its examples of ultimate subjects such things as a particular man or a particular horse. It shows no awareness of the possibility of analysing such things as compounds of form in matter, and its doctrine is now to be confronted with this analysis. Aristotle's first reaction is that this simply gives us *three* different kinds of things that are ultimate subjects, for now both the matter and the form must be accorded this status, as well as the compound of the two, which was all that the *Categories* had recognized. (I take it to be obvious that what the *Metaphysics* calls a compound of form and matter is the same thing as what the *Categories* had called a primary substance, e.g. a particular man or horse. For a different view, see Frede & Patzig, ad loc.) But this is immensely puzzling, for it seems to be built into the matter/form analysis that form cannot be an *ultimate* subject of predication; on the contrary, form must surely be predicated of matter, and apparently of the compound too. (For example, when the statue is made, the bronze comes to acquire a shape that it did not have before. But then, surely, that shape must be predicable of the bronze, and presumably of the statue too, for one may say of each of them that it is so shaped. But the second claim is disputed by Lewis [1991], ch. 7.) Anyway we expect form to be predicated of matter, and indeed Aristotle several times affirms that it is (*Z*13, 38^b4–6; *H*2, 43^a5–6; *H*3, 43^b30–2; *Θ*7, 49^a34–6; cf. *Z*17, 41^a26–8, $^b4$–9). *Pace* Brunschwig [1979], there is nothing at all mysterious about such predications. What is mysterious is that Aristotle should *also* characterize form as a subject (an 'underlying thing') rather than a predicate, as he does both here and at *H*1, 42^a26–31.

It has been proposed by Irwin [1988], 214–15, that we should understand the criterion for substancehood to be introduced in *Z*4, namely of being expressed 'without predicating one thing of another' (30^a10–11), as the 'clearer version' of the 'subject criterion' that *Z*3 desires (at $^a10$). Then we can say that form does satisfy this clearer version. But that is wholly unreasonable, for the *Z*4 criterion is demanding internal simplicity, which is not at all the same as being a subject rather than a predicate. Another suggestion, which Ross seems to accept, is that Aristotle does not really mean to call form an *ultimate* subject; his thought is that it is a subject, though it is also a predicate, like the secondary substances of the *Categories*. This is certainly a possible view of the passage at *H*1, 42^a26–31, where ultimacy is not mentioned. But on this account the present passage is a mistake, as was suggested long ago by Bonitz [1848], ii. 301. Perhaps the most straightforward explanation (adopted, for example, by Frede [1978]) is to suppose that Aristotle distinguished between forms as universals, which are predicated, and forms as particulars, which are not. But it is controversial whether Aristotle thought that there were such things as particular forms. On this, see the prologue to *Z*13. For a further suggestion about how forms may be counted as 'underlying things', see *H*1, 46^a26–31 n.

29^a5–7: 'If form is prior to matter . . . it will also be prior to the compound of both, for the same reason.' I suspect that this statement should not be pressed too closely. Aristotle surely does hold that form is prior to matter, but it is not at all clear what specific kind of priority he is here thinking of as the relevant one (cf. *Z*1, 28^a30–$^b2$ n.), or what he would give as the reason for it holding. Whatever these are, it seems improbable that the same reason, and the same priority, would hold of the form and the compound. For more on this topic, see *Z*10, *passim*.

29^a10–26

This paragraph divides into two parts. In the first ($^a10$–19) Aristotle offers an argument to show that only matter satisfies the proposed criterion; in the second ($^a20$–6) he begins by explaining what he means by matter, then gives a second version of the argument, and apparently concludes from this that matter must be as he has explained it. Let us take the first half first.

$^a10$–19: 'When all else is taken away,' Aristotle says, 'nothing apparent remains.' The phrase 'all else' might be taken to mean, in the context, 'everything but matter'. But then, while it is no doubt true that if you take away everything but matter then only matter remains, it would not seem to establish anything of interest. (Presumably it is equally true that if you take away everything but shape then only shape remains.) So it is perhaps best to take this phrase as meaning 'everything that admittedly is not substance, e.g. all qualities, quantities, and so on'. (That is why the parenthesis at $^a15$ reminds us that a quantity is not a substance; it is therefore legitimate to 'take it away'.) When we do 'take away' all these things that are not substance, then, Aristotle says, 'nothing apparent remains' (*ou phainetai ouden hupomenon*). This might be taken to mean that nothing *at all* remains, or that nothing *perceptible* remains. Schofield [1972] has offered an interpretation of the passage which takes the first alternative, and accordingly when Aristotle repeats his claim by saying 'we see nothing remaining, unless there be something which is determined by these' ($^a17$–18) he takes it that there is in fact nothing that is 'determined by these'. (In fact he prefers to see the 'unless' clause as 'an inept gloss', p. 99.) But I cannot see how, on this interpretation, Aristotle could think himself entitled to conclude that 'on this view it must appear that matter alone is substance' ($^a18$–19). So we must suppose that he means that something *does* remain, namely matter. (Similarly he says at *Physics* IV, 209^b9–11: 'When the boundary and the attributes of the sphere are taken away, nothing is left besides the matter.') But why, then, should he imply that this matter that remains is not perceptible? If we think in terms of the bronze statue, which has bronze as its matter, this seems rather mysterious. For to 'take away' its length, breadth, and depth is presumably to imagine it as altered in these respects (or perhaps to think of it as not yet specified in these respects). But if this thought-experiment is still to leave the bronze, with other or unspecified spatial dimensions, then surely it still leaves something perceptible? But the answer must be that we are *also* to 'take away' those other attributes of the bronze, such as its colour, weight, hardness, and so on, in virtue of which it is bronze, and perceived as such. This we are entitled to do because these attributes also are not substances. Then what we have left is merely 'prime' (or 'ultimate') matter, which indeed Aristotle does characterize as imperceptible (*GC* II, 332^a27, $^b1$; cf. *GC* I, 319^b8–18?). (His thought presumably is that any matter that one perceives must be perceived *as* matter of this or that specific kind—bronze or wood or water or whatever; one cannot perceive it just *as* ultimate matter.)

A difficulty with this interpretation (which is urged by Gill [1989], 23–6) is that Aristotle imagines us 'taking away' not only the spatial dimensions of our subject, and its other attributes (*pathē*), but also its *capacities* (*potentialities—dunameis*). But it surely must be impossible to take from any kind of matter its *capacity* to assume the appropriate form, while yet leaving it still matter of that same kind; and even prime matter is no exception to this. This difficulty must simply be admitted, and can only be met by supposing that Aristotle did not really mean to strip off *all* capacities. Presumably nothing whatever could survive the loss of *every* capacity for *every* attribute. (Gill in effect suggests that Aristotle thought that the 'receptacle' of Plato's *Timaeus* would be supposed to survive such a loss (pp. 26–30); but I see no probability in that suggestion.) Nor is it too surprising that Aristotle should be somewhat imprecise about just what one is to imagine taken away, for when one thinks about this question the weakness of this whole line of argument becomes apparent.

Aristotle's basic thought is that a genuine substance must be able to survive the loss of any of its non-substantial properties, i.e. its qualities, quantities, relations, and so on. So if we 'take away' all of these—and we can most simply envisage this as a matter of imagining them to be different—then what remains will be the genuine substance. But with any supposed substance other than pure matter there will always be some non-substantial properties that it cannot exist without. (For example, a statue cannot survive the loss of its shape, an animal cannot survive the loss of its capacity to perceive (Z1, 28^{a}33–4 n.), and so on.) Only pure matter, then, will pass this test, and it does pass just because none of its properties is essential to it. Two comments may be made on this argument. (i) Its cogency depends very much on what we are to count as the 'non-substantial' properties of a thing. Thus (*a*) having the ability to perceive is having a soul of a certain kind, and we shall learn that the soul of animal is its *essence* (see prologue to Z10). Are we entitled, then, to regard it as a 'non-substantial' property of the animal? Similarly, are we in fact entitled to regard the spatial dimensions of a statue as 'non-substantial' properties of it? Or again (*b*), in the other direction, if we are allowed to say that the property of filling space *is* 'non-substantial', then clearly matter cannot satisfy this test any better than anything else; for all matter must fill space. (ii) Assuming the argument to be cogent, it must nevertheless be convicted of *ignoratio elenchi*. It has no tendency to show that matter, and only matter, is an ultimate subject of predication, which is what was to be proved. At best it shows that matter, and only matter, is 'separable' from non-substances in a sense very similar to that desired in Z1, 28^{a}33–4 n. But clearly Aristotle himself cannot have seen the argument as establishing a suitable kind of 'separability' for matter, for he will very soon go on to complain that matter is *not* 'separable' (39^{a}26–8). Neither of these objections applies to the revised version of the argument to be found in the second half of this paragraph; it does not depend upon ignoring the distinction between 'substantial' and 'non-substantial' properties, and it is directed exactly to the point at issue.

^{a}20–36: What I have called the 'revised' version of the argument is just this: other things are predicated of substance, and substance of matter (^{a}23–4). It is very commonly supposed that when Aristotle here says 'substance is predicated of matter', by 'substance' he means 'form'. (According to Brunschwig [1979], 132, this view is universal.) But to take it in this way is to miss the point of the argument, which is supposed to show that *only* matter is an ultimate subject. So in particular it needs to be argued that what the *Categories* calls a primary substance—a particular man, or horse—is not after all an ultimate subject; no doubt other things are predicated of it, but *it* must be predicated of something further, namely its matter. Thus, when one says that this aggregate of flesh and bones here is Socrates, or again that the ('prime') matter here is *the* flesh and bones of which Socrates is made, in each case one is predicating a particular of its matter. From our point of view, this means simply that the 'is' of predication includes as a special case the 'is' of constitution. (For the 'is' of 'this matter is Socrates' is not an ordinary 'is' of predication, since that must be followed by a general term, but nor is it the 'is' of identity, since the same matter may persist while Socrates does not; it is, as we now recognize, a further kind of 'is' called the 'is' of constitution.)

One might therefore resist Aristotle's argument by insisting upon a distinction between predication and constitution, and this is in effect to distinguish between two senses of his technical term 'to underlie'. In what we may call the 'logical' sense a subject of predication is said to underlie its predicates, and in what we may call a 'physical' sense the matter of which a thing is made is said to underlie the thing so made. So in the physical sense only matter is an ultimate underlier, but in the logical sense any particular will qualify as such, since it is only universals that can be predicated (*Int* $17^a38-{}^b1$; *An. Pri* 43^a25-32). One might take it that Z13, 38^b5-6, is intended to state just such a distinction between two senses of 'to underlie'. With more certainty one may observe that Θ7 clearly reasserts that the particular man is an *ultimate* subject of predication, explaining that it is not him but his form that is predicated of his matter ($^a34-6$). So no doubt Aristotle *could* have resisted the argument that he gives here in Z3 for saying that matter is the *only* ultimate subject, and later on he certainly does (in Θ7, if not before). But one cannot be confident that that is how he was thinking here in Z3. The most that can be said is that such a distinction between different senses of underlying would serve very well to remedy the 'unclarity' complained of at $^a10$.

In what I have said so far I have presumed that we have *independent* grounds, resting in fact on Aristotle's theory of change, for affirming the existence of matter as something which has (almost) no properties 'in its own right'. But Aristotle's own thought seems to be that *any* ultimate subject of predication must be devoid of properties 'in its own right'. He claims that for any thing predicated there is something which it is predicated of, and which 'itself has a being different from each of the predicates' ($^a22-3$), and he goes on apparently to infer '*and so* the last thing will not be in its own right . . . anything at all' ($^a24-5$). This, however, is a mistake. For example, Socrates may be said to 'have a being different from' the predicate *man*, since Socrates is a particular and the predicate is a universal. And this predicate is truly predicated of Socrates. But it does not follow that Socrates is not in his own right a man. Similarly, we may predicate of any lump of matter both that it is matter and that it has such-and-such a mass, and it cannot *follow* that the lump is not matter, or is not of that mass, in its own right. No argument based simply on the nature of predication can show that there are things which have no essential properties. Consequently it is sometimes suggested that Aristotle does not himself endorse this premiss that subject and predicate always have 'a different being', and that in his own view the argument fails at this point. But one may reply that while the

Aristotle of the Logical Works should certainly view the premiss with suspicion (and similarly the Aristotle of *Γ*4, $1007^{a}20$–$^{b}1$), still the author of *Z*17 may well have been more content with it. For he is very scornful of saying that 'a thing is itself'.

$29^{a}26$–33

The conclusion to which we have been led is one which Aristotle now rejects as impossible. It is impossible, apparently, because matter is not 'separable' and is not 'a this'. Postponing for the moment Aristotle's explanation of *why* the conclusion is impossible, let us first ask *what* exactly he claims to be impossible. It is either (*a*) that matter should be *a* substance (see e.g. Owen [1978], 13–14; Burnyeat [1979], 11–13; Ackrill [1981], 125; Lear [1988], 277; Furth [1988], 187–8), or (*b*) that matter should be the *only* substance (see e.g. Kung [1978]; Irwin [1988], 207–11; Frede & Patzig, ad loc; Lewis [1991], ch. 10). On the face of it, it is (*a*) that he intends, for it is this that is directly stated to be impossible at $29^{a}26$–7, and this that had earlier been mentioned as problematic at $29^{a}10$. But it is implied that matter is a substance only a few lines later, when at $^{a}32$ form is said to be 'the *third* kind of substance', and this implication is amply confirmed by what comes afterwards. Matter is affirmed to be a substance in passing at *Z*10, $35^{a}2$, at length in *H*1, $42^{a}24$–$^{b}8$, and subsequently on several occasions in *H*2 ($42^{b}9$–10, $43^{a}14$–19, $43^{a}26$–8) and at *H*4, $44^{a}15$. (Similarly *Λ*3, $1070^{a}9$–13; *Anim* II, 1, $412^{a}6$–9.) Nor can we suppose (as Owen does) that these passages are to be reconciled with *Z*3 by supposing that in *Z*3 it is *prime* matter that is said not to be a substance, while elsewhere it is more familiar kinds of matter that are allowed as substances. For prime matter is evidently included as a material substance at *H*4, $44^{a}15$–25, and—more importantly—it is specifically prime matter that is said to be a substance at *H*1, $42^{a}24$–31, even though it is not 'a this', and—it is implied—not 'separable' either.

Now one might suppose that this argument in *Z*3 is simply incompatible with most of the rest of *Z* and *H*. (As we shall see, it is extremely difficult to avoid this conclusion about *Z*13.) The best version of this interpretation will be that the whole discussion of prime matter, from 'But it is not enough to say only this' in $^{a}9$ to 'would seem to be substance more than matter is' in $^{a}29$–30, is a later addition to an original version of *Z*3 that lacked this discussion altogether. So the supposed 'original' version of *Z*3 would just have said that there are three things that underlie—namely matter, form, and the compound of the two—and would have gone on to observe that form is prior to the other two, and most needs further discussion. This is certainly compatible with what is said elsewhere in *Z* and *H*. Then later Aristotle added this awkward problem about matter being a substance, but never got around to revising the rest of *Z* and *H* to take account of it. (One might suggest that this supposed later version of Z3 would belong to the same period as Z16, 40^b5–16, for that passage contains a line of thought which implies that matter cannot be a substance, but the implication is not fully explicit.) There are three points that one might urge in favour of this reconstruction. (i) It allows Aristotle to mean what he actually says at 29^a26–7. (ii) It explains, what otherwise seems rather odd, how the thesis that matter is a substance can be calmly accepted at 29^a2 but regarded as problematic at 29^a10. (iii) It does something to mitigate the rather surprising dismissal of matter as 'in a way evident' at 29^a32. For *prime* matter is surely not in any way 'evident' (*phaneron*), and Aristotle himself has just implied that it is 'not apparent' (*ou phainetai*, 29^a12). But, on the suggested reconstruction, it was not prime matter that this remark was aimed at, but only such ordinary matter as bronze (29^a4).

On the alternative interpretation, point (iii) just mentioned simply has to be accepted as surprising, and nothing more can be done with it. Points (i) and (ii) are met by the response that Aristotle has not quite said what he meant. He meant to introduce as problematic (at $^a10$), and then condemn as impossible (at $^a26$–7), the view that matter is the *only* substance. (So on this interpretation one is tempted to translate 'matter is substance' rather than 'matter is a substance'; but that is not the most natural way of taking the Greek.) This, after all, is the conclusion that his line of reasoning is meant to establish, as is stated at 29^a19. Moreover, the way in which he rejects this conclusion clearly does *allow* him to retain matter as a substance. For he says that separability and thisness belong *chiefly* to substances—he does not say that they belong to *all* substances—and hence he concludes that the form and the compound seem to be substance *more* than matter is. Since this reasoning is after all quite compatible with the claim of *H*1 that matter is a substance, though not separable and not a this, it may well be said that there is no call for the extravagant speculations of the first interpretation. All that we need to do is to recognize again, as at 28^b33–6, that Aristotle's expression can be somewhat imprecise. On the whole this second interpretation seems to me to be preferable.

On either interpretation of the argument, its moral must be that it is not true that 'what most seems to be substance is what ultimately underlies' (29^a1–2). For on any view matter is at least one of the things that ultimately underlie, but it is not what *most* seems to be substance. On a true view there are also other things which may be said to be, in their own way, ultimate underliers, namely the compounds of form in matter which the *Categories* had called 'primary substances'. Our present argument, failing to distinguish the relevant senses of 'underlying', has claimed that these are not ultimate underliers, though they are certainly restored to that status in Θ7, and possibly earlier at Z13, 38^b5–6. But in any case they too do not qualify as 'what *most* seems to be substance', for they are compounds of form in matter, and the form is prior to the compound, and so presumably has a better title to be substance (in view of Z1, 28^a31–2). Form, then, is what *most* seems to be substance. It is also the 'most puzzling' of the three candidates. So it is hardly surprising that Aristotle should now promise a further discussion of it. Unfortunately the further discussion does not much help to clarify the claim here that form *is* one of the ultimate underliers; nor does it really assist one in understanding how form should be 'separable' and 'a this' to a greater extent than matter is.

$^a28$: *Separability*. Aristotle's physical theory posits a single stuff, i.e. prime matter, out of which everything is made. When he wishes to distinguish this theory from (what he took to be) Thales' theory, that everything is made of water, or Heracleitus' theory, that everything is made of fire, he tells us that his single stuff is 'not separable' (e.g. *GC* II, 1, 329^a24–7; *Phys* IV, 9, 217^a21–6). It is clear that he means by this that it cannot occur 'on its own', but only in the form of one or another specific kind of stuff. It is not clear whether he would equally wish to say that a specific kind of stuff, say bronze, is 'not separable', on the ground that it cannot occur without some definite shape, even though no particular shape is essential to it. If so, then this line of thought seems to generalize to the view that a 'separable substance' must be such that all its properties, at any time, are essential to it, and the consequence would be that no material substance can be 'separable' (though God, perhaps, would still qualify).

At *H*1, 42^a26–31 we are unambiguously told that the particular material substances that are compounds of form in matter are 'separable without qualification'. It seems probable that the 'separability' claimed for substance at *Z*1, 28^a33–4 should be similarly understood as applying to substances of this kind, though I have not been able to suggest any suitable sense of 'separability' that would substantiate this claim. In the same passage in *H*1 the form is by contrast said to be 'separable in formula' (i.e. in definition), and the same phrase is occasionally used elsewhere (e.g. *Phys* II, 1, 193^b5). Somewhat surprisingly, in *Δ*8 the form is said to be 'separable' without such a qualification added (1017^b25–6), though apparently it is still forms of material substances that are in question. On the other hand we are explicitly told in *H*3 that the form of a house, or an implement, does not exist apart from the particulars, and hence does not count as 'separable', and it is hinted that the same applies to the forms of plants and of animals, with one possible exception. (See 43^b18–23 n.) If it is not to be a trivial truth that everything that has a definition counts as 'separable in definition', then the idea is perhaps this: the definition of a (substantial) form does not mention any other kind of thing, without which the thing defined cannot exist. (Contrast the definition of a finger, *Z*10, 35^b10–11.) Taken in a fairly natural way, this would imply that the particular substances that have those forms are 'separate from one another', as advocated by Morrison [1985]. But, as he notes himself (pp. 154–5), this seems a poor ground for saying that the form itself is either 'separate' or 'separable'.

Separability (or separateness) evidently indicates some sort of independent existence, but Aristotle never explains just what sort he is thinking of. One suspects that there is no one kind of independence that matter lacks, that the compound has, and that the form also has (though perhaps in a qualified way); and Aristotle does little to disarm this suspicion. It is a pity that book *Δ* contains no dictionary entry for 'separability', nor for 'thisness'.

^{a}28: *Thisness*. In the simple terminology of the *Categories*, the odd phrase 'a this' appears just to mean 'a particular' (*Cat* 3^{b}10–23). But by the time we come to the central books of the *Metaphysics* it is clear that Aristotle has given this phrase a much wider range of uses—so wide, indeed, that it is very difficult to see what significance he now attaches to it. We must, then, begin with a brief survey of the evidence.

There are, I think, three main uses to be distinguished. (i) The most straightforward is that in which it is applied to a particular as opposed to a universal. This seems to be the original use (as in *Cat* 3^{b}10, *SE* 178^{b}38–179^{a}10), and it is no doubt in this sense that he says at *Phys* I, 7, 190^{b}25 that matter *is* a this. The word is still used in this way in the *Metaphysics*. In book *Z* there are several clear occurrences at *Z*8, 33^{a}31–2, ^{b}21–4 (which includes an application to matter at ^{b}23); also at *Z*11, 37^{a}2; *Z*13, 39^{a}1 and ^{a}16. I would add *Z*14, 39^{a}30–2 and ^{b}4, and (more controversially) *Z*13, 38^{b}5. (ii) *Perhaps* because the only particulars that Aristotle recognizes are in the category of substance, he also uses 'a this' simply as a label for that category as opposed to others, e.g. at *Phys* III, 201^{b}26; *GC* I, 317^{b}8–11; *Anim* I, 402^{a}24 and 410^{a}13–15. There are examples of this use at *Z*1, 28^{a}12; *Z*4, 30^{a}19; *Z*4, 30^{b}10–12; *Z*7, 32^{a}15; *H*6, 45^{b}2; and I think we may add *Z*13, 38^{b}24–7. In some of these places one might suspect that Aristotle is thinking mainly of particular substances (e.g. *Z*1, 28^{a}12), but in others the context shows that it is only universals that are in question (*Z*4, 30^{a}19; *H*6, 45^{b}2; *Z*13, 38^{b}24–7). (iii) Finally there is the use in which 'a this' is applied to a form or essence. Sometimes the form is called a this in contrast to the privation, e.g. *GC* I, 318^{b}15–17 and ^{b}32. This is found at *H*1, 42^{b}1–3. More often the contrast is between form and matter, as at *Δ*8, 1017^{b}25; *Θ*7, 1049^{a}35; *Λ*3, 1070^{a}11; *Anim* II, 412^{a}7–9. This is found at *H*1, 42^{a}27–9. Occasionally it is the essence that is called a this as opposed to the coincidental attribute, as at *An. Post* I, 4, 73^{b}7. I suspect that this is the intended contrast at *Z*4, 30^{a}2–5 and at *Z*12, 37^{b}27. This has listed all the occurrences of 'a this' in books *Z* and *H*, save for the present occurrence at *Z*3, 29^{a}28.

If one asks what single conception of 'thisness' could hold together this wide variety of uses, then perhaps the best suggestion is that 'a this' is something definite and determinate, rather than indefinite or determinable (cf. Gill [1989], 31–4). Aristotle not infrequently characterizes the universal as indeterminate (*ahoriston*) by comparison with the particular (e.g. *Θ*7, 1049^{a}36–^{b}2; *M*10, 1087^{a}16–18; cf. *Z*1, 28^{a}27), he describes matter in the same way by comparison with form (e.g. *A*8, 989^{b}18; *Z*11, 37^{a}27), and he says the same too of the privation (e.g. *Phys* III, 201^{b}26).

On the other hand, one cannot see why Aristotle should choose the strange phrase 'a this' to express this idea, when the word 'determinate' is already available. An alternative explanation may be drawn from the occurrence at *An. Post* I, 4, 73^b7 (which I take to be relatively early; I think it is the only occurrence of 'a this' in the Logical Works that does not simply mean 'a particular'). Here Aristotle is clearly thinking of the demonstrative 'this' as introducing a subject of predication, but he also has views about what counts as a 'proper' or 'natural' subject (cf. Barnes [1975] ad loc). The right kind of subject-expression is of the kind 'this *X*', where '*X*' says what the subject is, i.e. gives its essence. (Hence 'this walking thing' and 'this pale thing' are *not* proper subject-expressions.) So it comes about that Aristotle thinks of the expression '*X*' as 'signifying a this' when it can appropriately be prefixed by the word 'this' to form a proper subject-expression 'this *X*'. That is just to say that it is essences which are thises, and on this suggestion they are called thises because they are what we need to introduce proper subjects of predication (cf. *Anim* II, 412^a7–9). Since Aristotle commonly takes it that form and essence are to be identified, this will of course explain why he calls the form a this. Since again he commonly refers to the category of substance as the category of essence (i.e. of 'what-it-is'), this will also explain why he can equally call it the category of what signifies a this. But this explanation does not give us a *single* conception of thisness, for the fact that the particular is also called 'a this' should now be regarded as a different, but of course connected, use of the expression. Whether Aristotle also has that different use in mind when he claims here that thisness belongs chiefly to substances may be doubted. At any rate it is the form rather than the compound that he insists is a this at *Δ*8, 1017^b25; at *H*1, 42^a26–31; at *Λ*3, 1070^a9–13; and at *Anim* II, 1, 412^a6–9.

According to the first explanation, then, matter is not a this because (in Aristotle's view) it must be counted as indeterminate; by contrast the form and the compound are each counted as determinate. It may well be doubted whether there is any one concept of 'determinacy' that would verify these three claims, but I shall not investigate that question further. According to the second explanation, matter is not a this because it is not the essence of what has matter, and therefore, is not suitable for introducing a subject of predication, whereas the form is. But if this is Aristotle's thought then again we must protest that it does not actually yield the conclusion he desires. No doubt it is true that matter is not the essence of what *has* matter, but it is equally true that matter is the essence of what *is* matter, so if it is matter that we wish to talk about then there is no better way of introducing our subject than by an expression such as 'this matter' (or, in a particular case, 'this bronze' or 'this water' or 'this earth' and so on). That is to say, on this way of understanding thisness, matter is in fact just as much 'a this' as form is. I suspect that we should get the same result on any plausible account of thisness.

To sum up, Aristotle considers that substances, which are the fundamental existents, should if possible be (*a*) things that ultimately underlie, and (*b*) thises, and (*c*) separable. To judge from *H*1, his view is that matter qualifies as a substance primarily on ground (*a*), form on ground (*b*), and the compound on ground (*c*), though all three do count as underlying things. But on the deeper question of *why* it is desirable that 'fundamental existents' should satisfy these three criteria (or others to be introduced later) there is nothing that one can say. Aristotle appears to have taken them to be wholly self-evident, and never offers anything that could be regarded as a justification of them.

29^a33–$^b12$

In this final paragraph Aristotle's thought is that, if we can first become clear about the familiar and perceptible substances, we shall then be in a better position to attack the question of what substances there are that are not perceptible. The thought is repeated, more succinctly, at *Z*11, 37^a10–18 and at *Z*17, 41^a6–9. (Cf. also *Z*2, 28^b27–32 and *H*1, 42^a22–4.) He also follows this plan in his own discussion in book *Λ*, where chapters 1–5 briefly summarize a number of points about perceptible substances before chapters 6–10 move on to non-perceptible substances. (One is, however, rather at a loss when trying to say just how the first investigation is supposed to have helped us with the second. For one rather drastic suggestion on this topic, see the prologue to *Z*13, pp. 185–6.)

CHAPTER 4

In chapters 4 and 5 Aristotle begins his discussion of 'what being is for a thing', i.e. the essence of a thing. This, he explains, is given by its definition. But the burden of the discussion in these two chapters is to place restrictions on what may be said to *have* a definition. It appears that, properly speaking, only species (i.e. forms) in the category of substance will qualify.

29^{b}1–13

The phrase which I translate as 'what being is (for a thing)', i.e. '*to ti ēn* (*hekastōi*) *einai*', is a phrase of Aristotle's own invention. A more literal rendering is 'the what [it] was (for a thing) to be', but the past tense of 'was' appears to have no significance. From as early as the *Topics* (101^{a}19–23, and *passim*) this phrase has been used interchangeably with 'definition'.

I use 'logical' to translate—or rather, to transliterate—'*logikōs*'. It is difficult to know quite what force to attach to the word, especially when, as here, it is not clear what it is contrasted with. In view of the fact that '*logos*' often means 'definition', it would be quite natural to suppose that Aristotle is proposing to begin by *defining* his notion of essence. In that case, the 'logical remarks' continue only to 29^{b}22, as suggested by Woods [1974/5], 170–1. But one might also suppose that 'logical remarks' are those which concern language, or 'how to express oneself' (*pōs dei legein*); in that case they are not brought to an end until 30^{a}27, as proposed by Ross, and by Owen [1960], 176 n. Yet a further suggestion is that we quite often find 'logical remarks' contrasted with 'physical remarks' (e.g. *Phys* 204^{b}4–10, *GC* 316^{a}11–14), where the contrast is between an approach that remains general and abstract and one that goes more deeply into the nature of the objects concerned. From this perspective one might suggest that all of chapters 4–6 discuss essence 'abstractly', and it is not until essence is viewed as form, in contrast to matter, that the 'abstract' approach ceases.

29^{b}13–22

The essence of a thing is what it is said to be 'in its own right' in Aristotle's most common usage of that phrase, i.e. what it is said to be in an essential predication. Thus, since you are not essentially artistic, being artistic is not your essence (nor, we may add, is it even any part of your essence). There is a clear implication in this remark that there is such a thing as your essence, but we should not be tempted by this to assume that your essence must be peculiar to you. On the contrary, the usual view is that your essence is exactly the same as mine, namely to be a man (in the sense, of course, of a human being). But it is somewhat awkward that Aristotle is about to go on to say that an essence is what is given by a definition, for your essence is not what is given by your definition. You have no definition (as is argued at length in Z15). Your essence, then, is given by the definition, not of you, but of what you are said to be in your own right, i.e. a man. This is a complication that Aristotle here pays no attention to. (It will surface again at Z6, 32^a6–10.)

But there is another complication that he does pay attention to, in $^b16$–20. In Aristotle's most common usage, a predication '*A* is *B*' is counted as a predication 'in its own right' when *B* is, or is part of, the definition of *A*. But he also has another usage, which needs to be marked off: *A* is *also* said to be *B* 'in its own right', not when *B* occurs in the definition of *A* but when *A* occurs in the definition of *B*. (This is the second sense of 'in its own right' given at *An. Post* I, 4, 73^a34–$^b5$; it is also described at Δ18, 22^a29–32, and will have a large part to play in the argument of chapter 5.) The example here (as in Δ18) is when one predicates of a surface that it is pale. For Aristotle holds that colours belong primarily to surfaces (and derivatively to the things that have those surfaces), and that this point should figure in the definition of any colour. As his reason for setting aside this kind of 'in its own right', as not what is intended here, Aristotle states that being for a surface is not the same as being for something pale. One may note that this *also* sets aside a further kind of '*A* is *B*' predication 'in its own right', namely where *B* is part, but only part, of the definition of *A*. For in such a case too it will not be true that being for *A* is the same as being for *B*. (For example, being for a man is not the same as being for an animal.)

Having remarked that being for something pale is not the same as being for a surface, Aristotle adds, apparently as an aside, that being for something pale is also not the same as being for a pale surface. His objection is not that 'is pale' is not equivalent to 'is a pale surface', but that in the supposed equation the left-hand side is repeated in the right-hand side, so that as a definition it would be blatantly circular. This then leads him to his final characterization of what an essence is: we have a formula which gives the essence of a thing where (*a*) this formula does 'express the thing' (correctly, one presumes), and (*b*) it is not circular by including [a mention of] that thing itself. (Other interpretations of this very elliptical passage are given by Ross; Woods [1974/5], 174–5; Frede & Patzig; Gill [1989], 117.)

The point of the final parenthesis at $^b21$–2 is not clear, but perhaps Aristotle means to indicate that the argument so far does not prevent us finding an account of what being is for a pale thing. For example, if Democritus was right to identify the pale surfaces with the smooth surfaces (*De Sensu* 442^b10–12), then, because of the special relationship between pale or smooth *things* and pale or smooth *surfaces*, we can equally identify the pale things with the smooth things, and being for a pale thing with being for a smooth thing.

29^b22-30^a6

In this paragraph Aristotle argues that certain compound items do not have an essence. The compounds he has in mind appear to be those expressed by coupling a term from the category of substance (e.g. 'man') with a term from some other category (e.g. 'pale', again). His opening words suggest that he has already been discussing a compound from some other category (or categories), and perhaps arguing that *it* has no essence. But, at least on my way of construing the previous paragraph, this latter suggestion is quite out of place. The compound 'pale surface' has indeed figured in the discussion, and this is a compound of two terms neither of which is in the category of substance; but we were not discussing whether *it* had an essence.

The general structure of the paragraph appears to be this. At $^b28$ Aristotle raises the question of what the essence of a pale man might be (supposing there to be a single word for 'pale man'). Then a reason is suggested for saying that it has no essence, and this reason is disputed down to $^a2$. The dispute appears to be left unfinished, but apparently the reason offered is found to be inadequate. Then at $^a2$ the question whether there is an essence of a pale man is raised once more, and a different reason is given (and accepted) for saying that it has none.

$^b28-^a2$: This section is in many ways obscure. First, it is not clear what is supposed to be the advantage of having a single word for 'pale man', and why the question 'What is the essence of a pale man?' could not have been raised directly. Next, the correct doubt to raise about this question would seem to be: 'But is there anything which a pale man is said to be in its own right?' I am inclined to think that the Greek *can* be taken in this sense, and will so take it, though one has to admit that it could more naturally be taken in a different way (i.e. as relying on the contrast between entities that *exist* in their own right and those that only exist coincidentally, as in Z6). Supposing, then, that this is what is meant, the reply seems to be: 'Why not? There are two ways in which a predication "A pale man is *X*" may fail to predicate *X* of the subject in its own right, and there is no reason to suppose that everything predicated of a pale man must fall short in one of these two ways.' However, the text that we have lacks this last claim, i.e. that there is no reason to suppose that everything predicated of a pale man falls short in one of the two ways explained, so one cannot be at all sure that the interpretation I suggest is indeed what Aristotle intended. (Moreover, I should remark here that the words 'It may be said' and 'But we may reply' are supplied by me (following Ross), and are not in the Greek, which simply has 'But' and 'or' respectively.)

The suggestion that there are *only* the two specified ways in which a predicate may fail to be true of the subject in its own right, i.e. may fail to be a definition of the subject, is surely an exaggeration. One of them is illustrated by giving, as the definition of 'pale', what is actually the definition of 'pale man' (and this is presumably the definition 'from addition'); the other by giving, as the definition of 'pale man', what is actually (the definition of?) 'pale'. It seems clear that an attempt to define 'pale man' *need* not fail in one or other of these ways. (And one may note, incidentally, that the illustration actually assumes that there *is* a definition of 'pale man'.)

(At $^b33$ the translation 'the reverse occurs' is a fudge, designed to fit the two illustrations we are given. More literally, the Greek says that in the first case what is defined is defined 'by it being added to something else', and in the second case 'by something else [being added] to it'. But there is no contrast between these two descriptions; defining *X* by adding *X* to *Y* is no different from defining *X* by adding *Y* to *X*. What is illustrated in the second case might better be described as defining *X* by *subtracting* something from it. Accordingly, Frede & Patzig propose inserting a 'not', so that the text reads 'by something else not [being added] to it'.)

$^a2-6$: Aristotle now switches to a different line of argument: an essence must be a this, whereas a compound such as 'pale man' is not a this. Indeed, he says, only a substance is a this, and compounds are not substances.

We may accept the premiss that a compound in which one thing is predicated of another is not a substance. At any rate, the compounds in question were introduced as compounded from the category of substance and some other category ($^b22-6$), and the categories were intended as classifying only simple items, not compounds. (Of course, this premiss appears highly contentious when considered in the light of the analysis of substances as themselves compounds of form and matter. But that analysis is not here in prospect, as I argue in my epilogue to chapters 4–6.) It is less clear why Aristotle should be entitled to claim that only a substance is a this, at any rate if he is thinking of thisness along the lines suggested in Z3, 29^a28 n. For that suggestion was that the description '*X*' counts as introducing a this if the phrase 'this *X*' is one that Aristotle will recognize as forming a proper subject-expression, i.e. one that gives the essence of the subject in question. But presumably there is nothing improper about such subject-expressions as 'this colour', or 'this length', when it is colours or lengths that we wish to speak of. Nevertheless, he would seem to be justified in his claim that a compound such as 'pale man' is not a this, i.e. that 'this pale man' is not a proper subject-expression. This is because (in our terminology) the essence of the item referred to is not to be a pale man, but simply to be a man. And the same will hold for any similar compound where the non-substantial component is not already a part of the essence of the substantial component.

But does it follow that the compound has no essence? Here we need to distinguish. The phrase 'the essence of a pale man' may be taken as generalizing over the essence of each particular pale man. Now Aristotle is prepared to distinguish the pale man from the man, since the one underlies the other (Z1, 28^a20–31 n.), and on this approach it will be reasonable to say that, whereas the man has an essence, the pale man does not. We would prefer to say rather that the essence of the pale man is just the same as the essence of the man, namely to be a man. In either case we can agree that there is no essence which is peculiar to pale men. But the phrase 'the essence of a pale man' can of course be taken quite differently, as speaking of the essence of a certain compound *universal* expressed by 'pale man'. When the phrase is taken in this way, the fact that this expression fails to introduce a this, in the sense explained, is neither here nor there. Nor can I see any other interpretation of 'a this' that would be more relevant. For the essence of a universal is what is given by its definition, and there is no reason to suppose that a compound universal cannot be defined. (On the contrary, it seems obvious that if the components of a compound can be defined, then so too can the compound itself.) Yet Aristotle's conclusion clearly is that a compound lacks a definition, so it surely should be the compound universal that is in question.

The argument, then, appears to rely on a confusion between two ways of taking the phrase 'the essence of a pale man'. (We shall see what seems to be a similar confusion at Z6, 31^a19–28.) But, formally speaking, the fault is that the opening premiss, namely 'an essence must be a this', is false. It is true that a this must be an essence, in the sense that a universal which introduces a proper subject (when prefaced by 'this') must be the essence of the *particulars* that fall under it. But there appears to be no good reason to claim that the essence of a universal must be 'a this', either in this sense or in any other.

(For the translation of '*estin hoper X*' as 'is just what is *X*' see Barnes [1975], 168, and compare *H*6, 45^a36–$^b7$.)

30^a6–17

In this paragraph Aristotle moves on to his positive claim about what does have an essence, and the word 'formula' (i.e. '*logos*'), which often does mean 'definition' in Aristotle, is here given a wider signification. In this paragraph any (meaningful) series of words is apparently counted as a formula—even that very long series of words, stretching for twenty-four books, which is the *Iliad*. But only a formula of a certain kind will be a definition (*horismos*), and the things that have essences will be the things that have formulae of that kind. These, he claims, will be just those things that are 'forms of a genus'.

The initial 'therefore' would seem to look back partly to the preceding paragraph, but also partly to the one before, which had claimed 'wherever, then, the formula expressing a thing does not include that thing itself, this is the formula of what being is for the thing' ($^b19$–20). It is this that licenses the conclusion that the things that have essences will be those whose formula is a definition, but it is the discussion of compounds in the last paragraph that must be taken to justify the extremely restrictive conditions that Aristotle proceeds to place on what, properly speaking, counts as a definition. No doubt it is fair to say that the *Iliad* is not the kind of formula that could be the definition of anything, even if we were to invent some single word that means the same as that whole poem means. (Or perhaps Aristotle supposes that we already have a word, namely 'the *Iliad*', that means what the *Iliad* means; if so, that would be a mistake on his part.) So there must be *some* restriction on the formulae that are to be counted as definitions. We might perhaps start with the idea that the formula must be a formula *of* something. But what Aristotle claims is that it must be a formula *of* something that is not a compound of the type just discussed. At any rate, he says that it must be 'of something primary', and then proceeds to explain that as simply meaning something that is *not* 'expressed by predicating one thing of another'. If there is any justification for this, it is the argument at $^a2$–6, that such compounds do not have essences because they are not thises.

Aristotle proceeds to claim that only 'a form of a genus' will count as primary in the sense stipulated. As I have mentioned in the prologue to Z3, the word '*eidos*', which I always translate as 'form', and which always is translated as 'form' when it is contrasted with matter (as often in the Physical Works), is the same word as is generally translated 'species' in the Logical Works, and contrasted with genus and differentia. So if Aristotle is aware of any potential ambiguity in the word, arising from these two different contrasts, then clearly he is indicating here that it is 'form' in the sense of 'species' that he intends. (But later, in Z10–11, we shall find him considering the view that within a term for a species, such as 'man' or 'horse', we can distinguish a formal and a material component, and then it will be the formal component that he calls primary. See 35^b27–30, 37^a5–7.)

Just as we have been given no satisfying reason for the claim that only things that are in a certain sense simple can have essences, so here we are given no reason at all for the claim that *only* forms, i.e. species, are in this way simple. It is claimed that they *are* simple. So if we are still to think of them as being defined, in the way familiar from the Logical Works, by genus and differentia, then we must infer that such a definition does not 'predicate one thing of another'. Presumably the locutions 'not by way of participation or as an attribute, nor coincidentally' are to be understood as alternative ways of expressing this same idea, or expressing it more fully. (On this, see Z12, 37^b14–24n.) But even if species are in the relevant way simple, what is more distracting is that it appears that genera and differentiae must *also* be simple—and, one would have thought, even more simple. How, then, can it be *only* species that satisfy the condition?

We may perhaps set aside here the question of differentiae, for in what is to come it will be suggested that the species, i.e. form, may simply be identified with the differentia (*H*2, *passim*; also Z12, 38^a18–

34). We may also note that in Z13 it will be argued that the genus has no existence apart from the species (38^{b}30–4) and is not present in the species 'in actuality' (39^{a}3–14), and hence is not a substance. But this does not appear to prevent us saying that it nevertheless *is* in the relevant way *simple*. There seem to be three possible responses to this problem: either (i) the phrase 'nothing but what is a form of a genus' is not intended to rule out genera themselves; or (ii) it is intended only to rule out *ultimate* genera (and this is reasonable because, although simple, they do not have definitions at all); or (iii) Aristotle means more by 'primary' than he has said. As in the last paragraph he had claimed that only a substance could be a this, so here he perhaps intends the extra condition that only a substance will count as primary. If so, then we can properly invoke Z13 for the premiss that a genus is not a substance.

Of these three responses, it is clearly (ii) that is the most economical, and on that ground one might very naturally prefer it. But in fact there is reason to suppose that (iii) is nearer the mark. For just as there would appear to be 'thises' that are not in the category of substance, so also there are species and genera of items that are not in that category, and non-substantial species are in no way prevented from having essences by the stipulation that only 'a form of a genus' will qualify. But the next paragraph begins in a way which presupposes that non-substances have already been shown not to have an essence, though it certainly has not been argued that they fail to be simple in the sense explained. (It *will* be argued in Z5.) It would appear, then, that when Aristotle says that only what is 'primary' will have an essence, he means to restrict the field to things that are *both* simple (i.e. not expressed by predicating one thing of another) *and* in the category of substance.

^{a}14–17: 'everything else as well will have a formula stating what it signifies'. It is not clear how much Aristotle means to include in 'everything else', but one guesses that he is primarily thinking of such compounds as 'pale man'. The appropriate 'simple formula' in this case is perhaps that the pale men are those things that (*a*) are (essentially) men, and (*b*) have pallor (coincidentally) belonging to them. That is how it states 'that this belongs to that'.

30^{a}17–27

This paragraph seems at first to introduce an alternative, and as it were less rigid, way of speaking. The previous paragraph had claimed that certain things just *do not have* definitions, and it is taken as having claimed this of all non-substances (not only of compounds). But now it is suggested that we may say instead that they (or some of them) *do* have definitions, and indeed essences, so long as we recognize that they do not have them in the primary way. However, it is not clear that each way of speaking is counted as equally good. On the contrary, the next paragraph opens with 'One should ascertain how to express oneself on each point, but not more than how things are', and it then proceeds to use the less rigid way of speaking to describe 'how things are'. So clearly the less rigid (and less shocking) way of speaking is to be preferred. The present paragraph, then, *corrects* the previous paragraph; it was a mistake to say blankly that non-substances do not have definitions or essences, for the fact is that they (or some of them) do, although not in the primary way. In arguing for this point the paragraph thus provides a further reason for saying that only substances have essences in the primary way.

The argument is evidently this. (i) The verb 'is' applies, in its primary sense, only to substances ($^a21-2$). Hence (ii) the notion of a what a thing is applies, in its primary sense, only to substances ($^a18-20$, $22-7$). Hence (iii) what being is, and therefore definition, applies, in its primary sense, only to substances ($^a17-18$). Now in the prologue to Z1 I offered two accounts of the way in which 'is' has several senses, and if we adopt account A given there, this argument is wholly indefensible. For on that account the verb 'is', meaning 'exists', applies in its primary sense to particular substances. It cannot follow from this that 'what it is' applies in its primary sense to particular substances, since this 'is' is not the 'is' of existence but the 'is' of essential predication. Moreover, if we do take (ii) as claiming that 'what it is' applies in its primary sense to particular substances, then (iii) cannot follow from it. For (iii), as elucidated in the previous paragraph (at $^a9-10$), claims that 'what being is', and hence definition, applies primarily to the *species* of particular substances, and not to particular substances themselves. However, if we take the alternative account B, then the first objection is automatically absorbed, since it is built into account B that the being (= existence) of any item is to be equated with what that item essentially is, and this again with what being is for it. Moreover, account B yields no priority to particular substances as opposed to their species (and genera), because it is concerned throughout with items that are taken to be definable. Admittedly there is doubt over just how substance does acquire its priority on account B, but it is clear that Aristotle does claim the relevant priority for it. (See Z1, 28^a34-6n. and epilogue.)

The present passage must, then, be taken as endorsing the conflation characteristic of account B, provided it is taken as propounding an argument. But the defender of account A might perhaps reply that we should not try to find an argument here at all. Perhaps, that is, (ii) is not supposed to *follow* from (i), but is merely presented as something to be *expected*, by analogy with (i). Just as 'is' applies to certain things in a primary way (namely to particular substances), and to others in a dependent way, so it is reasonable to expect that 'what it is' will apply to certain things in a primary way (namely to species of substances), and to others in a dependent way. But if this is all that Aristotle means to suggest, then the reply is that his analogy is extremely weak, as my next comment will show.

$30^a27-{}^b7$

This paragraph evidently endorses the 'less rigid' way of talking introduced in the last. It proceeds to add an explanation of how 'primarily' and its opposite are to be understood, namely as a case of what Owen [1960] has called 'focal meaning', whereby the primary use of an expression figures in the paraphrase of the dependent uses. Thus the word 'medical' applies primarily—according to Aristotle—to the art, skill, or knowledge of medicine (i.e. to the *tekhnē* = *epistēmē* of medicine). Other things are called 'medical' by reference to this. For example, a patient is called a medical patient because he or she is being *treated by* the art or skill of medicine; an operation is called medical because it is *performed with* that art or skill; an instrument is called medical because it is *used in* medical operations, i.e. operations *performed with* that art. And so on. Thus the word 'medical' is used, not meaning one and the same thing, nor yet equivocally, but with reference always to one and the same thing. And we have been told at *Γ*2, $1003^a33-{}^b10$ that the same applies to 'what is'.

Aristotle comments that for present purposes 'it makes no difference' if we prefer to say, not that 'is' is used focally (i.e. 'with reference to one thing'), but that it is used 'by adding something and subtracting something'. What he appears to be thinking of here is adding or not adding such qualifying phrases as 'being *for a quality*' or '. . . *for a quantity*'. At any rate, that is what is illustrated by the example of the unknown being said to be known ($^a33-4$), where we must add the qualifying phrase 'known *to be unknown*' (*Rhet* 1402^a6). (Similarly with 'what is not is' at $^a25-6$ earlier.) But simply to insist on suitable qualifications in this way is not yet to give any account of why the one use is to be regarded as 'primary', and the others as dependent. That is just what the focal explanation does provide, and at the same time it supplies a reason for saying that we do have different uses to distinguish.

Evidently Aristotle is endorsing the focal explanation. If we take the previous paragraph to be meant as an argument, then all that he need be doing here is reiterating its premiss, that 'is' (i.e. 'exists'?) has a focused variety of uses. But if the previous paragraph is intended only to suggest an analogy, then he is claiming here that 'what it is' and 'what being is' and 'definition' can equally be seen to have a similarly focused variety of uses. But this seems to make very little sense. It implies that when we speak, say, of 'the definition of pallor', then what we mean has a complex paraphrase in which the same word 'definition' occurs, but this time in the context 'definition of a substance'. One has no idea how to supply such a paraphrase. The truth seems to be that the meaning of 'definition' does not in *any* way vary with the category of the item defined, but it surely does not vary in the 'focused' way that the analogy would require.

30^b7–13

Up to this point it has been conceded only that (on the less rigid, and preferred, way of speaking) items in categories other than that of substance may be said to have, in a secondary way, both a definition and an essence. According to the *Categories*, these items are all simple items (*Cat* 1^b25–7), so the concession would not imply that a compound such as 'pale man' may also be said to have, in its own way, a definition and an essence. But it now appears that Aristotle is prepared to concede this last point too. He still insists that there must be *some* restriction on the formulae that can be taken as expressing definitions: such a formula must be a formula 'of a unity' (or more literally a formula 'of one thing'; see *Z*12, 37^b8–14n.); moreover, the thing must be a unity 'in one of the ways in which we speak of unity', and these are no more than 'the ways in which we speak of being'. Apparently this is still held to rule out some candidates, in particular the *Iliad*, but it is now taken to permit such a compound as a pale man, which has being coincidentally and is one coincidentally.

Comparison with *H*6, 45^a12–14 (and cf. *An. Post* 93^b35–7) strongly suggests that Aristotle wishes to say that the *Iliad* is itself 'one by being bound together' (*sundesmōi hen*), and if so then the kind of 'binding' that he is thinking of is no doubt that done by connecting particles such as 'and', 'but', 'after that', and so on. For at *Int* 5 exactly the same phrase is used of just this kind of 'binding'. (Cf. also *Poetics* 1456^b20–1, $^b38$–1457^a6, $^a28$–30.) If so, then we may probably draw two morals. (i) Despite initial appearances, Aristotle is not meaning to say that there can be no definition of *anything* that is one by being continuous. On the contrary, in his view the things that are one by being continuous form a major division of things that are one in some perfectly good way (cf. *Δ*6, esp. 1015^b36–1016^a17; *I*1, esp. 1052^a15–29). What he is concerned with is a particular kind of continuity, namely that due to connecting particles. (ii) What lies behind his remark is just a muddle. There is no reason why one should not define what is unified by connecting particles—e.g. why one should not define 'an epic poem' or 'a sonnet' or simply 'a conjunction of two sentences'. What Aristotle is thinking of is that a sequence of words which is unified only in this way is not *itself* a definition. (Cf. 30^a8–9 and *H*6, 45^a12–14.)

CHAPTER 5

This short chapter begins with a problem about 'things that are coupled and not simple', for example snubness. The problem is, it appears, that an attempt to define them must run into insuperable difficulties. Then at the end of the chapter Aristotle claims that the same problem affects *all* non-substances, thus providing further support for his claim that, properly speaking, only substances can be defined.

$30^{b}14$–28

Snubness must be explained as concavity in a nose. It is because one must mention both concavity and noses in the explanation that snubness is a coupled thing. (According to the usage of $31^{a}5$–7 it would be not 'snub' but 'snub nose' that expresses something coupled; this discrepancy is of no importance.) But, says Aristotle, this means that a formula defining snubness would have to be one 'constructed from an addition', and, he implies, such formulae cannot be definitions. But what exactly is a formula 'constructed from an addition'?

Early in chapter 4 a proposed definition of 'pale' as 'pale surface' was rejected 'because it itself is being added on' ($29^{b}18$–19). The objection there seemed simply to be that the definition would be circular. But in this example the Greek word for 'added' was not the same as the one used here. Later in chapter 4 precisely the same phrase 'constructed from an addition' was used, and apparently applied to the case where one defines 'pale' by *the formula of* a pale man ($29^{b}29$–33). Since there seems no particular reason to suppose that the word 'pale' must occur in the *formula* of a pale man, the objection to this definition is not that it is circular. The most natural objection to raise is of course that there are things that are pale but not pale men. But *this* objection seems not to apply in the case of snubness. If Aristotle's thought is that in order to define 'snub' one has to give the formula of a snub *nose*, and that is why the definition is 'from an addition', then this is precisely because there is not, and could not be, anything which is snub but not a snub nose. (Snubness is predicated of noses 'not coincidentally . . . but in its own right' ($^{b}18$–20), i.e. in the *second* of the two senses of 'in its own right' mentioned at the beginning of chapter 4, and spelled out at length here at $^{b}23$–6.) But what, then, is wrong with the suggestion that we may define 'snub' by giving the formula of a snub nose? The truth is that Aristotle nowhere explains what his objection is.

The only objection that one can see as justified by what has been said so far is this. First, since it is part of the meaning of 'snub' that only noses can be snub, it is indeed true that one can only define 'snub' from an addition, i.e. by giving what is in effect the formula of a snub nose. But second, a snub nose is just a concave nose, and a concave nose is a *compound* item 'expressed by predicating one thing of another', i.e. in a predication that is coincidental. (For, despite what Aristotle says at $^b18$–20—which, on this account, is just a slip—the predicate 'is concave' does not seem to attach to the subject 'a nose' in its own right in either sense of that expression; noses do not have to be concave, and concave things do not have to be noses.) Thus although 'snub' is a single word, one could define it only by giving the formula of a compound item, and just such a compound as has been argued in chapter 4 not to have a definition, or anyway not in the primary sense. If this is right, then we do not have a new argument here, but simply the application of an old one.

It is certainly an objection to this interpretation that Aristotle *does* say, at $^b18$–20, that concavity is an attribute of the nose in its own right, whereas on this account he is relying on the point that it is *not*. If his thought is as suggested, this carelessness is difficult to explain. But I postpone consideration of a different interpretation until we have considered the 'further difficulty' in the next paragraph.

30^b28–31^a1

The 'further difficulty' begins with a logical mistake. It is true that a snub nose and a concave nose are the same, but it does not follow from this that snubness and concavity are the same. (Compare: the square of 2 is the same as the double of 2, but it does not follow that being the square of is the same as being the double of.) Since we must evidently reject the supposed consequence, Aristotle infers that we must reject the premiss, and he appears to suppose that it should be replaced by 'a snub thing and a concave nose are the same'. This, of course, is equally correct (and reflects the suggestion with which we began at $^b16$–18, that snubness is to be explained as concavity in a nose). From this he infers that a snub nose will be the same as a concave nose nose, and hence that in the expression 'a snub nose' the same thing is said twice. This inference seems to be correct. For a snub nose is something which is both snub and a nose, and hence (by our premiss) both a concave nose and a nose, i.e. both concave and a nose and a nose. But there is not, as Aristotle seems to suppose, anything wrong with the conclusion. After all, many perfectly idiomatic phrases do in this sense say the same thing twice, e.g. 'a nose which is a concave nose'. Of course, when one does in this way say the same thing twice, then saying it the second time adds nothing that makes any difference. Thus to say that something is both concave and a nose and a nose is, for all logical purposes, just the same as to say simply that it is both concave and a nose. Hence the premiss that Aristotle began by rejecting can in fact be deduced from the alternative premiss that he suggests in its place. To put it briefly:

Suppose

(i) A snub (thing) = a concave nose

Then, as Aristotle infers

(ii) A snub nose = a concave nose nose

But, as I have just urged

(iii) A concave nose nose = a concave nose

From which we infer

(iv) A snub nose = a concave nose

Aristotle has begun by rejecting (iv), so he is bound in consistency to reject (iii) as well. And this is exactly what he does. He supposes that the expression 'a concave nose nose', if it is admitted at all, will have to mean something *different* from the expression 'a concave nose'. But then, since one cannot suggest any suitably different meaning for it, he is drawn to conclude that the expression should not be admitted. So, using (ii), the expression 'a snub nose' should not be admitted either, i.e. it will be impossible to speak of a snub nose. Yet this conclusion is equally absurd. 'And therefore it would be absurd if such things [as snubness] had an essence' (b34–5), for a statement of the essence would be bound to license the equation (i), which we have just found to be untenable.

It is true that one cannot see how equation (i) by itself might be argued to give rise to a *regress*, which is Aristotle's last claim in this paragraph. The regress Aristotle surely has in mind—for it is the one he gives, with a different example, when discussing this topic at *SE* 13, 173a34–8—in fact begins from the different premiss

(v) A snub (thing) = a snub nose

(One may of course deduce this premiss from (i) and (iv) together.) Given this, then by the same reasoning as before we have

A snub nose = a snub nose nose
A snub nose nose = a snub nose nose nose
etc.

But one is rather at a loss to supply Aristotle's ground for saying that if snubness has an essence then *both* (i) *and* (v) must be accepted. (For of course, if both are accepted, then (iv) will follow at once; but the discussion began by rejecting (iv).)

For this reason, the argument has been construed differently, as resting upon the dilemma: if snubness has an essence then *either* (i) *or* (v) must be accepted. (See e.g. Hare [1979], 174; Balme [1984], 308–9; Frede & Patzig.) The argument then goes: if (i) is accepted then (ii) follows, so that 'the same thing will be said twice', and if (v) is accepted then the regress follows, so that 'it is impossible to speak of a snub nose'. Aristotle rejects both conclusions, and therefore rejects the premiss too. However, I think it is quite clear that in our text both horns of the dilemma stated at b32–3 are rejected before the regress is mentioned, and that the regress is represented as a *further* consequence of the hypothesis that snubness has an essence. So I am inclined to think that Aristotle has failed to notice that the regress in fact requires a different premiss. In any case, the argument is wholly unsatisfactory. The regress in question is quite harmless, and the truth is that there need be nothing wrong with saying the same thing twice. In the *Sophistici Elenchi* Aristotle classifies it as a kind of logical error (in ch. 3), but that is just a mistake on his part.

Snubness is mentioned in *SE* 13 as giving rise to this alleged problem over saying the same thing twice ($173^b5–11$), and in *SE* 31 Aristotle apparently offers a solution for this case, though it is difficult to understand. He ends the discussion there by saying that one should not grant that a snub *thing* is a concave nose, but only that snub*ness* is concavity *of* the nose, and that it is not absurd to say that a snub nose is a nose which has concavity *of* the nose ($182^a3–6$). His point *seems* to be that one may use the word 'nose' twice if it occurs once in the nominative and once in the genitive (as suggested by Balme [1984], 308), but if that really is all he means then it is surely a subterfuge of no philosophical significance (*pace* Ross), and Z5 must be right to pay it no attention. But I suspect there may be more to it.

Let us first notice something that he has said earlier in the *SE* passage, namely that although the word 'concave' *reveals the same thing* (*to auto dēloi*) when applied to noses and to other things, nevertheless in the compound phrase 'concave nose' it *signifies* snubness (*sēmainei to simon*), as it does not in other such compounds ($181^b37–182^a2$). This appears just to be a contradiction. But it is a contradiction that recurs in Z5, where at $^b18–20$ Aristotle says that concavity is predicated of a nose in its own right, apparently supposing that 'nose' appears in the definition of 'concave' when we speak of a concave nose, yet at $^b30–2$ he insists that this holds of snubness but *not* of concavity. While this *may* be just carelessness, one wonders whether perhaps there is an indication here of some aspect of his thinking which is not being clearly expressed.

There is in fact something right about the suggestion that 'concave', when applied to noses, *means* concavity *of the nose* (and something correspondingly wrong about my earlier statement that a concave nose is just something which is both concave and a nose). For when we speak of the shapes of noses—as with 'a straight nose', 'a hooked nose' and the like—what we have in mind is the shape of the profile of a certain part of the nose when seen from a certain angle. So the sense which 'concave' actually bears in the expression 'a concave nose' indeed cannot be explained without reference to noses. And here I think we approach what is *really* in Aristotle's mind as the special problem over 'coupled things', namely that they are *not* straightforward compounds as 'a concave nose' appears at first sight to be. They arise when we have an attribute *X* which is confined to subjects of a special kind, the *Y*s, and where it is not possible to explain the things which are *X* as the *Y*s which are *Z*, for *any* attribute *Z* which is not *also* confined to the same range of subjects. Evidently this description fits Aristotle's *other* examples much better than it fits snubness. Presumably we cannot explain the things that are feminine as the animals which are *Z*, for any attribute *Z* which also applies to non-animals. Similarly, we cannot explain the things which are odd as the numbers which are *Z*, for any attribute *Z* that is not itself confined to numbers. A 'coupled thing', then, is a compound of kind, but of a special kind where it is not possible to analyse that compound as a compound of two *independent* elements. But of course it has to be admitted that even if this is the right explanation of why Aristotle felt such things to be special, it was not something that he himself was very clear about. For snubness is not a very good example, and to open the discussion by taking it to be obvious that snubness is concavity in a nose is to begin with a point that is wholly misleading.

31ᵃ1–11

Aristotle here generalizes his result that snubness has no proper definition to the somewhat sweeping claim that *no* predicate has a proper definition, except for those in the category of substance. His reason is that *all* other predicates will be predicated of some subject in its own right, as snubness is predicated of a nose in its own right, and hence they could only have definitions 'constructed from an addition'. It can hardly be said that he offers us any very explicit argument for this claim. All that we are given is one further example, the predicate 'odd' which applies only to numbers, to add to several that we have been given already—namely that 'feminine' and 'masculine' apply only to animals (ᵇ21), that 'equal' applies only to quantities (ᵇ22), and that 'pale' applies primarily, not to men (ᵇ25), but to surfaces (29ᵇ17).

It is important to distinguish the present claim from a different way in which Aristotle generalizes from snubness to a wide variety of other things. Earlier in the *Metaphysics*, at *E*1, 1025ᵇ28–1026ᵃ6, snubness was used as a paradigm of something that has matter included in its definition. (Similarly *Phys*, II, 194ᵃ1–15; *Anim* III, 429ᵇ14; *Z*10, 35ᵃ1–6.) Here it is a paradigm of something that is predicated of a subject 'in its own right' (in the second sense of that expression) so that that subject must be mentioned in its definition. *Pace* Hare [1979], 168 and Furth [1985], 110–11, these features of snubness are not the same. In the passage at *E*1 snubness is contrasted with concavity (1025ᵇ31–4) and likened to all the things studied in physics, in particular to animals and plants and their parts (1026ᵃ1–3). Here in *Z*5 snubness is contrasted with animals and plants, in so far as these are in the category of substance, and presumably it is likened to concavity. For one would suppose that shapes, like colours, are predicated of some subject in its own right, either a surface or a line (i.e. the profile of a surface). One certainly would *not* suppose, from anything that we have had so far, that concavity is itself being counted as a *substance*, and therefore as something that does have a definition in the primary and unqualified way. (Contrast *Z*11, 37ᵃ29–33; and see my comments ad loc.) But although it is quite easy to supply a suitable 'first recipient' for concavity, to be mentioned in its definition, it is still not very obvious why Aristotle should think that this can always be done for *every* predicate that is not in the category of substance.

If we attempt to supply an argument, then the only line of thought that I can see is this. According to the limited ontology of the *Categories*, all predicates other than predicates in the category of substance are predicated of substances. But Aristotle must have come to realize that this scheme is too simple. For example, his discussion of time in *Physics* IV, 10–14 recognizes that times are predicated of changes, and not of substances (as the *Categories* had claimed, but very obscurely in view of 2^a2). However, he no doubt still wishes to maintain that these changes, of which times are predicated, are themselves predicated of substances. To judge from the examples given here in Z4–5, it is the more liberal doctrine that is now being presupposed. Thus equality is predicated of quantities, which are not themselves substances. But those quantities are either predicated of substances, or of something else (e.g. a change?) that is predicated of substances, and so on. Similarly, oddness is predicated of numbers, which are not substances for Aristotle. But those numbers in turn are predicated of something else, no doubt collections of substances. Again, colours (and shapes?) are predicated primarily of surfaces, which also are not substances. Perhaps it is a little odd to say that those surfaces in turn are *predicated* of the bodies that have them, but at any rate they are *explained* in terms of those bodies. (Similarly, snubness is predicated of noses, and we shall find in Z16, 40^b5–16 that noses are not actually substances; but still they are to be *defined* in terms of the animals that have them, which are substances.) Thus everything that is not a substance depends, either directly or indirectly, on what is a substance. It may perhaps be a little misleading to say that this dependence is in all cases a matter of predication, but I think it is an over-simplification that does no great harm, and so I shall continue with it.

This more liberal ontology, then, brings with it a new thought. There are predicates of various kinds, and not only of a kind to be predicated of substances. But to understand any predicate one must understand what kind of predicate it is, and this requires a knowledge of what it may be predicated of. Consequently, the definition of any predicate must specify which things it is predicated of 'in their own right'. It appears to follow from this that every predicate *whatever* must be defined 'from an addition', but we need to make a special exception for predicates in the category of substance. It is here that we invoke the hierarchical ordering that I have supplied (and which is not to be found explicitly stated anywhere in Aristotle's writings, so far as I am aware). In the definition of any predicate we must specify what kind of thing it is predicated of, and in the definition of this in turn we must specify what kind of thing *it* is predicated of, and so on, until eventually we come to substances. (Thus, in the definition of anything there will, eventually, be some reference to substances, as Z1 has affirmed (on one interpretation).) But with the definition of particular kinds of substances, this is no longer so. We do not need to 'add' an account of what kind of thing that predicate is predicated of, since the predicate itself tells us. The role of such a predicate is precisely to give us the 'what it is' of the thing of which it is predicated. Thus, in order to be equal, a thing must be something *else* first—in fact a quantity, as Aristotle here says—and the definition of equality must tell us this. Again, in order to be pale, a thing must be something *else* first (Z1, 28^a33–4n.)—in fact a surface, or something that has a surface—and again the definition must 'add' this information. But in order to be a man or a horse there is *nothing else* that the thing has to be, for a man or a horse is 'just what it is'. That is why no 'first recipient' needs to be mentioned in this case: the explanation of the predicate itself simply *is* the explanation of 'what receives it'.

This account is, of course, a speculation. We know that in the Logical Works Aristotle is assuming a very simple structure for the whole of language. We can point to many instances in his later writings where his own claims show that this structure is too simple. We have no direct evidence for saying that he ever attempted to work out a more complex structure, but only little hints here and there. The present passage is, in my view, one of the most significant of these hints. As the choice of examples shows very clearly, it is not true that all predicates are predicates of substances; on the contrary, there are predicates of many different kinds. Yet Aristotle is confident that *all* of them (except predicates in the category of substance) will have 'first recipients', and so will need to be defined 'from an addition'. Why should he be so confident? It cannot be that he has seriously looked for exceptions and failed to find any, for there are several predicates, of the sort that he himself recognizes, which are clear exceptions. Consider, for example, predicates of place such as 'in the Lyceum' (*Cat* 2^a1). All kinds of things may be said to be in the Lyceum—for instance a person, a quarrel, snow, darkness, the end of the nature-trail, the ugliest juxtaposition of different building-styles to be found anywhere in Athens, and so on and on indefinitely. There is surely no hope of finding a 'first recipient' for such a predicate. Yet Aristotle assures us that there must be one, for this predicate and for every other. Surely, he must be in the grip of some theory.

CHAPTER 6

In the two preceding chapters Aristotle has argued that only a substance has an essence. In this chapter he argues that a substance in fact *is* the essence that it has. At least, he claims that this identity holds for 'things spoken of in their own right', though not for 'things spoken of coincidentally'; but it is not entirely clear how we should take this distinction. I return to this question in my epilogue to these chapters.

31^a15–18

Aristotle introduces his question with the claim that 'it is thought' that each thing is identical with its own substance. Though he does not spell this out for us, it seems likely that what 'is thought' is, more exactly, that each thing *which is a substance* is identical with its own substance, i.e. that if *X* is a substance then *X* is the substance of *X*. We are offered no basis for what is introduced here as a received opinion, but the thought behind it seems likely to be this: if *X* is the substance of *Y*, where *X* and *Y* are different, then *X* is prior to *Y*; but the genuine substances are those that are prior to all else, so in this case *Y* cannot be a genuine substance. Assuming, then, that for any genuine substance there must be something which is the substance of it, this can only be itself.

The correct answer to Aristotle's question about essence would appear to be this. Since it has been explained in chapter 4 that the essence of *X* is what is given in the definition of *X*, and since one does not define this or that particular *X* thing but rather the universal character that all *X* things share, and since a definition states an identity, it must follow that *X is* the same as the essence of *X* wherever *X* is taken to be a (definable) universal character, and that *X* is *not* the same as the essence of *X* wherever *X* is taken to be anything else (e.g. a particular pale man). This, evidently, is not how Aristotle expresses his own answer, which is that the identity holds where *X* is 'spoken of in its own right', but not where *X* is 'spoken of coincidentally'. In his usual usage of this phrase, it is clear that Aristotle counts a compound term such as 'pale man'—even when taken universally—as a term for something 'spoken of coincidentally'. On some occasions he will also count the simple items in categories other than that of substance as 'spoken of coincidentally' (e.g. *An. Post* I, 4, 73^b5–10), and so he *appears* to do here at 31^b22–3 below; on other occasions he will count them as 'spoken of in their own right' (e.g. Δ7, 1017^a22–3). But to determine just how he means his own answer to be understood, we must of course look to the arguments that he offers.

31ᵃ19–28

This paragraph first offers an argument for saying that a pale man and the essence of a pale man are not the same (ᵃ21–4), then it apparently suggests an objection to that argument, and a reply that would meet that objection (ᵃ24–8). The arguments seem to be put forward somewhat tentatively throughout. The second part of the paragraph is very difficult to interpret, but the first part seems straightforward enough.

ᵃ21–4: Suppose that:

(i) a pale man = being for a pale man.

Then, in view of the fact that

(ii) a pale man = a man ('as they say')

and the further (unstated) assumption, evidently reasonable in the light of (i), that

(iii) a man = being for a man

we can apparently conclude

(iv) being for a pale man = being for a man.

But (iv) is evidently false, so (i) must be rejected. One may note at once that the force of this argument does not in any way depend upon using the compound term 'a pale man' in the initial supposition. In place of 'a pale man' we could have written 'a pale thing' or indeed 'an animal' throughout, and the argument would be unaffected. But the expression 'an animal' is not usually regarded as introducing 'a thing spoken of coincidentally'.

To evaluate this argument from our perspective, we first note that, if premiss (ii) is to be acceptable, then it must be taken to concern some particular pale man (for it is not true that *all* men are pale men). Consequently the argument is valid only if it is that same man who is in question in premisses (i) and (iii) as well. But, for any general term '*X*', the supposition that there is some particular *X* which is identical with what being is for *any X* must surely be dismissed as absurd. And perhaps that is indeed the moral that Aristotle means to draw from this argument. But then we may object that it is not strictly relevant to the question which is supposed to be at issue, for that question was framed, at the beginning of the chapter, as the question of whether each thing is identical with what being is for *it*. (This formulation is most explicit at 31ᵇ6–7 and at 32ᵃ5–6.) If we reinterpret the argument so that it does address *this* question, i.e. by taking the initial supposition as 'a pale man = being for *that* pale man', then the conclusion to which it leads is that being for that pale man is the same as being for that man. But one cannot say of *this* conclusion that it is evidently false.

Whatever it is that Aristotle sees as a potential objection to the argument, it is surely not this.

ᵃ24–8: As a preliminary to attacking this obscure passage, I first note that Aristotle's grasp of the logic of identity, at least as displayed in the

Topics and *Sophistici Elenchi*, is not as secure as one might desire. For most of the *Topics*, one has little to complain of. At 103ᵃ33–9 he is clear that 'Socrates is the man who is now talking' is an identity-statement, and he calls it a coincidental identity, evidently because the predication 'Socrates is now talking' is coincidental. At 133ᵃ33–4 and at 152ᵇ25–9 he announces the general principle that if x is identical with y then whatever is predicated of x will also be predicated of y (with various special cases at 133ᵃ24–32, 152ᵃ33–7, 152ᵃ39–ᵇ5). But at *SE* 179ᵃ32–ᵇ4 (cf. 169ᵇ3–6) he denies this principle for a coincidental identity. He is led to do this by a mistaken diagnosis of the fallacy in:

You do not know [who] the man approaching [is].
The man approaching is Coriscus.
∴ You do not know Coriscus.

On his account, it can be truly predicated of the man approaching that you do not know him, but it cannot be truly predicated of Coriscus that you do not know him, even though it is true (but 'coincidentally') that the man approaching is Coriscus. His position appears to be that the item signified by 'the man approaching' and the item signified by 'Coriscus' are in one way the same (i.e. coincidentally) but in another *not* (i.e. they are not the same 'in substance', or—elsewhere—'in being', or 'in definition'). It is because there is also a way in which they are *not* the same that something can be true of the one but not of the other. Earlier in the *Topics*, at 133ᵇ17–36 we find the same thought applied to 'a pale man' and 'a man', where these expressions certainly seem to be envisaged as referring to what we would call the *same* thing. Aristotle tells us that indeed it is not right to say without qualification that [the items signified] are two *different* things (*heteron*), but we must count them as *other* (*allo*), on the ground that their being is different. (For discussion of these and other passages see White [1971], K. T. Barnes [1977], and Matthews [1982]; cf. Z1, 28ᵃ20–31 n.) With so much by way of preamble, let us now come to the text in hand.

The Greek at this point is extremely elliptical. A literal rendering of the objection raised at ᵃ24–5 would be

Or [is it] not necessary that things in accordance with coincidence are the same? For not in the same way do the extremes become the same.

On the interpretation I propose, which is partly embodied in my translation, the suggestion that 'things in accordance with coincidence' might not be the same casts doubt upon the truth of premiss (ii). In conformity with the passages just cited from the *Topics* and *Sophistici Elenchi*, it suggests that a mere coincidental identity should not really be counted as a case of *sameness* at all; at best it is a matter of being 'not different . . . but other'. This, it is suggested, would block the argument, for the argument was not proposing that its extreme terms, i.e. being for a pale man and being for a man, would become the same only in this way, i.e. coincidentally, which is not really a way of being *the same* at all. (To expand on this objection a little: the peculiar relation of coincidental identity, which is a kind of being the same while also not being the same, is a relation which does hold between what is signified by 'a pale man' and what is signified by 'a man', in suitable cases. But it cannot hold between such terms as *being* for a pale man and *being* for a man. If these are the same at all, then they must be the same in the *proper* way (i.e. 'in substance', or 'in being' or 'in definition'). But the argument cannot establish this, since premiss (ii) is not an identity of this kind.) However, Aristotle replies to this objection, at ᵃ25–8, by saying that it *would* seem to follow *from the argument* that the extreme terms must be coincidentally the same; yet this does not seem to be the case, so we are still entitled to reject one premiss of the argument, namely premiss (i).

It is certainly a drawback to this interpretation that it has no explanation to offer of why, in the course of his reply at ᵃ25–8, Aristotle should change his example of the extreme terms, from 'being for a pale man' and 'being for a man', to 'being for a pale thing' and 'being for an artistic thing'. On the account suggested, this makes absolutely no difference to the merits and demerits of the argument. An alternative text in ᵃ27, followed by Ross and many others, alters the sense so that it seems at first sight to yield an explanation of this point. On this alternative text, Aristotle's reply is:

> However, it would perhaps seem to follow that the extreme terms would be the same *if they are* things [spoken of] coincidentally, e.g. . . .

So on this account he is suggesting that the objection he has raised would be avoided if we rewrote the argument with 'a pale thing' in place of 'a pale man', and 'an artistic thing' in place of 'a man', throughout. To explain how this would improve matters, Ross proposes to understand the objection at ᵃ24–5 in this way:

> Or [is it] not necessary that [the essences of] things [spoken of] in accordance with coincidence are the same [as the essences of the simple terms contained in them]? For not in the same way do the extreme terms become the same [as their respective middle terms—i.e. the essence of a man does not 'become the same' as a man in the same way as the essence of a pale man is (supposed to) 'become the same' as a pale man].

On this account of ᵃ24–5, it is suggested that the substitution of the new 'extreme terms' for the old would correct the defect here complained of, and so restore the force of the original *reductio ad absurdum*. (Essentially the same account of ᵃ24–5 is given by Frede & Patzig, though they adopt at ᵃ27 the same text as I do.) I can only say that this reading of ᵃ24–5 seems even more far-fetched than mine, and that it constitutes even more of an insult to Aristotle's logical acumen.

One further comment may be made on this paragraph. The initial claim that a pale man and what being is for a pale man are not the same is put forward only tentatively ('the two would *seem* to be different'). The argument then given for it is also tentative; a vital premiss is qualified by 'as they say', and, whether or not it is this premiss that is later objected to, at any rate some objection is raised. But the objection itself seems only tentative, and the reply to it (which is explicitly prefaced by a 'perhaps') even more tentative. It would appear that nothing definite has yet been established. One might *hope* that this is because we have not yet been introduced to a crucial distinction that Aristotle is going to make at 31^b22–8, and that this distinction will clarify the disputed premiss that a pale man is a man. For, in the light of that passage, we may say that it is important to be clear about whether the expressions 'a pale man' and 'a man' are each being used to signify an attribute, or a thing that has that attribute. In the first case the premiss is straightforwardly false, and in the second case it is straightforwardly true, so we can set aside the obscure idea that what they signify is in a way the same but also in a way not the same. But I postpone to the epilogue a consideration of whether it is reasonable to attribute this line of thought to Aristotle.

31^a28–$^b11$

In this paragraph Aristotle turns to consider the things that are 'spoken of in their own right', and at once offers a further characterization of such a thing: it is a substance such that no other substance is its substance, and nothing else is prior to it. Let us call this a characterization of a 'fundamental substance'. Now he does not actually say that *everything* that is spoken of in its own right is a fundamental substance, but only that the fundamental substances (if there are any) would be *examples* of things spoken of in their own right. But if there are any other examples we do not seem to hear of them. I return to this point in the epilogue.

As an alleged example of such things, Aristotle considers the Platonic forms, which he himself does not believe in. (I use 'Form', with a capital 'F', to translate '*idea*' rather than '*eidos*'. Aristotle uses '*eidos*' both for his own forms and for Platonic forms (e.g. Z2, 28^b20; Z14, 39^a27; Z16, 40^b27), but he reserves '*idea*' for Platonic forms. The locution '*X*-itself' is a characteristically Platonic idiom for a Platonic form.) Perhaps Aristotle chooses these examples here because he does not feel it appropriate to offer his own examples yet. Admittedly, he has already told us in Z4 that only the species of a genus have essences in the primary way, so one might have expected him to use these as examples, but we shall find as we read on that this was only a rough-and-ready characterization. In chapters 10 and 11 we learn that these species must be understood in a certain way if it is to be true that no other substances are prior to them, and it is not until chapter 13 that it is argued that the genus is not —despite initial appearances—prior to the species. If Aristotle is writing here with these future developments in mind, one might expect him to be cautious about claiming at this point that the species of a genus do satisfy the characterization of fundamental substances. Alternatively, or in addition, one might suggest that he turns to the Platonic forms here because he wishes to make a polemical point about them, namely that the only way in which one can understand these alleged entities is by simply identifying them with entities which Aristotle takes to be more comprehensible, namely essences. (An essence is something which is simply a universal; it is not *also*, and inconsistently, supposed to be a special kind of particular. Cf. Z15, 40a8–9.) But one must not press this line of thought too far. For Aristotle himself does not even believe that there is any universal character corresponding to the supposed Platonic forms of goodness-itself (*auto to agathon*) or being-itself (*auto to on*), because goodness and being are 'spoken of in many ways' (*EE* I, 8; *EN* I, 6). And while there is no doubt a universal character corresponding to animality-itself, it is not an essence if indeed it is only species and not genera that have essences.

Presumably Aristotle supposes that the argument he offers will establish that, where *X* is a fundamental substance as specified, then *X* and the essence of *X* must be identical, *whatever* the fundamental substances turn out to be. The argument may be split into three parts, a31–b3, b3–10, and an afterthought at b11.

a31–b3: At first sight the reasoning here is straightforward. A fundamental substance, by definition, is one that has nothing else as its substance. But if it is not identical with its essence, and if essence indeed is substance, then it will have something else as its substance, namely its essence. Hence a fundamental substance must be identical with its essence. One can only note that Aristotle here feels entitled to assume that the essence of a thing and the substance of that thing are the same, though that had seemed to be an open question when the chapter began (a18). One may also note a further assumption, which at first sight appears to be this: fundamental substances must *have* essences, even if we are supposing that it is Platonic forms that are the fundamental substances. But on further reflection we see that this second assumption is a little more complex, for again the essence that is being assumed is not quite the essence *of* the thing it is identified with. Aristotle does not assume that, if the Platonic form goodness-itself is a fundamental substance, then there must be such a thing as what being is for *it*, i.e. for goodness-itself; what he assumes is that there must be such a thing as what being is for *a good thing*, i.e. *any* good thing. To state the assumption generally, then, it is this: any fundamental substance will be associated with some universal and definable characteristic which will be its substance. It then follows that if our original substance is indeed fundamental, it must itself *be* this universal and definable characteristic.

b3–10: The text at this point appears to be incomplete. It offers a further argument based on the supposition that the fundamental substance and its essence are 'divorced from one another', but this supposition is introduced by an 'on the one hand' which is nowhere answered by an 'on the other hand'. Since it can hardly be supposed that if *X* and *Y* are not identical then they must always be 'divorced from one another' in the sense here specified, this argument appears to be seriously incomplete. But on closer inspection we find that the argument is at least nearer to being complete than this comment suggests. The hypothesis of divorce is fairly clearly the hypothesis that neither belongs to the other (though Aristotle has simplified 'goodness-itself does not belong to the essence of a good thing' to 'being good does not belong to the essence of a good thing'). But it is clear that the intolerable consequence that the essence is not a being is deduced just from one half of this hypothesis, i.e. from the premiss that the Platonic form does not belong to the essence. It also appears that the (equally intolerable?) consequence that the form is not knowable is deduced just from the other half of the hypothesis, i.e. from the premiss that the essence does not belong to the form. So what the argument aims to show is in fact that *each* of the two *does* belong to the other. But we are left to speculate on whether Aristotle would take it to follow from this that they must be identical. (The truth, of course, is that it does not follow.)

The first consequence stated, that the form will be unknowable, is held to follow just from the claim that to know a thing is to know its essence (cf. *Z*1, 28^a35-^b2). Later in this chapter, at 31^b18-22, this claim will be taken to show by itself that every knowable thing is identical with its essence. The reasoning, one supposes, must be something like this: if to know a thing is to know its essence, and yet the thing is not identical with its essence, then to know the thing is to know something other than that thing, which does sound somewhat paradoxical. But here it appears that Aristotle does not see this result as wholly paradoxical, or at any rate he does not wish to press his argument so far, for here he infers only that every knowable thing must at least have an essence *belonging* to it. Perhaps one can elucidate the thought in this way. A *fully* knowable thing must *be* an essence, but there are also other things which are partly knowable, because they do at least have essences belonging to them. They will be, perhaps, compounds of essence and something else, e.g. matter. But if there is anything to which no essence even belongs, e.g. prime matter, then it will not be knowable at all (*Z*10, 36^a7-9). If this is right, then Aristotle is contenting himself here with the rather weak thesis that it would be intolerable to have a fundamental substance that was not even *partly* knowable, and hence inferring that there must at least be some essence that belongs to it. (And he is assuming, as is reasonable, that if there is any essence that belongs to the Platonic form *X*ness-itself, it can only be the essence of an *X*.) But it is perhaps because he has here made only a rather weak claim that he reverts to the same line of thought later in order to make the stronger claim: relying this time on the thesis that a fundamental substance must be fully knowable, he infers from this alone that it must *be* an essence.

As for the validity of this reasoning, the apparent paradox with which I began evidently rests on a misunderstanding of the phrase 'know what

X is'. For the basic thought, which Aristotle inherited from Plato, is that to know *X* is the same as to know what *X* is (or, in a frequent Greek idiom, 'to know *X*, what it is'). Now suppose that the right answer to the question 'What is *X*?' is that *X* is *Y*. Then the basic thought is clearly to be understood in this way: one knows *X* if one knows *that X* is *Y*. That is to say, knowing an object is equated with knowing a certain *fact* about that object. So even though *Y* is what *X* is, and to know *X* is to know what *X* is, it is a confusion to suppose that it follows that to know *X* is to know *Y*. So there is in fact no danger of the paradoxical result that knowing one object, namely *X*, *might* turn out to be knowing *a different object*, namely *Y*. This is a wholly spurious ground for supposing that the fact about *X*, which must be known if *X* is to be known, has to be a fact of the form '*X is identical with Y*'.

Let us turn to the second argument. The supposition that the form does not belong to (i.e. is not predicated of) the essence is taken to be a perfectly general supposition about *all* forms and their corresponding essences. So it implies not only that the essence of a good thing is not itself good, but also that the essence of a thing that is is not itself a thing that is. But then Aristotle argues, evidently illegitimately, that *this* conclusion can be generalized to all essences, yielding the result that no essence is a thing that is. One might certainly have expected a little more caution here, especially as Aristotle's *own* position is that the essence of a thing that is indeed is *not* a thing that is. (That is, he holds that there is no such thing as the essence of a being, an essence that absolutely every being would share.) But there seems no more to be said than that the argument is plainly illegitimate: there is no reason to suppose that anything that holds of one essence must hold of every other essence too.

b11: The last sentence of this paragraph, stating that the essence of a good thing belongs to everything that is good, is introduced as a 'further' point, from which, however, Aristotle appears to draw no consequence. One *possible* way of extracting a relevant consequence from it would be this: both the essence of an *X* thing and the form *X*ness-itself belong to whatever is an *X* thing, and to nothing else. That is to say, they belong to all the same things (including, as b3–10 has just argued, very unwisely, to one another). What, then, could be the point of insisting upon distinguishing them? But, obviously, this is a speculation that goes well beyond anything that is actually said.

31b11–18

Aristotle concludes that goodness and the essence of a good thing are the same, here dropping the title 'goodness-*itself*', which indicates that it is a Platonic form that is under discussion. For, as he goes on to say, the same result holds for anything that is 'primary, and spoken of in its own right', whether or not such things are Platonic forms. In fact, as my comments have shown, the argument at 31^a31–$^b3$ holds for any fundamental substance which has an associated essence, and the argument from knowability within $^b3$–10 (to be repeated at $^b18$–22) is supposed to hold for anything that is (fully) knowable. (The other arguments establish nothing relevant.) Presumably we should not understand Aristotle as here committing himself to the view that goodness and beauty *are* either fundamental substances or fully knowable. At any rate, they are surely not examples of what he had meant earlier at *Z*4, 30^a11–13 by 'forms of a genus'.

The paragraph ends (at $^b15$–18) with what appears to be a polemical aside, directed against the Platonic forms: if there are such things, then what underlies will not be substance (as *Z*3 had suggested). But Aristotle's reason is not, as one might have expected, that Platonic forms would be substances that do not underlie, but rather that Platonic forms would be substances whose existence did not depend upon something underlying them, i.e.—in more Platonic language—upon something participating in them. (This is, of course, a perfectly correct point to make about Platonic doctrine.) The implication is interesting. For Aristotle's own forms, i.e. essences, do owe their existence to the things they are predicated of (see, e.g., *H*3, 43^b14–23) and apparently he is suggesting here that this is what allows him to hang on to the principle that what underlies is substance. It is not that his forms are *themselves* underlying things, as was claimed (very obscurely) at *Z*3, 29^a2–3, and will be claimed again at *H*1, 42^a28–9. The more relevant point, apparently, is that the form depends for its existence upon the things that underlie it, as equally they depend for their existence upon the form. So there is a mutual dependence, each is equally fundamental in its own way, and each can be said to be, in its own way, a substance. But if there were no such dependence—for example if there were both 'underlying things' and 'forms', each existing independently of the other — then apparently neither could count as a substance, or at any rate the 'underlying things' could not. But perhaps this pushes rather too far the implications of what is only an aside.

31^b18–22

See 31^b3–10 n. (The word '*ekthesis*', for which I have borrowed Ross's rendering 'exhibition of cases', means more literally 'setting things out'. It is not at all clear what method of argument Aristotle means to indicate by it in the present context. See Ross on *A*9, 992^b10.)

31^b22–28

Aristotle returns here to 'things spoken of coincidentally'. This time his examples are introduced by simple terms from categories other than substance, not by a compound term as at 31^a19–28. The implication of

31ᵃ27–8 (at least as I read that passage) had seemed to be that it makes no difference which kind of term we take, but one could wish that the point had been stated more explicitly.

The point that he now wishes to make is quite clear: we must distinguish between the attribute itself and the thing that has it, and the attribute is the same as the essence, while the thing that has it is not. In Greek this distinction is indeed the diagnosis of an ambiguity in a single expression, literally rendered 'the pale' (*to leukon*), which can mean either the attribute (pallor, paleness, being pale, etc.), or pale things in general, or the pale thing in question. When Aristotle says 'that to which the attribute attaches and the attribute itself are both pale', we need not think of him as meaning to imply that the attribute of being pale is itself a pale thing (and that being round is a round thing, being heavy is a heavy thing, etc.). He probably means only to say that the word 'pale' (especially in the phrase 'the pale') can be used both to refer to the attribute and to describe what has it. He gives no reason here for saying that the attribute is identical with its essence, but presumably the reason is to be supplied from the immediately preceding remark that to know a thing is to know its essence. So the unstated assumption is that the attribute is knowable.

One would have thought that the distinction between the attribute itself and what has it is a distinction that needs to be made in *all* cases, not only for 'things spoken of coincidentally' (both simple and compound), but also for 'things spoken of in their own right'. There is certainly no suggestion of the latter application in this passage (but see 32ᵃ4–11 n.). We are left to speculate on whether Aristotle means what he says here to include compounds spoken of coincidentally.

31ᵇ28–32ᵃ4

In this paragraph Aristotle offers a further argument to show that some things at least, and in particular essences, must be identical with their essences. In the first part of the paragraph (ᵇ28–30) he apparently sees an absurdity in the suggestion that the essence of the essence of *X* should be different from the essence of *X*, but it is not very clear at first sight what that absurdity is. Then at the end of the paragraph he claims that we should have an infinite regress if the two were always different (ᵃ2–4). It is convenient to begin by considering the regress.

Consider the infinite series of terms:

(1) *X*
(2) The essence of *X*
(3) The essence of the essence of *X*
(4) The essence of the essence of the essence of *X*
etc.

Clearly if (1) and (2) are identical, then all these terms are identical. Equally, if (2) and (3) are identical, then all the terms from (2) on are identical. But Aristotle seems to claim that if (*n*) and (*n* + 1) are not at any stage identical, then all the terms in the series will be distinct from one another. This does not follow without a further premiss, for there is so far nothing to prevent us supposing that (*n*) and (*n* + 1) are always distinct, but (*n*) and (*n* + 2) always identical, so that there are just two items in all. But it is not difficult to supply a further premiss. For any *X*, if *X* and the essence of *X* are not identical, then the essence of *X* *abstracts* from *X* its essential part or aspect or something of the sort. Thus at each stage (*n* + 1) is either identical with (*n*) or 'more abstract' than (*n*). Aristotle's result then follows simply from the truism that the relation 'more abstract than' is transitive and irreflexive. Using the same supplementary idea, we can further explain why Aristotle should take it for granted that the regress would be vicious. For if (*n* + 1) is always in some sense a *part* of (*n*), then our second term, the essence of *X*, will have infinitely many distinguishable and successively more abstract parts. But Aristotle has always insisted that an essence must be finite (e.g. *An. Post* I, 22, $82^b37–83^a1$; cf. *H*3, $43^b35–6$).

The argument is correct, then, on the assumption that for any term in the series *there is* such a thing as the essence of it. Now it might seem that at the beginning of the paragraph it is just this assumption that Aristotle is finding absurd, i.e. it is absurd that there should be such a thing as the essence of the essence of a horse. But he certainly ought not to be finding this absurd if it is coupled with the admission that it is the same thing as the essence of a horse. (For, as we have observed, if (1) = (2) then it *follows* that (2) = (3), and hence that (3) exists.) The initial claim, then, should be that it is absurd that (2) and (3) should both exist and be different. Using the same supplementary idea once more, we can now offer an explanation of this. For the supposition that (2) and (3) are different is the supposition that (3) abstracts from (2) its more essential aspect. But since (2) is a similar abstraction from (1), it follows that (3) also gives an essential aspect of (1), and one that is more essential than that given by (2). Hence it is (3), and not (2), that should have been given as the essence of (1) in the first place.

Admittedly, this interpretation of the first part of the paragraph supplies a great deal that Aristotle does not actually say. We could avoid this if we suppose instead that the 'absurdity' with which the paragraph begins is really the same as that with which it ends, i.e. that if one wishes to distinguish between the essence of a horse and the essence of the essence of a horse, then clearly there is a *danger* of a regress. But in that case the 'further' at $^a2$ does not actually introduce a *further* point; it merely elucidates what the initial point was.

Between what I have been calling the first and the last part of the paragraph, i.e. at $^b31–^a2$, Aristotle betrays once more that he is now assuming a thesis which had been left undecided when the chapter began, i.e. that there is no distinction to be drawn between the substance of a thing and the essence of that thing. This, he seems to say, makes it easier to believe that some things are identical with their essences, presumably because he has begun by citing it as a received opinion that each (?) thing is identical with its substance. He also adds that his argument shows that where *X* and the essence of *X* are identical, this identity is not merely coincidental, since their definitions must also be the same. This comment is correct, given that an essence is just what is expressed by a definition, as Z4 has said. (For if (1) = (2) then (2) = (3), as we have observed, but '(2) = (3)' says that the definition of (1) is the same as the definition of (2).) In the course of this comment the example changes from the essence of a horse, which *is* an essence for Aristotle (at least until Z10, 35^b27–31), to the essence of a unity—or more literally the essence of a thing that is one thing—which is not. There appears to be no reason why he should at this point return to an example more acceptable to the Platonists than to himself.

32^a4–11

Aristotle concludes that things which are primary and spoken of in their own right are identical with their essences. Though he does not say that it is *only* such things that are identical with their essences, it is quite natural to suppose that this is what he means, in view of the fact that this sentence appears as a summary of the result reached in the chapter as a whole. The word 'primary' has not hitherto been used in this chapter. One might suppose that it is intended to pick up the characterization of a 'fundamental substance' at 31^a28–31, in which case being primary is either identified with, or is a special case of, being spoken of in one's own right. But it is no doubt better to suppose that the word is to be understood here in accordance with the explanation given at Z4, 30^a10–11 as meaning 'not expressed by predicating one thing of another'. (At any rate Z11, 37^a3–$^b7$ would support this view.) However, we have already seen that there is a doubt over whether this is supposed to include or to exclude simple items in categories other than that of substance. There is the further doubt over whether being primary and being spoken of in one's own right are intended as two different expressions for the same condition, or as two distinct conditions which must both be satisfied, or possibly—by reinterpreting the scope of 'and' — as two distinct conditions of which at least one must be satisfied. It cannot be said that this summarizing statement clears up the obscurities already noted in this chapter.

Aristotle then baffles us further by referring to an apparently *familiar* debate on whether Socrates is or is not the same as the essence of Socrates, and remarking that the argumentative moves familiar from that debate may also be applied to 'sophistical objections' to his own position. We, who are not familiar with that debate, can only speculate on what these argumentative moves are, and on what he takes the result of that debate to be. On the one hand, one might suppose that Socrates, as an example of what the *Categories* calls a primary substance, should count as 'spoken of in his own right' and indeed as 'primary' in the sense of Z4, 30^a10–11. (Even if it is true that one cannot 'express' Socrates without bringing in the fact that he is a man, still this does not count as predicating one thing of *another*. For Socrates does not have to be something *else* before he can be a man; on the contrary, he is just what *is* a man (*An. Post* I, 22, 83^a1–14; Γ4, 1007^a20–$^b6$).) On this account it would seem that Socrates must, in Aristotle's view, count as being identical with his essence. But on the other hand, it is quite clear that Socrates is a particular rather than a universal, and from the perspective of the *Metaphysics* he is regarded as a compound of form in matter. Such a compound is not 'primary' either in the sense of Z4, 30^a10–11 or in the sense of Z6, 31^a29–31, since it is 'expressed' when we predicate Socrates' form, not of *him*, but of his matter, and the form is *prior* to the compound (Z3, 29^a5–7). But, more straightforwardly, it is *only* universals that can be identical with their essences, as (eventually) Z10, 35^b31–36^a9 manages to imply. Thus Socrates is not identical with his essence. He can be said to *have* an essence (cf. Z4, 29^b14–16), but his essence is exactly the same as Callias' essence. i.e. the essence of a man (Z8, 34^a5–8). So he cannot possibly be identical with it.

I have suggested here some fairly straightforward points to be made on either side of the question. Whether they at all resemble points that Aristotle may have had in mind, one does not know. Some interpreters have taken it to be evident that Aristotle is implying that Socrates is identical with his essence (e.g. Owen [1965], Woods [1974/5]), and some have taken the opposite view to be equally clear (e.g. Lear [1988], 279–80; Furth [1988], 235–6). All that one can say with confidence is that this text can be taken either way. (I shall discuss the general issue in the prologue to Z13.) There is, however, a small hint in the phrasing that Aristotle uses here that *might* be taken as indicating his own view. The most straightforward way to express his general position is by saying that some things are, and some things are not, identical with their essences. But his remarks on 'the pale' at 31^b22–8 would encourage a different phrasing: a thing is identical with its essence when taken in one way, but not when taken in another. Now it is in fact this latter phrasing that Aristotle uses in the last sentence of the chapter, and it is plausible to suppose that it is the recent mention of Socrates that has led to it. If this is right, then his own answer to the question about Socrates takes this form: Socrates, taken in one way, is the same as his essence, but taken in another way he is not. As for what these two ways of taking Socrates might be, it is natural to refer forward to the obscure suggestion of Z10–11 that he may be taken either as a compound of form in matter or as his form (i.e. soul) alone (35^a7–9, 36^a16–17(?), 37^a7–8). Then, presumably, it will be Socrates 'taken as form alone' that is identical with the essence of Socrates. But how this is to be understood is itself controversial; see the prologue to Z10.

Epilogue to *Z*4–6

These three chapters pay no attention to the distinction between form and matter. The word 'matter' does not occur in them at all, and the word 'form' occurs only twice: once in the phrase 'a form of a genus' at $30^{a}12$, where it evidently means 'species', and once at $31^{b}14$–15, where it refers to Platonic forms. From this point of view the chapters belong with the Logical Works, rather than the Physical Works (and that is perhaps a reason for saying that all three chapters are governed by the opening of *Z*4, 'and first let us make some logical remarks'). In this respect they resemble *Z*1, and we may add *Z*13–14 (setting aside $38^{b}1$–8), but no other chapters of *Z* or *H*. There is accordingly another way in which they seem to belong with the Logical Works, and to be somewhat removed from at least most of *Z* and *H*, and that is that their view of what counts as a substance is apparently governed by the familiar distinction between the category of substance and the other categories. It is true that this way of contrasting substances with other things is used explicitly only in *Z*4, first at $29^{b}22$–7 (to explain the kind of compounds there under consideration) and then at $30^{a}17$–27 (where it is the basis of a central argument). But we are given no hint, as we read on, that this contrast is about to be superseded—as it evidently *is* superseded in *Z*7–11—by the different idea that substance (or essence) is form as opposed to matter. So far as *Z*4–6 is concerned, it appears to be the familiar category of substance that remains central.

In broad terms one might say that the main claims of *Z*4–6 are (*a*) that only a species in the category of substance has an essence, and (*b*) that such things in fact are the essences that they are also said to have. But, to be fairer, one must weaken claim (*a*). The strong version is what appears first (in *Z*4, $30^{a}2$–17), and it reappears later when it is said to be 'absurd' that snubness, and things like it, should have an essence at all (*Z*5, $30^{b}28$–$31^{a}1$). But it is superseded by a weaker claim, that other things may indeed be said to have essences, though not in the primary way. This is applied to the simple items in categories other than substance at $30^{a}17$–27, extended to compounds such as pale man at $30^{b}7$–13, and apparently conceded also to snubness at $30^{b}26$–8 and at $31^{a}7$–11, i.e. both before and after an essence of snubness is dismissed as 'absurd'. Indeed, such a concession must be granted to snubness if it is to be maintained for any predicates other than those in the category of substance, for at $31^{a}1$–5 it has been claimed that *all* such other predicates are in the same position as snubness (i.e. they have 'first recipients' which must be mentioned in their definitions). But although it is this weaker view that prevails, still it is clear that *Z*4–5 do maintain a distinct preference for items in the old category of substance.

By contrast, it may well be said that *Z*6 in the end turns out to show no such preference. Certainly it is always ready to grant the existence of any essence that may be proposed—e.g. of a pale man ($31^{a}19$–21), of a pale thing ($31^{a}27$ and $^{b}22$–4), of Socrates ($32^{a}8$), of the essence of a horse (31^b28–32^a4 n.), and even of goodness, being, and unity (31^b12, 32^a2). But it is not clear just which things it allows as identical with their essences. It argues first that all 'fundamental substances' are so, and this apparently includes all species in the category of substance (31^a28–31). But it also argues that all (fully) knowable things are so, and it appears to be on this ground that the attribute pallor is admitted, though not pale *things* (31^b20–8). The same ground evidently admits compound attributes too, for if being pale and being a man are each knowable things, then surely being a pale man is also knowable. But one cannot be quite sure that Aristotle has seen this point. Since he has conceded that compounds do have definitions, he evidently *ought* to concede that they may be known by knowing their definitions. And since he has in fact argued that even an apparently simple attribute such as pallor is really a kind of compound (for its 'first recipient' must be mentioned in its definition), he evidently *ought* not to have felt that being compound is a stumbling-block. I am inclined to think, therefore, that he should be given the benefit of the doubt on this point, and that he has in fact reached, by a somewhat circuitous route, the conclusion which I originally said was the 'correct' conclusion (31^a15–18 n.): *any* universal and definable characteristic is identical with what is given in its definition, and hence with its essence; nothing else is. But there are two reasons for regarding this interpretation as too optimistic.

(i) The claim at 32^a4–6 that the identity holds for things that are primary and [for things that are?] spoken of in their own right would certainly seem to be intended as a summary of the chapter. If so, then one would *expect* it to be intended to carry the implication that it is *only* for such things that the identity holds. Now, a (superficially) simple attribute such as pallor could be held to be primary in the sense explained at Z4, 30^a10–11, i.e. not expressed by predicating one thing of another. (But I did suggest in my note on that passage that Aristotle seems to have held there that only substances satisfy the condition, and this certainly is the implication of Z5, 31^a1–14.) Alternatively, or in addition, such an attribute could be held to be spoken of in its own right, in conformity with Δ7, 1017^a22–4, and despite Z6, 31^b22–3. For once we have firmly distinguished between a use of 'the pale' that refers to the attribute, and a use that refers to what has that attribute, it could well seem reasonable to say that it is only the latter that speaks of something 'coincidentally'. Thus all the *explicit* claims of Z6 can be harmonized with the suggested implication that it is only things that are primary *and* spoken of in their own right, or only things that are primary *or* spoken of in their own right, that are identical with their essences. But one cannot reasonably suppose that a compound attribute counts either as primary or as spoken of in its own right. So if compound attributes are to be included as identical with their essences, we cannot read an implied 'if *and only if*' into this sentence.

(ii) If the obscure coda on Socrates and the essence of Socrates is to be taken in the way my note suggested, then Aristotle has not reached the 'correct' solution unless he supposes that when Socrates is 'taken as form alone' he is also taken as universal and definable. This is quite hard to believe, though the view has been defended (e.g. by Woods [1974/5]). But in any case I think it best to preserve a scepticism on whether Aristotle does mean to suggest, in this passage, that Socrates can be 'taken in two ways'. And if he does not, then we do not know what the passage indicates about whether Socrates is or is not identical with his essence. So I shall continue to set it aside.

Returning to clear examples of universals, we may anyway conclude that the doctrine of Z6 is not particularly restrictive. Even if compounds are still scurvily treated, at any rate all simple attributes, from whatever category, are allowed to be the same as their essences. It is in Z4–5 that a preference is found for attributes (and in particular species) from the category of substance, and it is the fact that only these have essences in the primary way that allows Aristotle to accept the proposed identification between substance and essence (as he does, by implication, at 31^b2–3 and $^b31$–2). For what he accepts comes to this. First, the essence of any thing and the substance of that thing are indeed the same. (This identity has in fact been presupposed all through the Logical Works.) But second, by the argument of Z6, what has an essence is that essence, and so is in this sense a substance. This seems at first sight to destroy the concept of substance by making every definable thing equally a substance. But it does not do so, because it is only the species in the category of substance that have an essence in the primary way, and so only these that are essences, and in this sense substances, in the primary way. Admittedly, every other definable thing will have an essence, hence be an essence, and hence also be in this sense a substance; but we must add 'not in the primary way'.

That, then, is the result to which these chapters lead, and the reasoning relies throughout on the perspective of the Logical Works. By contrast, at the end of Z11 there is a passage which summarizes the doctrine of Z6 from a quite different perspective, in which the contrast between form and matter is all-important (i.e. 37^a33–$^b7$). Just before this is a passage which is usually seen as attempting a similar summary of Z5 (i.e. 37^a29–33). But if that is right, then one can only say that the new perspective has distorted Z5 out of all recognition, and so should not be trusted as an elucidation of Z6 either. For further discussion of this issue, see my comments ad loc.

CHAPTER 7

Prologue to *Z*7–9

As many commentators have observed, there is good reason to suppose that the discussion which now appears as chapters 7–9 of book *Z* was not originally written for its present position in book *Z*. First, on the most probable MS reading it begins abruptly, with no connecting particle or any other link to what now precedes it. Second, its topic is the general nature of coming to be, and it is not at once clear why this topic should be considered in a discussion of essence begun in *Z*4–6 and continued in *Z*10–11. To some extent this does *become* clear, for form and essence are to be identified, and the topic of coming to be shows us the contrast between form and matter in a setting that is natural to it (cf. the prologue to *Z*3). Moreover, one of the points made during the discussion of this topic, namely that form is not itself produced or created (*Z*8), is a point that Aristotle evidently does regard as relevant to his concerns in book *Z*, and it is natural to suppose that it is largely because the discussion does make this point that he decided to incorporate it here. It is this point that is emphasized in the conclusion to the whole discussion (*Z*9, 34^b7–19), and this point that is afterwards cited as established (*Z*10, 35^a28–30; *Z*15, 39^b26; *H*1, 42^a30; *H*3, 43^b16; *Θ*8, 49^b27). But one cannot believe that when the discussion was first written, its purpose was only, or mainly, to make this point. For the somewhat obscure discussion of spontaneous generation that occupies most of chapter 9 would then have to be set down merely as a lengthy and distracting aside, and the same might be said of much of the elaborate parallel drawn in chapter 7 between natural and artificial generation.

The discussion has been touched up, here and there, to suit it for its present context. No doubt the concluding passage at 34^b7–19 was added then, for although it is evidently meant as the conclusion to all three chapters it clearly focuses on the doctrine of chapter 8, omitting chapter 9 altogether, and with only an oblique reference to chapter 7. This conclusion uses the word 'primary' apparently in the sense explained at *Z*4, 30^a10, to apply to simple items in all categories. There are also three brief asides equating form with essence (and, in the first case, with primary substance too), at 32^b1–2, 32^b14, and 33^b7. It is easy to suppose that these asides are later additions to an original discussion which paid no attention to the notion of essence, and in the first two cases there are positive advantages in so doing. (See my notes ad loc.)

Now even if *Z*7–9 did once form an independent fragment, it does not follow from this that there was once a version of book *Z* that lacked these chapters. For they may have been incorporated at the same time as *Z* itself was first written. The main reason for supposing that they are a later addition is that they are not mentioned in the summary at the end of *Z*11, which is otherwise fairly full. On the other side, I have noted that the doctrine of *Z*8 is cited several times in what comes after, and in particular at *Z*15, 39ᵇ26 it is clearly cited as something that has already been said. This must imply that *Z*8 was already in its present position when *Z*15 was written. (The contrary implication of *H*3, 43ᵇ16 should be set aside, since that paragraph of *H*3 is itself misplaced. See *H*3, 43ᵇ14–23 n.) In any case, we may leave this question open. It will not affect the interpretation of these chapters.

32ᵃ12–15

This opening paragraph states the general theses about coming to be that will be developed in detail in what follows. The verb which I translate 'come to be' (i.e. '*gignesthai*') can be used either with a complement, as is illustrated here, or without one, in which case it means 'come into being' or 'come to exist'. Aristotle presumes here that we always have a complement, though he surely does not wish to rule out consideration of '*X* comes into being'. Rather, he takes this to be covered by 'something comes to be *X*', and where this is a case of *X* coming to exist the expression '*X*' will standardly be from the category of substance (e.g. 'a man', as at 32ᵃ18, or 'a house' as at 32ᵇ12).

Aristotle claims elsewhere that coming to be takes place *only* with respect to the four categories illustrated here, i.e. substance, quality, quantity, and place (*Phys* V, 224ᵇ35–226ᵃ26). This is an unnecessarily restrictive doctrine, which he does not seem to be insisting upon here. Clearly 'a this' in ᵃ15 is standing in generally for terms from the category of substance. There is a dispute, which I consider in my next note, over whether Aristotle is thinking of particular substances or of kinds of substances. Nothing can be inferred from the fact that he chooses the expression 'a this' to refer to the category (cf. *Z*3, 29ᵃ28 n.).

32ᵃ15–26

The word 'generation', which translates '*genesis*', can be used to cover any kind of coming to be, but is most naturally used when what is in question is coming into being. This is how it is used here, of the coming into being of natural substances, such as a man or a plant. Presumably Aristotle does not wish to deny that a thing, once brought into being, can undergo further natural changes, but that is not his topic here. The paragraph contains first a general statement of Aristotle's position on natural generation (ᵃ15–19), then a digression on the necessity for matter (ᵃ20–2), then a further reflection on the 'natures' involved in this natural phenomenon (ᵃ22–5). It will be convenient to postpone comment on the digression to the end, for the interpretation of the other two passages is closely linked.

What a man comes from is on our theory an ovum and on Aristotle's theory the 'menstrual fluid' (*ta katamēnia*, *H*4, 44ᵃ35). Since it will make no important difference, I shall speak in terms of our own theory. It seems, then, that the ovum is 'what we call matter' in this instance. But actually this is not quite right, as we may see in this way. The matter of a change is supposed to be something that *persists* throughout that change (*Z*3, prologue), but we evidently do not want to say that the ovum still remains as the adult human that comes from it. To suit Aristotle's theory we must therefore say this. First, the process by which a man is brought into existence is the relatively brief process of conception, in which the ovum is fertilized and transformed into a living thing. The matter of this change is the matter that first constitutes the ovum and then the living foetus; this is (on Aristotle's theory) exactly the same matter all through. Thereafter there is a long process of growth and development, until we finally have a mature adult, but this is not strictly a *generation*, for it is the alteration of an already existing substance and not the creation of a new one. What remains the same throughout this change is simply the substance itself—i.e. we have the same human being all through, now in one phase and now in another—but the matter that it is made of will be different at different times, as 'some flows out and some flows in' (*GC* I, 5, 321^b24–7). (So we need to distinguish the matter that a thing comes *from* and the matter that it is at any time made *of*.)

What a thing comes from is what Aristotle also calls the 'material cause' of the process that generates it. What it is brought into being by is what he also calls the 'efficient cause', that which begins the change, that from which it originates (33^a24–5). One might naturally suppose that the efficient cause of conception is the sperm, and that is just what Aristotle does say at *H*4, 44^a35. But here it is relevant that his own theory of this process is different from ours. He holds that the sperm does not contribute any matter to the resultant individual; rather, it transfers to the ovum a *form* which it carries from the father. So he prefers to say here that that 'by which' a man comes to be is itself a man (i.e. the father), or more strictly it is the form conveyed from him and imparted to the ovum at conception. Given his own theory of how animal reproduction occurs, it seems at first perfectly reasonable that he should call this form its efficient cause. It looks rather less reasonable if we turn our attention from animals to plants. Presumably the matter 'from which' an oak tree comes into existence is the matter of the acorn, and one would have supposed that the efficient cause 'by which' the acorn is thus transformed is whatever it is that starts that acorn into life, e.g. a suitable moist, warm, earthy, environment. But Aristotle will still say that the efficient cause is the form that the acorn somehow inherited from the tree on which it grew, and which may in fact remain for a long time dormant within it. One has to say, I think, that there is something rather forced about Aristotle's insistence that the one factor that deserves to be picked out as 'efficient cause' is always just the form and nothing else. (The same point evidently applies too to what the next paragraph will say about the efficient cause of generations effected by skill.)

Anyway, the position so far is that in natural generations 'that from which' is the matter, and 'that by which' is the form. Given this, it might seem very natural to suppose that the third factor that Aristotle distinguishes, i.e. 'what the thing comes to be', will be the particular compound of matter and form that results. On the other hand, one might equally well say that we have so far mentioned the material cause and the efficient cause, so one expects that the third factor will be a further kind of cause, and in that case it must surely be the form, here functioning as both formal cause and final cause. (The *locus classicus* for Aristotle's doctrine of 'the four causes' is *Physics* II, 3 and 7; at 198a25–6 he is thinking of natural generations when he remarks that the formal and final causes are often the same, and the efficient cause is also the same as them 'in form'.) So when Aristotle says here at a18–19 that 'what a thing comes to be is a man or a plant or something else of this sort, which we most strongly affirm to be substances', on one view (adopted by Ross) he is speaking of particular compounds, but on the other view (argued by Owen [1978/9], 16–21; Loux [1979], 1–2, Frede & Patzig) he is speaking of forms.

The clearest argument is a parallel with Λ3, 1069b36–1070a2. There we find a similar list of three factors involved in any coming to be, namely what changes, by what it is changed, and to what. Unambiguously these are further identified as, respectively, the matter, the efficient cause, and the form. (Aristotle does not there elaborate upon the relation between the efficient cause and the form, no doubt because he is speaking of all changes and not just of generations.) Now of course he may have changed his mind, between writing Z7 and Λ3, on which three features of a change deserve to be emphasized, but it does not seem particularly likely. A second argument may be drawn from the opening of Z8, where Aristotle reminds us again of that by which a thing comes to be, that from which, and the something that it becomes. He changes his example of the something from 'a man or a plant' to 'a sphere or a circle', and at once he goes on to say that just as one does not make the matter so equally one does not make *the sphere*. It is quite clear that he *means* by this last remark that one does not make the *form* of a sphere, though in fact that is not what his words actually say, and this inappropriate language recurs several times in the first paragraph of Z8. The explanation that immediately suggests itself is this. His view is that when we say what a thing becomes we specify a form, i.e. that in the phrase 'to become a sphere' the words 'a sphere' stand for a form, since they introduce a kind of thing but not a particular thing of that kind. (This claim can be presented in a way that is defensible, as Owen urges on pp. 18–19.) Hence Aristotle supposes that one can express the point that people do not make that form by saying that they do not make that sphere, namely the sphere that is mentioned when we say that something becomes a sphere. Given, then, the premiss that what a thing becomes is a form, we have an explanation both of his sequence of thought at the opening of chapter 8 and of the otherwise strange misuse of language that accompanies it. But if his view is that 'a sphere', in the context 'becomes a sphere', stands for a particular compound of form in matter, then the beginning of chapter 8 surely cannot be explained at all.

These two arguments together are quite convincing. I should mention a third argument, which is that at 30^b1–2 we will be told that the form, i.e. the essence, is 'the primary substance'. This is difficult to reconcile with the suggestion that at $^a19$ it is the compound, not the form, that is 'most strongly' affirmed to be a substance. But I would put little weight on this point, since it seems to me probable that 30^b1–2 was added when Z7–9 was adapted to its present context in book Z. It would not be very surprising if the addition did not jibe too well with one aspect of the original.

On the other side there is of course the obvious point that in Z7 form is explicitly mentioned several times in connection with 'that by which' (the efficient cause), but *never* in connection with 'what' the thing comes to be. Moreover, the implication of $^a22$–5 would seem to be that it is *only* 'that by which' that does involve form. In this passage we are told that each of the three factors mentioned 'is a nature'. The sense in which matter *is* a nature is obscure, but I think it likely that the point is that the matter *has* a definite and specific nature, which gives it the potentiality of becoming an animal or plant only of one definite species. (For example, one cannot bring a dog into being by trying to impose the right form on matter supplied by a cat.) Then we are told that as what comes into being *has* a nature, so 'that in accordance with which' it comes into being *is* a nature. You would have thought that this nature must be a form, whether it is the form or the compound that is being counted as 'what' the thing comes to be. But just as Aristotle's language distinguishes this nature from the nature 'from which', so it *also* distinguishes it from the nature 'by which', and it is only the last that is said to be 'the nature spoken of in accordance with form'. It is very difficult to avoid the conclusion that the other two are *not* spoken of 'in accordance with form', and hence that neither of them can *be* forms. (*Perhaps* the contrast intended is that they are to be taken as peculiar to the particular animal in question, e.g. as together forming its 'nature' in the sense of its 'inner cause of changing and resting' (*Phys* II, 1, 192^b8–32); whereas the nature which is form is universal.)

We have a conflict of evidence. Perhaps the simplest resolution is to say that in Aristotle's view 'what' a thing comes to be is to be regarded as a (universal) kind of thing rather than a (particular) thing of that kind, and is indeed just what he usually calls a form. Where this kind of thing is specified as 'a sphere', as at the beginning of Z8, then indeed it is a form. But when it is specified as 'a man' or 'an oak', which is what we are considering here, Aristotle is now unwilling to call it a form. For he is going to tell us in the next chapter, at 33^b24–6, that a universal such as 'man' is actually a universal compound of form in matter, on a par with the clear compound 'bronzen sphere', which has matter as well as form in its definition (33ᵃ1–5). That is perhaps why he here calls it somewhat vaguely 'a nature', and apparently distinguishes it from the nature which is form.

ᵃ20–2: A more literal translation of these lines is 'each is capable both of being and of not being, and this *is* the matter in each'. But it is difficult to make any sense of the idea that the matter in a thing simply *is* its capacity both to be and not to be, and presumably what Aristotle intends to say is that the matter *explains* this capacity.

Aristotle clearly holds that every generated thing, whether generated naturally or in any other way, comes *from* matter. For it would be impossible otherwise to account for its generation (cf. 33ᵇ11–13, in the next chapter). His sequence of thought here might be reconstructed in either of two ways. (*a*) Generated things come *from* matter; therefore, throughout their career, there is always matter *in* them; therefore they are always capable of ceasing to exist, i.e. because that matter may at any time lose the form that it must have in order to constitute the thing. (*b*) Things which come into being must also be capable of ceasing to be (*De Caelo* I, 12); to explain this, we must suppose that they always have matter *in* them; to explain this in turn we must suppose that they come *from* matter. That is, it is not entirely clear what is supposed to be the premiss and what is supposed to be the conclusion, but Aristotle's wording seems to suggest (*b*) rather than (*a*). In any case, the argument is paying little attention to the distinction between coming *from* matter and being made *of* matter.

32ᵃ26–ᵇ14

Under the heading 'natural generations' Aristotle has considered how substances come to be by nature, but not how things come to acquire by nature predicates from other categories. (In fact, he has considered only the generation of *living* things; the coming into being of a swallow's nest, or a spider's web (*Phys* II, 199ᵃ26–7) would not fit anywhere into his present discussion (cf. 199ᵇ26–8).) Under the heading 'other generations' one would therefore expect him to be considering how artefacts and so on come to be, as indeed the word 'production' (or simply 'making', '*poiēsis*') might well suggest. But in fact his main example under this heading is the production of health in a patient, which is a case of a thing coming to have a certain quality. The points that he wishes to make about producing health he applies equally to the production of, e.g., a house (ᵇ12), but I suspect that he has in fact been misled, in the last two paragraphs of this chapter, by paying insufficient attention to the distinction.

All productions, he claims, are effected 'either by skill (*tekhnē*) or by some capacity (*dunamis*) or by thought (*dianoia*)' (cf. *E*1, 1025ᵇ22). Presumably skill is a special kind of thought, namely thought that is based on correct principles and successfully applied. It is not clear what he intends by 'some capacity' (which seems not to be meant to cover the further case of spontaneous productions, a topic mentioned here but postponed for later treatment). Whatever it is, it is not illustrated in the ensuing discussion, which concentrates on productions effected by skill. The main point that he wishes to make about these is that the form of what is so produced is present beforehand in the soul of the producer, and he evidently means to count this form as that 'by which' these generations are effected, i.e. their efficient cause (cf. 32^b21-3). In this way productions and natural generations resemble one another. (For some comment on what Aristotle means by 'the soul' (*psukhē*), see the prologue to Z10.)

Having told us that the form of what is produced is in the soul of the producer, Aristotle at once adds 'and by its form I mean what being is for it, and its primary substance'. This is the first identification of form and essence, relating Z7–9 to the discussion of essence in Z4–6. In fact we have more than an identification, since it is added that the form or essence of a thing is also its 'primary substance', which is the first occurrence of this phrase in book Z. (It is used again at 37^a5, $^a28$, and $^b1-4$ in Z11.) Clearly, it does not mean here what it meant in the *Categories*. It is not obvious whether it means here the same as was meant by 'primary' in Z4–6, because although 'primary' was there defined simply as 'non-compound' (30^a10-11), there remained a suspicion that it was intended to be confined to items in the familiar category of substance. Evidently 'primary substance' here is not so confined, for we are about to be given the form of health as an example (and this is called a substance at $^b4$ and at $^b14$). It appears that 'form', 'essence', and 'substance' are here being used with very little restriction to cover any characteristic that may be acquired or lost in a change (cf. Z3, prologue).

I suggested in my prologue to Z7–9 that this link back to Z4–6 is a later addition to an original text, and it is plausible to suppose that it has displaced something once in the original. This would be some statement to the effect that, although a skill is always a 'skill of opposites' (Θ2), nevertheless we need not suppose that the soul of one who has the skill will contain a form for each of the two opposites. This seems needed to give a suitable connection to the next sentence, which is introduced as *explaining* something by the fact that, in a way, opposites have the same form. But in the text as we have it there is no statement that needs any such explanation. (As for the explanation offered, it is surely oversimple; but let us not fuss about that.)

At $^b6-10$ Aristotle sketches how the practical reasoning of the doctor will begin from the thought of what health is, i.e. of its form or essence. The account is amplified in the next paragraph, and seems sufficiently clear. Then at the end he returns to his parallel with natural generation, that that 'by which' the generation is effected is the same form as is acquired in the generation, but 'in another'—in the one case in a material thing (the parent), but in the other merely in the mind.

Apparently equating the original notion of 'that by which' (*hupo tinos*) and the skill in question (*apo tekhnēs*), he is led to conclude that the skill *is* the form. Evidently this cannot be accepted quite literally. (At best, the skill is *knowledge* of the form—and, one should add, the ability to work out how it may be produced in other things.) Finally he reminds us again that by the form, i.e. 'the substance without matter', he means the essence. Again, it helps to suppose that this reminder is a later addition, since it seems to be incorrectly placed. It attaches to the clause 'the one that has matter from the one that does not', and not to what follows it.

32^b15-26

This paragraph seems sufficiently clear, save for its last sentence. The doctor's thinking is presumably completed by the thought that the patient should be rubbed, and the rubbing which he then proceeds to is the start of that part of the process which is called production. Does Aristotle mean to imply that in a spontaneous production of health the starting-point would also be a rubbing, but one which occurred spontaneously? Or does he mean rather that it would be a production of warmth by some other spontaneous means? From the nature of the case, and from the fact that Aristotle says it is the warming (not the rubbing) that is the starting-point, the second appears to be the more probable alternative. But then the example does not really illustrate what it is meant to. So perhaps it is better to take the first alternative. At any rate in chapter 9, where spontaneous generation is the main topic of interest, the example of health is used once more, and it is described as stemming from 'the warmth in the movement' (which causes 'the warmth in the body'). This 'movement', one supposes, is again a rubbing of some kind.

32^b26-33^a5

In this paragraph Aristotle apparently sets himself to argue that if anything is produced then some part of it must be present beforehand. The theme is resumed in chapter 9, 34^a21-32, but apparently abandoned in the conclusion to that chapter (34^b16-19). As it is presented at the beginning of the paragraph, i.e. in its application to health ($^b26-31$), the claim is clearly mistaken.

One can see why Aristotle should suppose that when health is produced by warming, that is because warmth is part of health. For health, according to a prevalent Greek theory, is a correct balance in the body between the hot and the cold, the wet and the dry, and so on. One can also see why, being cautious of affirming this theory, Aristotle should wish to hedge, and allow that warmth might not itself be a part of health but instead lead to something else—more or less directly—which is a part of health. (Of course there is also the possibility that warmth is not a part of health but leads directly *to health*, and not to some part of it.

See $34^a25–32$ n.) But neither of these views would justify the claim that, if health is to be produced, then some part of health must be present beforehand, i.e. before the whole process *begins*. For the supposed part of health is envisaged as arising *during* the production, and is not present before it begins. (Thus, when one produces warmth by rubbing, no 'part' of the warmth is present beforehand.) Generally, when the change we are concerned with is the acquisition of some property not in the category of substance—e.g. a quality (as here), or a quantity, or a position—one cannot usually say what might count as a 'part' of this property, and there should be no temptation to suppose that it must be 'partly' present before the change begins. But that is just what Aristotle is doing. He is treating health as if it were a substance, with warmth and so on as its *matter*, as the comparison with a house makes clear. This is evidently a mistake.

On Aristotle's general principles, it is fair to say that in any change there must be *something* that is present beforehand, as he does say at $^b30–1$. If we adopt a wide use of the technical term 'matter', and a somewhat loose use of 'part', then we can go on to say that the matter of the change is always present beforehand, and persists through the change, and hence is a 'part' of what results ($^b31–2$). But in this use, when an animal becomes healthy it is the animal itself that is counted as the matter of the change, and as a 'part' of the healthy animal we end with (Z3, prologue). Perhaps because he dimly recognizes that *this* way of relying on matter has no relevance to what he has just been saying about health, Aristotle proceeds to ask whether there must *also* be present beforehand some part that occurs in the definition of what results ($^a1–2$). His thought, one supposes, is that matter will not occur in this definition. But then his reply is profoundly unsatisfying, for he simply says that we may always include matter in the definition if we wish. We can choose to regard the result, not just as a circle, but in particular as a circle made of bronze, and define it accordingly.

$33^a5–23$

The linguistic point that Aristotle offers to explain in this paragraph is difficult for the translator, since it would not be correct as a point about English. He tells us that we do not say that a statue 'is stone' or 'is bronze', whereas in English we do say just this, for our words 'stone' and 'bronze' are used not only as nouns but also as adjectives. To represent the adjectival use of the word, which in Greek has a different termination, I have therefore resurrected the ancient word 'bronzen' (by analogy with 'wooden' and 'brazen'), and have stuck to this throughout Z7–9 (though not elsewhere). But I have shrunk from the similar coinages 'stonen' and 'bricken', using instead 'of stone' and 'of bricks'. Thus Aristotle's text in $^a7$ does not present the two alternatives '*of that*' and '*that-en*', but only the second alternative, which he uses in all his examples.

There is a second difficulty which is more vexing. In order to show clearly that 'stone', 'wood', and 'bronze' are functioning in this paragraph as nouns, and not as adjectives, it is necessary to supply them with an indefinite article. But one does not quite know whether they are to be taken here as count-nouns, which take the indefinite article 'a' (and also take a plural), or as mass-nouns, which take the indefinite article 'some'—unaccented and pronounced 'sm'—and do not take a plural (except in certain idioms). Many English nouns function in both ways—as witness the well-known ambiguity in 'Mary had a little lamb'—and the same is true of Greek. 'Stone' in Greek is usually a count-noun; 'wood' in Greek may easily be either (for 'a wood' means 'a log' or 'a stick'); but 'bronze' is, I think, *always* a mass-noun. I have therefore imposed some uniformity on the passage by taking all these nouns as mass-nouns throughout, and inserting in square brackets the appropriate article 'some' in all cases. But one doubts whether Aristotle himself could even have understood the question 'Did you mean to contrast the stonen statue with a stone or with some stone?' For there is no Greek word that corresponds either to 'a' or to the unaccented 'some'.

Aristotle sets out to explain what at first appears to be a linguistic oddity. In a non-substantial coming to be, as when a man becomes healthy, the end product is still said to be a man; but in a substantial coming to be, as when some bronze becomes a statue, the end product, i.e. the statue, is not still said to be some bronze; rather, it is said to be bronzen. His explanation is that there is a difference in how we describe what the end product comes *from*. In the first case we have a description which contrasts with being healthy, namely being sick, and so we can say that the man came to be healthy from being sick; we do *not* say that he came to be healthy from being a man. But in the second case there is no suitable description to apply to the bronze, which contrasts with its being a statue, so here we *do* say that the statue came into being from some bronze. But the proper way of using the word 'from' is the first, whereby what a thing comes *from* does not remain. Influenced by this, and since we *do* say that the statue comes from some bronze, we are unwilling to say that after it has done so it still is that bronze. That is why we change the ending, and say instead that it is bronz*en*. But, Aristotle adds, it would be better not to say at all that the statue comes *from* the bronze, precisely because the bronze does remain. It is an implication of this recommendation that, if we did speak in the better way, then we would be able to see that, just as a healthy man is indeed a man, so a statue *is* actually some bronze, even though this is not what we normally say. And the more general implication is that although language does in fact use different forms to speak of those changes in which a persisting substance acquires a new attribute, and those in which a new substance comes into being, the difference is of no significance; it arises only through a lack of vocabulary.

These implications are certainly mistaken. When a new substance comes into being, from some persisting matter, we have *two* ways of describing what results, i.e. either as a bronzen statue or as some bronze in the shape of a statue. But these are not descriptions of the *same* thing, since the statue will generally have a shorter career than the bronze. Thus the statement 'The statue we end with is the bronze we began with' is certainly false if the 'is' is read as an 'is' of identity, though it may be acceptable if the 'is' is taken as an 'is' of constitution. By contrast, 'The healthy man we end with is the man we began with' is a perfectly correct statement of identity. And if we wish to preserve a parallel with the case of the statue, we shall have to find some other way of describing what results when a man becomes healthy, a new entity created by that change and constituted by the man. One might indeed say that the change results in some 'human health' (changing the noun 'man' into the adjective 'human'), but to say that that health is 'made of' the man, as the statue is made of the bronze, would be excessively bizarre.

We may conclude that Aristotle has failed to see the true reason for our way of speaking on this topic, but it is probably rash to suppose that he saw and accepted the 'implications' that I have extracted from his recommendation. His discussion of the same idiom in Θ7, 49^a18–$^b2$ seems rather better. There he says that we are right to say that the statue is bronzen, and is not (some) bronze, comparing this to the way we say that a man is healthy, but not that he is health; the change of ending has a similar explanation in each case. Here it is clearly implied that the statue and the bronze are not identical. (There is also a discussion of the idiom at *Physics* VII, 3, 245^b9–246^a4, but that is concerned to make quite a different point.) In any case, the recommendation that he has just made, about how the 'from' locution should properly be used, is not one that he makes any attempt to conform to himself. On the contrary, he stipulates at the beginning of the next chapter that we are to understand what a thing comes *from* as being the matter, and not the privation (33^a25–7), which of course was how he had used the locution initially (32^a17). (But by 34^a22 the usage has changed again.)

33^a7–8: 'By contrast, a healthy man is not said to be that from which he came to be healthy.' The contrast, as I understand it, is that sickness is not in *any* way predicated of the healthy man; he is not said to be sick nor said to be 'sick-en'. But one is tempted by Frede & Patzig's proposal to read *ekeininon* in place of *ekeino* in $^a8$. Then the translation is: 'A healthy man is not said to be that-en, [with reference to] that from which he came to be healthy.' This gives a much more straightforward contrast.

CHAPTER 8

In this chapter Aristotle argues that one does not make a form, and elaborates on this by saying that a form is not a this (*tode*) but is such a kind of thing (*toionde*). This point leads him into an objection to the Platonic view of forms.

33^a24–$^b19$

In these first two paragraphs Aristotle states and argues for his claim that one does not make a form, e.g. a shape. The language that he uses in the first paragraph is simply contradictory. For he says that when one makes a bronzen sphere, just as one does not make the bronze, so also one does not make the sphere, despite the fact that the bronzen sphere one does make *is* a sphere ($^a28$–31). (His remark that this fact is merely 'coincidental' does not seem to help at all.) Then again at $^a33$ he repeats his claim that one does not make the sphere, and a little later the contradiction seems even more explicit: 'from this, which is bronze, one makes this, which is a sphere; but this itself [one does not make]' ($^b2$–3).

I have suggested an explanation of this confusing language at 32^a15–25 n. of the previous chapter (p. 122), and there is no need to repeat it here. At least it does become clear, as Aristotle reformulates his point again and again throughout these paragraphs, what that point is meant to be. It is that to make a bronzen sphere is to bring it about that some bronze has a certain shape, i.e. is spherical; but just as one does not, in this process, make the bronze, so also one does not make *the shape*. The shape itself is not the kind of thing that is made. Having formulated the point, let us consider the arguments that Aristotle gives for it. There may be what is intended as an argument at $^a31$–2; there is certainly an argument at $^a34$–$^b1$, which is given more fully in $^b11$–16 in the second paragraph; there is also an argument at $^b3$–5.

$^a31$–2: Aristotle *may* be suggesting that since a bronzen sphere is a compound of form in matter, we should regard both the matter *and the form* as underlying it, and there is a general principle that one does not make what underlies. As an argument this would be weak, for lack of proof of the supposed general principle. After all, one can and does make bronze (from copper and tin)—a point that Aristotle seems to forget until 34^b12–13; and it *could* be that in making some bronze one was also at the same time making a bronzen sphere. But it is not clear that Aristotle even means to suggest that the form *underlies* the compound, for certainly that is not his usual use of the notion of underlying, and although the phrase 'what in general underlies' (*to holōs hupokeimenon*) is certainly obscure, still it does not very clearly suggest '*both* the things that underlie' (i.e. both the matter *and the form*).

^b3–5: The argument is that if the form were made, there would be an infinite regress of makings. This, however, is a non sequitur. After all, the bronze *is* made, as I have just observed, but no infinite regress of makings results from this.

^b11–16 (with ^a34–^b1): The argument is that if the form of a sphere were itself made, then it would have to be made *from* something (a principle announced right at the beginning, 32^a12–14, and perhaps argued for at 32^a20–2), and hence it would itself have to be some kind of a compound of matter and form. But, it is suggested, we cannot reasonably view it in this way, since its definition is just 'a shape everywhere equidistant from its centre'. Now one might of course say that this definition can be viewed as defining a compound of a kind, namely one that compounds a genus (shape) with a differentia (equidistant from the centre). And one might go on to observe that Aristotle himself seems at times prepared to accept that genus is to differentia as matter is to form (*Z*12, 38^a5–9 n.). Or, more interestingly, one might object that the definition is wrongly phrased: a sphere is rather a *part of space* so shaped that its boundary is everywhere equidistant from its centre, and this definition does mention matter of a kind, namely space (*H*6, 45^a33–5 n.). But clearly these objections carry little force. A form is, as Aristotle reminds us again at ^b7, an essence, something specified by a definition; and it really is not very clear how one could *make* such a thing, given Aristotle's general principle that what is made must be made from matter that previously existed in another form.

But if forms cannot be created and similarly cannot be destroyed, it appears that they must exist eternally. And from this it seems further to follow that their existence must be independent of the existence of the things that have those forms. But this, surely, is Plato's attitude to forms, and not Aristotle's? We shall see later that Aristotle does not accept these inferences, and he will claim that it does not follow that forms are eternal (*Z*15, 39^b20–7; *H*3, 43^b14–23 n.). But what he does here is to distinguish his own theory from Plato's in a different way.

33^b19–26

Aristotle argues that if there were a sphere apart from the particular spheres (i.e. a Platonic form of the sphere), then no other particular sphere could ever have come into being. His reason is that if the form is to exist separately, then it must be a this in the sense of a particular (*Z*15, 40^a8–9), but no particular can be in numbers of distinct particulars (*Z*14, 39^a24–^b2); only a universal can achieve this (*Z*16, 40^b25–7). This is because a universal is 'such a kind of thing, and not a determinate this'. The text that is usually adopted for ^b21 means: 'No, for no this could ever have come into being, if it were in this way', i.e. if the form existed apart from the particulars. This version of the argument employs the notion of a this rather differently, and is even more elliptical than the version I have preferred. But presumably the argument is to be filled out in essentially the same way in each case: if the form of a sphere were the kind of thing that could exist apart from the particular material spheres, then it could not also be put into particular lumps of matter to create material spheres.

Two points may be noted about this argument. (*a*) It seems simply to be one of Aristotle's fundamental assumptions that a universal cannot *as such* 'exist separately' (i.e. independently of its particular instances); if it is to exist at all it must exist either in particulars or as a particular. (*b*) Even if we grant that no universal exists separately, and that it is universals that are needed to explain coming to be, still Aristotle's conclusion does not actually follow. There might *be* a Platonic paradigm sphere, existing independently of any material spheres, even if it is not that entity but the universal that is put into matter in coming to be. To this Aristotle will naturally reply that no purpose is served by positing such a thing, and that indeed seems to be exactly what his thought is in the following paragraph. But before I come to that I add a further note on the present paragraph.

$^b21$–4: *Thises and suches.* On the usual text for this passage, we may say that in this paragraph Aristotle simply denies that a form is a this; rather it is such a kind of thing (not *tode* but *toionde*—a contrast that hails from Plato's *Timaeus* 49 D–E, and will reappear at Z13, 38^b34–39^a3). Then throughout Z8 only particulars will be called thises. (Of course the word 'this' is used as a demonstrative to refer to the form, e.g. at 33^b19, but I am speaking of its use as a descriptive noun in the phrase 'a this'.) However, on the text that I prefer, it is allowed that the form may be a this *in one way* (as required by *H*1, 42^a29), so long as it is not *also* the kind of this that could exist separately, or (as this account has it) 'a *determinate* this'. (The word 'determinate', '*hōrismenon*', is a word that must be interpreted according to its context. On this account, in the present context it means 'particular', and contrasts with the 'indeterminate' nature of universals (cf. Z1, 28^a27; Θ7, 49^a36–$^b2$; *M*10, 87^a16–18). Elsewhere it can certainly be said that a form is determinate, in contrast to the indeterminate nature of matter (e.g. Z11, 37^a27).)

On any view there are at least two other kinds of entities called thises in the present paragraph, both the matter from which generation proceeds ($^b23$) and the 'this of such a kind' that results ($^b24$). On my translation, the latter is also referred to as 'the complete this', though this translation is insecure. (The phrase '*to hapan tode*' might simply be rendered 'this whole thing'.) It would seem that the *only* reason for calling the matter a this is that it is a particular chunk of matter, and the conflict with Z3, 29^a28 can hardly be avoided.

(On the suggestion that the universals 'man' and 'animal' are 'like bronzen sphere in general', i.e. a kind of universal compound of matter and form, see further Z10, 35^b27–31 n.)

33^b26-34^a8

This paragraph is introduced as though it followed from the previous one, and the previous paragraph did indeed contain a reason for saying that we do not need to posit forms existing separately (as 'substances in their own right' ($^b29$) or as 'paradigms' ($^a2$)) in order to account either for coming to be in general or for the coming into being of substances in particular (which I take to be the force of 'coming into being *and* substances', $^b28$). But to the thought of the previous paragraph it is wholly irrelevant that in natural generations, where what is generated is 'what is most assuredly a substance' ($^a4$, cf. *Z*7, 32^a19), the form is present beforehand in the parent. In fact there is a shift, from one paragraph to the other, in the relevant conception of 'the causality of the forms'.

The previous paragraph had concerned the form as formal cause, i.e. as 'what the thing becomes', as what gets combined with matter in a generation. It had been argued that for this purpose it is no use to posit a form that exists separately, since that is not the kind of thing that could be combined with matter. But in the present paragraph Aristotle is evidently returning to the idea of the form as 'that by which' the change occurs, i.e. as the efficient cause, and is claiming that separately existing forms are not needed in this role either. It is a familiar complaint of his that Platonic forms cannot function as efficient causes (e.g. *A*9, 991^b3-9), but here his point seems to be somewhat different: Platonic forms would anyway be superfluous as efficient causes, for in practice we can always find some other, more accessible, efficient cause. For example, in the generation of a living thing the efficient cause is the Aristotelian form, existing beforehand in the parent. Now of course this one example does not show that alternative efficient causes can *always* be found, and perhaps Aristotle would not actually wish to claim so much. At any rate, his thought here is that he does not need to claim so much, for if Platonic forms are not needed to account for the most important kind of coming to be, i.e. the generation of 'what is most assuredly a substance', then there would be a kind of absurdity in supposing that they were needed for less important cases. For if they exist at all, they must be important. (A similar line of argument is quite often employed, these days, against the existence of God.)

$^b33-^a2$: Aristotle incidentally notes the mule as an exception to his thesis that man begets man. In fact mules are sterile, and are begotten by horses upon asses (or, more usually, the other way round). By way of lessening the exception, he comments that in this case what usually applies to the species can at least be applied to the genus, for the horse and the ass share a genus, and the mule shares it too. (I take it that the somewhat odd claim that it, i.e. the genus, 'would be both' ($^a1$) should be taken as meaning that both the horse and the ass 'would be it', i.e. would fall under it, and in fact do fall under it, apart from the unimportant fact that we have no name for it.) Even so, the exception is somewhat awkward for his claim for the priority of the species in the reproduction of living things. See further $34^a33–^b7$ n. in the next chapter.

$^a5–8$: The indivisible form that Socrates and Callias share is evidently the form of the species man. Aristotle does not suppose that we can subdivide this into, say, the form of the Greeks and that of the Persians, or of white men and black men. Given the fact that all kinds and races of men can interbreed with all others, and Aristotle's principle that parent and child always share the same form (unless we have something 'contrary to nature', $^b33$), this conclusion is indeed required. (But it is not without problems. See *Z*9, $34^b1–4$ n.) As for the statement that what makes Socrates and Callias different is their matter, this seems to be Aristotle's standard view (cf. *Δ*6, $1016^b31–5$; *I*3, $1054^a32–5$; *Λ*8, $1074^a31–5$; there is a useful discussion in Cohen [1984*b*]). We shall find that in *Z*10, $36^a2–12$ and *Z*11, $36^b32–37^a5$ he is even prepared to invoke 'intelligible matter' to account for the distinctness and particularity of those 'intelligible' and perfect circles that are studied in geometry. One could of course offer other ways in which any two different men must be different—e.g. that they do not occupy the same position at the same time—but Aristotle's view seems perfectly acceptable.

CHAPTER 9

This chapter returns to the topic of spontaneous generation, mentioned but only briefly treated in chapter 7. The first two paragraphs concern the spontaneous generation of things that may also be generated by skill, and the third that of things that may also be generated by nature. It ends with what is evidently a summary of all of chapters 7–9, though it is focused almost entirely on chapter 8.

34^a9–21

The text and interpretation of the first two paragraphs are bedevilled by Aristotle's obscure thesis that, if health is generated, it is generated from some part of itself, such as warmth. Since it is the only example he gives of something that may be generated both by skill and spontaneously, one might expect it to be playing an important part in his thinking on this topic. But let us begin by simply setting it aside, and supposing that he is concerned with the generation of a material thing such as a house (by skill) or, say, a sand dune (spontaneously). In that case, we can take the 'matter' that is spoken of in this paragraph in a straightforward way.

In any generation the matter 'begins the process' simply in the sense that all generation is 'from' some pre-existing matter. It is a little unexpected to be told that this matter contains some *part* of the (resulting) object, but we may suppose that Aristotle means that the matter with which we begin will be or contain within it all the matter which will form the 'material part' of the thing generated. Then his point is that this matter can sometimes be set in motion in the right way spontaneously, and sometimes not. At first he speaks of the matter moving *itself* (^{a}13–16), and here his view must be—despite what he actually says—that *all* matter can move itself to some extent, e.g. fire upwards and earth downwards, but some kinds of matter can initiate more complex motions. Then he speaks of the matter being moved by something else, where this other thing is not moved by any relevant skill (^{a}19–21). (Again he does not express himself quite accurately: he loosely says that what *results* is set in motion by something else, not that its matter is. Let us treat this simply as a slip.) Presumably we should regard these two as alternatives: the matter may move itself, or it may be moved by something else. He adds that in the case where something else sets the matter in motion, if the generation is to be spontaneous, then this something else must lack the skill, and so must whatever moved it in turn; and I presume we may add 'and so on'. One supposes that he is thinking here that in a case of production by skill it may well be that the matter (e.g. wood) is 'moved' by some implement (e.g. a plane or a saw) which does not itself possess the skill (of carpentry), but is in turn moved by something that does. This, then, must be ruled out if we are to have a case of spontaneous generation.

However, although this account (taken in the way that I have taken it) is reasonably clear, one is at a loss to supply examples. No doubt, a house will do perfectly well as an example of something that cannot be generated spontaneously: the bricks cannot set themselves in motion in the required way, and nor can anything else (e.g. the wind) which is not guided by human agency. If one wants an example, fitting what is said here, of something that is spontaneously generated, then one naturally turns to Aristotle's views on the spontaneous generation of some forms of animals. For example, he tells us in *GA* III, 11 that many shellfish are generated spontaneously from mud and seawater, the 'useful' part of the matter being 'concocted' to form the shellfish, and a 'useless residue' being left behind. One could perhaps suppose that this is a case of the matter moving itself, but it is no doubt better to say (despite 34^b4–6) that the matter is moved by something else, namely the heat of the sun. However, this example does not illustrate the thesis under discussion, which is that some things can be generated both spontaneously *and by skill*. Somewhat lamely, I suggested a sand dune, which of course is normally generated spontaneously but no doubt could be deliberately constructed. (Similarly caves, lakes, mounds, and so on.) But Aristotle's own example is the generation of *health*. Was the account really meant to apply to that, and—if so—how?

One *can* apply the account to the generation of health by supposing that the matter of this generation is just the body that becomes healthy. But then it will be very tempting to suppose that the 'part' of the resulting object that this matter already contains ($^a12$–13) is not just the body once more (as the previous account requires) but is instead something like the warmth in the body, whose role as a 'part' of health Aristotle is so keen to stress (32^b26–30, 34^a25–30). This, of course, introduces the difficulty that the account is interpreted differently for each of the two examples Aristotle gives, i.e. the generation of health and of a house. There is also the worry that in Z7 Aristotle appeared to be thinking that warmth, as one of the 'ingredients' of health, should be counted as part of its *matter*. So is this perhaps what he has in mind when he speaks of the matter beginning the whole process ($^a11$)? But finally, I think that one needs to take quite seriously the hypothesis that the account in this paragraph does not apply to health, and that Aristotle has temporarily lost sight of his own example. In that case, the words 'or from a part', which have been added at the end of the paragraph, are possibly Aristotle's own attempt to mend matters. (If not, they are a copyist's attempt; for they are surely present only because the case of health, which the next paragraph will elaborate, does not seem to be covered otherwise.)

In fact the words 'or from a part' at $^a21$ make the wrong connection between the two paragraphs, for Aristotle's overall position in this chapter appears to be this. (i) Spontaneous generation occurs when the matter is moved spontaneously. (ii) The matter may move *itself* spontaneously, and this is what happens in the spontaneous generation of living things (34^b4–7). Or (iii) the matter may be moved by something *else*, and this is what happens in the spontaneous generation of non-living things, of the kind that can also be brought into being by human agency. For in such a case the moving cause (e.g. warmth) will be a part of what results—or, at any rate, it will lead to such a part, more or less directly (34^a25–30). If this states the overall position correctly, then the right way to connect this paragraph with the next would be to end it: 'It is because they are set in motion by things which do not possess the skill . . . and which *are* parts (of what results).'

34^a21–32

$^a21$–5: Since the text of the opening sentence of this paragraph is disputed, we must begin with that. The manuscript reading may be translated:

> It is also clear from what has been said that in a way everything comes from something of the same name, as things [that are generated] by nature, or from a part of the same name, for example a house from a house, . . . or from a part, or what has some part, unless it comes to be coincidentally.

(The MS A^b lacks the last occurrence of the words 'or from a part' ($^a24$), but otherwise there is unanimity.) This text presents us with four alternatives:

(*a*) from something of the same name
(*b*) from a part of the same name
(*c*) from a part
(*d*) from what has some part.

Logically (*b*) can be dropped at once since it is just the conjunction of (*a*) and (*c*). But in fact (*b*) should be dropped because it can only be understood as a repetition of (*a*), as Ross very clearly argues. (The whole paragraph is concerned only with the kind of things that may be produced by skill, so the clause 'as things that are generated by nature' is a comparison and not an example, and therefore the example 'a house from a house' would have to be taken as illustrating both (*a*) and (*b*) if both are retained.) I therefore delete (*b*). This gives us a very straightforward contrast: it is the things produced by skill that come from something of the same name (i.e. the form in the mind of the producer), and the things produced spontaneously that come from a part (or what has some part), for example health from warmth (or from rubbing). It merely muddles things to add that the form in the mind of the producer may also be viewed as a kind of 'part' of what results, and it is wholly mistaken to suppose that in spontaneous production the whole and the part 'have the same name'. For example, health and warmth (or rubbing) do not have the same name.

The final caveat 'unless it comes to be coincidentally' may be ignored. Unless Aristotle is begging the question entirely, he is referring here to what he calls 'coincidental causes', which are just ordinary causes under a 'coincidental description', i.e. a description which does not indicate the way in which they are causes. Thus a pale man may be the cause of a statue, but he causes it not *qua* pale but *qua* sculptor. See *Phys* II, 3, 195^a26–$^b21$.

$^a25$–30: Aristotle begins by confining attention to causes which are 'primary' and 'in their own right'. Here 'in their own right' is used simply as the negation of 'coincidentally' in the previous sentence; and a 'primary' cause is no doubt an 'immediate' cause, i.e. one which causes directly and not via a number of intermediate links (cf. *H*4, esp. 44^b1–2 and $^b15$–20). Such a cause, he claims, always is a part of what it produces. Thus suppose that health results, more or less directly, from a warming movement (presumably rubbing, as at 32^b26). Then he considers that we have these possibilities:

(i) warmth is health
(ii) warmth is a part of health
(iii) warmth is followed by health
(iv) warmth is followed by some part of health.

In case (i) the primary cause of health is the warmth in the movement, which is a 'part' of the warmth in the body, i.e. the health in the body. In case (ii) the primary cause of health is the warmth in the body, which both produces health and is a part of health. But what are we to say in case (iii)? Assuming that neither (i) nor (ii) applies, and that the warmth is directly followed by health without further intermediate steps, then in case (iii) warmth is the primary cause of health but *not* a part of it. Thus Aristotle's own principle requires that an instance of case (iii) always is an instance of case (ii). Similarly with case (iv). For here warmth is (we may suppose) the primary cause of something else *X*, which in turn is the primary cause of health. Then, on Aristotle's principle, *X* will be a part of health, as he says, but *also* warmth will be a part of *X*. So again warmth is a part of health after all, and we are back to case (ii) again. To generalize, if we may assume that 'is a part of' is a transitive relation, and that any case of causation may be broken down into a series of primary cases, it follows that a cause, however remote, will always be a part of what results from it. This surely reduces the principle to absurdity.

$^a30$–2: How does what Aristotle has just said of health confirm the view that even in spontaneous generation the starting-point is always the 'what-it-is', i.e. the substance given by the definition? His assumption must be that those 'parts' of a thing that can be its 'primary causes' are always 'parts' that are mentioned in its definition (cf. *Z*7, 33^a1–5). One can only note the assumption and pass on.

34^a33–$^b7$

Aristotle proceeds to the spontaneous generation of 'things formed by nature'—or perhaps 'things that hold together by nature' (*ta phusei sunistamena*)—by which he evidently means living things. Though his remarks here are extremely brief, still they manage to disagree in two ways with the much fuller treatment of the topic in *GA* III, 11. He tells us that in this case the matter moves *itself*, whereas in *GA* he insists upon the importance of warmth from the sun (762^b12-15, cf. 737^a1-5), and he appears to imply here that all living things spontaneously generated can *also* be generated from seed (similarly Z7, 32^a30-2), whereas *GA* denies this (761^b24-6, 762^a8-9, $^b21-8$). This clash could be partly avoided by supposing that he is speaking of different phenomena in the two places, i.e. in *GA* of the regular generation of certain species of animals without seed, and here of the irregular and unusual generation, without seed, of animals that are standardly generated from seed.

Whether the topic here is regular or irregular spontaneous generation, in either case Aristotle seems much less puzzled by it than one would expect him to be. For why should creatures that are generated *without* the influence of any form from a parent nevertheless always belong to one or another recognizable species? Does this not tend to undermine what Aristotle sees as the need for form in the explanation of natural phenomena? But perhaps it is unfair to take issue with him on the somewhat recherché topic of the breeding of shellfish. Where he can more reasonably be pressed is on the implications of his further digression on the mule—i.e. further to 33^b33-34^a2 of the previous chapter—where he is faced with the opposite difficulty: form is acting as efficient cause in the usual way, but the species is not preserved.

$^b1-4$: (The word '*anthrōpos*', which I elsewhere translate 'man', covers both sexes. So in this passage it must be rendered by 'human', to bring out the contrast with a different word '*anēr*' which means man as opposed to woman. My translation of this passage transposes clauses in a way that Ross's punctuation is intended to allow for. But it would certainly be easier if one transposed the text itself.)

One would not have expected Aristotle to qualify with 'in a way' his usual claim that parent and offspring just *do* have the same name in the normal case, nor to suggest that fathers and daughters are in any way an abnormal case, comparable to the mule. But in fact the cases *are* entirely similar, according to his own theory. For on his theory the form is supplied by the male parent (conveyed by the sperm), and the female parent supplies the matter. But this matter has a nature of its own, and when a female child is begotten this is due to a 'failure' in the male sperm: it has failed to 'master' the matter supplied (*GA* 776^a18-24, cf. 766^b15-17). He is bound to give exactly the same explanation of the mule. In fact when one thinks through the implications of his theory of heredity in *GA* IV, 1–4, one finds that no special pre-eminence is assigned to the form as *species*, and indeed the notion of form is here used in a much narrower way (see e.g. Balme [1980], 1–4). For example, Aristotle admits that Socrates and Coriscus can each pass on to their children their different and distinguishing features ($767^b24-768^a2$), including such inessential features as the shape of the nose (768^b2) or the colour of the eyes (inessential according to $778^a16-{}^b19$, but evidently inherited, as 778^b1-2 implies). But the mechanism for this is still supposed to be the transference of form from the father, working against the 'nature' of the matter supplied by the mother. It evidently follows from this theory that the form which is relevant to heredity—i.e. the form that Aristotle likes to point to by reminding us that 'man begets man'—cannot be identified with essence. For the purposes of heredity Socrates and Coriscus are not of (exactly) the same form, and the form that they share must therefore be 'further divisible' (contra 34^a8). Thus the theory of inheritance in *GA* IV, 1–4 is simply inconsistent with the claims about form and essence made in *Z*7–9, and Aristotle was verging on very dangerous ground when he dropped this slight hint in the present passage that there *is* a similarity between daughters and mules.

34^b7–19

Summing up the whole message of *Z*7–9, Aristotle concentrates upon the claim that form is not generated, making it clear that this applies not only to forms in the old category of substance but to anything that is 'primary'. Here at least it is clear that this expression applies to simple items in all categories, and evidently his argument in *Z*8 entitles him to this. For the reasons that are taken to show that shapes are not generated will apply to other qualities, quantities, and so on, without more ado. (One may note that both 'substance' in $^b8$ and 'what a thing is' in $^b13$ are used to refer to the old category of substance; but 'substance' has been applied to all primary things at 32^b1–2, and 'what a thing is' may also be applied in this wider way, in view of its equivalence to 'what being is', i.e. essence.)

Finally, Aristotle observes that it is peculiar to substances (i.e. substances in the *old* sense) that their generation requires the pre-existence of 'another substance, actually existing'. (On the word 'actually', i.e. '*entelekheia*', see *H*1, 42^a28 n.) Presumably we must understand here 'another substance *of the same name*'; so we need not ask whether the matter that must pre-exist *any* generation is here denied the title of 'a substance, actually existing'. It is plausible to suppose too that the form in the mind of the maker would not count as 'a substance, actually existing', so this point need not be intended to cover the production of such things as houses. No doubt Aristotle means it to apply primarily to living things. But in that case he seems already to have forgotten the topic of all the rest of chapter 9, i.e. spontaneous generation. For he has given us no reason to suppose that the spontaneous generation of, say, a limpet does depend on some other limpets existing beforehand.

It may be noted that he no longer wishes to insist on his mistaken claim that when a quality (such as health) is generated, some 'part' of it must be present beforehand. He now claims merely that the quality must 'pre-exist potentially', which appears to mean only that there must exist beforehand something capable of acquiring that quality. That would not appear to be a controversial claim.

CHAPTER 10

Chapters 10 and 11 discuss definition, and are mainly centred on the question 'What parts of a thing are parts of its definition?' During the course of these chapters Aristotle introduces his idea that the definition of an animal is the definition of its soul (*psukhē*), and this is an idea extraordinary enough to deserve some preliminary comment. I concentrate upon the account in the *De Anima*.

Prologue to *Z*10: The Soul

In many places where Aristotle speaks of 'soul' we would more naturally speak simply of life, and at least it is clear that soul and life always go together for him. Thus living and non-living things are contrasted as those that do and do not have soul (*ta empsukha*, *ta apsukha*), and in this contrast plants certainly count as living things. But if soul in general is correlated with life in general, Aristotle also insists upon our recognizing different kinds of soul, or life. In chapter 2 of book II of the *De Anima* he lists his main subdivisions in this way. Lowest in the scale is what he calls 'the nutritive soul', which is primarily correlated with being nourished by food, though Aristotle also associates it with growth (413^a25, 416^a25–7) and with reproduction (415^a23, 416^a19). Next comes 'the perceptive soul', which is also associated with imagination and desire, on the ground that where there is perception there is also pleasure and pain, and where these are there is bound to be desire too (413^b22–4). After this comes 'the locomotive soul', which is found in animals that are capable of moving about from place to place, and finally 'the thinking soul' (or intellect). If we may confine attention to mortal and perishable things, these various kinds of soul are hierarchically arranged. Thus all living things, including plants, have a nutritive soul, whereas it is definitive of animals that they also have perception, at least in its most primitive form, which is touch. (This is taken to include taste, 414^b6–14, 422^a8.) Some animals also have higher forms of perception, of course, and among these some have the power of locomotion (434^b25–7). Finally, no animal except man has the power to think, and man has *all* the kinds of soul here distinguished. The general idea is evidently this: different kinds of creature manifest life in different ways, and to say that they have this or that kind of soul just *is* to say that they have this or that kind of life. So a soul, it appears, just *is* a kind of life; it is not (in our sense) the *cause* of that life, but the life itself.

This, at any rate, seems to be a fair inference from Aristotle's explicit definition of the soul in chapter 1 of book II. He begins by reminding us that a substance is a compound of a certain form in a certain matter, where the matter is a potentiality and the form an 'actuality' (412^a6–10). Then he at once proceeds to say that, in the case of a living thing, the body is its matter and the soul its form. So 'the soul is the substance, as form, of a natural body that potentially has life. The substance is actuality, so the soul is the actuality of a body of this kind' (412^{a}19–22). Clearly 'substance' in this definition means 'essence'. Two further points may be made in elucidation. First, it is obvious that Aristotle does not mean that the soul is the essence of a body that has life *merely* potentially, and not actually. He means that bodies which are actually alive have soul as their form, essence, or actuality (412^{b}25–6), and he has put in the word 'potentially'—somewhat misleadingly (cf. Z16, 40^{b}5–16 n.)—only because he so constantly associates matter and potentiality. Second, he goes on to explain that the soul is 'the first actuality' rather than 'the second actuality', meaning by this that the soul is the disposition to act in suitably life-manifesting ways, and not the actual acting in those ways. For an animal has life, and therefore soul, even when it is asleep (412^{a}22–8).

So it appears that to have soul is to have life, a kind of soul is a kind of life, and the soul itself simply is that life. That is why we need not ask how soul and body are one, for it is simply in the way that form and matter are one, as when some wax has a certain shape (412^{b}6–9). But a better comparison is where the form of a thing is not just its shape but its function, as with an axe or an eye (412^{b}11–22). For the form or essence of such a thing, what it is to be an axe or an eye, is to have the capacity to perform the appropriate function (i.e. chopping or seeing, respectively). The difference is that an axe is merely an artefact, and does not chop by itself, but needs an agent to wield it. In this respect the comparison with the eye is better, but still not entirely appropriate, for the eye can only be an eye (properly speaking)—i.e. it only has its capacity for seeing—when it is part of a larger whole, the whole animal. 'But if the eye were an animal, sight would be its soul; for this is the substance [i.e. essence] of an eye as given by its definition' (412^{b}10–22).

However, in the course of making these comparisons, which seem to speak so strongly for the simple identification of soul and life, Aristotle also says something which heralds a discrepant theme. A living body, unlike an axe, is a body that exists by nature. But that is to say (in accordance with *Physics* II, 1, 192^{b}8–32) that it has within itself a 'principle' (*arkhē*) of motion or rest, i.e. of changing or not changing (412^{b}15–17). If 'principle' here means 'cause', as it very frequently does, then the kind of body that has a soul is one that has within it a *cause* of its behaving as it does. But then, will it not be natural to take the soul to be, not the mere disposition or capacity to behave in a way that manifests life, but rather the cause of this behaviour? Moreover, at the end of this very chapter, in which Aristotle has defined the soul as 'the actuality' of the living body, he says something which one can only take as saying that this possibility has not been ruled out, namely 'It is not clear whether the soul is the actuality of the body in the same way as the sailor is of the ship' (413^{a}8–9). But, one protests, this is perfectly clear. If there is any sense in which the sailor may be said to be 'the actuality' of the ship, it is not the sense in which 'actuality' is used in the definition of the soul. It is astonishing that Aristotle apparently does *not* think that what he has said so far is enough to rule out this image of the soul as the sailor of the ship.

But almost everywhere else in the *De Anima* it is this image that prevails. I mention two examples from chapter 4 of book II, where it is claimed that the soul is the formal, final, and efficient 'cause and principle' of the living body (415^b8–27). The argument to show that the soul is the formal cause, i.e. the cause as essence, begins from the premiss that, for living things, to be is to be living. From this Aristotle *ought* to have inferred that the essence, i.e. what being is, for such a thing is simply its being alive; but what he actually says is that since the essence of a thing is the *cause* of its being, the essence of a living thing is the 'cause and principle' of its being alive, i.e. its soul (415^b12–14). Now if in this remark 'cause' really does mean '*formal* cause', in the way that the formal cause of being healthy is simply health, then there is no fallacy. But one cannot help noticing that Aristotle never does directly say that the soul *is* life, even where (as here) his argument very clearly demands it; he prefers always to say that it is the 'cause' or 'principle' of life, or to use some similar locution. But it is more significant that in the same passage Aristotle directly claims that the soul is an *efficient* cause. In support of this he says that it is that whence locomotion begins, and that—in living things that do not have the power of locomotion—at any rate perception and growth are 'in accordance with soul' (416^a21–7). The latter claim we may set aside as being too vague to establish anything to the purpose, but the former is more informative. What is needed to initiate an animal's movement is a desire of some kind, and this in turn may be aroused by a perception. So if we suppose (as would be a perfectly ordinary Greek idea) that it is properly speaking the soul that perceives, and the soul that desires, then it will be reasonable to infer that it is the soul that initiates movement. But this requires us to say that it is indeed the *soul* that *does* these things.

In the *De Anima* (and indeed elsewhere) Aristotle constantly speaks of the soul as itself being the thing that thinks, that desires, and that perceives. But to speak of the soul in this way is to envisage it as some special *part* of the man, and a part that is thought of as ruling and controlling the other parts, as the sailor controls his ship. It is true that at one point he says one should speak of the *man* as doing these things rather than his soul (408^b1–18), but when one looks at the passage more closely one finds that it simply reinforces, and does not in any way retract, the idea that the soul is a special *part* of the man. For his thought in this passage is that although one might at first sight say that the soul 'is moved' (or: 'is affected') by such things as joy, fear, anger, perception, and thought, it is better to say that it is the man and not the soul that is thus 'moved' ('affected'). And this is because the man is moved *by* his soul: in anger, the soul causes the heart to move; in perception, the relevant movement is one that reaches *to* it; in memory, it is one that reaches *from* it. But it is not the soul itself that 'is moved'. However, this clearly *affirms* the view that the soul is a special 'part' of the man (and adds that it is a part 'incapable of being affected' (*apathes*), as 408^b18–31 goes on to elaborate—but quite unreasonably). The whole picture still consorts very well with the idea that the soul in the body is just like the sailor in his ship, and is quite inconsistent with the view that the soul is rather 'the actuality' of the living body.

Thus what Aristotle says of the soul in the *De Anima* is simply inconsistent. According to his official definition, the soul is the form, essence, or actuality of the living body; it is what we give as the definition of such a body, i.e. what it is for such a body to be actually living. It is also what that body is for, as sight is what the eye is for, and chopping is what the axe is for. For when a thing has a function, then what it is to be that thing is also what the thing is for. But at the same time the soul apparently is not thought of simply as *being* life, or even as the particular kind of life that that body has; rather, it is what is *responsible* for that life, its cause or explanation. In this latter role it is thought of as a special part of the living thing, ruling and directing its life-manifesting behaviour. It is in particular that part of it that thinks, desires, and perceives, and as such it has a special location in the body (which in fact is not the brain but the heart, on Aristotle's account). Conceived in this way, it makes sense to ask whether the soul of a living body could exist 'separated' from that body. Drawn by his *other* view of the soul, as the 'form' of the body, Aristotle firmly says that this cannot happen with the 'lower' parts of the soul, i.e. the nutritive, perceptive, and locomotive parts, for they are simply the 'actuality' of a material thing. And yet in the case of the 'thinking part', he evidently regards this as a real question, precisely because the thing in us by which we think must be regarded as immaterial. His final answer to the question is controversial, and I must refrain from discussing it here. But if it can even be thought of as a serious question, that must be because the image of the sailor in his ship is exerting a strong influence.

The significance of this problem for the *Metaphysics* lies in its possible implications for 'particular forms', i.e. forms which by their very nature belong to one individual and no more. While we adhere to the official definition of the soul as the form, essence, or actuality of the living body, and while we recall that the soul is to the body as sight is to the eye, or as the ability to chop is to the axe, there is little temptation to suppose that the form is anything other than a universal. So, since Socrates and Callias are the same in form, their form being indivisible (Z8, 34^a7–8), Socrates and Callias have the same soul. But this, of course, is a decidedly unusual way of thinking of the soul, and for most of the time Aristotle adopts a way of talking that is inconsistent with it. He speaks of Socrates' soul as that in Socrates which thinks, desires, perceives, and so on. But then of course Socrates' soul cannot be the same thing as Callias' soul, for what Socrates thinks is not always the same as what Callias thinks. I shall return to this issue in the prologue to Z13. For *most* of Z10–11 we can adhere to the view that a form, and hence a soul, is always a universal, but in some few passages there will at least be a temptation to think otherwise (35^a7–9, 36^a17, 37^a5–10).

34^b20–32

Aristotle apparently introduces two questions to be discussed in this chapter, the first at $^b20$–8 and the second at $^b28$–32.

$^b20$–8: The initial statement that 'as the formula stands to the object, so do the parts of the formula stand to the parts of the object' should be regarded as a rough-and-ready, prima-facie generalization. In effect, Aristotle is raising the question whether and to what extent this generalization is correct, when he asks which of the parts of a thing should be counted as parts of its formula.

As he actually frames the question here, it asks whether *the formula of* the parts should or should not occur in the formula of the whole, which apparently presupposes that each of the 'parts' we shall be concerned with does have a (defining) formula. This leads to what he would certainly regard as a vicious regress. For if every defining formula has parts ($^b20$), and every such part itself has a defining formula, then when a definition is fully spelled out, with definitions everywhere substituted for names, that definition must be infinitely long. But Aristotle would certainly reject this as an impossibility (*Z*6, 32^a2–4 n.). He appears to recognize in *Z*17 that definitions must eventually end in indefinables (41^b9–11; cf. *H*3, 43^b23–32), but it is a point that he quite often seems to overlook (cf. *Z*1, 28^a34–6 n.; epilogue to *Z*4–6). Nevertheless, it is not a point that much affects his discussion in this chapter (or the next), for we can generally take him as asking whether the definition of the whole should or should not *refer to* this or that part. We shall not need to assume that the part itself can be defined.

$^b28$–32: Aristotle's opening question, then, we may take in this way: which of the parts of a thing are mentioned in its definition? It is not altogether clear whether we should understand the last two sentences as introducing a second and distinct question, namely: which of the parts of a thing are prior to it? Certainly, if there are two distinct questions here, then they are treated by Aristotle as very closely connected questions, both to be answered on the same basis. His initial answer at 35^a9–$^b3$ seems to be directed mainly to the first, though the second is also treated (somewhat obliquely) at 35^a24–31. At 35^b3 he says that he will 'take up the question again', which suggests a further examination of the same question, not a change to another. But from there onwards what he says is mainly directed at the question of priority, and his final summary at 36^a12–25 focuses entirely on this question. Yet just before this summary, at 35^b31–36^a12, there has apparently been a return to the first question.

It seems that the right conclusion to draw from this is that Aristotle saw both questions as raising essentially the same issue, and requiring to be answered in essentially the same way, namely by being clear about exactly what the thing is whose 'parts' we are enquiring into. The crucial point to be clear upon is whether we are speaking of the form alone, or of that form compounded in some way with matter.

One may note what appears to be a slip in the last line of this paragraph. Aristotle certainly holds that a finger cannot exist except as part of a living man, while the man can exist without his finger (35^b22-5). But presumably he does not really hold that an acute angle cannot exist without a right angle.

34^b32-35^a9

In this paragraph Aristotle introduces the distinction between matter, form, and the compound of the two, which will be the foundation of his answer. He represents it here as if it were a kind of ambiguity in the notion of a part, and he begins by mentioning, only to set aside, a different ambiguity in this notion. In one sense, a part is indeed a measure of quantity, i.e. one finds the quantity of a thing by finding the number of discrete parts that it contains equal to one another and to some given unit of that quantity (cf. *Δ*25, 1023^b12-17; *I*1, 1052^b20 ff.). But this use of the notion is clearly irrelevant here. What we need to consider, he tells us, is the 'parts' of a substance.

35^a1-7: If *Z*10 was written before *Z*7–9 were adapted to precede it, then these lines return to the contrast between matter and form for the first time since *Z*3. Clearly the contrast is here taken to be familiar, but so it was in *Z*3, and no conclusion about *Z*7–9 can be deduced from this. The difficulty with the present passage—and, indeed, with the whole of the chapter—is to be clear about how 'matter', and hence 'the compound', are to be understood.

Normally when Aristotle mentions his familiar trio of matter, form, and the compound of the two one thinks of the matter in question as a *particular* chunk of matter, and hence of the compound as a particular individual, compounded from that chunk of matter and a (universal) form. That is how *Z*3, 28^b36-29^a10 is naturally taken; it is the only consistent interpretation of *H*1, 42^a26-31; it is clearly how the notion of a 'form in matter' was understood throughout *Z*8, and the same word 'a combined whole' (*sunholon*) was used of the compound in *Z*8 (at 33^b17) as is used here ($^a6$). But we have already seen that Aristotle is also prepared to talk of something having matter as a part, where the 'matter' in question is not a particular chunk of matter but a *kind* of matter, e.g. bronze (*Z*7, 32^b31-33^a5; *Z*8, 33^b25-6), and in what is to follow in this chapter he will make the point quite explicitly, using again the same word, 'a combined whole' of the *universal* compound so formed

($35^{b}27$–31). Thus nothing can be inferred from the occurrence of this word. (It is also true that nothing can be inferred from the occurrence of a similar, and apparently synonymous, phrase, 'a thing taken together [with matter]' (*suneilēmmenon* [*tēi hulēi*]), that we shall meet shortly. This is surely used of the universal compound at $36^{a}27$, but of the particular compound at $35^{a}34$.) Thus we must look to the context to determine which kind of matter/form compound, particular or universal, is in question on each occasion.

In the present context it at first appears to be universal compounds that are meant. For Aristotle at once cites the example of snubness, making the point that flesh (which is a *kind* of matter) is in a way a 'part' of it. (So his point here is that of *E*1 and not that of *Z*5; see *Z*5, $31^{a}1$–14n.) Apparently it must be the universal characteristic of being snub that he is here referring to, since he uses the explicitly abstract noun 'snubness' (*hē simotēs*). Yet a doubt enters in the very next sentence. For if one is considering the *universal* 'statue', but as a combined whole, why should one suppose that *bronze* in particular is a 'part' of it? After all, statues can be made of all kinds of different materials. So it seems much better to suppose that it is this particular statue that has bronze as a part, not the universal statue. Moreover, the point seems to be strongly confirmed in the next paragraph, where Aristotle insists that the compounds he is talking of can be destroyed by being resolved into their matter ($35^{a}17$–22, and often subsequently). It seems to make no sense to suppose that a *universal* compound can be destroyed in this way. I am inclined to think, then, that it was particular compounds of form in matter that Aristotle *meant* to introduce in this paragraph, and that it is these that his argument is supposed to concern. As we shall see, universal compounds are mentioned again as the discussion proceeds, but always they seem to upset, rather than help, the line of argument that is pursued for most of the chapter.

$^{a}7$–9: Aristotle opened this paragraph by suggesting that there is some ambiguity in the notion of a part, and that in *one* way the matter of a thing can be counted as a part of it, but not in another. But this supposed ambiguity seems not really to be a case of ambiguity at all, since it simply depends upon *what* thing we are talking about: the matter is a part of the compound, but is not a part of the form. However, here at the end of the paragraph the idea of an ambiguity returns, but is relocated: the trouble arises because the same word is used both of the compound and of the form alone. If he means to say that the same word may be used both of the universal compound and of the form alone, then this (somewhat improbable) doctrine is one that is unambiguously presented at *H*3, $43^{a}29$–$^{b}4$. The word 'house', he there says, may signify a shelter made of bricks and stones arranged in a certain way, or it may simply signify a shelter. Similarly, the word 'man' or 'animal' may signify a soul (i.e. life?) in a body or it may simply signify a soul. Since the passage is concerned with alternative *definitions* of 'house' and 'animal', it must be universal compounds that are there in question. If, however, he means to say here that the same word may be used both of the particular compound and of the form alone, then the simplest way of taking his claim is as illustrated below at 35^b1–3: the word 'circle' applies both to what is without qualification a circle (i.e. the form) and to particular circles 'there being no name peculiar to the particulars'. (Cf. *Z*6, 31^b22–8, on 'the pale'.) This may, indeed, be all that needs to be said.

But one may well suspect that there is more to it. Aristotle's language here is extremely compressed, but it can quite easily be taken to say that each thing may be said to be *identical* with its form, and not merely that its form may be predicated of it. (One might, indeed, *translate* the passage so that it appears to admit only of this interpretation, i.e. as 'the form, and the thing *qua* having the form, may be said to be each thing'. Thus Ross [1928]; and cf. Furth [1985] and Irwin [1988], 239. But in fact none of these authors think that the passage does propound an identity.) The identity interpretation would *appear* to be what is contemplated at 36^a17, and again at 37^a7–8, where the example is that Socrates may be taken to be a compound of soul in body but he may *also* be taken to be simply a soul. It is also what is suggested by *Z*6, 32^a6–11, if that passage claims that in one way Socrates is the same as his essence. But of course one cannot suppose that a particular thing is literally identical with its form unless one also supposes that its form is a 'particular form', found in it and in no other particular.

As I noted in the prologue, there evidently is a temptation to make just this supposition where the form in question is a soul, as at 36^a17 and at 37^a7–8. But in our present passage souls have not yet been mentioned, and the forms that have been mentioned are shapes (i.e. the shape of a snub nose and the shape of a statue). There is no noticeable temptation to suppose that the shape of a particular nose or statue must be peculiar to it. I am therefore inclined to think that at least there is no *need* to introduce 'particular forms' at this point. It is adequate to suppose that each thing may be said to *be* its form just in the sense that it may be said to be 'a so-and-so' (e.g. 'a statue', 'a circle'), where this phrase 'a so-and-so' is taken as specifying the general form which, in another idiom, we say it *has*. (Cf. *Z*7, 32^a22–5 n.) But it is rather more difficult to 'explain away' 37^a7–8 in the same way.

35^a9–22

Here Aristotle applies to the circle and the syllable, which were the examples he used to illustrate his first question (34^b24–8), the distinction just introduced between the material and formal 'parts' of a thing. The semicircles are not mentioned in the definition of the circle, he tells us, because they are parts of the matter of the circle, not of its form. (He grants that they are 'closer' to the form than is the bronze of a bronze circle. One guesses that his point here is that a circle does not have to be made of bronze, but it does have to contain two semicircles.) By contrast, the letters are mentioned in the definition of the syllable—and he shows that he means letters *as types*, not particular tokens—because they are parts of the form and not of the matter.

This reply is profoundly unsatisfying. It is very natural to construe the letters of a syllable as its matter, and Aristotle himself will take them in this way in Z17, 41^b12–33, esp. $^b31$–3. If it is the syllable as type that is to be defined—as of course it should be—then no doubt it will be letters as types that figure in the definition. But that is just to say that the letters in question will be 'taken universally', and there seems to be no reason why they should not *both* be matter *and* taken universally. Aristotle's position here seems to depend upon ignoring this possibility. As for the semicircles, he has no ground that one can see for claiming that these can only be construed as material parts. As he himself has said earlier, the circle is 'divided into' its semicircles *just as* the syllable is divided into its letters (34^b26–8). No doubt he now wishes to say that although a particular token syllable, written on paper, can be destroyed by being thus divided, this does not destroy the syllable as type, i.e. as form. But obviously we can say exactly the same of the circle and its semicircles. I do not see that there is any answer to this objection in the present paragraph.

Later, Aristotle will offer a different argument, that the semicircle is defined in terms of the circle, and not vice versa (35^b9–10), whereas the letters are not defined in terms of the syllable. This does indeed seek to make a relevant distinction between the two, though it is still not entirely satisfactory. For clearly one *can*, if one wishes, first define the semicircle independently, and then define the circle in terms of it.

35^a22–$^b3$

At the end of the previous paragraph Aristotle has said that the material parts of a thing 'are parts of the combined whole, but not parts of the form or of what has the formula'. It is natural to understand 'or' as 'i.e.', so that the form *is* what has the formula. At any rate, it is certainly implied by this sentence that the combined whole does not have a formula. There are many other places in Z10–11 where it seems to be being assumed that *only* the form has a formula. The claim at 35^b34 that 'only the parts of the form are parts of the formula' is perhaps the most explicit. We infer, then, that there is not such a thing as the formula of a compound. But in that case what are the two kinds of formula that are distinguished at the beginning of the present paragraph?

Frede & Patzig propose this interpretation. The one kind of formula is like that of the syllable, which does contain a reference to 'such parts' as its letters. These are parts into which the syllable is destroyed, and they are 'principles' of it ($^a24$–5). But they are not material parts of the syllable, for it has been explained that they are parts of its form (^{a}11). The other kind of formula is like that of the circle, which does not contain a reference to the parts into which it is destroyed, namely its semicircles. For if it were to contain such a reference, then it could only be understood as 'a formula of the thing taken together with matter'. But Aristotle's doctrine is that there can be no such formula.

This is a bold attempt to see Aristotle's text as free from contradiction, but I am afraid that it does not work. The suggested interpretation of the phrase 'such parts', as referring back all the way to the parts of the syllable last mentioned at ^{a}10–11, strikes me as distinctly implausible. But the crucial objection is this. The interpretation requires one to maintain that the compound things which are said to be destroyed into their material parts at ^{a}25–7, namely a snub nose and a bronze circle, have no formula at all. But Aristotle goes on at ^{a}28–9 to contrast them with things not compounded from matter, and he describes these latter as 'things whose formula is a formula of the form alone'. But on the present interpretation there is no point whatever in this description, since it is claimed that *every* formula is a formula of the form alone. The only relevant point to make about formulae would be that non-compound things do have a formula whereas compounds do not. But clearly that is not the point that our text does make.

I see no alternative to the view that in this paragraph Aristotle is supposing that only *some* formulae are 'of the form alone', and others are of form and matter combined. There are many places outside *Z*10–11 where he is very ready to speak of the formula of such a compound. For example, it is his standard description of the formulae that concern the physicist (e.g. *E*1, $1025^b28-1026^a6$; *K*7, 1064^a23-8; *Phys* II, 194^a12-15 and 200^b7-8; *Anim* I, 403^a24-^b16). Within *ZH* one might also point to *Z*4, 30^b12-13 and *Z*5, 31^a7-14; *Z*7, 33^a1-5 and *Z*8, 33^b25-6; *H*2, 43^a7-26 and *H*3, 43^b28-32. (I would also add *H*6, 45^a34-5, but that depends on a controversial interpretation.) In view of all these parallels from elsewhere, it is not at all surprising that Aristotle should here be recognizing that there is such a thing as the formula of a compound. Nor is there really any contradiction with the passages that imply that no compound has a formula. For it is the *particular* compound that Aristotle wishes to say has no formula of its own (as is quite explicit at 35^b31-36^a8), whereas it must presumably be the *universal* compound that he is thinking of when he assumes that a compound does have a formula. So one might suggest that the appearance of a contradiction arises only because he does not make clear which kind of compound he is talking of at each point. But I fear that that over-simplifies the problem.

In the present paragraph, as in the previous one, it must presumably be particular compounds that are destroyed into their material parts, and certainly it is a particular man, and particular circles, that are given as examples at $^a33-^b3$. Accordingly, it should be particular compounds that have their material parts as their 'principles'. (This implies, presumably, that their material parts are prior to them, and so is a first statement of Aristotle's answer to the question about priority raised at 34^b28-32.) But the words 'for this reason' at $^a24$ show that Aristotle's thought is that the material parts are 'principles' *because* in this case they are mentioned in the definition. This apparently presupposes that in so far as the particular has a definition, it is the definition of the universal compound, which indeed does appear to be Aristotle's doctrine in passages where he is explicitly recognizing the existence of the universal compound (as at *Z*11, 36^b28-30 and 37^a5-10). But elsewhere he says that in so far as the particular has a definition, it is the definition of its form alone (as is implicit in 35^a9-22 and 35^b3-14, and explicit at 35^b31-36^a9 and at 37^a26-30 of the summary). When he is thinking in this vein it is because he is not recognizing that there is such a thing as a universal compound.

(The claim at $^a28-30$ that forms themselves cannot be destroyed may perhaps be intended to recall *Z*8, but the caveat 'or at any rate not in this way' presumably arises because Aristotle is thinking of his point that it does not follow that forms are eternal. This point has not been made in *Z*8, but will be made briefly in *Z*15, 39^b24-6 and more at length in *H*3, 43^b14-24.)

35^b3-14

In this paragraph Aristotle focuses more directly on the question of priority. The parts of the formula, he claims, 'are prior, some or all of them' ($^b5-6$, $^b14$). He fails to specify what they are prior *to*, but it is natural to suppose that in the first instance they are prior to what is given by the whole formula, which is again being taken to be the form. In that case, the kind of priority in question will be what is elsewhere called 'priority in formula (i.e. in definition)' (e.g. *Z*1, 28^a34-6), and it is clearly a relation between universals. This claim will be repeated in the summing up at 36^a22, and it seems perfectly straightforward. It is true that in the next paragraph he will say that the parts of the formula (some or all of them) are prior *to the compound* (35^b19), and this claim will also be repeated in the summing up at 36^a20. But it seems very improbable that that is what he intends here. For he adds also that 'the parts that are material, and into which the thing is divided as into its matter, are posterior' ($^b11-12$). Again he does not specify what they are posterior to, but it must surely be the *same* thing as he says that the parts of the formula are prior to. In that case, it can only be the form. For he will tell us in the next paragraph that the material parts are *prior* to the compound (35^b20-2, repeated in the summary at 36^a19-22)—at least in one way. So his overall position is evidently this: (i) the parts mentioned in the formula are prior to the form as a whole ('some or all of them'); (ii) the form, and its parts, are prior to the matter, and its parts; (iii) *both* the form, and its parts, *and* the matter, and its parts, are prior to the compound. Claims (i) and (ii) are stated in this paragraph, and claim (iii) will be stated in the next. (One may note, incidentally, that claim (iii) conflicts with the general principle announced at *M*7, 1081^a27–9, that if *X* is prior to *Y* then also *X* is prior to the compound *X* + *Y* and *X* + *Y* is prior to *Y*. I *suspect* that *Z*3, 29^a5–7 means to rely on the *M*7 principle rather than on claim (iii) here, but one cannot tell.)

Claim (i) seems, as I have said, to be entirely straightforward. Why, then, does Aristotle qualify it with 'some or all of them'? (The qualification is nowhere elucidated.) The only explanation I can see is that given by Ross, who draws attention to the doctrine of *Z*12, according to which the final differentia in a definition is—or should be—equivalent to the whole definition. In that case it might seem to be a 'part' that could not be prior to the whole.

Claim (ii) is one that we have met before, at least in the simplified version that form is prior to matter, at *Z*3, 29^a5–7. But the kind of priority that is in question was not explained there and is not explained here. We shall see that in the next paragraph the 'compounds' under discussion seem still to be treated as particular rather than universal compounds, so that the priority claimed here should be that form is prior to particular chunks of matter, and not that it is prior to universal kinds of matter. If so, then one may speculate that the kind of priority in question may again be a kind of priority in knowledge (as priority in definition is a kind of priority in knowledge), roughly on these lines: a universal form may be grasped directly by the intellect, but a particular chunk of matter, in so far as it can be 'grasped' at all, can be 'grasped'—i.e. identified—only via some universal form that it possesses. (Cf. 36^a2–9.) But the truth seems to be that the priority of form to matter is so much an unquestioned axiom for Aristotle that one cannot be sure that there was any one definite kind of priority that he intended.

35^b14–27

Here Aristotle introduces his idea that the form or essence of a living thing is its soul. It is the first time in this chapter that form and essence have been explicitly identified, but this identification is equivalent to the assumption that only form is defined (since an essence is just what is given in a definition). Whatever doubts one might have about the conception of the soul that is actually at work in the *De Anima* (for which see my prologue), here in *Z*10–11 it is clear that a soul *ought* to be regarded as something universal. It is the substance of an animal as given by a (defining) formula, and in this way its form and essence (35^b15–16). But a (defining) formula is always of what is universal (35^b34, 36^a28–9), and moreover only a universal is identical with its essence, and the soul is identical with its essence (36^b1–2). So let us take it that a soul just is a way of living.

Having claimed that a soul is the essence of 'a body of this sort' (i.e. a natural body that potentially has life—and has life 'potentially' because it has life actually), Aristotle apparently offers an argument for it, an argument which aims to deduce the essence of the body as a whole from the essence of its parts ($^b15$–18). The argument is hardly cogent. The premiss that *every* part of the body has a function, and is defined by that function, is surely an exaggeration; so too is the further premiss that in *every* case the function will presuppose perception. Nor is it very clear how it would *follow* from this that the body as a whole will therefore have a function presupposing perception, and will be defined by that function. But that is apparently what Aristotle is suggesting. At any rate he does believe that the body as a whole has a function, for it is a kind of tool or instrument for living with (*PA* 645^b15–20, cf. 642^a12–14), and accordingly that function, i.e. living a suitable kind of life, will be its essence. But the suggested argument for that conclusion was, no doubt, something of an aside, and we need not pursue it further.

Aristotle now returns to his concern with what is prior to what, and I take what he has to say in two parts.

$^b18$–20: The parts of the soul will be distinguishable aspects of whatever kind of life is in question, e.g. this or that kind of perception, or locomotion, or reasoning. These ('some or all of them') will be prior to the whole soul as in the previous paragraph, i.e. in definition. Aristotle now adds that they will also be prior to the compound, presumably because the whole soul is prior to the compound, and here again we must ask whether it is particular compounds or universal compounds that he is speaking of. The right answer at first appears to be 'both', for the clause at $^b19$–20 'and similarly in particular cases' seems to show that both particular and non-particular cases are in question. But thereafter it is only particular compounds that are mentioned. It is the particular that is divided into its material parts at $^b21$–2, and presumably destroyed thereby (as at 35^a17–19, $^a27$, $^a31$–$^b1$). It is the particular again that Aristotle is speaking of at $^b22$–3, when he tells us that its material parts are in one way prior to it, though not in another. The priority relations of the universal compound are entirely ignored throughout this discussion, except for the present statement that the form is prior to it.

There is again no elucidation of what kind of priority is in question, but if we are to take seriously the suggestion that the form is *in the same way* prior both to the universal and to the particular compound, then I think only one account is possible. The form is prior to both just because it is a *part* of both, and a part is automatically prior to that of which it is a part. At any rate, I do not see how to explain the next few lines without supposing that this is *itself* counted as one kind of priority.

$^b22$–7: Aristotle claims here that the material parts of a compound are always prior to it in one way, though he adds that they need not be in another. The way in which they need not be prior is clear, namely, they need not have the capacity to exist separately (34^b31–2). (This is the priority that was somewhat oddly called 'priority in time' at *Z*1, 28^a33–4.)

So far as this kind of priority is concerned, the man is prior to his finger, since he can exist without it while it cannot exist without him (for a severed finger does not properly count as being a finger at all). The man is not prior to all his parts in this way, for he cannot exist without his heart any more than it can exist without him. But anyway, we have here a sense of priority, i.e. priority in separate existence, in which the part need not be prior to the whole. In the previous paragraph we were told of another sense of priority in which the part need not be prior to the whole, i.e. in definition, for on the contrary the whole (taken universally) may well be prior in definition to the part (taken universally). (And one presumes that in this way the whole animal is prior not only to the finger but also to the heart.) But Aristotle claims a third sense in which the material part is always prior to the material whole. What is this? Frede & Patzig must, I think, be right to say that it is just that the one is a part of the other, and that that *itself* is a kind of priority.

An alternative explanation (proposed by Gill [1989], 128) is that what is to count as the matter of an animal may be taken in two ways. The proximate matter consists of the shaped bodily organs, of which the finger and the heart are examples (similarly the hand, 36^{b}30–2). These are what the animal is 'immediately' made of, and Aristotle constantly claims that, since they cannot function when separated from the whole animal, they equally do not exist then. But they in turn are made of stuffs such as flesh and blood, bone and sinew, which is therefore matter at the next level down (*GA* I, 715^{a}9–11). Now, elsewhere Aristotle does argue that since flesh and blood also have functions to fulfil—for example, the function of flesh is to be sensitive to touch (*PA* II, 653^{b}19–25)—they too do not count as existing when they are no longer part of a living body (e.g. *GA* II, 734^{b}24–34, 741^{a}10–11; *Meteor* IV, 390^{a}14–15). But he also says at one point that in a dead man we seem to have flesh and bone 'more' than we seem to have a hand or an arm (*GC* I, 321^{b}29–32), and here in Z10 he seems to be supposing that flesh and bone do indeed survive the death of the animal. At any rate he tells us that a man is destroyed when he is dispersed into flesh, bone, and sinew (35^{a}17–19, ^{a}31–3), and this way of putting it certainly seems to carry that implication. This then, leads Gill to suggest that his point in the present passage is that the *proximate* matter of a man cannot exist without the man himself, but the more *remote* matter can, and *it* will therefore have the familiar priority of separate existence.

Now it seems to be true that we must recognize the distinction between proximate and remote matter in order to see how Aristotle is not contradicting himself when he claims that material parts (such as hands and fingers) do not survive death and also implies that material parts (such as flesh and bones) do survive it (cf. Irwin [1988], 241). But all the same I do not see how this point can be the explanation of his claim that in one way the matter is prior to the compound. For the text at ^{b}22–3 cannot be translated as making a distinction between two different kinds of bodily parts. Unambiguously it distinguishes between two different ways of being prior, and applies both of them to the same bodily parts. I therefore conclude that in Aristotle's own view the part must always count as prior to the whole in *one* way, simply because it is a part. The apparent difficulties which seemed to affect this principle when it was first mooted at 34^b28–32 are to be met by distinguishing between this kind of priority and other kinds.

35^b27–31

In this brief paragraph it is explicitly recognized that there are both universal and particular compounds, and that species such as man or horse count as examples of universal compounds. The idea presumably is that a man may be defined as such-and-such a kind of body (or such-and-such an arrangement of flesh, bones, and so on), living such-and-such a kind of life. The next chapter will pay some attention to these compounds, but here it is simply mentioned that there are such things, and we are calmly informed that they are not substances. This clearly rejects the claim of Z4, 30^a11–13, that the substances are just those things that are forms, i.e. species, of a genus. (When it is said that the particular case is compounded from 'the ultimate matter', we should presumably understand 'ultimate' (*eskhaton*) to mean a *particular* lump of matter. There is no need to see it as also importing a reference to prime matter.)

The paragraph is not closely attached either to what precedes it or to what follows it, and I strongly suspect that it is a later addition. It makes explicit a point that has in fact been implied several times already, but the point is one which has awkward implications for Aristotle's discussion of his main topic, and he has always ignored it so far. As we shall see, he continues to ignore it for all the rest of this chapter as well. It is difficult to see how he could have so ignored it if the point was firmly in his mind when he was first writing this chapter. I presume that the paragraph is a note added later, when the discussion of Z11 had focused his attention on the topic, and that he added it without pausing to reflect on how it affected his main line of argument in Z10.

35^b31–36^a12

It is at once clear that the argument of this paragraph depends upon ignoring the possibility of universal compounds. For it claims that the parts of the form are the parts of the essence, i.e. those mentioned in the defining formula. Then, in order to prove that the parts of the combined whole are *not* mentioned in the definition, it claims that definition is always of what is universal, and there is no definition of a combined whole because it is particular and not universal. Evidently, this is flatly inconsistent with the admission just above that there are wholes which combine a form and *matter taken universally*. One cannot believe that

Aristotle wrote the two paragraphs one after the other, as they now stand.

It may be noted that at $^b31-3$ we hear for the first (and last) time of *three* kinds of parts, the parts of the form, of the compound, and of the matter. One may speculate that the parts of the compound are such parts as hands and fingers, which can only exist as parts of the compound, whereas the parts of the matter are such parts as flesh and bones, which Aristotle here counts as continuing to exist after the compound is destroyed. But I have already observed that the distinction between these two kinds of 'bodily parts' is not playing any role in the argument of the chapter (35^b22-7 n.), and the speculation must therefore be very tentative. (Besides, the text at this point is insecure. The distinction between parts of the compound and parts of the matter arises only from an emendation of the manuscript reading, which can be questioned. In fact Frede & Patzig do not adopt it.)

It should be observed that the implication of the parenthesis at $^a1-2$ is that only a universal can be identical with its essence. Cf. *Z*6, 32^a4-11 n. For comment on the argument at $^a5-9$ to show that particulars cannot be defined, see *Z*15, 39^b20-40^a7 nn., where this argument is given at greater length. I devote the rest of this note to 'intelligible circles' and their 'intelligible matter'.

$^a9-12$: The phrase 'intelligible matter' occurs in Aristotle's writings only here, and at 36^b32-37^a5 in the next chapter (which adds little to what we are told here), and at *H*6, 45^a33-6 (where its interpretation is disputed). Setting *H*6 aside until we come to it, we may say that here at least 'intelligible matter' is identified with 'the matter of the objects of mathematics' ($^a11-12$) and this is a topic mentioned at the end of *Z*11, and set aside for later treatment (37^a10-13). It is also mentioned as a topic for discussion at *K*1, 1059^b14-21 (a passage which corresponds to nothing in book *B*). It is not clear that any passage in the *Metaphysics* does contain the desired discussion.

Aristotle tells us (as Plato's own dialogues do not) that Plato supposed that there were on the one hand forms, and on the other the perceptible particulars that participate in them, but *also* an 'intermediate' kind of entity, 'the objects of mathematics'. These were like the forms in being eternal and changeless, but like the perceptible particulars in that there were many all alike (*A*6, 987^b14-18. Cf. *Z*2, 28^b20). Amongst these 'objects of mathematics' there will be the 'intelligible mathematical circles' mentioned here, studied by the geometer, and which Plato will insist are unlike any perceptible circles because they are genuinely *perfect* circles. Moreover, there must be many of them, for the geometer will prove such things as 'Any two circles can touch one another at only one point, and can intersect one another at only two points.' This would not make sense if there were only one 'intelligible' perfect circle. Aristotle accepts that there is something right about this picture, for indeed geometers do talk about perfect circles, and they do not conceive them as circular disks of bronze, wood, or other such perceptible matter. But, for Aristotle, if two things share the same form, then they must differ in their matter (*Z*8, 34a5–8), so there must be 'intelligible matter' for these 'intelligible circles' to be made of. It is what makes it possible for there to be many of them. (We might prefer to say that the two circles would differ by their position, but this makes little difference in the end, since the supposed positions are again positions in a merely 'intelligible' space.)

The picture that I have sketched so far still seems to be basically a Platonic picture, and we might go on to suppose that 'intelligible matter' (or 'intelligible space') is located not in this world but in some other world, accessible from this one not by perception but by thought alone. But this is not Aristotle's view at all, as the last sentence of this paragraph is designed to show. On his view, the 'intelligible matter' that the geometer apparently needs is just ordinary perceptible matter, but conceived 'in abstraction from' its perceptibility. That is, when the geometer proves something about any two circles, what he is actually doing is proving a result about any two circles made of ordinary perceptible and changeable matter, but since the nature of the matter involved does not in any way affect his proof, he rightly ignores it. All actual matter (at least, in the sublunary sphere) is in fact perceptible and changeable, but geometry is not at fault in 'abstracting' from this, and treating its matter as if it were imperceptible and unchanging (cf. *M*3, *passim*, and e.g. *Phys* II, 193b22–194a12). A question that may still be raised is whether geometry *is* in some way 'at fault' in supposing that the circles with which it deals are *perfect* circles. Aristotle would evidently wish to say that it is not, but quite how he justifies this reply is obscure. (See, e.g., Mueller [1970] and Annas [1976], 29–34.)

It is suggested by Jaeger that the last sentence of the paragraph, which indicates (very obscurely) Aristotle's own view of the situation, is a later addition. It seems to me that this is quite a probable conjecture. See *Z*11, 37a10–17n.

36a12–25

Summing up the conclusions reached in this chapter, Aristotle surprisingly does not draw attention to an important part of his solution, that a thing may be prior in *one* way but not in *another* (35b22–7n.). Instead he mostly relies on the principle that the parts of a thing are prior to it, and draws our attention to the need to be clear about just which thing it is that we are referring to. But there is something rather odd about the general structure of his answer, which is this. If a thing may *also* be identified with its form, so that we have *two* ways of taking it, either as compound or as form alone, then the answer is complex in this way . . . But if the thing is not to be identified with its form (so that, apparently, we have only one way of taking it, i.e. as the compound), then the answer is still complex. However, the answer on the first hypothesis is that the form without the matter is posterior to the parts in its formula, but prior to the material parts in the particulars, whereas the form with the matter is posterior to both of these. A little reflection shows that the answer on the second hypothesis must actually be exactly the same answer again. So it seems that Aristotle would have done better just to give this answer first, and then to note (as the structure of his actual answer implies) that it may be disputed whether a compound of form in matter can also be identified with its form alone. (The mooted 'identification' is evidently that of 35^a7–9. I suggested in my comment on that passage that we do not *need* to take it as seriously proposing an *identification*, but simply as remarking on an ambiguity. When we ask about the parts of 'a circle', we might be meaning to ask about the parts of particular circles or about the parts of the form of a circle, for the same word 'a circle' can be used to ask either question.)

It appears that Aristotle is continuing to ignore the universal compound. One might suppose that it is introduced in the clause 'if we take the thing as combined with matter, either the bronze right angle or that formed by particular lines' ($^a20$–2). But although 'the bronze right angle' might certainly be used as an illustration of a universal compound, if we do take it in this way then we are lacking any explanation of why it should be posterior to 'the parts of the particular right angle'. So it is very much simpler to suppose that each disjunct in 'the bronze right angle or that formed by particular lines' is to be taken as an example of a particular right angle, i.e. either one made of bronze or one made of 'intelligible' matter, like the 'intelligible circles' at 36^a3–4.

But in that case how are we to understand the way in which Aristotle introduces his 'first hypothesis' at $^a16$–17: 'If the animal or living thing is also the soul, or if each thing is its soul . . .'? Does it not seem as if this first proposes an identity between the *universal* compound 'animal' (or better, 'living thing') and its formal element 'soul', and then goes on to propose instead, or in addition, an identity between *particular* compounds and their formal elements? That could, of course, be so. We have already seen several occasions in this chapter where universal compounds are in fact mentioned, only to be subsequently ignored (35^a4–6, $^a21$–2, and quite probably $^b18$–20). But we are not forced to take the words in this way. The simplest alternative is that the second 'or' is merely epexegetic, i.e. that it means 'or in other words', or (in other words) that it means 'i.e.'. Then we can certainly suppose that it is particular compounds that are in question throughout. The suggestion will be that a particular animal (or living thing) may also be taken to be its soul, i.e. that each man, horse, and so on, may be so taken. There are also, of course, many other suggestions that one might make.

CHAPTER 11

36^a26-31

Here Aristotle introduces the question to be discussed in this chapter. From its initial formulation one might suppose that it was very much the same question as was discussed in the preceding chapter, but in fact it turns out to be rather different. For it concerns those universal compounds that the last chapter did mention, but then altogether ignored, and in effect I think it asks us to recognize that there are such compounds. Nevertheless, the introductory paragraph still appears to presuppose that a material component can never be universal, for it claims that 'definition is of the form and the universal' ($^a28-9$), strongly suggesting that *only* the form is universal.

Now in a sense this could be accepted. For when matter has to be mentioned in a definition, it will always be matter of this or that specific kind, as, for example, one might have to mention flesh in the definition of snubness (35^a4-6). But a specific kind of matter is itself to be regarded as a compound, consisting of some more underlying kind of matter—and eventually prime matter—*with* a specific *form*. Thus there is such a thing as the form of flesh, and of bronze, and the same holds generally for any kind of matter that can come into being (cf. *Z*9, 34^b11-13). So, as Aristotle says at *GC* I, 321^b19-22: 'Flesh, bone, and all such parts are twofold, as are the other things that have a form in matter. Both the matter and the form are called flesh and bone.' We can, therefore, maintain both that definition is always of the form and that some definitions define universal compounds, i.e. universals which combine formal and material components, for it is always the form and not the matter of the material component that is relevant. But although this would be a possible line for Aristotle to take, it does not seem to be the line that he does take. At any rate, he never suggests that when matter is 'taken universally' then it is in fact being 'taken, in a way, as form'.

36^a31-^b7

Here Aristotle explains his problem more fully. It is easy to see that something is not a part of the form when there are examples of the form existing without it. But it could happen that something always found with the form is nevertheless not a part of it, though it would be difficult in such a case to separate the form in thought. An example of this problem is that the form of man is always found in flesh and bones.

Aristotle appears to offer us just two alternatives: either the flesh is part of the form, or it must be possible to separate the form in thought, i.e. to envisage the form without that matter. One would suppose that both of these alternatives would seem to him to be impossible. In the previous chapter he has constantly characterized flesh and bones as material parts of a man, and has treated them as what survives when the form is lost. So he must be strongly disposed to think that they are not parts of the form. Yet he surely could not imagine creatures with that form, i.e. living the life of a man, which were not of flesh and bone, but had been put together from—say—metal, plastic, silicon chips, and so on. Just as, in his view, it is not an accident that a saw must be made out of metal, if it is to fulfil its function (*Phys* II, 200^a10-13), so one would certainly expect him to hold that it is not an accident that men always are made of flesh and bones. If this elucidation of the problem is right, then what is needed for its solution is an account of how certain features may be implied by, but not 'part of', the form. It is not at all clear that Aristotle himself responds to the problem in these terms.

Some interpreters have taken the last sentence of this paragraph to be stating that flesh and bone are not parts of the form (e.g. Balme [1980], 294; Lear [1988], 283; Gill [1989], 132; Frede & Patzig). This, however, reads too much into it, for it is simply phrased as a question which permits either answer. Nevertheless, we can be fairly sure that this was Aristotle's view, for at 36^b10-12 in the next paragraph he apparently accepts that flesh and bones stand to a man as bronze and wood to a statue (Heinaman [1979], 260–1). (But perhaps we ought not to be *quite* sure, for 36^b10-12 is after all presented as part of an opponent's line of thought.) Unfortunately, we need to take notice of such hints as these, for when Aristotle comes to offer his own view explicitly, at 36^b21-32, what he says is extremely enigmatic.

(As we find from 36^b24-5, the comparison in this paragraph between circles of bronze and men of flesh was drawn by Socrates the Younger. He is a character familiar to us from several of Plato's dialogues, i.e. *Theaetetus* (147 D), *Sophist* (218 B), and *Politicus* (*passim*). (Also *Letter* XI, 358 D.) From the *Theaetetus* passage it appears that he was, at least in his youth, a mathematician.)

36^b7-20

Aristotle pursues his question, not with the form of a man, but with the form of a circle or a triangle or a (straight) line. The suggestion is that these supposed forms are really compounds of a more basic form *in* a particular kind of matter. In the case of the circle and the triangle it is suggested that the 'matter' might be 'lines and continuity', but no more basic form is specified. In the case of the line the more basic form is specified as that of twoness (or duality), but no 'matter' for this form is suggested. (We can hardly take it to be, again, '*lines* and continuity', but should probably understand just 'continuity' to be carried forward from the first two examples to the third. This is what is found at *Anim* III, 429^b18-20. But *H*3, 43^a33-4 suggests not continuity but length.) The details of this 'reduction of things to numbers' are thus left in some obscurity, but we probably will not be too much astray if we take the basic thought to be that two points determine a line, three a triangle, and so on. This would seem to be in accordance with Pythagorean thought—at any rate, it fits well enough with what we are told of the Pythagorean Eurytus at *N*5, $1092^b8–13$—but one has less confidence about 'those who believe in the Forms', i.e. are Platonists of some sort ($^b13–17$). They may perhaps have had something more subtle in mind, but—if so—we do not know what it was.

Aristotle distinguishes two groups of these Platonists. Some hold that the Platonic phrase 'the line-itself' should be taken to refer just to the formal element in lines, i.e. twoness, while others hold that it refers to the compound of both elements—twoness-in-continuity, say—and hence that 'the line itself' should be distinguished from 'the form of the line'. In their view 'twoness-itself' may be identified with 'the form of twoness', presumably because twoness is not *itself* a compound of form in matter, 'yet this does not hold in the case of the line' ($^b17$). It appears, however, that Aristotle disapproves of both groups equally (*pace* Heinaman [1979], 262), for both are engaged upon a 'reduction of things to numbers' ($^b12$), and both are open to the two objections that he proceeds to bring.

His first objection is 'that there will be one form of many things that evidently differ in form' ($^b17–18$). To be convincing, this objection requires more discussion of examples. No doubt the position implies that there will be one form for things that are evidently different, e.g. for bronze circles and for wooden circles, but it would seem to be begging the question to claim that it will lead to one form for things evidently different *in form*. One can sympathize with the thought that, if numbers are the only forms there are, then there will not be enough variety among the forms. But in order to be sure one needs to know more about the principles of the proposed reduction. (After all, there are infinitely many numbers.)

Aristotle's second objection is that it will be possible to set up just one 'form-itself' for everything, and that 'this has the result that everything is one'. (I take it that the expression 'form-itself' is an ironic coinage, and that Aristotle means that it will be possible to suppose that there is only one form, and that it will be the only thing that deserves (for some *X*) the title '*X*-itself'. This single form might perhaps be 'the-one-itself'.) The second part of this objection is certainly unfair. Our Platonists are not taken to be denying that there are different matters, both different kinds of matter and different particular lumps of matter. So they can perfectly well maintain that there are many things, even if there is only one form. The first part would seem to be unfair as well. At any rate, *some* of our Platonists think that 'the line-itself' and 'twoness-itself' are distinct entities, both deserving the title '-itself' even though the formal element of each is the same. Moreover, these at any rate, and probably the others too, claim that 'twoness-itself' is *not* a compound of some more basic form in a certain kind of matter. Aristotle is presumably alleging that their own method of argument could be used to drive them to the result he states, but that we cannot tell without knowing what their method of argument was.

36^b21–32

Aristotle has now explained the problem with which he began the chapter, and gives us his own reaction to it. The problem was: which of the parts are parts of the form? Two specific cases were raised: (i) Is flesh part of the form of a man? (ii) Are lines and continuity part of the form of (say) a triangle? We may add a third question, arising from this last: (iii) are there in fact any forms other than numbers? One can be fairly sure that his own answer to (i) is 'no' (36^a31–$^b7$n.) and that his own answer to (iii) is 'yes', though he seems to preserve an open mind about (ii) (*Anim* III, 429^b18–20). But the main problem in the interpretation of the response that we actually find here is to see how it replies at all to the questions that have been raised. The solution that I shall suggest is that the response is addressed to a *presupposition* of these questions, namely that we need to be able to answer them *because* it is only form that is defined (36^a28–31). Aristotle now wishes to say that we can also define (universal) compounds, and therefore we do not have to decide whether our definition does define a form or a compound. (For example, we can continue to maintain that lines must be mentioned in the definition of a triangle—as at *An. Post* I, 4, 73^a34–7—while leaving question (ii) unsettled.) If this is right, then the present chapter rejects a crucial presupposition of the previous one.

The main claim comes in the first half of Aristotle's reply, at $^b21$–4. Then at $^b24$–32 he applies this to the problem of the definition of man, but in a way which still leaves one somewhat puzzled.

$^b21$–4: His first claim is that 'it is useless to reduce everything in this way, and to eliminate the matter'. It is not clear whether he is thinking specifically of the reduction 'to numbers' introduced in the last paragraph (36^b12), and there objected to, or of some more general 'reduction to form' that might be taken to be suggested by the earlier part of the chapter. But in either case, what exactly is this 'reduction' which 'eliminates the matter'? Well, the comparison which Socrates the Younger used to draw does not suggest that bronze be somehow 'eliminated' from the universe, but that it should be eliminated from the definition of a circle. And it goes on to suggest that flesh and bones might similarly be eliminated from the definition of a man. Moreover, *one* group of those who attempt to 'reduce everything to numbers' apparently wish to eliminate the matter of the line (i.e. continuous space?) from its definition, for they regard 'the line itself' as referring only to the form of the line, i.e. to duality. If we generalize from these points, then the 'reduction' and 'elimination' in question is just the claim that only form, and not matter, should figure in definitions. So this is what Aristotle is now condemning as 'useless'.

If we seek to avoid this conclusion, then we may suppose instead that the 'reduction' in question is an attempt to eliminate from the notion of form all material aspects. Thus Socrates the Younger may be taken as presuming that we do not count bronze as part of the form of a bronze circle, and going on to recommend that we should not count flesh as part of the form of a man, though he need not be taken as objecting to including material aspects in a definition (e.g. if what is to be defined is 'a bronze circle', as at *Z*7, 33^a1-5). Similarly, the *second* group of those who attempt to 'reduce everything to numbers' are perfectly happy to accept that 'the line-itself'—and hence, the definition of the line?—should include both formal and material components of the line, but they do wish to insist that these components are of different kinds. So, on this second view, what Aristotle is condemning as 'useless' is an attempt to press to an extreme the contrast between what counts as form and what counts as matter, by eliminating all matter from the form. On this view, the moral might be that we can stick to the claim that definition is always of the form, so long as we are suitably relaxed about how the distinction between form and matter is to be taken. It is 'useless' to be pernickety about it. (Cf. 36^a26-31 n.)

But it must be the first view, and not the second, that is supported by Aristotle's continuation: 'Some things *are* one thing in another, or certain things in a certain state.' This does not play down the distinction between form and matter, but on the contrary reasserts it. For a compound of form and matter is exactly one thing (form) in another (matter), or certain things (matter) in a certain state (form). As we are about to be told in 37^a5-7, and as we have been told already in the forward-looking note at 35^b27-31, the species man is precisely such a compound, taken universally. It is true that neither of these passages explicitly *says* that the *definition* of the species will therefore specify both the formal and the material aspects of the compound, and for an explicit statement to this effect we must look elsewhere, e.g. to *E*1, $1025^b28-1026^a5$ (cf. *Phys* II, 200^b4-8; *Anim* I, 403^b2-9). But we can at least confirm from the later discussion in *H*2, 43^a7-26 that there is henceforth no bar on matter figuring in a definition. I conclude, then, that the approach that Aristotle now condemns as useless is indeed the approach he took himself in *Z*10, and which he appeared still to be continuing with at the beginning of *Z*11, that a definition can *only* mention form, and never matter.

$^b24-32$: Aristotle now returns to the comparison between men of flesh and circles of bronze, and says that it is misleading: it misleads one into supposing 'that there might be a man without his parts, as there can be a circle without bronze'. Now evidently there can be circles made not of bronze but of wood or other similar materials. This suggests that there might perhaps be men made not of flesh but of something else, equally solid and perceptible. But also there can be circles which are at any rate conceived as made of purely intelligible matter, imperceptible and unchangeable. So this perhaps suggests that there might similarly be men who are made of no perceptible matter at all. On the face of it, it is this second suggestion that Aristotle replies to, and we may therefore presume that it was the second suggestion that Socrates the Younger intended to propose. At any rate, a Platonist could well think that this was a good way of describing the Platonic form of man (except that it would need to be added that there was only one such form). Aristotle's reply is that a man is necessarily a living, and therefore changing, thing, which he could not be if he did not have properly material parts. (At $^b28$ the MSS all have 'an animal is a perceptible thing', but it is quite tempting to follow Frede & Patzig by emending this to 'an animal is a perceiving thing'—*aisthētikon* for *aisthēton*. Aristotle defines animals by their ability to perceive, and perception implies change, so it would genuinely follow that animals 'cannot be defined without reference to change'.)

If this is the correct account, then Aristotle simply fails to consider whether a man might be made of some other kind of perceptible matter. But in that case why does he say, at the end of the paragraph, that only a living hand is a hand? He apparently offers this as a reason for his claim that a definition cannot ignore 'the state of the parts', and from this it must follow *a fortiori* that a definition cannot ignore *which* parts a man must have. In fact one can easily provide a justification for this thought. For if one thinks of the definition as specifying the kind of life that a man leads, then it must automatically imply something about his parts. For example, there must be organs for seeing, hearing, and tasting; there must also be suitable limbs for moving about, for using tools, and so on. But that is just to say that a man must have such parts as eyes, ears, and tongue, and again legs and feet, arms and hands, if we may assume that all such parts are defined simply by their functions and by nothing else. Thus, in the terminology of the note on Z10, 35^b22-7, the 'proximate matter' of a man is actually implied by his form, i.e. his life.

But then, does not the implication extend to his 'more remote' matter too? Certainly, if we think of flesh and blood, bone and sinew, as equally defined by their functions, then it will follow in the same way that a man must be made of these stuffs. (Thus, if a certain plastic fulfils all the functions of flesh, then it simply *is* flesh, on this approach.) In theory it appears that one could carry the same approach on further, to the immediate ingredients of these stuffs in turn, and so on right down to prime matter. (*Meteor* IV, 12, appears to be exploring this idea.) Alternatively, even if bone (for example) is not defined by its functions, still it might in fact be the only material that can sustain those functions (as metal is the only material suitable for sawing wood). Pursuing this idea in a similar way, we would again reach the conclusion that every aspect of the matter of a man is in fact necessitated by his form, i.e. his kind of life. (And *Phys* II, 9, appears to make just this claim, applying it quite generally to all things that exist by nature.) So Aristotle might perhaps be wishing to claim that the matter of a man is actually dictated by his form at all levels.

Some interpreters suppose that Aristotle means, in this paragraph, to rely upon the distinction between proximate and remote matter (e.g. Irwin [1988], 238–47; Gill [1989], 126–38). He has implied earlier in the chapter that such stuffs as flesh and bone are not 'parts' of the form, but he is implying here that organic parts such as the hand are 'parts' of it. If we recall that this same distinction seems to be needed in order to understand the position adopted in Z10 (see 35^b22–7n.), and if we presume that Z10 and Z11 are in harmony with one another on this issue, then this proposal seems quite plausible. On the other hand, there is not really a distinction of principle between the two kinds of matter, as I have just observed, and certainly Aristotle's usual practice in the biological works is to count flesh and blood as defined by their functions no less than eyes and hand. This might lead one to suppose that neither kind of matter is being counted as a 'part' of the form, though both are in a way 'implied' by the form and hence 'parts' not of the form but of the compound (cf. Heinaman [1979], Frede & Patzig). This is perhaps the most consistent position for Aristotle to take, though he does not himself draw the needed distinction between 'part of' and 'implied by'. Moreover, the interpretation brings to light a further doubt about this passage. When Aristotle says that it is a mistake to suppose 'that there might be a man without his parts', does he mean to be speaking of the *form* of man, i.e. soul, or of the compound? If he is responding here to the problem that he raised at 36^b3–7, then it should be the form that he is talking of, since that problem clearly concerned the parts *of the form*. On the other hand, the moral that he appears to draw, both before the present passage (36^b22–4) and after it (37^a5–7), is that 'man' signifies a compound. In that case, then certainly there cannot be a *man* without material parts, but the question about the *form* of man seems simply to have been ducked.

I do not believe that one can reconstruct Aristotle's position with any confidence. Perhaps that is because he had not thought it out very clearly himself. (See further the end of my epilogue to this chapter.)

36^b32-37^a5

Since Alexander it has been suspected that this paragraph is out of place, and indeed it is impossible to make sense of it in its present setting. In the last paragraph it has been claimed that a man is a (perceptible and) changing thing, and so must have changeable matter. It has been inferred, or will be inferred at 37^a5–7, that the material parts of a man must be mentioned in the definition of a man. This paragraph begins with the thought that the objects of mathematics, e.g. mathematical circles, are not perceptible (or changeable) things. But what one might expect from this contrast is that while the matter of a man *will* be mentioned in the definition of a man, the matter of a circle *will not*. However, our paragraph appears to suppose that there is an expectation that the matter of the circle, e.g. its two semicircles, *will* be mentioned in the definition of a circle. Now *this* one might explain if the sequence of thought was: mathematical circles are conceived of as made of purely intelligible matter; so perceptible matter such as bronze and wood will not figure in their definition, but one might expect the intelligible matter, and its parts (e.g. the semicircles), so to figure. (This is Ross's explanation.) But if this is what lies behind the question, then Aristotle's reply to it is wholly incomprehensible. For his reply is that mathematical circles do have intelligible matter, so the semicircles will be parts of this matter, and *therefore* parts of particular circles, and *not* parts of the universal circle (which is what is defined). The reply insists upon a point that was already taken for granted in the raising of the question, and wholly ignores the comparison that gave rise to that question. For the point was that the material parts of a man, *taken universally*, *do* figure in the definition. (Ross himself agrees that the answer will not do, but seems not to notice that—in the setting he has provided—it is wholly incongruous.)

In fact the setting which this paragraph appears to require is the setting of chapter 10, in which the possibility of taking some material constituent universally is constantly ignored, and indeed denied. It supposes that it has been argued that the material parts of a thing can only be parts of the particular, because they are perceptible (or, more relevantly, because they are changeable). Then it points out that this argument will not apply to the imperceptible parts (such as semicircles) of an imperceptible thing (such as a mathematical circle). But it replies that the same argument does apply in a way, since there is imperceptible (and unchangeable) matter too, namely intelligible matter. Our paragraph thus belongs with the thought of the paragraph at 35^b31-36^a12 of chapter 10, and I think it is an attractive hypothesis that it was originally written for that position. But then it was rejected from there when Aristotle determined to rewrite that paragraph (possibly adding 35^a9-12 in the process), and by pure accident has survived here in chapter 11, where it is quite incongruous. In any case it is clearly out of place where it now is.

37^a5-10

I have already commented sufficiently on the idea that 'man' and 'animal' should be taken to be universal compounds. But it is worth noting here what is said of the particular man. First, there is some hesitation over whether it is quite correct to say that Socrates *is* his soul. For some further remarks on this, see the prologue to Z13. Second, taking the more straightforward view that Socrates is a compound of soul and body, Aristotle expresses the position in this way: the universal 'man' is a compound of soul and body taken universally, i.e. with *both* components taken universally; but a particular man, such as Socrates, is a compound of 'this soul and that body', and in this way 'the particulars correspond to the universal'. This might well be taken to suggest that as the universal 'man' is a compound of two universals, so the particular man is a compound of *two particulars*, and naturally one will take it this way if one supposes that Aristotle's ontology includes particular souls. But if we do not begin from that supposition, then the language used here cannot force us into it. For the 'correspondence' that Aristotle wishes to draw attention to may simply be that both the universal and the particular man will be compounds.

37^a10–20

This paragraph mentions two questions that are postponed for later treatment.

$^a10$–17: The first is actually raised as a double question: (*a*) whether there is matter other than that found in sensible substances, and (*b*) whether there are substances other than perceptible substances, e.g. numbers. It is a little surprising to find Aristotle raising question (*a*) as if it were so far unconsidered, for he has certainly *mentioned* 'intelligible matter' already, as the matter of the objects of mathematics. But I have suggested that the very recent mention in 36^b32–37^a5 is out of place where it is, and is best relocated in an earlier draft of *Z*10, 35^b31–36^a12. Moreover, if that earlier draft did not include the lines that now form 36^a9–12, then Aristotle has not yet given his own explanation of what 'intelligible matter' is. Since he is writing here as one who has not yet considered this question, there is a strong temptation to suppose that 36^a9–12 did not precede this passage when it was first written.

In any case, although Aristotle has, in our present text, told us what he thinks of the matter of mathematical circles, he has said nothing at all about a supposed matter of *numbers*. But it would appear, from the way in which he links questions (*a*) and (*b*), and goes on to instance numbers as an example to which (*b*) applies, that he did see some connection here. One may speculate that the connection is this. Suppose that a number is, 'as some say', a combination of units (*Z*13, 39^a12–13; *H*3, 43^b33–4). Then the three units in the number three, which are the same as one another in form, must differ from one another by having different matter. This matter too is regarded by the arithmetician simply as 'intelligible matter'. So if either numbers or circles are held to be independently existing substances, the 'intelligible matter' that they both require must also be held to have an independent existence. But, in Aristotle's own view, it does not in either case. For the 'intelligible matter' of a mathematical circle is, as we have seen, just ordinary perceptible matter such as bronze or wood, abstractly considered. Similarly, the 'intelligible units' of the mathematical number three are again just ordinary units such as three men or three horses, but again abstractly considered. So the matter that differentiates them is really just the ordinary matter that differentiates three men or three horses, and numbers are no more independent substances than circles are.

The question of whether numbers should be counted as substances is a main theme of books *M* and *N*. But it is not clear that any passage in those rather disjointed books would count as the promised discussion of the matter of mathematical objects. The topic of *Z* and *H* continues to be the study of perceptible substances, which Aristotle seems to admit to be really a part of Physics rather than Metaphysics. (Cf. *Z*3, 29^a33–$^b12$; *Z*17, 41^a7–9; *H*1, 42^a22–5.)

$^a18$–20: The second question raised and postponed for later treatment is the question of 'the unity of a definition'. We have noted that *Z*4 inevitably raises this question when it claims that the things that have definitions in the primary way are 'the forms of a genus', since these are *not* 'expressed by predicating one thing of another' (30^a10–14). So too, of course, does the whole of *Z*10, with its basic assumption that 'a definition is a formula and every formula has parts' (34^b20). We shall find some treatment of this question in *Z*12, *H*3, and *H*6.

37^a21–$^b7$

This long paragraph summarizes, and brings to a close, the discussion of form and essence begun in chapter 4, though not in the order in which we have read it. I take the paragraph in sections.

$^a21$–2: Aristotle explained what an essence is at the beginning of *Z*4, namely that the essence of a thing is what it is said to be in its own right, if we take the phrase 'in its own right' in an appropriate sense. But he does not seem to have explained 'in what way it is itself in its own right'. I am therefore quite strongly tempted to emend the text at this point, by deleting the letters '*au*' from the word '*auto*' in $^a21$. The literal rendering would then be:

> and in what way [it is] the in-its-own-right

which could be taken as an ellipsis, entirely in Aristotle's usual manner, for:

> and in what way it is what a thing is in its own right.

Given this emendation, the summary here corresponds closely to the later summary at *H*1, 42^a17–18.

If, however, we stick to the text that we have, then the best explanation would seem to be this. The main doctrine of *Z*4 is that it is only things that are 'primary' that have essences (at least, in the primary way). We may plausibly equate the things that are primary in *Z*4 with the things that are spoken of in their own right in *Z*6, and observe that in *Z*6 these are identified with their essences. It follows that it is only things spoken of in their own right that are essences, or in other words that it is essences, and only they, that are spoken of in their own right. So this last statement is a way of putting the main claim of *Z*4, but in the vocabulary of *Z*6 and presupposing the doctrine of *Z*6.

It is not quite clear why Aristotle should wish to emphasize that he has stated what an essence is 'universally and in all cases', unless perhaps this phrase is intended to recall the point made in *Z*4 that things of different kinds have essences in different ways—some primarily, and others in various dependent ways.

$^a22-9$: This section summarizes much of chapter 10: the formula of an essence will not mention material parts, since they are not parts of the essence at all, but of the combined whole; and this has no formula expressing all of it, but only a formula of its formal component. As in almost all of chapter 10, the idea of a universal compound is here disregarded, and a combined whole is taken to be a form in a *particular* chunk of matter. It is this that is said to be 'indeterminate' ($^a27$), as in *Z*10 it is said to be 'unknowable' (36^a9). In fact the doctrine of *Z*11 is almost explicitly denied. For at $^a28$ we are offered the illustration 'thus a man has the formula of the soul', and the context shows that it is a particular man being spoken of. But *Z*11 has claimed that the formula of a man is inevitably a universal compound, mentioning not only the soul but also the body (taken universally), and has added that in this way the universal corresponds to the particular (36^b28-30, 37^a5-10). So it should surely be this compound formula that is the formula of the particular man, in so far as he has a formula.

$^a29-33$: The only place where Aristotle has already said explicitly that the substance proper is the form, and that the combined whole is called a substance derivatively from this, is at *Z*8, 33^b17-18. But the point is one that he might have made almost anywhere, and it seems improbable that he here means to refer back to *Z*8 in particular. (It would be his only reference, in *Z*10–11, to any of *Z*7–9.)

By contrast, we surely must see a reference to *Z*5 in the next sentence, if at $^a31-2$ we retain the words 'for in these the nose will occur twice'. This clause is found in all MSS, but Ross proposes to delete it as 'irrelevant in this context', and certainly it is wholly inept. As the text stands, the fact that there are two noses in a snub nose (and even in snubness, apparently) is given as a *reason* for saying that these things are compounded from concavity and the nose. But that is plainly absurd, and the connecting 'for' cannot be taken seriously. If the words are retained, then their point is simply to remind us that snubness was discussed at some length in *Z*5. One might not unnaturally expect a reference to *Z*5 at this point, since it is very clear that we have a reference back to the doctrine of *Z*6 in the next section ($^a33-^b1$). On the other hand, it seems to me that *any* reference to *Z*5 at this point would actually destroy the consistency of this whole concluding paragraph. From this point of view, matters are very much improved if we may follow Ross and delete the suspected clause, for then we can say that this mention of snubness is only a further recollection of the discussion of *Z*10, which gave snubness as its first example of a compound at 35^a1-6 (cf. $^a26$).

I shall take up later, at the end of this note, the question of whether any reference here to the doctrine of *Z*5 would be consistent. But we can observe at once that if such a reference is intended, then Aristotle is quite ignoring the differences between what he is saying here and what has been said in *Z*5. *Z*5 did not argue that a snub nose is not a primary substance because it has matter in it; nor did it go on to compare snubness with a particular such as Callias, who also has matter in him; nor did it suggest a contrast with concavity, which lacks matter. On the contrary, *Z*5 argued that any definition of snubness would have to be 'from an addition', and hence not a proper definition. It of course did not suggest that Callias would have to be defined 'from an addition', which would be nonsense, but it *did* claim that concavity would have to be. For it said that its point would apply to all predicates not in the familiar category of substance, on the ground that they all had 'first recipients' which had to be mentioned in the definition; and concavity is surely not an exception to this. So the truth is that any reference to *Z*5 at this point would betray a forgetfulness of what *Z*5 actually said. But no doubt Aristotle could sometimes be forgetful (cf. *H*1, 42^a4-6n.).

$^a33-^b7$: This concluding section evidently refers to *Z*6, but not in the terminology of *Z*6 itself, since the distinction between matter and form is not used in any of *Z*4–6. As I observed in my epilogue to *Z*4–6, there is some doubt over what the doctrine of *Z*6 is, so there must be a corresponding doubt over whether its doctrine is here correctly rephrased in the new terminology, or whether it has been somewhat altered as a result of Aristotle's new perspective. (If in the previous section he means to refer to *Z*5, then we certainly cannot rule out such an alteration.) I return to this point after briefly mentioning a couple of textual matters.

At $^b2-3$ both Jaeger and Frede & Patzig delete the words 'Thus crookedness and being for crookedness will be the same, if crookedness is primary.' Their main reason is that the example seems to them inappropriate. But it is an example of just the same kind as concavity, which has been used a few lines above to illustrate the substance that is form ($^a29-30$). (Indeed, I suspect that Aristotle's mind is still running on the shapes of noses; cf. *Phys* II, 194^a6-7; *Cael* I, 278^a29-31.)

At $^b5$ I retain the MS reading, since it seems to me to give a perfectly good sense: when Socrates is taken as a whole combined with matter, he is not even coincidentally the same as his essence (i.e. human soul). The observation has a special point if, as on the interpretation I offered, Z6, 31a19–28 is concerned with the possibility of a coincidental identity.

I devote the remainder of this note to the question of the internal coherence of the whole of this summary at the end of Z11.

First we may note that the summary does not anywhere allude to what has preceded it in Z11, and that in what it recalls from Z10 it very clearly conflicts with Z11. The obvious explanation for this is that the summary was written before the rest of Z11 was added, and that it once stood as the conclusion of Z10. I see no problem with that conjecture. If I am right in supposing that the explicit mention of universal compounds at 35b27–31 was a later addition to the text of Z10, then it is natural to extend the conjecture by supposing that the summary also precedes this later addition. Moreover, the summary pays no attention to the themes of Z7–9 (for we may discount 37a29–30), so we may if we wish suppose that it was written before these chapters were incorporated. In that case it was written before universal compounds were explicitly mentioned at Z7, 33a2–5 and at Z8, 33b25–6. It is a possibility, then, that the idea of a *universal* compound of form in matter had not occurred to Aristotle at the time when he was writing this summary. Alternatively, even if the idea was one that he had already used in other contexts, still we may suppose that it was not in his mind here, and that the compounds that he is actually thinking of in this passage are all supposed to be particular compounds.

In order to defend the summary we must invoke this possibility. For at a24–7 it restates the argument of Z10, 36a5–9, and this argument very obviously assumes that a compound of form in matter has to be a particular compound. If the summary is consistent, then, whenever it speaks of a compound we should understand it as meaning to refer only to particular compounds. It is not too hard to suppose that this is the correct interpretation of its final section, which recalls Z6. When we read there that something which is taken together with matter, as 'one thing in another', is not the same as its essence, then of course if we have Z11 in mind we shall think of the universal 'man', which is there described in just this way. Or if we have in mind the definition of 'primary' in Z4, and the attempt in that chapter to deny that a compound such as 'pale man' has an essence, then again we shall probably think of this compound as something universal. But as I have argued (in the epilogue to Z4–6), it is a possible interpretation of Z6 that it means to allow that *all* universals are the same as their essences, and even if that was not what Aristotle did actually intend when writing Z6, still it may be what he intends now, when looking back on it. The compounds that he means to refer to in this passage *need* not be taken to include universal compounds.

Now if we omit the doubtful clause at a31–2, so that the text can be taken as containing no reference to Z5, little more needs to be said. It is true that the explicit abstract noun 'snubness' at a31 does in fact introduce a universal compound, but so it did at 35^a4–6 in Z10, where, however, the subsequent discussion showed that was not how Aristotle was thinking of it. On the contrary, his argument in Z10 depends upon the compounds in question all being particulars. The same may well apply here, for, as soon as he has mentioned a snub nose and snubness in $^a31$, he at once goes on to couple a snub nose and the particular man Callias at $^a33$, as each contains matter. So perhaps here too he is actually thinking that the trouble with matter is its particularity, which makes it unknowable (36^a5–9) and hence indefinable (37^a24–7). But if on the other hand we retain the MS reading, so that a reference back to Z5 cannot be avoided, then what must we say? As I have already noted (above, $^a29$–33 n.), the doctrine of Z5 is actually quite different from the doctrine presented here, and if it is rephrased as a doctrine about certain 'combined wholes', then they evidently must be understood as universal combined wholes. (Z5 itself says that it is concerned with certain *attributes* (*pathē*, 30^b24) or *predicates* (*katēgoriai*, 31^a2).) So the result is that at $^a24$–7 Aristotle reminds us that *every* combined whole is particular, and for that reason indefinable, and then at $^a30$–3 he reminds us that snubness is a universal combined whole, and is indefinable for a quite different reason (i.e. because any attempt to define it must lead to saying the same thing twice). And we have to say that he apparently sees no conflict between these two reminders.

I conclude that there is much to be said for abandoning the MS reading, and seeing no reference to Z5 at this point. (And I note that if we do take this course, then we can with more confidence rely on $^a33-{}^b7$ to elucidate the doctrine of Z6.)

Epilogue to Z11: Form So Far

Z4–11 constitute the discussion of essence and form promised at the beginning and the end of Z3. There is more to come in later chapters that is relevant to a final assessment of Aristotle's position, and I shall return to the topic in my final epilogue. But it is convenient to review here what we have had so far.

In Z4–6 the topic was essence, rather than form. This was explained as what is given by a definition, and the proposed identification of substance and essence was accepted, but with some qualifications. For it was held that the notions of essence and definition are 'spoken of in many ways', as is the notion of being, and this yielded a privileged status for essences in the old category of substance.

By contrast, in Z7–9 the topic was form, rather than essence, and we were in effect introduced to Aristotle's basic trio: form, matter, and the compound of the two. The main point argued for was that it is only the compound that is generated and is destroyed. (It is true that specific kinds of matter—e.g. wood—are also generated and destroyed, but that is because they too are compounds. The matter that is genuinely indestructible is prime matter.) It is obvious that the compound that is generated and destroyed is the particular compound, and this was the centre of attention in Z8, and again in Z10. But Z7–9 did not restrict attention to generation in the intuitive sense, whereby it is particular items in the old category of substance that are generated and destroyed. On the contrary, the section opened with a promise to consider coming to be quite generally, including cases where what a thing comes to be is specified by an adjective from some other category, e.g. 'healthy'. In fact the generation of health was an example that received a great deal of attention. So health too is counted as a form (explicitly at 32^b1–6), and we should not strictly say that health *itself* is generated or produced; rather, what is generated is a 'compound' of health *in* a particular body.

In Z7–9 there is therefore no preference for the old category of substance. There is, certainly, a special feature of the generation of living substances to which our attention is drawn: in their case the form acquired in the generation must be present beforehand, in a specially strong sense (34^b16–18). But it does not seem to be suggested that these forms must therefore be assigned any privileged status *as forms*. Rather, *any* universal characteristic that can be acquired in a coming-to-be is counted equally as a form, and hence as itself ungenerated, with the sole rider that it be a simple characteristic (if that is what 'primary' means at 34^b7–10). Moreover, form and essence are identified, and identified too with 'primary substance' (32^b1–2), so that this notion is now wholly divorced from the old category of substance. We should not be surprised, then, that from this new perspective concavity and crookedness can be suggested as examples of primary substances (37^a29–$^b4$).

The position does not change in Z10, where it is assumed (*almost* everywhere) that a compound will be a particular compound, and that there are such things as the form or essence of a circle or a right angle, and (by implication) of a semicircle, an acute angle, and indeed a finger. (For it is assumed that these things can be defined (35^b6–11), and we know that a definition states an essence, and an essence is a form.) Such forms are not in the old category of substance, and indeed that category itself is pretty well abolished. For Z10 opens up a wholly new line of thought when it abandons the familiar species-terms 'man', 'horse', 'oak', and so on, and insists that the form of a living thing is actually its *soul*. In what I take to be the original version of Z10 (lacking 35^b27–31), the implications of this point are not seen. But in Z11 they are seen (or anyway some of them), for Aristotle at last recognizes not only that there are universal compounds but also that his discussion needs to pay them more attention. It is here that the notion of form begins to become, as Z3 has said (29^a33), 'most puzzling'.

Z4 did at length grant that there is such a thing as the definition, and hence essence, of the compound 'pale man', though it insisted upon adding 'not in the primary way' (30^b12–13). Z7 was happy to say that one can define the compound 'bronze circle', and apparently saw no need for any such qualification (33^a2–5). I have argued that Z10 does also admit definitions of 'snub' and of 'bronze circle' (35^a22-30), though indeed the admission is not consistent with its main claims. For of course Aristotle does not think that 'pale man', 'bronze circle', and 'snub' are expressions for forms. More interestingly, 'man' is surely amongst those universals that *Z*4 counts as having a definition and an essence in the primary way, i.e. the 'forms of a genus' (30^a11-12). But when Aristotle reflected on his view that the form of a man is his soul, and took it to follow that 'man' and 'soul' should be distinguished, he apparently did conclude that 'man' does not express a form after all. Hence in the passage later added to *Z*10 (i.e. 35^b27-31) he tells us that the universal man is *not* a substance. But in *Z*11 he does not withdraw the view that man can be defined; rather, the definition of man, like many other definitions, will take the form 'one thing in another, or certain things in a certain state' (36^b23-4). We must then abandon the equation between definition and form (i.e. substance), but whether this is best done by abandoning the equation between definition and essence, or that between essence and form, is not at present very clear. It appears from what comes later (e.g. in *H*2) that we do better to stick to the view that form and essence are always the same, but to allow that it is not only forms or essences that can be defined.

But the problem that has here surfaced is a deep one. For we are now, for the first time, putting some real weight on the idea that a form has to be *simple*. And this raises a question about all kinds of other examples, besides man, that were previously accepted as forms without more ado, e.g. the circle. For perhaps this universal too will turn out upon analysis to be some kind of compound of matter and form (as, indeed, some Platonists have actually claimed)? But this gives rise to a yet more general problem, and one which brings us back once more to the old problem of the unity of a definition. For perhaps it is the case that with *every* definable universal the definition will reveal it as a kind of compound of form in matter, and so not itself a form after all? But if that proved to be so, then we should have to admit that genuine forms are indefinable, and apparently Aristotle *does* come to make this admission at *H*3, 43^b28-32. But that must lead to the complete disintegration of this alleged equation between form, essence, and definition. I shall not pursue this thought any further now; instead I turn to consider once more what is implied by *Z*11 about its own problem, the relation between 'man', 'soul', and the matter of a man.

If a soul is a way of living, then it must imply suitable 'material parts' to enable the animal to live the kind of life in question. No doubt, most other forms too will imply something about matter. For example, in Aristotle's own view even the form of a circle implies matter, and hence perceptible matter, for you cannot have a wholly immaterial circle. But circles can be made of any kind of matter whatever, and for the sake of argument we may allow the Platonist to suppose that there is a special kind of matter—imperceptible and unchangeable, but intelligible—out of which the geometer's perfect circles are made. But it would be absurd to suppose that the same could apply to the matter of a living man; it is only very specific kinds of matter that can sustain life, and a soul must necessarily be in matter of this kind.

But if all this is right, then how does the form 'human soul' differ from the compound 'snub'? The only difference seems to be that snubness may be analysed as concavity in noses, and concavity is not itself confined to noses, whereas there is no *X* such that human souls are *X*-ness in a certain material, and *X*-ness can also occur in other materials. But that is just to say that 'human soul' is *more* snubby than 'snub' itself (as are 'feminine', 'odd', and 'equal'; cf. Z5 $30^{b}28$–$31^{a}1$ n., *ad fin.*). The reasons for claiming that the snub has no proper definition, and therefore cannot be a substance, apply to the soul with even more force, not with less. But it is very difficult to believe that Aristotle himself saw and appreciated this point. He seems to suppose that if we distinguish 'man' and 'soul', then we can safely admit that 'man' signifies a compound *without* having to say the same of 'soul'.

CHAPTER 12

Prologue to *Z*12

At the end of chapter 11 Aristotle noted two issues which he postponed for later treatment (37^a10-20), and one of them was the problem of the unity of a definition. Both *Z*12 and *H*6 announce themselves as discussions of this problem, and neither chapter recognizes the existence of the other. (The problem is also treated during *H*3.) It seems to me most improbable that when Aristotle postponed the issue at the end of *Z*11, and proceeded to sum up his discussion of essence, he was intending to treat of it immediately afterwards in the very next chapter. For, since the issue clearly does affect our understanding of essence, it would seem much better in that case to include its treatment in the main discussion of essence and postpone the summing up. In any case, it is clear that *Z*12 is only a partial treatment of its topic. First, it evidently recognizes at 37^b27 and at 38^a24 that it has considered only one kind of definition (namely 'definitions obtained by division'), and it allows for there being other kinds. Second, it explicitly characterizes its own discussion as merely a 'first statement' at 38^a24. Third, this characterization is clearly merited, for as it stands the discussion at 37^b27-38^a9 is quite needlessly confused, and overlooks a very simple point of logic. The chapter, then, is unexpected in its present position, only a fragmentary treatment anyway, and in fact one that could quite easily have been improved.

It is overwhelmingly probable that whoever first edited the *Metaphysics* (according to tradition, Eudemus) found amongst Aristotle's papers what is now *Z*12, perhaps bundled in with the other papers that are now books *Z* and *H*, but not securely attached to any one place. Anxious to fit it in somewhere, so that it should not be lost, he added it after *Z*11, where its topic had just been explicitly raised. Admittedly there is a mild awkwardness with this hypothesis, for presumably the same account applies too to the papers which are now the later chapters of book *H*. They also are fragmentary discussions of miscellaneous issues, related to the subject-matter of *Z* and *H*, but not worked into any continuous treatment. But in this case our editor added them at the *end* of the continuous treatment, for that is apparently concluded at the end of *H*2. Why should he not have done the same with *Z*12? Well, the obvious suggestion is that he wished to preserve at least the superficial *appearance* of a continuous discussion, even though the papers he was dealing with do not form one. But this could hardly be done if *Z*12 and *H*6 were placed near to one another, since each announces itself as opening the discussion of the same topic. So he hit upon the present arrangement, which separates them by a wide margin.

Was there, then, any reason for him to choose *Z*12, rather than *H*6, to go between *Z*11 and *Z*13? The only reason one can suggest is that he might have thought that *Z*12 provided the more complete treatment.

This is because *Z*12 distinguishes two kinds of case, the simple case where a definition contains a genus and just one differentia, and the complex case, where there are many differentiae, and most of its discussion then centres on the complex case. By contrast, *H*6 makes no such distinction, and never discusses the case of several differentiae at all. So *H*6 might well appear to be even more fragmentary than *Z*12, and therefore better relegated to the end. Nevertheless, I think it is clear that *H*6 is in fact the more mature treatment. I return to this point in my epilogue to the chapter.

37^b8–14

Aristotle begins by referring us to his *Analytics*. One suspects that this itself is a sign of the relatively early composition of *Z*12, since this is the only place in the *Metaphysics* where a passage from the *Analytics* is named explicitly. (But *Δ*30 apparently has in mind *An. Post* 75^a18–$^b2$ when it says at 1025^a34 that a certain account has been given 'elsewhere'.) Aristotle did indeed discuss definition at *An. Post* II, 3–10 (with some further advice on how to obtain definitions by division in II, 13), and the requirement that a definition should be a unity was mentioned, but not discussed, at 92^a29–30. (Also at *Int* 5, 17^a13–15.) The suggested definition of man as 'two-footed animal' is not seriously intended as a complete definition. Further differentiae such as 'going on foot' and 'wingless' will be suggested as we proceed, and adding these would lead to just the kind of definition that is contemplated in the *Analytics*. But we may note that it is certainly not the kind of definition of man that one would expect after reading *Z*10–11, with their emphasis upon the point that the essence of a man is his soul.

It is difficult to see quite what this problem is that Aristotle calls the problem of the unity of a definition. One should first observe that where my translation uses such phrases as 'a unity', or 'something unitary', this is in a sense an over-translation, for Aristotle himself just uses the simple phrase 'one thing'. (The same applies to *all* occurrences of 'unity', 'unitary', and so on, throughout the translation.) Thus a more literal translation of *Z*11, 37^a18–20, where the problem is first stated, would be:

> In the case of definitions, we must consider later in what way the [things] in the formula [are] parts, and why the definition [is] one formula. (For evidently the object [is] one, but by what [is] the object one? At any rate, it has parts.)

Similarly, a more literal translation of the present passage ($^b10$–14) would be:

> I mean this problem, whyever [that thing], the formula of which we call a definition, is one, for instance the two-footed animal [which is the formula?] of the man; for let this be its formula. Then why is this one and not many, animal and two-footed?

The simple answer to this question, as posed, is that, if we speak in our usual (but loose) way, there is no difficulty at all about the same thing being one *X* but many *Y*s. Thus a series of words may be one formula but [made up of] many words; a property such as being a man, defined by that formula, may equally be one (complex) property but [made up of] several (simpler) properties. But I do not imagine that this answer would satisfy Aristotle at all. He would ask, I think, 'But what is it that *distinguishes* the basic and simple property of being a man from the complex and derivative property of being a pale man?' Thus what is at issue, I think, is actually a problem about simplicity and complexity. Where Aristotle writes 'one', and where I translate 'a unity', I guess that what lies behind his thought is the notion of something simple. How can something be both simple and defined?

But one has to say that although this may perhaps *lie behind* Aristotle's problem, it is not how he formulates it himself. His own way of putting it is more like this. It appears that a definition has several parts, and it therefore appears that these must correspond to parts of the thing defined. But then we are at once faced with the question: 'What is it that holds these parts together, so as to make them parts of some *one* thing?' Roughly, the solution he offers in the present chapter is that, when you look at it closely, you can see that the definition does not have parts at all. But the solutions proposed in *H*3 and *H*6 are rather different.

37^b14–27

(In the opening line of this paragraph Aristotle unexpectedly uses the Greek equivalent of quotation marks around 'man' and 'pale', as if he were meaning to talk explicitly of the words rather than what they signify. But there seems to be no significance in this departure from his usual practice.) The general structure of the paragraph is that Aristotle first mentions one way in which two things (or words) may form a unity, but claims that genus and differentia do not form a unity in *this* way ($^b14$–21). Then he adds that, even if they did, it would not solve the problem, for it could not explain the case where there are many differentiae ($^b21$–4). Then he states his problem once more in general terms ($^b24$–7).

$^b14$–21: A particular pale man is one thing, and therefore the compound phrase 'a pale man' can signify one thing, i.e. when it is used to describe that man. This is because the attribute of being pale belongs to the man in question. In an exactly similar way, a particular two-footed animal is one thing, and therefore the compound phrase 'a two-footed animal' can signify one thing, i.e. when it is used to describe that animal. This is because the attribute of being two-footed belongs to the animal in question. But Aristotle correctly observes that *this* will not yield a solution to his problem, for in the definition 'man is a two-footed animal' no *particular* man, or animal, is being described. The 'unity' that he wishes to explain is not how a compound phrase 'two-footed animal' may be used to describe a single particular, but how it manages to express a single universal. We could explain this 'unity' in a similar way, he suggests, only if we could also say that being two-footed belongs to the *genus* animal, not to this or that particular animal; in an alternative locution (cf. Z4, 30a14–15), only if we could say that the genus participates in the differentia. But this, it seems, we cannot say (Z4, ibid.). For in the natural sense of 'belonging to', or 'participating in', this would be to construe the genus as itself a particular thing, with the property of being two-footed. But then, since the compound phrase 'four-footed animal' must equally express a single universal, on this account the same genus 'animal' will also have the property of being four-footed. This apparently leads to a contradiction, since nothing can be both two-footed and four-footed.

Now we do not have to stick to what I have called the 'natural' sense of belonging to, or participating in. In fact in the *Topics* the locution '*X* participates in *Y*' has mainly been used not for singular predications at all, but for universal ones, i.e. where *all* instances of *X* are also instances of *Y* (see, e.g., 121a10–19, 122b18–24, 123a20–7, 126a17–25, 132b35–133a11). Clearly, this is of no help here, since it is not true that all animals are two-footed, or that all animals are four-footed. But perhaps it may be suggested that we can count *X* as participating in *Y* (or *Y* as belonging to *X*) so long as it is true that *some* instances of *X* are also instances of *Y*. Then certainly the genus does 'participate' in the differentia, but no problem is solved by this. For in exactly the same sense 'man' participates in 'pale' (i.e. some men are pale), but Aristotle will not be willing to infer that the compound 'pale man' does, in the *relevant* sense, express something unitary, i.e. a single universal. His own objection, however, is rather different and very ingenious: even if we do allow that the same genus 'animal' can be said to 'participate' both in the differentia 'two-footed' and in the differentia 'four-footed', still our problem has a complexity which shows that this could not provide its solution.

b21–4: For consider now a case where there is more than one differentia, e.g. 'two-footed wingless animal'. If we are to explain how this phrase manages to express a single universal on the same suggested model, i.e. by analogy to the way in which 'pale artistic man' may be true of a single object, then the explanation is that the same man may participate both in being pale and in being artistic. Applying the model, then, our account must be that the same genus 'animal' participates both in 'two-footed' and in 'wingless', and *that is why* the whole phrase 'two-footed wingless animal' expresses a single universal; it is simply because the same genus participates in both. But clearly this explanation explains too much. For we are granting, for the sake of argument, that the genus 'animal' does participate both in 'two-footed' and in 'four-footed', so it will now follow that the whole phrase 'two-footed four-footed animal' expresses a single universal. But that is absurd, since it simply expresses a contradiction. That is, it is absurd that '*all* the differentiae should form a unity' (b24), though that is a result that we cannot avoid if we try to base our explanation on this model.

This is a very nice argument to show that the suggested model is of no help, and it holds however exactly we construe the suggestion that the genus may 'participate in' the differentia (or, in an alternative locution, that the differentia may be 'present in' the genus, b23). (I observe, incidentally, that it is because Aristotle is pursuing this model that he considers only the possibility that the genus might participate in the differentia, and pays no attention to the possibility that the differentia might participate in the genus, although he has actually claimed that neither participates in the other (b18).)

b24–7: This model having proved inadequate, Aristotle restates the problem. The definition defines a substance, and a substance is some *one* thing, but the difficulty is to explain how this can be so. Evidently the substance in question should be taken as substance in the sense of form, essence, and universal, and it is this kind of substance that Aristotle claims to 'signify a this' (as at Z4, 30a2–6). Whether he means to include here substances, i.e. essences, from all the categories is not clear. At any rate, the only definitions he explicitly considers in this chapter are definitions of such things as animals.

37b27–38a9

Here Aristotle begins upon his solution, restricting it to definitions 'obtained by division'. To practise such a division, one begins with a suitably wide genus, and divides it by adding a differentia that applies to some, but only some, of its members. Then one divides again by adding a further differentia that applies to some, but only some, of the things characterized so far. And so one continues until only a single species, not further divisible, remains. The result is to form a definition which consists of an initial genus followed by a string of differentiae, and where the initial genus together with *some* of the differentiae following can itself be regarded as a subgenus, differentiated by the remaining differentiae. For present purposes, it is the structure of the definition finally reached that is more important than the method of reaching it. Aristotle evidently concedes that not all definitions have this structure, and indeed that is already obvious from some of the examples offered in Z10 (e.g. a semicircle is defined as half a circle, 35b10, and this definition surely does not begin with the bogus genus 'halves'). It is admitted, then, that the positive solution that he is about to offer covers only some of the ground.

The sequence of thought in this paragraph is wholly mysterious. Aristotle first points to the fact just noted, that we can always regard the initial genus, taken together with some of the differentiae following it, as forming a subgenus. This leads him to say 'it makes no difference whether the constituents are many or few, nor therefore whether they are few or just two' (^{a}1–3). The moral of this would appear to be that the complex case of a genus followed by many differentiae can be reduced to the simple case of a genus followed by a single differentia, namely by taking all of the definition except the final differentia as introducing a (narrow) genus. So, if we can solve the simple case, we are done. Then, at the end of the paragraph, Aristotle offers a solution to the simple case: the genus does not exist apart from its species (NB 'form' = 'species'), or perhaps it does exist but if so only 'as matter', and it may therefore be discounted (^{a}5–9). But he does *not* conclude that the problem is now resolved. On the contrary, he seems to think that it is only the *initial* genus that may be discounted in this way, and we *still* have to show how a whole string of differentiae can be seen as 'forming a unity'. It is to this latter problem that the whole of the rest of the chapter is devoted. But in that case, what was the relevance of the remark that 'it makes no difference whether the constituents are many or few'? I see no explanation of this problem except one that relies upon the suggestion that Aristotle's stated reasons for discounting the genus are not his real reasons, and that his real reasons apply more convincingly to the initial genus than they would to subgenera formed along the way.

To illustrate this, suppose that we are seeking to define a man, and that we have so far reached 'wingless two-footed animal'. Someone points out that this does not yet distinguish men from all other animals, since some dinosaurs were both wingless and two-footed. He goes on to suggest that a distinguishing mark which would do the trick is that men are warm-blooded, while dinosaurs are not, and this is accepted. Then, on Aristotle's principles, we can treat 'wingless two-footed animal' as a genus, with 'warm-blooded' as its differentia. And for the reason given in ^{a}5–9 the genus can then be discounted, so that men can simply be defined as 'things which are warm-blooded'. But of course this result is absurd, and the subgenus certainly cannot be discounted. But the *initial* genus 'animal' perhaps can. This is because it is already entailed by each of our positive differentiae, namely 'two-footed' and 'warm-blooded', so that it does not need to be separately stated. In general, the justification that is needed for omitting any original constituent from a definition is that it is already entailed by the remaining constituents. Clearly, Aristotle himself uses this line of thought quite explicitly when he is considering how a string of differentiae might be argued to 'form a unity'. He surely should have used it too as his ground for discounting the genus. Elsewhere he has himself implied that the differentia will entail the genus (*Cat* 3, $1^b16–20$; *Top* VI, $144^b12–20$), and in an ordinary definition by division this is quite likely to be true of the initial genus, though much less likely to be true of the subgenera formed along the way. So one may sympathize with his instincts, though not with what he offers by way of argument.

$^a5$–9: We are offered two versions of the argument. The first is that the genus does not 'in an unqualified sense' (*haplōs*) exist apart from the species. There is a straightforward sense in which this is fairly uncontroversial, i.e. that every member of the genus must be a member of one of its species. One might suppose that Z13, 38^b16–34 is arguing for some stronger sense in which the genus has no existence apart from the species. But in either case the reply is that this is irrelevant; it has no tendency to show that the genus need not be mentioned in the definition of the species. And the same reply must be given to the alternative argument, that the genus exists only 'as matter' to the species. Whatever truth there might be in this rather obscure suggestion, it would not affect the point at issue. For if the rest of the definition does not entail the genus, then one cannot simply omit the genus without altering the purport of the definition. That, and only that, is what matters.

The suggestion that the genus is the 'matter' of the species is found elsewhere in Aristotle only at *Δ*28, 1024^b8–9 and at *I*8, 1058^a1–2, $^a23$–4. (Some think that it occurs also at *H*3, 43^b30–2 and at *H*6, 45^a33–5, and that it plays an important part in the argument of *H*6. I shall argue against that interpretation.) The implication of the present passage seems to be that the point of this suggestion is very much the same as the point that the genus does not exist apart from the species, and it makes little difference which one says. Moreover, the role of the example that Aristotle supplies, namely 'voiced sound' (*phōnē*, i.e. the kind of sound one makes when talking), seems to be to supply a case which you could equally well regard either as a genus or as matter. (For example, *phōnē* is called a genus at *B*3, 998^a20–5, and is called matter at *GA* V, 786^b21.) The idea is that the various kinds of sound—such as 'vowel', 'sibilant', 'guttural', and so on—may be regarded as 'made of' sound as well as being species of it. So you could look at things either way, and nothing much will hang on the question. (Similarly at 1058^a1–2.) But of course the truth is that in most cases it will seem a very strained metaphor. Could one, for example, regard the genus 'animal' as something that the various species of animal are *made of*? Or could one think of the genus as something that survives a *change* from first being one species to then being another? The genus is not well suited to either of the two main roles that matter is called upon to fulfil (Z3, prologue). One could say, I suppose, that both genus and matter may be counted as 'indeterminate' by comparison with the species-form, but that does not seem to me a very significant point of similarity.

38^a9–35

Aristotle here makes the perfectly correct point that a string of differentiae will reduce just to the last member if each is entailed by its successor. We have only to add (as suggested) that the first differentia should entail the genus, and we can fairly deduce Aristotle's conclusion:

a properly formulated definition will reduce to its last differentia alone, so there is really no problem over how its parts 'form a unity', for it does not actually have distinct parts at all.

Evidently he recognizes that definitions are not in practice formulated in the way his argument requires, but he apparently supposes that if we tried hard we could conform to his recommendation. There is, however, a point that he appears to overlook at $^a14$, namely that each further differentia must be a *positive* determination of its predecessor if the entailment is to hold. Thus, if one divides the footed animals into those that are cloven-footed and those that are *not*, then either 'not cloven-footed' will not entail 'footed' (being equally true of animals without feet at all, e.g. fish), or if it does then 'not cloven-footed' is understood as *meaning* 'footed but not cloven-footed'. But in that case one might well object that 'not cloven-footed' is itself being understood in a way that does not 'signify a unity'. There is also the further objection that a negative differentia cannot have any place in a series of differentiae such as Aristotle is recommending, because one cannot take the differentia *of it* in turn. (E.g. one cannot specify the different kinds of footless animals by specifying the different kinds of feet that they lack; *PA* I, 3, 642^b21–5.) Thus positive differentiae are required throughout, and ones that are not simply compounds of two independent differentiae. This is well illustrated by the example 'cloven-footed', which certainly cannot be analysed as '*both* cloven *and* footed'; it shows very well what Aristotle means by 'taking the differentia of the differentia'.

Epilogue to *Z*12

In *PA* I, 2–3 Aristotle himself attacks the kind of definitions described here, i.e. those that are obtained by a division 'properly carried out', as being both useless and impossible. While the details of his argument there can sometimes be obscure, his general moral is, I think, uncontroversial: any useful way of defining a species of animal will need to differentiate it from others by *many different* lines of differentiation. Usually, one cannot define a species at all by using only one such line (e.g. footedness); and even if with some species it can be done, still it is not useful for biological purposes to attempt it. For when it comes to explaining why the parts of animals are as they are, all kinds of *different* groupings need to be considered.

We must, I think, conclude that *Z*12 was written before *PA* I, 2–3, and I believe we can go further: *Z*12 must antedate practically all of Aristotle's serious work in comparative biology. For it must have struck him very early on in his biological research, as soon as he began to seek for some order and system in the great wealth of biological data that he was accumulating, that the kind of definition recommended in *Z*12 simply does not work. But it has been convincingly argued that Aristotle's biological observations took place mainly in his middle period, i.e.

between his two periods of residence at Athens, and that many of them date from the early part of that period. So this suggests a relatively early composition for *Z*12, perhaps not much after the *Analytics* to which it refers. On the other hand, there is reason to suppose that Aristotle's view of the soul as the form of the body superseded some earlier views, and it is usually counted as his 'late' view. Since it is clear that *Z*10–11 are entirely familiar with this 'late' view of the soul, one may reasonably conjecture that *Z*12 antedates *Z*10–11, and perhaps several other portions of *Z*, by several years. (For a useful survey of these and other chronological points, see Ross [1957].)

Now *Z*12 announces itself at $37^{b}10$ as a contribution to Aristotle's 'discussion of substance' (*hoi peri tēs ousias logoi*), so it was clearly written for the *Metaphysics*. But its basic approach to the problem with which it deals is rejected in the other attack on that problem in *H*6. For *H*6 first cites the problem in its usual form ('Why is man not an animal *and* two-footed?'), but then continues: 'Those who proceed with definitions and explanations in this way, as they usually do, will not be able to give an account that solves the problem' ($45^{a}21$–2). What it proceeds to recommend is a new style of definition, combining matter and form, which—it claims—dissolves the problem at once. This, I shall argue, involves abandoning the idea that we define things by genus and differentia, where neither element of the definition is predicated of the other ($45^{a}20$–33 n.). *Z*12, then, works with the old conception of a definition, found in the Logical Works and earlier in *Z*4, especially $30^{a}11$–14, according to which it is true that neither element 'participates in' the other. (See, e.g., *Top* VI, $144^{a}28$–$^{b}3$; *An. Post* II, $90^{b}34$–8.) But in *H*6 we find Aristotle advocating a new conception, which has gradually emerged from *Z*17, *H*2, and *H*3.

Thus the solution recommended in *Z*12 is rejected in *PA* I as impossible in practice, and rejected in *H*6 as mistaken in principle, since it employs an inadequate conception of what a definition is. It is a relatively early attempt, and one that Aristotle himself discarded.

CHAPTER 13

Prologue to *Z*13

This chapter is certainly the most vexing chapter in the whole of book *Z*. It opens by returning to the programme outlined at the beginning of *Z*3, and proposes a discussion of the claim of the universal to be substance. There then follow four paragraphs of argument in which this claim is dismissed, though a final paragraph adds that this conclusion leads to a problem. Omitting the introduction, I label the remaining paragraphs for ease of reference:

(1) 38^b8–16
(2) 38^b16–34
(3) 38^b34–39^a3
(4) 39^a3–14
(5) 39^a14–23

Paragraph (1) gives two reasons for saying that *no* universal is a substance. We may note here that the first of these is also repeated at *Z*16, 40^b16–27, where a third reason is added. Paragraph (2) opens with the concession that a universal cannot be a substance in quite the way that an essence is, but goes on to suggest that a *genus* may still be allowed to be a substance in a different way. The discussion of this suggestion is extremely confusing, and I shall argue that something must have gone wrong with the text at this point, but at any rate the paragraph clearly ends by rejecting it. The short paragraph (3) says that the discussion so far shows that *no* universal is a substance, and mentions a further line of argument as leading again to the same conclusion. Then paragraph (4) offers an alternative line of argument, apparently as leading to the same conclusion once more, though this is not explicitly stated. (In fact it is not clear what conclusion this fourth paragraph has in view.) Finally paragraph (5) notes that the argument appears to lead to the clearly unacceptable consequence that neither substance nor anything else can be defined.

There are two major problems of interpretation. One concerns the internal coherence of the chapter, and the other its relation to the rest of *Z* and *H*. In this prologue I concentrate on the second, but the central issue is much the same in each case. How are we to reconcile the claim that no universal is substance and the claim that an essence *is* a substance? For surely essences are universals?

On one interpretation, no reconciliation is possible, and Aristotle is acknowledging that his demands on the concept of substance cannot be jointly fulfilled (cf. Lesher [1971]; Sykes [1975]; Graham [1987], chs. 8–9). The arguments of *Z*4–11 require substance to be universal (so that it can be defined, *Z*4; so that it can be identical with the essence that is its definition, and hence fully knowable, *Z*6; so that it can play the appropriate role in generation, without being generated itself, *Z*8; and *perhaps* so that it can be pure form without any admixture of matter, *Z*10). But the arguments of this chapter show that substance cannot be universal, and this contradiction must simply be accepted. The conclusion to be drawn is, apparently, that there are no substances—or at any rate that there are no *perceptible* substances. For this line of interpretation may offer it as Aristotle's (unstated) conclusion that there is only one thing that satisfies *all* the criteria for substance, namely God. God is not a universal, but he is pure form, and so it would seem that he might well be both knowable and definable. Moreover, he does have an appropriate role to play in generation, without being generated himself, since he is the first and unmoved mover of the universe as a whole.

Now one might offer to support this line of interpretation on the basis of the difficult first chapter in book *E*, perhaps with some further hints from *Z*16, 40^b27-41^a3, for several commentators have claimed that the message of *E*1 is that it is only God who can really qualify as a substance (e.g. Owens [1951], ch. 7(b); Patzig [1960]; Frede [1987*a*]). However, it has to be admitted that this speculation receives little support from elsewhere, and in particular the further suggestion that the role of *Z*13 is to destroy the concept of perceptible substance is surely contradicted by all the rest of *Z* and *H*. For nowhere do we find any awareness that this concept has even been put in doubt. One might say that there *is* an awareness that the criteria for being a substance cannot be jointly satisfied, but Aristotle's reaction to this seems to be that we must therefore admit as substances *each* of the three candidates, matter, form, and the compound of the two, one because it satisfies one criterion and another because it satisfies another. This, at any rate, seems to be the moral of *H*1, 42^a26-31. But we do not anywhere find him suggesting that there are not really any perceptible substances at all. For the time being, then, I shall simply set aside this line of interpretation, though I return to it at the end of my epilogue to the chapter.

There are basically two directions in which one might move when attempting to harmonize the claims that an essence is a substance and that no universal is a substance. One may suggest either that Aristotle does not mean quite what we expect by 'essence', or that he does not mean quite what we expect by 'universal'. Let us take the first suggestion first. It can hardly be denied that for *most* of *Z*4–11 the forms or essences under discussion were universals, such things as what being is for a man, i.e. for *any* man. But on some occasions it appeared that Aristotle might *also* be recognizing individual and particular forms or essences, e.g. a form that was Socrates' form and for that reason could not be anyone else's. So the suggestion is that the moral to be drawn from *Z*13 is that it is only these *latter* forms and essences that do in fact deserve the title 'substance'. Modern debate on this suggestion stems mainly from Sellars [1957] and Albritton [1957]. Among many who have argued for it are Harter [1975]; Heinaman [1980]; Lloyd [1981]; Frede [1985]; Frede & Patzig, i. 48–57; Irwin [1988], ch. 12; among many who have argued against it are Woods [1967, 1991]; Loux [1979]; Modrak [1979]; Burnyeat *et al.* [1979]; Code [1984]; Lear [1988], ch. 6(6); Furth [1988], §20(iii); Lewis [1991], ch. 11.

The main evidence in favour of particular forms or essences is this.

(i) In *Z* and *H* there are three occurrences of the expression 'what being is for *X*' where '*X*' is clearly an expression for a particular. One is at *Z*15, 39^{b}25 ('being for this particular house'), but I shall argue that it is a mistake to see this phrase as intended to mention an essence at all. Another is at *Z*4, 29^{b}14–15 ('being for you'), where I have pointed out that there is no *need* to suppose that being for you is intended to be something different from being for me. The third is at *Z*6, 32^{a}8, where we have an enigmatic reference to the question of whether Socrates and being for Socrates are the same. But we may also note an occurrence elsewhere, in *Δ*18, where Aristotle is discussing the senses of 'in its own right'. He says there that one of these senses is what being is for a thing, 'for example Callias is in his own right Callias and what being is for Callias' (1022^{a}25–7). Here it certainly appears that Callias is identified with his essence as he is with himself.

(ii) We have noted the similar thesis that a thing may be identified with its form. Where this first occurs (*Z*10, 35^{a}7–9) it is tempting to give an explanation which does not actually suggest an identity at all, but simply an ambiguity. But in later occurrences (*Z*10, 36^{a}12–25, and particularly *Z*11, 37^{a}7–8) that explanation seems less convincing, and the suggestion does seem to be that Socrates and his form, i.e. his soul, may literally be taken to be the same thing. One must add that in these later occurrences Aristotle does not actually affirm the identity, but mentions it only as a view that one might take. But if it is to be a serious option at all, we must surely suppose that the form in question is a particular form.

(iii) More usually Aristotle distinguishes the form, as cause, from the particular thing of which it is the form, but of course this is quite compatible with supposing that the form itself is also particular. There is a passage in *Λ*5 which very clearly implies this. It begins by saying that although causes may be spoken of universally, still 'those universal causes do not exist, for the cause of what is particular is itself particular. Man is universally the cause of man, but there is no universal man; it is Peleus who is the cause of Achilles, and your father of you' (1071^{a}19–22). Then, elaborating upon the idea that the causes are different in different cases, the passage goes on to say that even for things in the same species they are different, 'not in form but because it is another particular, your matter and form and efficient cause, and mine; but they are the same in their universal formula' (^{a}27–9). This is the clearest endorsement of particular forms to be found anywhere in Aristotle. *Perhaps* it is a slip, and he did not really mean to say of the form what he clearly does mean to say of the matter and the efficient cause; but the text is quite explicit.

(iv) In several places Aristotle implies that forms need not be eternal; he denies that they are ever in the process of coming to be or ceasing to be, but he nevertheless speaks of them as capable of existing at some times but not at others. This of course could apply to universal forms, if at some times they do have instances and at other times they have none. One can easily interpret in this way passages such as *E*3, 1027^{a}29–30; Z10, 35^{a}28–30; Z15, 39^{b}22–7; *H*3, 43^{b}14–21; *Λ*3, 1070^{a}15–17. But in a few places such an interpretation is hardly possible, and Aristotle certainly seems to be supposing that a form ceases to exist when an individual ceases to possess it, e.g. *H*5, 44^{b}21–9; *Λ*3, 1070^{a}22–6. This could only apply to particular forms. A similar moral can be drawn from the fact that Aristotle speaks of souls as ceasing to exist at death, either simply (*PN* 465^{a}19–26), or with the qualification that the thinking part of the (human) soul might perhaps be an exception (*Λ*3, 1070^{a}24–6; *Anim* II, 413^{a}3–5, ^{b}24–9). Such a soul must be a particular soul, and therefore a particular form. (We have also noted, in the prologue to Z10, several other indications that Aristotle thinks of the soul as a particular.)

(v) I observed at Z3, 28^{a}36–29^{a}10 n., that the simplest way to explain Aristotle's claim that form is an ultimate subject of predication is to suppose that he means that particular forms are not predicated. This point, however, cuts both ways. For the claim that form is an ultimate subject appears to be dropped at the beginning of Z13 (see 38^{b}1–8 n.), though on this interpretation you would expect it to be emphatically repeated, since Z13 will claim that whatever is a substance cannot be predicated of a subject (38^{b}15–16).

(vi) Several commentators have supposed that Aristotle would not have called the form 'a this' unless he had thought of forms as particulars. In view of Z3 29^{a}27–8 n., I find this argument quite unpersuasive.

Most of this evidence consists of hints and suggestions. As Albritton [1957] noted, it provides quite a convincing case for saying that book *Λ* is committed to particular forms, but with books *Z* and *H* the case is altogether weaker (cf. Code [1984]). The meaning of the relevant passages is often doubtful, or they are capable of a different interpretation, or it could be said that Aristotle's phrasing may be careless, and he does not mean quite what he says. For one must not forget that there is evidence on the other side too. Perhaps the main point is that Aristotle *never* explicitly distinguishes the two kinds of form—universal and particular—that this interpretation demands. Moreover, he standardly takes it for granted that forms and essences are universal, and apart from the few places just noted he seems everywhere to ignore particular forms, even where his argument demands some consideration of them. (A conspicuous example is Z15; see 39^{b}24–5 n., where there is also some discussion of how particular forms should be construed.) Furthermore, forms and essences must be universal in order to satisfy the requirements on substance that Z4–11 have introduced, as we have already observed.

It follows that even if Aristotle did very firmly believe in particular forms, still this would not yield any *reconciliation* of Z4–11 on the one hand and Z13 on the other, so the interpretation does not actually deliver the result desired. (It may be said that *M*10 attempts a partial reconciliation, for *M*10 tries to argue that actual knowledge is of the particular and not the universal. But even if this is the point of *M*10, still it does not help us with the question of what Aristotle meant to be doing in book *Z*.) I therefore turn to consider the alternative approach already mentioned.

If forms are to be understood in the usual way, i.e. as universals, then in order to maintain their claim to be substances we must apparently say that Z13 does not really mean to argue that *no* universal is a substance. There have been various attempts to maintain that Z13 does not even *say* this. Thus Woods [1967] argues that the message of Z13 is that universals *which are predicated universally* are not substances, but that a species-form is a universal which is *not* predicated universally. A variation on this, proposed by Loux [1979] and by Code [1984] and by Lewis [1991], is that Z13 argues that no universal is the substance of what it is predicated of, that a species-form is a universal and is the substance of the members of the species, but it is not predicated of them; it is *predicated* only of their matter. (The suggested explanation is that 'this statue is statue-shaped' does not count as a predication because one cannot identify the statue without already relying on the fact that it is statue-shaped.) All such suggestions, it seems to me, are in clear conflict with what our text actually says. Within Z13 the thesis that is argued for is stated as 'nothing predicated universally is a substance' (38^b9), 'nothing predicated of an underlying thing is a substance' (38^b15), 'nothing that belongs universally is a substance' (38^b35); and in a similar passage in Z16 we find 'nothing that is common to many things is a substance' (40^b23). Subsequently, the doctrine of Z13 is described as the doctrine that 'nothing predicated universally is a substance' (Z16, 41^a4), 'the universal is not a substance' (*H*1, 42^a21), 'no universal can be a substance' (*I*2, 1053^b16–17). (Compare also *B*6, 1003^a7–8; *K*2, 1060^b21; *M*10, 1087^a2, $^a10$.) In the face of this, one cannot feasibly maintain that there are only *some* universals that Aristotle *says* are not substances.

An alternative version of this line of interpretation agrees that Aristotle says that no universal is a substance, but claims that he is now attaching an unexpected *sense* to the word 'universal' (e.g. Burnyeat *et al.* [1979], Lear [1988], Furth [1988]). The idea is that he still conceives of essences as in our sense universal, but they are no longer to be counted as universal in his sense, for in his sense, 'universal' now means '*more* universal than is the indivisible species-form'. The thesis that he is opposing in this chapter is a thesis that he evidently credits to his Platonist opponents, i.e. that the *more* universal something is, the *more* it counts as a substance. (The thesis is perhaps hinted at in Z16, 40^b16–

27; it is rather more clearly stated in the summary at *H*1, 42ᵃ13–16.) By contrast Aristotle's substances are the *least* universal of universals, and that is why he shifts his ordinary usage in this chapter in order to count them as simply *not* being universals at all.

One objection can be noted at once. This interpretation certainly posits a *change* in Aristotle's use of the word 'universal'; for example, essences were explicitly called 'universal' at Z10, 36ᵃ1. Yet, when Aristotle explains in this chapter what a universal is, he says that it is 'what is of a nature to belong to more than one thing' (38ᵇ11–12), and this is just the same explanation as he has *always* given (e.g. *Int.* 7, 17ᵃ38–ᵇ1; cf. *PA* 644ᵃ27–8). Thus *he* does not appear to be conscious of any such change. On the proposed interpretation, this is very difficult to understand. But the more powerful objection is that when one looks in detail at his arguments it becomes clear that they apply to all universals in the old and familiar sense of 'universal'. Naturally, this objection must be argued point by point as we go through the arguments. But if I may anticipate my verdict, then it is clear that all the three lines of interpretation I have sketched are faced with very serious difficulties. However, I have no fourth line of interpretation to suggest.

I return to the issue in my epilogue to the chapter, where I shall also be concerned with the problem of its internal coherence.

38ᵇ1–8

Z3 began by proposing four claimants for the title of substance, namely essence, universal, genus, and what underlies. It went on to subdivide what underlies into matter, form, and the compound of the two, but by the present stage form and essence have been very firmly identified. It now appears further that form, i.e. essence, is no longer counted as a subdivision of what underlies, for our opening paragraph says that what underlies does so in *two* ways, and not in three (ᵇ5; contrast *H*1, 42ᵃ26–31). One of these is explicitly characterized as the way that matter underlies, and the other is underlying 'by being a this, as the animal underlies its attributes'. Since Aristotle is prepared to call a form a this (Z3, 29ᵃ26–9n.), it *could* be that this phrase is intended to indicate how form underlies. But against this: (*a*) you would expect Aristotle to say 'the man' or 'the soul', rather than 'the animal', if he had meant to indicate not a compound but a form or essence; (*b*) since this passage twice contrasts essence with what underlies, it is natural enough to suppose that it is not here being counted as itself one of the things that underlie; and (*c*) the claim that the compound underlies is anyway much more plausible than the claim that the form does, so it would be strange to find the plausible claim dropped in favour of the implausible one.

Even if we admit that 'what underlies', as used here, is not taken to include form or essence, still the phrase is being used somewhat ambiguously. In its second occurrence at ᵇ5 it explicitly includes both matter and something else (which I take to be the compound), but in its first occurrence at $^b2$ it applies only to matter. For substance is indeed said to be matter, essence, and the compound of these: but it is *not* said to be the compound, essence, *and* the compound *of these*. There is what I take to be a further looseness of language in this passage. Having mentioned *four* claimants to the title of substance—i.e. what underlies (= matter), essence (= form), the compound of these, and the universal—Aristotle adds that *two* of them have already been treated of. So, if we take him strictly at his word, the compound has not been treated of. But while it is true that *Z*3, 29^a30–3 did not promise any discussion of the compound, it is difficult not to see both *Z*7–9 and *Z*10–11 as including such a discussion. I prefer to suppose, then, that when he says 'two' he means 'three', and that this is comprehensible since the discussion of the compound was not (of course) a separate discussion. (To avoid both of these difficulties, Frede & Patzig propose to delete the phrase 'and the compound of these' from $^b3$.)

Anyway, we come in this chapter to consider the claim of the universal (and, as a special case, the claim of the genus). This is advocated by some on the ground that the universal is 'a principle, and in the highest degree a cause'. This is the first mention in book *Z* of 'causes and principles' (see further *Z*16, 40^b19–22; *Z*17, 41^a6–10; *H*1, 42^a4–6). The discussion that follows does not shed much light on quite *why* the universal is held to be 'a principle and a cause', but this has been a prominent theme in book *B*, especially chapter 3.

38^b8–16

This first paragraph of argument opens on a tentative note ('it *seems* impossible'). But it then proceeds to two arguments, in $^b9$–15 and $^b15$–16, which do not appear to be tentative at all. At any rate, there is nothing tentative about the first, though perhaps there is about the second, which begins 'A substance is *said* to be . . .'.

$^b9$–15: Aristotle lays down the premiss that the substance of a thing is peculiar to it, and does not belong to anything else. In *Z*6, 31^a17–18 it was said that 'a thing is thought to be no different from its own substance', but that implies an *identity* between a thing and its substance. The premiss here does not envisage an identity but a one-to-one correlation, for it supposes that the substance of *x* is not *x* itself but does belong to *x*, and belongs to nothing else. This is confirmed by the repetition of the present argument in *Z*16, which claims that 'a substance belongs to nothing but to itself and to that which has it, i.e. that of which it is the substance' (40^b23–4). So the premiss is not one that we have had before (save much earlier, in the discussion of problems at *B*4, 999^b20–2), and it is not clear why Aristotle feels entitled to assert it here. But he plainly does assert it, and it must follow that if forms or essences are still allowed to be substances at all, then only particular forms and essences will qualify.

Actually we must strengthen this premiss a little if the argument is to be completely watertight. By definition a universal is 'of a nature' to belong to more than one thing, but it might for all that happen to belong only to one thing. To save the argument from this objection, it is natural to strengthen the premiss to this: for any *x*, it is 'of the nature' of the substance of *x* to belong to *x* and nothing else. It will then follow straightforwardly that no universal that belongs to *x* can be the substance of *x*, and equally that no universal that does not belong to *x* can be the substance of *x*. Hence no universal can be the substance of anything. If we add the principle (canvassed in Z3, 28^b33–6 n.) that any substance must be the substance of something, it then follows that no universal is a substance. This completes the argument.

In fact the argument continues for another four lines ($^b12$–15), but perhaps the best way to look at this continuation is as offering support for the opening claim that the substance of a thing is peculiar to it. This is deduced from 'things whose substance is one have the same essence, and so are themselves one' ($^b14$–15). The deduction appears to be this. Suppose that the substance of *x* belongs to *x* and to other things too. Then either it will be the substance of all the things to which it belongs, or of none of them. But it cannot be the substance of none of them, since by hypothesis it does belong to *x* and is the substance of *x*. (Aristotle does not put in this step; I supply it for him.) Equally, it cannot be the substance of all of them, *because* (*a fortiori*) it will then be the substance of one, and so—by the premiss just cited—all the others will be this one. But that is absurd. (Thus in effect I understand Aristotle to mean 'because' where the text has 'but'. I see no other way of understanding the argument. For a criticism of some alternative readings, see Code [1978].)

From the point of view of one who wishes to claim that universal essences are substances, there are in a way two false premisses in this argument. First, the universal 'man' (or 'human soul') is in a sense the substance, and essence, of all the particular men, though these are not identical with one another, so it is not true that 'things whose substance (and essence) is one are themselves one'. No doubt they may be said to be one 'in form' or 'in definition' or 'in substance', but they are not one 'in number', which is what our premiss here evidently means. (The meaning is made explicit in the repetition at Z16, 40^b17.) But in another and stricter sense particular men do not have definitions, and so do not have essences, i.e. substances. In this second sense, there is only one thing that the universal essence is the essence or substance of, namely itself (as Z6 affirms). So if we count it as belonging both to the particular men and to itself, then it is in this stricter sense the substance of just one of the many things to which it belongs, so it is not true that 'it must be the substance of all or of none'; while if we count it as belonging to the particular men but not to itself then it is a substance but 'is the substance of none' of those things to which it belongs. There is, therefore, only one way of *accepting* all of Aristotle's premisses in this argument, and yet *still* maintaining that universal essences are substances, and that is by supposing that the universal essence does not count as 'belonging' to the particular things of which it is the essence; it perhaps 'belongs' to itself, but not to anything else. But unless we suppose further that particular things are somehow excluded from the universe of discourse of this argument, that is surely impossible. For 'belonging' is one of Aristotle's most general expressions. Besides, we have noted that the repetition of this argument at *Z*16, 40^b23–4 does suppose that a substance will *belong* to something other than itself.

It seems to me, then, that there is no way of accepting this argument while still maintaining that the species-form is a substance. It also seems that we cannot accept the argument while still maintaining that it is particular men, i.e. particular compounds of form in matter, that are substances. For it is difficult to say of these that they belong to, and are the substance of, something other than themselves. So this argument will allow as substances *only* the particular forms or essences, that belong to one object and no more.

$^b15$–16: The premiss that a substance is always a subject of predication and never a predicate was, of course, the suggestion explored in *Z*3. In that chapter it was argued to lead to the conclusion that only matter is a substance, and this conclusion was rejected as impossible. So you would suppose that the premiss is now discredited. But we saw that Aristotle would be able to resist the argument of *Z*3, and the beginning of our present chapter very much suggests that he is now resisting it, since he claims there that there are two distinct ways in which things underlie (38^b5–6). Thus, apparently, both matter and the compound are permitted to be substances by this premiss. One could suppose that it would allow particular forms as well, but it is difficult to believe that Aristotle was bearing that point in mind when he began the chapter. For it would surely lead him to speak of *three* ways of underlying, as at *Z*3, 29^a2–3 and at *H*1, 42^a26–31, and not just of two. This second argument, then, does not seem to harmonize too well with the first.

If we attempt to accept the premiss of this argument while still retaining the species-form as a substance, then we must say the same as before. Not only are these universal forms not to be counted as 'belonging' to the particular compounds that fall under them, but also they are not to count as 'predicated' either of them or of their matter. But this is surely impossible.

38^b16–34

In the suggestion with which this paragraph begins it is apparently being taken for granted that a species such as 'man' or 'horse' is an essence and *is* a substance. (I return to this point at the end of the present note.

Meanwhile I assume it.) Then the suggestion is that a genus such as 'animal' admittedly cannot be counted as a substance in quite the same way as these are, but yet can be counted as a substance in a different way, because it is 'present in' the species. But it is not immediately made clear why this might entitle it to be called a substance. Let us call this the thesis of the paragraph. For ease of reference I divide the discussion of this thesis into four sections thus:

(i) $^b18-23$: 'In that case there is evidently . . .'
(ii) $^b23-9$: 'Further, it is absurd and impossible . . .'
(iii) $^b29-30$: 'Further, it will be present in Socrates . . .'
(iv) $^b30-4$: 'In general it follows . . .'

Whereas it is clear that section (iv) concludes against the thesis, the bearing of sections (i)–(iii) is rather less clear. For example, both Ross and Frede & Patzig suppose that all of (i)–(iii) argue against the thesis, Woods [1967] that they all argue for it, and Hughes [1979] that (i) argues for it, while (ii) and (iii) argue against it. (Woods has now revised his view [1991].) Since section (ii) seems to me to be the clearest of the three sections, I shall begin with it.

(ii) $^b23-9$: The main claim here seems to be quite clear, namely: any component of a substance would itself have to be a substance (cf. *Phys* I, 6, 189^a34-5). Moreover, the main line of the argument for it seems to be quite clear too: the components of a thing are prior to it, but a non-substance (such as a quality) cannot be prior to a substance. There is then a subsidiary argument for this last claim, which would appear to be this: what is prior to a substance 'either in formula or in time or in generation' would have to be 'separable', but (we supply) a non-substance cannot be 'separable'. Finally, it seems to me that there is not much room for doubt about how this argument bears upon the thesis of the paragraph: it gives an argument *for* it. For the thesis was that the genus must be allowed to be a substance, since it is 'present in' the species, and the species is agreed to be a substance. We have only to supply this little link: since the genus is present in the species, the genus is a component of the species. It then follows from this argument that since the species is a substance the genus must be one too, which is just what the thesis claims.

The main line of argument, one may observe, is one that is well supported by what Aristotle has himself said elsewhere. A substance such as a species has a definition which is given by a formula (Z4, 30^a6-14). Every such formula has parts, and the parts of the formula are prior to that of which it is the formula (Z10, *passim*). The genus 'animal' will in fact be a part of the formula of the species 'man' (Z12, 37^b12-14, and often elsewhere). It follows that the genus is prior to the species. But 'substance is prior in every way' (Z1, 28^a31-3), so indeed a non-substance cannot be prior to a substance. Thus, if the species is a substance, as is assumed, then the genus must be. Admittedly, the subsidiary argument seems to be fallacious. For the priority of genus to species that has been argued for is a special case of the priority of part to whole, namely priority in definition. But it was not *this* priority, but what is called here and in Z1 'priority in time' that was equated in Z1 with separability (28a33–4). Moreover, Z10 has pointed out in connection with a different case of the priority of part to whole that this priority does *not* necessarily bring with it the priority of separate existence (35b22–7). So we need not accept the subsidiary argument, which claims that *any* kind of priority must entail separability. But still the main line of argument seems to be quite soundly based, and the thesis of the paragraph is well supported by it.

(For 'priority in generation' in b28, see Z1, 28a31–b2 n. It is tempting to emend 'in generation' (*genesei*) to 'in knowledge' (*gnōsei*) so that the three kinds of priority mentioned here match those mentioned in Z1. But nothing hangs on this.)

In 39a3–14 we find a reply to this argument, namely that it is a mistake to suppose that a substance has components at all (from which it would follow that, if the species is a substance, then the genus cannot after all be a component 'present in it'). Ross, who sees this section (ii) as directed *against* the thesis, supposes that that is what Aristotle is saying here. On his account, the thesis that genus is in some way a substance is already refuted by the previous paragraph (38b8–16), and the present section (ii) is drawing the moral that since it is a non-substance it cannot count as 'present in' the species. But (*a*) it is not clear why the thesis should have been put up for consideration at all if it is taken to be already defeated by the previous paragraph; and (*b*) on this reading Aristotle must be presuming here that the genus *is* 'a quality' and 'an attribute' of the kind that he calls 'coincidental' (i.e. a *pathos*; see Z1, 28a19 n.), simply because it is universal. This consequence is accepted by Frede & Patzig, and by Hughes [1979], 118–19. But of course Aristotle usually *contrasts* a genus such as 'animal' with a mere quality, and on my reading that is just what he is doing here. He cites a quality as an evident example of something that is not a substance during an argument designed to show that that very different thing, the genus, must be allowed to be a substance.

(i) b18–23: If, as I have argued, section (ii) offers an argument *for* the thesis of the paragraph, then one certainly expects that the intervening section (i) will be speaking for it as well. I offer a paraphrase of the section on this assumption.

The thesis claims that the genus is present in the essence [i.e. as part of its definition]. In that case, it will itself have a definition [as assumed in Z10; see 34b20–32 n.]. This definition is not a definition of everything in the substance [i.e. the species], but that makes no difference, for it does nevertheless express the substance of something. [In one sense it expresses the substance of the species,] just as the species 'man' in its turn expresses the substance of the particular man [but without expressing everything in the particular man, for it does not express his matter]. So the same thing will happen again [i.e. the relation between particular men and the species 'man' will repeat itself in the relation between the various species of animal and the genus 'animal'. For equally, in another and stricter sense] the definition of the genus will express the substance of that thing in which it and it alone is present [i.e. of the genus 'animal' itself]. On this reading, section (i) does not so much argue for the thesis as explain what it is; the argument comes in section (ii).

Now of course I read a great deal between the lines to obtain this paraphrase, and the section can be read quite differently. Ross, for example, takes this section to be an attack on the thesis, and would offer a paraphrase on the following lines. (This adopts the alternative translation noted for $^b19$–20.)

The thesis is that the genus should be counted as a substance. In that case, it must have a definition [since every substance has. But the genus does not have a definition, or at any rate a *summum* genus does not. However, we may waive this point, for] it makes no difference even if there is not a formula of everything in the substance [i.e. even if the genus has no formula]. Nevertheless the genus will be the substance of something in the same way as the species man is the substance of particular men. So the same objection can be made again. For the genus animal will be the substance of [all animals, since the class of all animals is] that in which it is present as something peculiar to it. [But we have already proved, in 38^b8–16, that nothing can be the substance of many things, and the thesis must therefore be rejected.]

Ross's supplements to the text are, no doubt, no more speculative than my suggestions, but the argument that he extracts from it does seem to be a ludicrously bad one. The leading premiss is that nothing is the substance of many things. Then, in order to show that if the genus is a substance it will have to be the substance of many things, Aristotle claims that the species *is* the substance of many things, and that the genus will be similar. But then it is completely obvious that what disqualifies the genus disqualifies the species too; yet even Ross does not think that Aristotle means here to disqualify the species. It is surely much better to suppose that at least in *this* paragraph Aristotle is *not* insisting upon the point that nothing can be the substance of many things. If this is granted, then it seems to me very difficult to see this section as raising an objection to the thesis (except that its *first* sentence, claiming that the genus will have a definition, *could* certainly be seen as raising an objection).

On anyone's view, this section must be regarded as extremely elliptical, and one may make various further suggestions as to how the thought should be filled in. (The versions given by Woods [1967] and by Hughes [1979] are both different in detail from mine, and from each other, though we all agree that the section aims to speak for the thesis rather than against it. The versions given by Heinaman [1980] and by Frede & Patzig are also different from one another and from Ross, though they all agree that the section objects to the thesis.) There are, moreover, several further translations available at various points in the passage, some of them based on variant readings of the text which are not without support. I conclude that one's interpretation of this obscure section (i) of the discussion must be dictated by one's interpretation of the rather clearer section (ii) that follows it.

(iii) $^b29$–30: The bearing of this brief remark is obscure, and the text is also insecure. An alternative reading (adopted by Jaeger and by Frede & Patzig) is 'Further, it will be present in Socrates as his substance, so that . . .'. It seems to me probable that this cryptic pronouncement is intended to attack the thesis rather than to support it, but one cannot, I think, be at all confident. Speculation seems to me unprofitable.

(iv) $^b30$–4: Sections (i), (ii), (iii), and (iv) begin 'In that case. . . . Further. . . . Further. . . . In general it follows . . .'. So what one *expects* is that section (iv) concludes, and perhaps summarizes, the several points leading up to it. This expectation is evidently disappointed, for section (iv) clearly concludes Aristotle's *attack* upon the thesis of this paragraph. It says that 'it follows' that if man and other such things—i.e. other species, presumably—are substances, then no component in the definition of such things can be the substance of anything. There is no doubt that we are meant to add 'and therefore no such component can be *a* substance', so the thesis of the paragraph is rejected. The genus is not a substance (though the species is). It is also claimed to follow that the genus does not exist apart from its particulars, and this again very probably means 'its particular species'. But what are these conclusions supposed to follow *from*? Nothing that has yet been stated, it appears. We can only conclude that our text is awry; some lines must have fallen out between sections (ii) and (iv), which gave the argument from which (iv) is said to 'follow'.

Now a relevant argument is given later in the chapter, in the fourth paragraph at 39^a3–14, and particularly in 39^a3–8. But this is clearly presented as an *alternative* line of argument, both in its opening sentence at $^a3$ and again at $^a8$ ('for this reason *also*'). So we cannot mend matters by transferring these lines to an earlier position, to fill the gap in the reasoning. In fact it seems to me that we just do not know what the argument might have been that Aristotle first used to counter the interesting objection of section (ii). (There is perhaps a slight hint to be extracted from 39^a15 below, but it is too slight to be of any real help.) But even if I am wrong about the relation between paragraphs (1) and (2), and it is really paragraph (1) that is supposed to supply the argument—despite the fact that that argument so obviously disqualifies the species as well as the genus—all the same, we still have to say that there must be something wrong with the text of this paragraph. For the structure 'In that case. . . . Further. . . . Further. . . . In general it follows . . .' cannot be used to open with a defence and to end with an attack.

My discussion of this paragraph has presumed that when the thesis of the paragraph is stated at the outset it is being assumed that the (universal) *species* is a substance, and that this assumption is still retained when the thesis is finally rejected. Since this point is a crucial part of the dilemma presented by Z13 as a whole, I now re-examine it.

There are features of my translation which embody this presumption. Thus at $^b18$ I translate 'as for instance animal is present in man and horse', whereas one might equally translate 'as for instance the animal is present in the man and the horse', or 'as for instance an animal is present in a man and a horse'. Similarly at $^b21$ one might translate 'as the man is the substance of the man in whom it is present', and again at $^b30$–1 one might translate 'if a man and other things spoken of in the same way are substances'. No argument can hang on whether a translation contains 'the' or 'a' or no article at all, and what Aristotle is talking about can only be gathered from what he says of it.

Here the most salient point is that what he is talking about is said to have a definition. This must rule out the view that it is particular men such as Socrates and Cleon (Z15, 39^b20–40^a7, 40^a27–$^b4$). It should also rule out the suggestion that he is speaking of the particular forms of these men, i.e. their souls, for a particular form is no more definable than a particular compound. At any rate, the arguments of Z15 would apply equally to both. But in that case it must be the universal man that is under discussion. A further argument is this. Suppose that one is convinced by the arguments of paragraph (1), and accepts that no universal can be in the fullest sense a substance. But suppose also that one wishes to claim that universals can be substances in some weaker sense. Then what candidates might one suggest? A full-blooded Platonist would no doubt think of the *highest* universals, such as unity and being, as the best candidates (Z16, 40^b16 ff.). One more in tune with Aristotle's way of thinking would surely opt for the *lowest* universals, i.e. the indivisible species. But who would pass over both of these suggestions, and instead advance the claims of the *genus*, as the *best* candidate for a universal substance, because it is present in particular substances? This is surely absurd. It is only sensible to put forward the genus, on the ground given here, if one takes it that the species is already accepted as a substance.

I therefore conclude that paragraphs (1) and (2) cannot be harmonized; (1) argues that the species is not a substance, but (2) presumes that it is.

38^b34–39^a3

This brief paragraph would follow very happily after 38^b8–16 and before 38^b16–34. It is not specially concerned with the status of the genus in contrast to the species, or more generally with the ingredients of the definition of a substance, but once more with *any* universal. The two arguments presented in 38^b8–16 may certainly be summarized as showing that 'on this basis, *none* of the things that belong universally is a substance', and the further reason alleged here is equally general: *no* universal 'signifies a this, but rather such a kind of thing'. It was, of course, urged in Z8, 33^b19–26 that a form must signify such a kind of thing, and not a determinate this, if it is to be able to play its appropriate role in generation. But in Z8 it was not inferred that a form could not therefore be a substance. Here the inference is drawn (as it also is in B6, 1003^a5–9), though here we are offered a different reason for saying that a universal must signify such a kind of thing, namely that we cannot otherwise avoid 'the third man' (and other objections).

The argument of 'the Third Man' is well known to be the argument stated in Plato's *Parmenides* at 132 A–B, though Plato originally applied the argument to large things, and the debate soon transferred it from large things to men. In outline, the argument goes thus. Suppose that the various particular men are all men by virtue of their shared relation to some one form, the form of man. (This is the One-over-Many assumption.) Then this form of man is not the same as any of the particular men that share this relation to it (the Non-Identity assumption). But it is itself a man (the Self-Predication assumption). Hence, both it and the particular men we began with share the common characteristic of being a man, which is to say that there is some one form to which they share a relation (the One-over-Many assumption again). But this latter form cannot be the same as any of the things that share this relation to it (the Non-Identity assumption again). It is therefore a 'third man', over and above both the particular men and the form of man that we began with. (And since it too is a man, by the Self-Predication assumption, there must by the same reasoning be a 'fourth man' as well, and similarly a fifth, and so on, *ad infinitum*.) To confirm that this was how Aristotle himself saw the argument, see fr. 4 (Ross) of his *Peri Ideōn*.

Now it seems obvious to us that the simplest way of blocking this argument, as stated, is by denying the Self-Predication assumption, i.e. by claiming that the form of man is not itself *a man*. From Aristotle's perspective, one might try to put the point in this way. Admittedly, the form of man is 'what a man is', i.e. what is defined when one defines 'a man'. And so in some sense the form of man is man. But it is *not* another *particular* man. Or, in other words, the form of man is 'such a kind of thing', and is not 'a this'. That is why we cannot say that it, and the particular men, *share* a relation to some 'third man', for it simply is not the right kind of thing to *share* any such relation, since it is not a this, while particular men are. That is very much what Aristotle seems to offer, as his reply to the Third Man, at *SE* 178^b36–179^a10; it is also the reply that he indicates here. (Whether the reply is adequate is of course another question. No doubt it is correct to say that the form of a man is not itself a man. But can we equally say that the form of a unity is not itself a unity, and the form of a being is not itself a being?)

The problem of 'the Third Man' is clearly a problem that affects *all* universals (i.e. universals in *our* sense of the word). As the title itself indicates, there is no special immunity for universals that are, as Aristotle would say, 'indivisible forms and essences'. So Aristotle's claim in this paragraph is that 'man' and 'horse' signify such a kind of thing, and not a this, and *therefore* are *not* substances. This fits very well with his arguments in paragraph (1); it is evidently quite inconsistent with what is presupposed in paragraph (2).

39^a3-14

The claim of this paragraph is that a substance cannot be composed of substances, or at any rate not of substances 'present in it in actuality'. (This qualification is dropped at $^a8$, repeated—but apparently disregarded—at 39^a14-15, and dropped in the summarizing sentence at the end of Z16.) The most obvious suggestion concerning the relevance of this claim is that it counters the argument at 38^b23-9, which attempted to show that if the species is a substance then so is the genus. For that argument presumed that the genus was a component of the species, in fact a component of its definition, and it inferred (in accordance with Z10) that the genus must therefore be prior to the species. It added that what is prior to a substance must itself be a substance (apparently in accordance with Z1, 28^a32). But we are now told that, if the species is a substance, then either it has no components at all (cf. 39^a17-18), or—if it does—those components are not substances (at least, not 'in actuality'; they may perhaps be substances potentially). Thus, either the doctrine of Z10 is rendered pointless, since there never are parts of a substance which are parts of its definition; or the doctrine is denied, since the parts of a thing which are parts of its definition are no longer allowed to be prior to it; or it is admitted that there may be something prior to a substance which is not itself a substance, e.g. the genus to the species. Aristotle does not tell us here which of these alternatives he wishes to adopt, because indeed he does not himself say anything about how the claim of this paragraph bears upon the rest of his discussion. It is a suggestion of mine (which I shall reconsider later on) that it is intended to offer an alternative argument for the conclusion stated in paragraph (2), namely 'that nothing in the formula of such things [i.e. species] can be the substance of anything, [nor therefore can it be *a* substance]' (38^b31-2).

As for the argument proposed, it is the rather astounding claim that nothing whatever can be both one thing and two things. I call this astounding, because Aristotle takes it to imply that nothing whatever can both be one thing and *composed of* two things; hence, nothing has parts. He attempts to soften the claim by conceding that what is one thing may be *potentially* two, so that the parts of a thing may be allowed a potential existence while they are together and constitute the thing, on the ground that they are capable of an actual existence, i.e. when the thing is separated into its parts and no longer enjoys ('actual') existence itself. But still, he is claiming that when the parts are together they do not actually exist. And his reasoning is evidently this: if the parts did actually exist, they would have to be many. Hence the one thing that they are parts of would have to be many. But that is a contradiction. The argument is quite general, and Aristotle applies it to things of all kinds, not only to substances. (It is applied to lines at ^{a}6–7 and to numbers at ^{a}11–14, but neither of these are substances.) So understood, the argument cannot possibly be defended. But it might perhaps be defended if we took it as propounding a special principle *about substances*, as is suggested by the remark on Democritus at ^{a}9–11: it was because Democritus made atoms his *substances* that he was right to say that one of them could not also be or become two.

Actually, this remark introduces a new point. It has been conceded that in general a thing may be one thing and also *potentially* two, since it may be divided into two parts which would *then* exist actually. But Democritus did not concede this for his atoms, and presumably Aristotle would not concede it for a species-form. As forms in general cannot be created (*Z*8), so also they cannot be destroyed ('or anyway not in this way', i.e. by being separated into their components (*Z*10, 35^a30)). A species-form, then, is one thing and not even potentially two. If it has components, then they do not have even the *potentiality* for existing 'actually', i.e. in separation from it. This makes it appear that a substance cannot have components at all, and such a claim should not surprise us. For it is merely another form of the demand—which has been with us, in one way or another, ever since *Z*4, 30^a2–6—that substances should be in some suitable way 'simple'.

The demand naturally raises the question: can there be a definition of what is in this way 'simple'? Accordingly, the final paragraph of the chapter draws our attention to this problem.

My remarks so far have supposed that this 'alternative' argument in paragraph (4) is to be understood as an 'alternative', not to the argument of paragraph (3), but to the argument of paragraph (2). So its aim is to show that the genus should not be allowed to count as a substance, even if it is in *some* sense a 'part' of the species, and the species is a substance. That is, I think, the most natural way of taking it. But could it instead be construed as an alternative to the argument of paragraph (3), that *no* universal is a substance? Well, it would seem to be possible. One would take it as an argument against the claim of the most favoured kind of universal, i.e. a species or species-form such as man or human-soul.

For suppose that one is now convinced by the arguments of paragraphs (1) and (3) that only such things as *particular* men can count as substances. Nevertheless, these things have consistently in *Z*7–11 been taken to be *compounds*, namely compounds of a universal form in a particular chunk of matter. (If Aristotle recognizes such things as particular forms, then they also would seem to be analogous compounds; on this see *Z*15, 39ᵇ24–5 n.) By the argument of this paragraph, then, the components of such a compound cannot themselves be admitted as substances. Thus a particular chunk of matter is not a substance, or anyway not a substance 'in actuality' (cf. *Z*3, 29ᵃ26–7? *H*1, 42ᵃ27–8?), but also *nor* is the other component, the universal form. That is, an argument which is naturally seen as granting that the universal 'man' is a substance, in order to argue that its component, the genus 'animal', is not, *could* also be seen as one that grants that the particular man is a substance, in order to argue that its component, the universal 'man', is not. And, given Aristotle's general approach, we can very naturally infer that if a universal such as 'man' is not to be allowed as a substance, then no other universal will be allowed either.

It is possible that this is how Aristotle intended his argument to be taken. The argument of 'the Third Man' mentioned in paragraph (3) shows that the universal man is 'such a kind of thing', and not 'a determinate this'. When this point was mentioned in *Z*8 (in connection with a different argument, 33ᵇ19–26), it was not concluded that the universal therefore cannot be a substance; but just this conclusion is drawn in our paragraph (3). The supposedly 'alternative' argument then spells out why. For if the universal is 'such a kind of thing', then it can only exist *in* the particulars that are of that kind (*Z*8, 33ᵇ19–26 n.). That is to say, it will be a kind of 'component' of these particulars. Hence, by our argument in paragraph (4), if they are substances, then it cannot be.

So construed, paragraph (4) *can* be seen as correctly placed after paragraph (3). But it is certainly an objection to this construal that the comparison with Democritus then becomes inept. For Democritean atoms are indestructible, and so are Aristotelian species, whereas it is clear that particular men are not. On the other hand, this construal would explain why Aristotle does not here press his argument to the strong conclusion which his comparison suggests. He does not say that substances cannot have parts at all, but only that they cannot have parts *which are substances*.

39ᵃ14–23

The concluding paragraph notes that the result raises a problem over definition. For it has been argued (*a*) that no substance is composed of universals, and (*b*) that no substance is composed of (actual) substances, and from this it appears to follow that no substance is composite. Yet it also seems that only what is composite can be defined.

It is not at once clear whether Aristotle's thought is that (*a*) and (*b*) *together* generate the unwelcome conclusion, or that each *separately* does so. In the first case he would seem to be supposing that the two ways of being composite mentioned in (*a*) and (*b*) are together exhaustive of all possible ways of being composite, but this is surely very implausible. To avoid this, one might suggest that they need only exhaust those ways of being composite that are a prerequisite for definability, but this then invites the response that (*a*) by itself does that. For in Aristotle's view only universals are defined, and they are defined in terms of other universals. So in fact (*a*) by itself will generate the problem, without assistance from (*b*). By contrast, (*b*) will generate the problem only if we assume in addition that what is mentioned in the definition of a substance must itself be an (actual) substance, and one can hardly take (*a*) as supplying that assumption. So perhaps the best suggestion is that each of (*a*) and (*b*) separately is supposed to lead to the problem, but that (*b*) does so only with the help of rather more of the discussion of paragraph (4) than just this one thesis quoted from it. For we have already noted that the problem does seem to arise from paragraph (4) taken as a whole.

While it is perfectly clear that 'no substance is composed of substances' is quoted from paragraph (4), it has not actually been said anywhere in this chapter (as our text now stands) that no substance can be composed of universals. It has of course been said that no substance *is* a universal, and in paragraph (3) the claim that a universal signifies such a kind of thing, and not a this, was offered as a reason for this. Since the same claim is offered as a reason here, we must suppose, with our present text, that we have a reference back to paragraph (3). So the reasoning to be supplied is apparently this. By paragraph (3), no substance is a universal. By an auxiliary assumption, what is composed of universals must itself be a universal. Hence, as asserted here, no substance is composed of universals. By a further auxiliary assumption, only what is composed of universals can be defined, i.e. it is only this kind of composition that permits definition. Hence no substance can be defined. But what an extraordinarily roundabout way of reasoning! The two auxiliary assumptions are no doubt perfectly plausible in themselves, but why bother to introduce them at all? There is a much simpler argument, which goes like this. By paragraph (3), no substance is a universal. By *Z*10, 35ᵇ34–36ᵃ2 (or by *Z*15), only universals can be defined. Hence no substance can be defined. Why should Aristotle avoid this very simple argument in favour of one that is much more circuitous?

I am therefore tempted to the following conjecture. We have seen that paragraph (2) contains a lacuna, for it is lacking any satisfactory argument to show that the genus is not a substance while the species is. We now note that this concluding paragraph cites the thesis that no substance can be composed of universals as if it were a thesis that had already been established, though in fact it has not even been stated. (No doubt it would *follow* from the claim that no one thing can also be two things, but here it seems to be contrasted with the conclusion that is actually drawn from that claim in paragraph (4).) So perhaps this thesis was once part of the text and formed part of the missing argument in paragraph (2). If that is so, then presumably it was not *there* justified by the fact that a universal signifies such a kind of thing, and not a this. For it is quite clear that that justification would disqualify the species as well as the genus. At some time, however, the original statement of the thesis and its justification both fell out of the text. So it appeared here in the concluding paragraph without any obvious justification in what had gone before, and someone then added the justification that we now find here. Given the preceding paragraph (3), and a further but very plausible assumption, this *does* indeed justify the thesis. But it appears to justify too much. For it introduces the thought that *no* universal is a substance. That thought leads at once, and very simply, to the conclusion that no substance can be defined. But our concluding paragraph never states that very simple argument; it offers more circuitous arguments which would allow one to suppose that a species-form is a substance, and is a universal, and so is at least the right kind of thing to be defined. But, it points out, it is quite difficult to see how there could actually be a definition of it if, as has been argued, it must be regarded as incomposite.

On this account, the problem which our concluding paragraph is pointing to is the problem of 'the unity of a definition': it is the problem of explaining how a thing that does not have parts can nevertheless be defined by a definition which does have parts. To find the clarification of this problem 'in what follows' we should therefore look to *H*6, and perhaps also *H*3, and possibly to *Z*12 too. But a difficulty with this suggestion is that these discussions of the unity of a definition do not anywhere suggest that 'in a way [the species] can be defined, while in a way it cannot' ($^a21$–2). That is, they do not seem to suppose that 'in a way it cannot' (but cf. *H*3, 43^b30?). We could make rather more sense of this proposed solution, that 'in a way it can while in a way it cannot', if we supposed that it was particular compounds of form in matter that were now being counted as substances. For in one way these cannot be defined, since no particular can be defined; but in another way they can, in so far as their formal aspect can be defined. However, there seems to be no clarification of this 'in what follows', and perhaps the clearest statement of the point is one that we have had already, i.e. in *Z*10, 36^a5–9 and in *Z*11, 37^a26–9. The third suggestion, of course, is that it is particular forms that are now being counted as substances, and no doubt one could similarly say of these that their universal aspect can be defined and their individuality cannot. But there is nowhere where the *Metaphysics* could be said to clarify *this* point.

Epilogue to *Z*13

Our present text of this chapter contains two distinct and incompatible lines of thought. In paragraphs (1) and (3) it is argued that no universal is a substance, and these arguments cannot be understood as intended to allow that the universal species-form is an exception. Yet in paragraph (2) it is presumed that the species-form *is* a substance, and argued that for that reason the genus is not. Moreover, it is natural to take paragraph

(4) as continuing the line of thought of paragraph (2). So not only do we have two incompatible lines of thought both present, but also—as the text stands—they are interwoven. Moreover—as the text stands—they are brought together in the concluding paragraph (5), which refers back both to paragraph (3) (at 39^a16) and to paragraph (4) (at 39^a17). But quite apart from this, which is the main dilemma, we can anyway be sure that *something* must be wrong with the present text, since paragraph (2) makes no sense even on its own. The best hypothesis here seems to be that a crucial argument has fallen out.

By relocating the paragraphs, so that the order runs (1), (3), (2), (4), (5), we can at least unweave the two lines of thought. By deleting from (5) its reference back to (3), we can prevent them from ever being brought together, and this deletion is not without some independent justification, as I have argued. But although we may in this way attempt to *separate* the two lines of thought from one another, nevertheless the main dilemma still remains if both continue to be present. It is very difficult to believe that Aristotle could have been so blind as to present both of them in the same chapter, without even remarking on their incompatibility.

I therefore proceed to a conjecture, which is that he never did intend both lines of thought to be present simultaneously. The conjecture is that there was an earlier version of the chapter in which the species-form *was* counted as a substance, and a later version in which it was not. The crucial part of the conjecture is that (2) was part of the earlier version and was not intended to be part of the later version at all. So it is a mere accident that (2) survives in any form. As it is, we have seen that (2) survives only in a mutilated form, missing its crucial argument, and this is because in Aristotle's own mind the whole of (2) had been consigned to the waste-paper basket. But by accident only its middle portion actually suffered that fate. The conjecture is, then, that the later version of this chapter contained paragraphs (1), (3), (4), (5) as we now have them. The earlier version clearly cannot have begun with paragraph (2), so I posit a paragraph (1*) which once opened the discussion with an argument to show that nothing *more* universal than a species-form could count as a substance. (One needs only to alter a few words of our present paragraph (1) to obtain such an argument. Its leading premiss would be that things whose substance is one are one *in form*, not that they are one *in number*.) I also posit an earlier version (5*) of our present (5), which differed from our present (5) by lacking the words 'since a universal signifies such a kind of thing, and not a this' at 39^a16, and *perhaps* also lacked the words 'but perhaps in a way it can while in a way it cannot' at 39^a21. So the posited earlier version of the chapter contained (1*), (2), (4), (5*).

In this earlier version, (4) was of course intended to present an argument alternative to that of (2). But we may suppose that, when he came to revise the chapter so that it argued for a much stronger conclusion, Aristotle himself saw the ambiguity in (4) that I have mentioned.

He therefore determined to retain it in the new context (and—presumably—he failed to observe that the comparison with Democritus was now out of place). So he altered (1*) to (1), dropped (2), added the new (3), left (4) as it was, and made only a minor change in (5*) to form (5) as we have it. For the problem posed by (5) also arises on either version of the chapter, as we have noted. This then yields the later version (1), (3), (4), (5). The two versions are wholly different in their implications, but at least each is now coherent in itself, despite the fact that they share a good deal of their material.

The problem of the internal coherence of *Z*13 seems to me to be insoluble without some such conjecture as I have proposed, which isolates from one another the two incompatible lines of thought. But we still have to reconsider, in the light of this conjecture, the external problem of how *Z*13 relates to the rest of *Z* and *H*.

The conjectured earlier version presents little difficulty. So long as the universal species-form *is* still allowed as a substance, the claim that anything *more* universal than this is not a substance fits well enough with Aristotle's doctrine elsewhere. But there are two qualifications to be made to this statement. First, I shall suggest that much of *Z*16 is more in harmony with the final version of *Z*13 than with its supposed earlier version. (Similarly, *I*2, $1053^{b}16-17$ recalls the final version.) Second, there are two points where the summary at the beginning of *H*1 needs a special gloss, if conflict is to be avoided. (See *H*1, $42^{a}12-16$n., $^{a}21-2$n.) Setting these points aside, the supposed earlier version of *Z*13 is in fair harmony with the rest of *Z* and *H* (except that the end of paragraph (2) must conflict either with *Z*10 or with *Z*1).

But the later version is clearly not in any such harmony. Whether this version is taken as implying that only particular men, horses, trees, and so on, could be substances, or whether it is taken as implying that only their particular forms could be substances, in either case it is clearly not consistent with the main thrust of *Z*4–11 (as I argued in the prologue). It is also contradicted by the opening of *Z*15, which implies that both universal forms and concrete particulars are substances, before going on to argue that no particular is definable. It is also at odds with the natural way of taking the bulk of *Z*17–*H*6, as we shall see. This must then be explained by the hypothesis that the later version is later than most of the rest of *Z* and *H*, and its effect is simply to destroy the overall coherence of the work. But why should Aristotle have wished to destroy his earlier discussion in this way?

Well, he must presumably have changed his mind over the acceptability of universal substances. This could have been because he had come to believe in particular forms, and had resolved to rely on them instead of universal forms; or it could have been because he came to give more weight to the criterion of independent existence, and to feel that only concrete particulars could satisfy it; or no doubt other motives could be suggested. It is possible that the interpretation which I mentioned first in the prologue to this chapter is on the right lines. Perhaps he had come to think that *all* kinds of perceptible substance were unsatisfactory candidates for that title, since all fail at least some of the desired criteria, and that only God could fully satisfy the requirements. But, for whatever reason, it seems that he must have changed his mind, yet also that he never carried out the reconstruction of *Z* and *H* that this change of mind so clearly demanded.

CHAPTER 14

This chapter professes to turn against the Platonic forms some arguments already stated in chapter 13. From the summary at *H*1 we see that the Platonic conception of forms was associated in Aristotle's mind with the idea that universals are substances. ('And the [Platonic] Forms are closely connected with the universal and the genus, for it is for the same reason that they are thought to be substances', 42^{a}15–16.) This no doubt explains why he now passes to the topic of Platonic forms, which occupies all of this chapter and much of the next. But it is less easy to say in what way the discussion of this chapter proceeds 'from the same considerations' as were also employed in chapter 13. I return to this question in my final note on the present chapter.

39^{a}24–30

The hypothesis to be refuted is introduced as the conjunction of two theses: (*a*) that the forms are 'separable substances', and (*b*) that the species-form is 'composed of' the genus and the differentiae, so that the genus is 'present in' the species. Thesis (*a*) is shortly re-expressed as the thesis that a form is 'separate and a this' (39^{a}30–1); it is natural to take this as implying that the form is a special kind of particular (cf. *Z*15, 40^{a}8–9, and *Z*8, 33^{b}19–26 n.). Thesis (*b*) reminds us of the thesis of paragraph (2) of the previous chapter (38^{b}16–18), which was there (allegedly) refuted without any reference to thesis (*a*). Whatever Aristotle meant when he said that this chapter proceeds 'from the same considerations' as the last, at any rate it is clear that the theses to be refuted are closely similar in each case. But the argument that he offers here appears to be quite different. It focuses on the question of whether the genus is *the same* in each of its various species, and that question was never raised in (our text of) chapter 13.

As he at once concedes, the genus 'animal' is the same *in formula* whether it is considered as something 'present in' the species man, or as something 'present in' the species horse. The question he wishes to raise is whether it is *numerically* the same in each case. One might suggest that Aristotle is relying on thesis (*a*) when he supposes that this is a fair question to raise, i.e. that he would grant that questions of numerical identity make sense only when it is particulars of some kind that we are considering.

(At ^{a}26–7 Aristotle's Greek is more literally rendered 'For if the forms exist, and the animal is in the man and horse . . .'. Occurrences of the noun 'animality' throughout my translation of this chapter represent occurrences of the phrase 'the animal' in the Greek; similarly for other abstract nouns. Cf. *Z*13, 38^{b}16–34 n., p. 198. For the specimen definition of man as a two-footed animal, see *Z*12, 37^{b}8–14 n.)

39^a30-^b6

In this paragraph Aristotle begins by claiming that, if there is a Platonic form of man, then there will also be Platonic forms of its components, and so in particular a Platonic form of animal. This presumably relies upon the thesis of chapter 13, that if a substance has components, those components must themselves be substances. Then in $^a33-^b2$ he argues very briefly that the animality in man and in horse cannot be the same, and in $^b2-6$ he adds a further difficulty for the Platonist, which is apparently something of a digression from his main line of argument. He returns to the main dilemma in the next paragraph, arguing antithetically that the animality in man and in horse must be the same.

$^a33-^b2$: Aristotle's argument is simple: the forms of man and of horse, he assumes, are 'separate' (or 'apart') from one another, so nothing that is 'in' the one can also be 'in' the other. But the argument is over-simple, for why are we bound to suppose that the forms of man and of horse are so separated? Why should we not say that these forms overlap, and so have a part in common, that part being the genus that is 'in' both? Clearly the text contains no answer to this question.

It seems probable that this gap in the argument arises because Aristotle intended to take over an argument from Plato's *Parmenides*, but failed to notice that it does not work so well in the application that he gives it. Plato's argument concerned not the relation of genus to species but that of form to particular. Supposing that the form was in some sense 'in' the particular, he had asked whether it was the whole of the form, or only part of the form, that was present in each particular. Then, construing the form as something that occupies a space in its own right, he had urged that the first alternative was impossible, since the form would then be 'separated from itself' (*Parm* 131 A–B). Plato's covert assumption that a form may be construed as occupying space, so that the terminology of part and whole is applicable in a fairly literal way, is perhaps reflected in Aristotle's overt assumption that the form is 'separate and a this'. But since Plato is talking about particulars, he is entitled to assume that two particular men (say) are 'separated from one another', and have no part in common. Aristotle, however, is considering the relations between forms themselves, and cannot just assume that two distinct forms, both species of the same genus, cannot have a part in common. In this case, the point needs arguing, and it is not at all clear what argument one might supply on his behalf.

$^b2-6$: Aristotle moves to a further objection, no better than the last, this time concerning the relation between genus and differentia. His thought appears to be this. Since it is true to say that some animals are two-footed, and since according to the Platonic theory the word 'animal' always imports a reference to the form of animality, and the word 'two-footed' always imports a reference to the form of two-footedness, there must be some relation between these two forms which is stated by 'some animals are two-footed'. But, he objects, the Platonist cannot say what this relation is supposed to be. It clearly will not do to say that the form animality 'participates in' two-footedness if this means that the form itself is a two-footed thing, for on the same principle it would also be a four-footed thing, and nothing can be both. (Cf. Z12, 37^b18-21.) But, having pointed out (quite correctly) that *this* account of the relation will not do, Aristotle seems at once to assume that no *other* account is available either. He dismisses, apparently as meaningless, the suggestions that the two forms might be 'in contact' or 'intermixed', and assumes that the Platonist must then be reduced to silence. But in fact it is quite clear how the Platonist should answer: 'Some animals are two-footed' says that the form animality and the form two-footedness are each parts of some 'larger' form (e.g. the form of man).

If this answer seems unexpected, it is because *we* now apply the terminology of part and whole, to describe relations between universals, in exactly the opposite way to that which is in question here. *We* consider the extensions of the (one-place) predicates involved, and treat the subset relation as the relation of part to whole. So on our account 'some animals are two-footed' is taken as 'saying' that the set of animals and the set of two-footed things have a common part (i.e. a non-null intersection). But then on our account 'man' is a part of 'animal', i.e. the set of men is a part (non-null subset) of the set of animals. Our Platonist, however, was initially credited with the view that 'animal' is a part of 'man', so he is naturally taken as using the part–whole relation in exactly the opposite sense from us, because he is thinking of intensions rather than extensions. This leads straightforwardly to the answer I have just given on his behalf.

39^b7-16

Aristotle now takes up the other half of his dilemma. He supposes that he has shown that the animality in man must be different from the animality in horse, but now proceeds to argue that that view too is untenable. The main argument, which is very confusing, is apparently completed by $^b14$. The last few lines indicate, without discussion, two further questions that might be pressed.

$^b7-14$: Aristotle's first observation is that, on the hypothesis in question, there will be very many things ('practically an infinite number') that have animality as their substance (i.e. essence). Since he offers as his reason for this claim that it is not coincidentally (but essentially) that man [or: a man] is composed of animality, it appears that the 'very many' things that he is thinking of are the various species of animals, or possibly the various particular animals. This, however, appears to be true in *any* case (if we may discount Z13, 38^b9-15), and is not specially a consequence of the hypothesis that the animality in each species is different. One might have expected him to say rather that there will be very many of these animalities, each of them having animality as the whole of its essence, for this might seem more perturbing (cf. $^b15$–16 below). But in fact it is not until the 'further' in $^b9$ that he comes to speak directly of these animalities.

At $^b9$ he claims that there will be many things which are animality-itself, and these things evidently are the animalities in the various species. To say that each of them *is* the form animality-itself is evidently to imply that they cannot in fact be different from one another, and hence that they are not 'many' after all. Apparently as an argument for this claim, Aristotle asserts:

(i) The animality in each [species] is its substance (since man is essentially an animal).
(ii) Everything that the species is composed of is a form.
(iii) In that case it [sc. the animality in each species] will not be the form of one thing and the substance of another.

Hence:

(iv) Each of these animalities will be animality-itself.

It is difficult to reconstruct a coherent train of thought from these assertions. Without much confidence, I hazard the following:

(*a*) By hypothesis (39^a26, $^a31$–3) the components of the species are Platonic forms.
(*b*) So the animality in man is some Platonic form or other, i.e. it is the form *of* something or other, and the question is: of what?
(*c*) But what it is the form of it will also be the substance of, and conversely.
(*d*) And it is the substance of an animal (since man is essentially an animal).
(*e*) Hence it is the form of animality.

Of these assertions, (*a*) corresponds to (ii), (*b*) is a link put in by me, (*c*) corresponds to (iii), and (*d*) is supposed to correspond to (i). It may be objected to this reconstruction that Aristotle introduces his (iii) with 'In that case' (*oukoun*), which could equally be translated 'So' or 'Accordingly', as if (iii) were an intermediate conclusion, whereas I introduce my (c) with 'But', making it clear that I construe it as a further premiss. To this I can only reply that I cannot see how Aristotle's (iii) can be understood as anything other than a premiss, and I do not think that its introductory particle *need* be seen as preventing this.

The main difficulty with the suggested reconstruction is with my clause (*d*). Aristotle's (i) is ambiguous, and it may be taken as claiming that the animality in each species is *a* substance (rather than *its* substance). I have adopted the translation 'its substance', since that is what the supporting argument apparently aims to establish. But in either case Aristotle's (i) does not say that the animality in each species is the substance *of an animal*. In reply I can say only that I see no other way of obtaining what looks like an argument from Aristotle's own assertions. But even so, it is not at all a good argument. From the premiss that man is essentially an animal one may perhaps infer that the animality supposed to be 'in' man must bear some essential relationship to the form animality-itself. But it cannot follow that it *is* that form, rather than a different form—say the form of 'human animality'—which is special to man, though still essentially related to animality-itself. So on my account of the reasoning it is admittedly fallacious. But I have no other account to offer.

39^b14–16: Aristotle adds two further questions which require an answer from one who holds that the animality in each species is different, namely: (i) What is each composed of, and how does animality-itself enter into its composition? (ii) If its substance (i.e. essence) is just animality and nothing else, how can it exist apart from animality-itself? These are both perfectly good questions to raise. Concerning (i), the opponent is apparently committed to holding that the animality in man must have animality-itself as a part. For he began (in 39^a26) by supposing that, since man is essentially an animal, the form of man must have animality as a part. Now he is (allegedly) forced to concede that the animality that is a part of this form is not animality-itself, but is essentially an animality, so similarly it too must have animality-itself as a part. But then we may ask what *other* parts it is supposed to have. And if the answer is that it has no other parts, then we may move to question (ii), asking how, in that case, it is supposed to be distinguished from animality-itself. While if the answer is that it does have some other parts, then certainly it will be difficult to say what they are, and besides, the whole argument may begin again. For we may ask whether the animality-itself that is a part of the animality in man is or is not *the same thing* as the animality-itself that is a part of the animality in horse. (It is a pity that Aristotle does not make this last point explicit.)

We may conclude that, despite the weakness (or alternatively, the unintelligibility) of what appears to be Aristotle's main argument in this paragraph at $^b9$–14, nevertheless his general position in the paragraph is a strong one. If one has begun by supposing that each species of animal has animality as a part, then it will indeed be difficult to maintain the position that the animality in each species is different. But, as I have observed, there is no need to try to maintain this, for there is no sound objection to the view that the animality in each is the same.

39^b16–19

The argument of this chapter has concerned the relations, particularly part–whole relations, between one Platonic form and another. Aristotle ends with the claim that the same problems arise when one considers the relations between forms and particulars, and yet further problems too which are even worse. It is reasonable to suppose that he has in mind mainly the problems developed in Plato's *Parmenides*, which do indeed begin with problems concerning wholes and parts (at 131 A–E), but also include further problems too (most famously 'the Third Man', at 132 A–B). Aristotle concludes that there are no Platonic forms. If this conclusion is supposed to be based on the arguments that he has *not* given, concerning the relations of forms and particulars, then we cannot ask whether it is fairly derived. But if the argument that *is* given in this chapter is supposed to be contributing to the conclusion, then we must say that that is a mistake, for two reasons. First, Aristotle's dilemma has a perfectly good answer, as we have seen, and second, Aristotle himself says, at the beginning of the chapter, that it aims to refute the conjunction of *two* theses, (*a*) that there are Platonic forms, and (*b*) that part–whole relations hold between them as described. But presumably one could hold (*a*) without also holding (*b*).

In fact, the role of thesis (*a*) in the argument as presented is not at all clear. A natural suggestion would be that Aristotle views (*a*) as a presupposition of (*b*), i.e. he thinks that one never would be tempted to suppose that part–whole relations obtained between universals unless one construed universals as Platonic forms (as 'separate substances' and as 'thises'). But against this one must observe that in the previous chapter thesis (*b*) was put forward (at $38^b16–18$) without presupposing (*a*), but—if anything—as a premiss from which one might deduce (*a*). (More accurately, the suggestion was that from (*b*) one could deduce that a universal such as a genus was a substance; there was no suggestion there that it would also follow that a universal was 'separate' and a 'this'.) Moreover, thesis (*b*) was (allegedly) refuted in the previous chapter without any help from (*a*). This leads one to conjecture that the aim of the present chapter is to offer a new refutation of (*b*), which, however, does require (*a*) as a premiss, as suggested in $39^a24–30$n. But then it is *very* difficult to see why Aristotle should end the chapter by concluding that (*a*) is false. Given a demonstration that (*a*) and (*b*) are together impossible, one is entitled to conclude that (*a*) is false only if either one has shown that (*b*) is true, or one has shown that (*a*) implies (*b*). Clearly Aristotle has not shown either of these. And while it is possible that he believes that (*b*) must be true in some sense—i.e. that there must be something right about the claim that being an animal is a 'part' of being a man—the indications of our text are strongly against this. For the previous chapter has surely rejected (*b*). (I add that (*b*) will be rejected once more in *H*3, $43^b4–14$ and $44^a2–9$, where a much more interesting argument is employed.) So it seems that he must believe that (*a*) implies (*b*). The belief shows itself again in the next chapter at $40^a17–27$, though it is difficult to see any rational basis for it.

Given this underlying belief on Aristotle's part, one can see why he might introduce the present chapter as stemming 'from the same considerations' as the last. For the last chapter had argued that (*b*) was false, and he now aims to develop the implications of this point to show that (*a*) is false also. That is why the chapter ends by concluding that (*a*) is indeed false. But one has to admit that what actually happens in the chapter is not the desired demonstration that (*a*) implies (*b*), but something quite different—a new refutation of (*b*) which uses (*a*) as a premiss.

CHAPTER 15

This chapter argues for the familiar claim (first found at *An. Post* II, 97^b26) that no particular is definable. The claim is first argued for ordinary perceptible particulars, and is made to depend upon the fact that they have matter, and are therefore destructible. It is then argued for Platonic forms, which are supposed to be a special kind of imperceptible and indestructible particular. Finally a third argument is given, which is applied in the first place to perceptible but indestructible particulars, such as the heavenly bodies; but it evidently does apply to destructible particulars too.

39^b20–31

Aristotle begins by recapitulating the doctrine of *Z*7–9. (For the significance of this, see the prologue to *Z*7–9.) We must distinguish, he says, between the form or essence on its own and the compound which is that form taken together with matter. (Note here (*a*) that each is unambiguously said to be a substance, despite the argument of *Z*13 that no universal is a substance; (*b*) that Aristotle clearly has in mind particular compounds, not the universal compounds mentioned in *Z*11 and in parts of *Z*10.) Referring back to *Z*8, he reminds us that the form on its own cannot be generated or destroyed, though he adds here (as he did not in *Z*8) that this need not be taken as implying that the form exists always. His point is that the form does not undergo a process of coming to be or of ceasing to be, though it may nevertheless exist at some times but not at other times. (For comment on this, see *H*3, 43^b14–23 n.) The compound, on the other hand, can be generated and can be destroyed, and he apparently takes this to follow from the fact that it contains matter. So his reasoning is: (i) particular perceptible things are compounds of form in matter; (ii) what contains matter is destructible; (iii) what is destructible is indefinable. Of these, (i) may be regarded as axiomatic; (iii) will be argued in the next paragraph; and (ii) is supported here by the claim that it is the nature of matter to be capable of being and of not being (cf. *Z*7, 32^a20–2).

It may be noted that this support is inadequate. There are (in Aristotle's view) particular perceptible things that are indestructible, namely the heavenly bodies. These have 'matter for locomotion' but not 'matter for generation and destruction'. (That is to say, their matter is capable both of being and of not being in a given place, but it is *not* capable both of being and of not being the heavenly body that it is. Cf. *H*1, 42^a32–$^b8$ n.) Aristotle turns to consider the possibility of defining such things at 40^a27–$^b4$, so the fact that they are not covered by his argument here is not a serious omission. (But he fails to note that his argument here requires a qualification.)

$^b24$–5: 'Being for a house cannot come to be, only being for this particular house.' In these words Aristotle seems explicitly to distinguish two items, on the one hand the universal essence of any house, which is not generated, and on the other the particular essence of this house, which is. But when we follow through the implications of this interpretation, it becomes impossible to sustain.

First, if particular essences are being mentioned here, then Aristotle is saying of them that they are compounds of form in matter, and for that reason can be created. But contrast with this *H*5, 44^b21–9, which also seems to mention particular forms. If it does, then *H*5 says of them that they do not contain matter, and hence cannot be created, but exist and fail to exist without any such process. So if this passage and *H*5 both concern particular forms or essences, then they evidently contradict one another. But one might reply that *H*5 is either mistaken on this point, or misinterpreted, for there are other indications that particular forms contain matter. At *Z*11, 37^a1–2, we find: 'Everything has matter of some sort unless it is not a this but a what-being-is and a form itself in its own right.' Now the theory that Aristotle believes in particular forms will certainly maintain that a particular form is a 'this', since that is supposed to be the explanation of why Aristotle so often calls the form a 'this'. So this passage too implies that particular forms (if they exist) must have matter, in contrast to the 'form itself in its own right', which must here be the universal form, and has no matter. (But I should remark that an alternative text for 37^a1–2, adopted by Frede & Patzig, would not carry this implication.) In any case, Aristotle's general principles would seem to require particular forms to have matter. For if a universal form such as the form of man is 'indivisible' (*Z*8, 34^a8), and if particular forms are in some way instances of it, then how else would Aristotle explain their differentness, one from another, if not by supposing that they have matter of some kind?

But then, what is the matter of the particular form of this house? If we say that it is just the matter of the house, then the house and its particular form are evidently identified with one another, since each is a compound of the same form in the same matter. In support of this, one might point to those places where Aristotle does appear to suggest an identity between a particular material thing and its form (see *Z*13, prologue, p. 187); against it, one could point to other places where he distinguishes the two (notably *Z*13, 38^b8–15; *Z*16, 40^b16–24; *Λ*5, 1071^a27–9). But in any case the proposal seems to me absurd (*pace* Irwin [1988], ch. 12). If no distinction is to be drawn between the form of this house and the house itself, then this is just a way of saying that there are no particular forms; for the word 'house' is then applicable to particular houses, to the universal form of a house, and to nothing else that is different from these.

The alternative is to suppose that the matter of the form of the house is some different kind of matter, perhaps an 'intelligible' rather than a perceptible matter (cf. *Z*10, 36^a2–12 n.). The effect of this would be that the form of this house would be an imperceptible particular, as one might quite naturally suppose that the forms of living things, namely souls, are also imperceptible particulars. But it is clear that in the present passage Aristotle is not envisaging any such thing. When he says at $^b28$ that his argument applies to 'particular perceptible substances', this is not because he wishes to exempt imperceptible ones—for his argument would apply equally well to either kind of particular, since each is destructible—but because he is assuming that all particular substances *are* perceptible. Moreover, there is no suggestion in this paragraph (or in the next) either that we have two different kinds of matter to consider, or that there are two different kinds of particulars in question.

The first conclusion to draw is that our passage does not mean to mention particular forms or essences at all, and that the phrase 'being for this particular house' must therefore be differently interpreted. I see no great difficulty in this: the claim that being for this house is the kind of thing that can come to be need not be any more than a roundabout way of saying that this house can come to be. Similarly at *Cael* I, 9 the context makes it quite clear that a contrast between 'being for a circle' and 'being for this circle' (278^a8–9), and again between 'being for a world' and 'being for this world' (278^a12–13), is just the familiar contrast between the form by itself and the compound of that form in this or that particular parcel of matter. If this is granted, then a second conclusion that one might draw is that, when he wrote this passage in *Z*15, Aristotle did not think that there were such things as particular forms. For otherwise he must have realized that they were highly relevant to his argument in this chapter, and yet in fact the chapter ignores them altogether, *despite* the suggestive phrase 'being for this particular house'.

39^b31–40^a7

At *A*6, 987^a32–$^b8$ (cf. *M*4, 1078^b12–30) Aristotle tells us that Plato held that one can only define unchanging things. In this paragraph he argues himself for the similar thesis that one can only define indestructible things. The argument has already been anticipated at *Z*10, 36^a2–11, and it is this. A definition must be a necessary truth, and incapable of being otherwise. It can therefore be known, in the strict sense of 'knowledge', which implies that what is known is always true. (Aristotle *says* that in this sense what is known is always *known*; it is charitable to correct this statement as I have done.) But a destructible thing can be known, in a looser sense of 'knowledge', only when it is perceived. At other times there is no guarantee that it still exists, and hence no knowledge of it, 'even though the same formula be retained in the soul'. But that is to say that such a thing cannot be known in the strict sense, and hence cannot have a definition.

This argument cannot be defended. Note first how it slides between knowing a truth and knowing an object. For example at $^a1$ the phrase 'what is capable of being otherwise' appears to be used of a contingent truth, but in the next line it is assumed to refer to a destructible object. To remedy this we may suppose that, when Aristotle appears to speak of knowing an object, he is thinking of knowing a certain truth about that object, namely a truth that states what it is. This, after all, is what a definition does. (Compare Z6, 31^b3-10 n.) But then the trouble with the argument is that it confuses knowing *what x* is with knowing *that x* is (i.e. exists). As long as 'the same formula is retained in the soul', we may surely continue to know what *x* is, even though—since *x* is subject to destruction and no longer being perceived—we have ceased to know that *x* is. Indeed, this must be admitted, if we can know (or rationally believe) that *x* has ceased to exist. For one must still know what *x* is, in order to know that *x* is not, otherwise one does not know what it is that is not.

Discussing definition in *Posterior Analytics* II, 8, Aristotle explicitly claims that one cannot know what something is without knowing that it is (93^a16-27; cf. 92^b17-18). (This is connected with his apparently odd idea—which we shall find also in Z17—that to know what a thing is is the same as to know why it is (93^a3-4; cf. 90^a14-23).) In the *Posterior Analytics*, of course, he was not explicitly considering the definition of particulars, and as a claim about knowledge of universals this is evidently controversial. But we may concede, for the sake of argument, that as a claim about knowledge of particulars there is *some* truth in it. However, the sense in which it is (or may be) true is a sense in which the 'is' is tenseless, or alternatively in which its tense may be adjusted to suit the case in hand. Thus perhaps I cannot know who Socrates is or was unless I also know that Socrates is or was, but this formulation deliberately allows for the possibility of simultaneously knowing both who he was and that he no longer is. So there is no good argument here for the thesis that destructible things have no definition.

It may also be observed, *ad hominem*, that Aristotle's own position apparently is that forms may exist at some times but not at others, even if they are not subject to destruction in the sense that they are ever in the process of being destroyed. This would apply to particular forms (if there are such things) and also to some universal forms (*H*3, 43^b16-23 n.). So his argument here, if valid, would show that none of these forms have a definition. But one would expect him to hold that all universal forms can be defined.

(I offer no comment on the connection between definition and scientific demonstration that is presumed here, since it is not important for the argument. It is discussed at length in *An. Post* II, 3–10.)

40^a8-27

Aristotle turns his attention to some supposed imperceptible and indestructible particulars, the Platonic forms. His discussion appears to equate the idea that these forms are particulars with the idea that they are separable (i.e. that they exist independently of the ordinary perceptible things that 'participate' in them).

He begins with the point that the definition of any Platonic form will use words already in common use, and that these are general words, true of many things. It would have been helpful if he had said at this point what exactly he meant to reject when he ruled out the possibility of coining a new word for the purpose. I return to this at the end of this note. Anyway, he proceeds to illustrate his point by remarking that one who tried to define you would list various characteristics that you have, e.g. that you are lean, pale, and so on, and that these characteristics apply to others besides you. He then makes the obvious suggestion that the *conjunction* of all these characteristics might apply to you and to nothing else, and apparently he grants that this might be so in the present case, i.e. when the object to be defined is you. But he claims that it cannot be so when the object to be defined is a Platonic form. The remainder of the paragraph then offers two arguments for this claim, the first at $^a15$–22 and the second at $^a22$–7.

$^a15$–22: First, he says, the names taken together, e.g. 'two-footed animal', will apply not only to [the form of] a two-footed animal but also to [the forms of] two-footed and animal. To back this up he then argues at length that, on the Platonic theory, the form of an animal and the form of two-footedness must both be separable. His argument here assumes (as in the previous chapter?) that on the Platonic theory the species-form *must* contain both the genus-form and the differentia-form as parts. And first he claims that they are parts of equal status, so that if one is separable the other is too, and then he seems to assume that it will be conceded that the genus-form is separable ($^a19$–22). As a further point he adds that both are 'prior in being' to the species-form—i.e. that it could not exist unless they do, while they each could exist without it—and this, I think, is taken to be a further reason for saying that both are separable ($^a22$–3). This completes his first argument.

Let us pass over the reasons for saying that on the Platonic theory there must be separable forms both of animality and of two-footedness. Granting this for the sake of argument, why should it follow that the phrase 'two-footed animal' will be true of both? The best that one can say seems to be this. It was part of the Platonic theory that the form of *X*-ness is itself an *X* thing (at least, until Plato saw the difficulties involved, e.g. the Third Man; see Z13, 38^b34–39^a3 n.). Aristotle appears to have held that the Platonic theory cannot avoid this if it insists upon construing the form as a particular, and that if the form is separable it must be a particular. Hence the form of animality will be an animal, and the form of two-footedness will be two-footed. If we bring in here the further point that whatever is two-footed is an animal, it can then be inferred that the form of two-footedness is a two-footed animal, i.e. that the phrase 'two-footed animal' is true of it, as well as being true of the form of man. But (*a*) it will not follow by any reasonable principle that I can see that the form of animality will be a *two-footed* animal, and anyway (*b*) Aristotle's objection only arises because of a special feature of his specimen definition of man. If we had defined a man as a wingless two-footed animal, there would be no reason to suppose that the whole phrase 'wingless two-footed animal' was true either of the form of animality or of the form of two-footedness or of the form of winglessness. One can only conclude that this first argument fails to establish its conclusion.

ᵃ22–7: The second argument begins like the first with a claim that on the Platonic theory there must also be a form of animality and a form of two-footedness, and it maintains that *these* must be predicated of many things. The reason given apparently supposes that *these* forms cannot be defined in terms of other forms, and so could not be known *via* such a definition, and hence must be known in some other way. While no doubt one might protest that 'two-footed' should be definable in terms of 'two' and 'footed', still we can accept the more general claim that there must be *some* forms that are not defined in terms of other forms; rather, other forms are defined (and known?) in terms of them. Aristotle's thought is, then, that these 'basic forms', as we may call them, can only be understood if they have instances, so that the word used to specify them (e.g. the word 'animal') is understood because it applies to many things, and in particular to things that exist in this world and are available to perception. This is an ingenious thought. On the Platonic theory the form of man does not depend for its existence on there being men, just as (I presume) the form of a unicorn does not depend for its existence on there being unicorns. So it cannot be argued that the word 'man' (or its definition), which by hypothesis is true of the form, *must* be true of other things too. But whereas Plato would wish to claim such ontological independence for all forms, Aristotle offers an epistemological reason for saying that it cannot be permitted for the basic forms, in terms of which the others are defined.

No doubt a Platonist would wish to distinguish between ontology and epistemology, but we need not pursue this issue further, for even if Aristotle's point is granted, it still will not yield the conclusion he is aiming for. On the position outlined, the Platonist is not claiming to be able to define the basic forms, but he does claim to be able to define other forms, by assigning to them a conjunction of characteristics. Each of these separately will characterize a basic form as well, and hence many other things too. But it still does not follow that the conjunction of all the characteristics will apply to anything other than the one form (as the case of the unicorn makes clear). So the second argument too misses its mark.

One might reply that even if the conclusion does not follow, nevertheless it is often true. From the Platonic viewpoint, Aristotle is exaggerating when he implies in his last words (ᵃ27) that *every* form is participated in.

Nevertheless a good number do have instances, including many that the Platonist will regard as definable, such as the form of man. So Aristotle can press his point in these cases, for the point that he intends is surely just this: what the Platonist will give as the definition of the form of man is simply the definition of *a man*. But then, what is given as a definition will be true of all men, and so cannot define one man in particular. It is curious that Aristotle never states his point in this simple way, but instead gives us two roundabout arguments which seem deliberately to avoid the premiss that there are men. For that reason, they fail in their purpose. But surely he did not think that the Platonist would deny this premiss?

The simple point is one that Aristotle does make elsewhere (e.g. *EN* I, 6, 1096^a34–$^b5$), but he there also suggests the Platonist's reply, which is that there are several characteristics that distinguish the form of man from other men. The form is (on this theory) a man, but it is a man who was never born and will never die, who exists eternally and without change, who is intelligible and not perceptible, and so on. If we build these characteristics into the definition of the form (as is suggested at *EE* I, 8, 1218^a10–12), then Aristotle's point is met. At the same time we meet the point that he probably had in mind initially, when he said that in defining a form the Platonist was not permitted to coin a new word ($^a10$). The 'new word' he was thinking of was no doubt the technical locution 'man-itself' (*autoanthrōpos*) or 'the very thing which is man' (*auto ho estin anthrōpos*), which is the Platonic locution for a Platonic form. He frequently complains that this locution needs explanation (e.g. Z16, 40^b30–4; *M*4, 1079^b3–11; also the passages just cited from *EN* and *EE*), and we have now suggested the explanation: the locution implies eternality, changelessness, intelligibility, and so on.

We may put the point more generally in this way. To refer to an abstract object one frequently uses a general term '*X*' together with what I shall call a prefix, which creates a singular term out of that general term. Plato used the prefix 'the *X* itself'; Aristotle uses the prefix 'what being is for an *X*'; we use such prefixes as 'the property of being an *X*', 'the class of all *X*s', and so on. Usually, if one is asked to *define* such an object, what one actually defines is the general term '*X*', not the prefix. As a rule, one cannot in any strict sense *define* the prefix, and Aristotle does not define his prefix any more than Plato defines his. But we understand the prefix in the light of the author's theory about the objects referred to by means of it, and I would say that we understand Plato's theory at least as well as we understand Aristotle's. So it was not a good idea, on his part, to complain that one cannot define the objects that this theory is concerned with.

What is wrong with Plato's theory—at least, the version of it that Aristotle is considering here—is not that it cannot be understood, but that it cannot be believed. It is quite absurd to suppose that something which has the other characteristics that Plato assigns to forms could also be a man. So modern Platonists (and, some hold, the later Plato himself) reject the view that the form of an *X* is itself an *X*. But they may still retain that feature of the Platonic theory that Aristotle evidently saw as the cause of the trouble, namely the thesis that forms have a 'separate existence'.

40^a27–$^b4$

In this final paragraph, Aristotle returns from the supposed imperceptible particulars posited by Plato to the more familiar perceptible particulars, but this time he pays particular attention to those that are (in his view) indestructible. His opening words 'As has been said' are surprising. There appears to be nowhere where he has already said that even indestructible particulars are indefinable.

We are tempted to suppose that his argument here relies on the principle introduced earlier, that a definition should state a necessary truth (39^b31–40^a2). If so, then his point is that it is merely a contingent truth that the sun possesses those attributes that one might use when trying to formulate a definition of it, e.g. 'going round the earth' or 'hidden at night' or—to add an instance from Plato—'being the brightest of the heavenly bodies' (*Tht* 208 D). (The attributes that Aristotle cites are cited in poetical vocabulary, and so are presumably quoted from someone; but we do not know from whom.) That is to say, there is no necessity that the sun should have these attributes, or that it should be the only thing that has them. But when one takes into account the fact that Aristotle's conception of necessity was different from ours—for example, he makes no distinction between physical necessity and logical necessity—this seems dubious. It is, for him, an eternal truth that the heavenly bodies behave as they do, and for that reason it would apparently qualify (in his eyes) as a necessary truth.

Alternatively, one might suggest that his point is that we do not, in the strict sense, *know* these things to be true, since they are truths concerning perceptible objects but go beyond what can actually be perceived (cf. *Top* V, 131^b19–30). This would relate his argument here to his previous claim that a definition can, in the strict sense, be known (39^b31–40^a2). But perhaps it is more plausible to suppose that his point is that we can at least *imagine* these things to be otherwise: we can imagine that the sun should stand still, or be visible at all times, or that there should be another body just as bright as the sun and behaving just like it. If so, then the underlying assumption is that a definition should state a truth that cannot be imagined otherwise. (In either case there will be a conflict with *H*4, 44^b12–15.)

These divergent accounts make a difference to the assessment of Aristotle's argument from a modern perspective. We are nowadays familiar with the claim that for each individual that comes into being there is a necessary truth true of it and of it alone, namely one that states which other individual(s) it must originate from if it is to exist (cf.

Kripke, *Naming and Necessity*, 112–15). So if all that is required of a definition is that it should state a necessary truth, it is nowadays controversial to claim that a particular individual cannot be defined. But if a definition should state something that can be known a priori, or that cannot be imagined otherwise, then the thesis of the necessity of origins poses no threat to Aristotle's position. We may also agree with him that definitions in this sense are inherently general, and that no 'concrete' (i.e. perceptible?) particular can be defined, though we should prefer to reserve our position on 'abstract' particulars (e.g. forms, classes, numbers, and the like) which perhaps do not deserve the title 'particular'. But both we and Aristotle will find it a problem to say whether God can be defined; it is a pity that Aristotle's discussion in this chapter fails to consider the question.

CHAPTER 16

This chapter has two parts. In the first, Aristotle returns to his list of the things commonly held to be substances in *Z*2, 28ᵇ8–15, and argues that most of them are not actually substances. In the second, he argues once more that no universal is a substance, and then offers a diagnosis of the Platonist's fundamental error. The two parts appear to be independent of one another, though the concluding sentence brings both together: it states once more that no universal is a substance, which is the claim of the second part, and that no substance is composed of substances, which is apparently taken as the moral to be drawn from the first part.

40ᵇ5–16

The 'things commonly thought to be substances' are no doubt the things listed at *Z*2, 28ᵇ8–15 as those which 'most clearly seem' to be substances, and listed again at *H*1, 42ᵃ6–11 as 'agreed by all' to be substances. Aristotle here tells us that most of them are 'potentialities', and presumably he means it to follow from this that they are not substances. (Cf. *Λ*3, 1070ᵃ18–20, with Jaeger's text.) The examples that he gives are the parts of animals and the elemental stuffs such as earth and fire and water. In the latter case it is clear from ᵇ8–10 that Aristotle wishes to say that they are only 'potentialities' because they are not 'unities'. It appears that he means the same point to apply to the parts of animals too, even though the word 'unity' cannot be understood in quite the same way in the two applications. But admittedly the text does not quite say this.

If we look just to the reasons that Aristotle states, they are these. First, at ᵇ6–8, he claims that an animal's parts do not exist, except as matter, when separated from the animal. From this he apparently infers that when not separated they are merely potentialities, and hence not substances. This inference is puzzling. Then, returning to the point at ᵇ10–16, he notes that one might wish to say that the parts (when attached) exist both potentially and in actuality 'on the ground that they have principles of movement deriving from something in the joints'. In some cases, he adds, the part retains this principle even when detached. (His usual examples are insects, such as centipedes, where he observes that the animal may be cut in half and both halves will continue to move as before, at least for a time. See, e.g., *Anim* 412ᵃ19–22; *PN* 467ᵃ18–22; *PA* 682ᵃ4–8; *IA* 707ᵃ24–ᵇ5.) Nevertheless, he bluntly concludes without further discussion that this would be a mistake: the parts only exist potentially, and then only when 'they form a continuous unity by nature', i.e. when they make up a whole animal formed as nature intended.

Now we know that, in Aristotle's view, nothing counts as, say, an arm or a leg unless it can fulfil the function of an arm or a leg, which is principally a question of its being able to move in certain ways. The second passage suggests that what Aristotle is concerned with is the *source* of this capacity. Does the arm contain within itself whatever it is that enables it to move as it does? His first suggestion is that it does not, because it evidently loses this capacity when detached from the rest of the body. But then he notes that there are exceptions, for in some cases the detached part can still move. This evidently suggests that its 'principles of movement' must be, to some extent, within it. Yet he seems to deny the significance of this point, for he simply reaffirms that the part only has a potential existence, though he gives us no explanations. We *can* supply an explanation if we bring in the thought that an animal is a unity in a way in which its parts are not. It is a unity in so far as the source of its activity is wholly within it, and so it exists and acts independently, i.e. independently of the activity of anything else. By contrast, the source of the activity of its parts is not wholly within those parts, so the part does not move independently. Even if, in some rare cases, a part of the body can move independently of the other parts when it is detached from the whole, still this is of no significance; and the reason is that the parts evidently do *not* move independently when they are *not* detached. On the contrary, the animal acts as a whole. It is, as one might say, a 'unit of action', while they are not.

Supposing that this is broadly correct, we still have a puzzling question to consider: why does Aristotle put his point by saying that the parts are 'potentialities', or that they only exist 'potentially'? It is of no help here to look back to the previous discussion in Z13 of the principle that the parts of a substance are not substances themselves. It was said there that what is actually one thing may be potentially two things, though it cannot actually be two things. Thus the two halves of a still undivided line cannot be said to exist actually, but they may be said to exist potentially, on the ground that they *can* exist actually, and will do if they are separated from one another (39^a4–7). But Aristotle cannot mean us to apply this line of thought to the parts of an animal, for he is insisting that a separated hand, not capable of fulfilling the function of a hand, is *not* actually a hand. What, then, is it that is merely 'potential' about a fully functioning hand that is part of a man? How could such a 'potentiality' be realized, so as to become a corresponding 'actuality'? And if no such realization is possible, then in what sense is it a 'potentiality'?

The explanation can only be this: when Aristotle says 'potentiality' what he means is just 'matter'. This is indicated by the phrasing of his opening sentence, where he first claims that a functioning part of an animal 'is a potentiality', and then adds that when it is separated and ceases to function 'then *too* it is as matter'. So to call it a potentiality is to imply that it is matter, and so far as one can see it is to imply nothing more. We have a parallel in Aristotle's definition of the soul as 'the substance as form of a natural body that potentially has life' (Z10, prologue). A body which has a soul as its form is not one that has life merely potentially; it is one that has life actually, and no further 'realization' of its potentiality for life is possible. Aristotle has put in the word 'potentially' because he so constantly associates matter and potentiality, and he wishes to emphasize that the body is the matter, and the soul the form, of this form-in-matter compound. As for the association between matter and potentiality, this arises because Aristotle always thinks of matter as 'capable both of being and of not being' (*Z*7, 32^a20–2; *Z*15, 39^b29–31; cf. *H*1, 42^a27–8; *H*2, 42^b10). When one thinks through the implication of this, the relevant potentiality that the living body has is not that it potentially *has* life, but that it potentially *lacks* life. That is, it is because the same body can persist *without* life that it counts as the matter of the living thing. Similarly, then, with the parts of the body. The potentiality that characterizes a functioning hand is that it can *cease* to function, and it is only in that sense that it 'is' a potentiality.

But, finally, one should note that from Aristotle's own perspective even this cannot be quite right. For on his account the hand cannot survive the loss of its functions, and so should not really be counted either as 'matter' or as 'potentiality'. According to the suggestion canvassed in *Z*10, 35^b22–7 n., it is only the flesh, bone, and sinew of which the hand is made that merits this description. According to further suggestions canvassed in *Z*11, 36^b24–32 n., we may need to retreat to even more 'remote' kinds of matter before we find something with the right capacity 'both for being and for not being'. Aristotle's paradoxical thesis that a dead hand is not a hand is here causing needless trouble.

$^b8$–10: The elemental stuffs earth, water, air, and fire are denied the title 'substance' because 'none of them is a unity, but as it were a heap, until they are concocted and some unity is formed from them.' In what sense is a clod of earth, or a drop of rain, 'not a unity'? It cannot be in quite the same sense as that in which a whole animal is a unity though its parts are not, for a clod of earth is quite capable of manifesting its own proper 'activity' independently—i.e. it will move downwards, seeking its natural place at the centre of the universe. In fact, what Aristotle says suggests a quite different reason: the earth is not 'a unity' because something better can be made of it. For example it, together with some other ingredients no doubt, might be 'concocted' into a more developed material, say wood, from which a genuine unity, such as a tree, was formed. ('Concoction' is Aristotle's regular word for the chemical transformation of a less developed into a more developed material; see e.g. *Meteor* IV, 2, *passim*.)

As I noted at *Z*2, 28^b8–15 n., Aristotle quite frequently shows that he thinks of things that exist by nature as forming a hierarchy from the less developed to the more developed, with the elemental stuffs at the bottom of this hierarchy and animals at the top. The development in question is a development from what is more in the nature of matter to what is more in the nature of form, and when he sets out this hierarchy at the beginning of *PA* II he adds that things lower in the hierarchy exist *for the sake of* things higher in it ($646^a8-{}^b10$). So this perhaps suggests another way in which the elemental stuffs do not 'exist independently', i.e. they would not exist at all if they were not needed for the composition of more developed things. Evidently the same could be said of the parts of animals too. But the point that is made here is different: in contrast to the animal part, the clod of earth is characterized as a 'mere potentiality' in the light of its potential to be developed into something better, and said to be 'not a unity' in comparison to the 'more unified' nature of that better thing.

$^b11$: For the translation 'and the closely related parts of the soul' see Ross's note. It is perfectly natural to think of the 'perceptive part' of the soul as 'closely related' to the organs of perception, the 'locomotive part' to the organs of locomotion, and so on (cf. *Z*10, prologue). Aristotle implies that his argument holds equally for these. No doubt they can be denied the title 'substances' on much the same ground, i.e because they do not function independently of one another. But it is even more difficult to suggest any sense in which they could be said to be 'potentialities', or to 'exist potentially', or to be 'matter'. (To avoid these problems, Frede & Patzig offer a quite different way of taking this clause. But their proposal introduces other problems, which seem to me even worse.)

$^b15-16$: In *GA* 773^a Aristotle gives several examples (including Siamese twins at $^a4$) of parts of animals that are unified 'by growing together' in an unnatural way. It is difficult to think of examples of parts unified 'by force', unless he simply means that two fingers might be tied or glued together.

40^b16-27

Aristotle turns abruptly, and without any explanation, from the 'commonly accepted' substances to the Platonic idea that the universal is a substance, and the more universal more of a substance. It is mildly odd that there is no acknowledgement in the present paragraph that the claim of the universal has already been discussed and dismissed in *Z*13. In fact the paragraph contains two arguments against the universal, and the first of them ($^b16-24$) is apparently a repetition of the first argument of *Z*13 (38^b9-15). It will be convenient to consider this first argument in three parts: $^b16-19$, $^b19-22$, $^b23-4$. The second argument at $^b25-7$ is new.

$^b16-19$: Elsewhere in Aristotle (e.g. *I*2, 1054^a13-19) the fact that unity is predicated in the same way as being, together with the premiss that being does not signify any one thing (*Z*1, 28^a10), is used to infer that the same holds of unity. Here, however, the point seems simply to be that whatever is is one, so that unity is a universal of the widest possible scope (cf. *B*4, 1001^a19–24).

Supposing that $^b13$ is to be translated 'the substance of unity is one', the argument is this. Assume that unity is the substance of the things that are unities. Then, since unity will be a single substance, all the various unities have the same substance. But things which have the same substance are the same thing, and this conclusion is manifestly absurd. This is an acceptable argument if its premisses are granted. The premiss that things whose substance is the same are themselves the same is Aristotle's premiss (repeated from *Z*13, 38^b14–15); the Platonist would not grant it. But the premiss that unity is a single substance is the Platonist's premiss, and Aristotle would not grant it. It would be fair for him to use it in an argument against the Platonist, *provided* that he made it clear that it was his opponent's premiss and not his own. For example, he could have arranged the argument (as I have just done) so as to present this claim not as a premiss but as a consequence of the thesis that unity is the substance of things. But that is *not* how the argument is actually presented in our text. In our text, Aristotle is clearly asserting this premiss in his own person. So either we must suppose that some suitable qualification has dropped out of the text (e.g. 'the substance of unity is one, *if there is such a substance*'), or we must look for an alternative interpretation.

The usual view is that the awkward premiss should be translated 'the substance of a unity is one', meaning: 'For anything that is a unity, there is only one thing that is its substance.' In context, this is not the most natural translation. Although the phrase *to hen* can certainly mean 'any unity' (or simply, 'any one thing'), and does mean this at $^b25$ below, still it can also mean 'unity' (or 'oneness'), and evidently does mean this both immediately before, and immediately after, its occurrence in $^b17$. The supposed change of use at $^b17$ is therefore unexpected, but not impossible. What is more difficult to explain is how, on this interpretation, the premiss is supposed to be relevant to the argument in hand. The best that one can say seems to be that it is intended to lead up to, or prepare the way for, the further premiss: 'Things whose substance is numerically one are themselves numerically one.' For in fact it is that further premiss that does all the work, and it needs no assistance from the claim that a single thing has but one substance.

$^b19$–22: Having argued that neither being nor unity can be the substance of things, Aristotle rather surprisingly adds that in the same way 'being for an element' and 'being for a principle' are not the substance of things ($^b19$), and a little later he adds [being for] a cause to this list ($^b22$). This suggests a connection between the present paragraph and the previous one. In the previous paragraph it was argued that various things are not substances because they are not (in a suitable sense) unities. Thus if x is a substance it must also be true that x is a unity. In the present paragraph Aristotle aims, amongst other things, to guard against a possible misunderstanding of his use of this criterion: he does not mean to imply that if *x* is a substance then unity is *the substance of x*. Similarly one might propose, as further criteria of substancehood, that if *x* is a substance it must also be true that *x* is an element (*stoikheion*) or that *x* is a principle (*arkhē*) or that *x* is a cause (*aition*). (Thus in Z13 the Platonists were said to hold that universals were substances because they were principles and causes (38^b7), and in Z17 Aristotle will adopt this criterion himself.) But again it must not be thought that this implies that being a principle, or being a cause, is the substance of *x*. Rather, to find the substance of *x* one asks *what* principle, or *what* unity, *x* is. (Why does Aristotle say 'being for a principle', where one expects him simply to say 'being a principle'? Perhaps because if being a principle were the substance of things, then it would be a substance, and according to Z6 it would then be identical with its essence; that is, being a principle would be the same thing as being for a principle).

Aristotle adds that being and unity have a better claim to the title 'substance' than do [being a] principle or element or cause, though he does not say why. (Alexander's explanation is that to say that *x* is a being, or unity, is at least to say something about *x* itself, whereas to say that *x* is a principle, element, or cause is to allude to how *x* is related to something else, since a principle is always a principle *of* something.) In any case he insists that neither being nor unity do deserve this title, for nor does anything else that is 'common to many things'.

$^b23$–4: The supporting argument for this claim is that: 'A substance belongs to nothing but to itself and to that which has it, i.e. that of which it is the substance.' This description of what a substance is clearly *allows* the species-form to be a substance, since it allows for there to be many things of which a substance is the substance. But the claim that nothing that is common to many things is a substance does not allow this. So the supporting argument fails to support what it is meant to.

In the epilogue to Z13 I conjectured that the first argument of that chapter (i.e. 38^b8–15) arose by modifying an earlier version, where the earlier version had allowed the species-form to be a substance, though the later did not. One might advance a similar conjecture for the similar argument here, pointing to the lack of fit between premiss and conclusion in these lines, and the difficulty over the opening lines at $^b16$–19 above, as indications that our present text is not the result of a single line of thought. But it is just as easy to regard these supposed 'indications' as no more than the result of some slight inattention to detail, and I think myself that the conjecture is without adequate motivation in the present case. Even if there were earlier and later versions of Z13, still it may well be that this part of Z16 was first composed as further support for the later version.

$^b25$–7: The second argument puts forward two premisses, (*a*) that a unity cannot be in many places at once, and (*b*) that what is common is in many places at once. From these we immediately infer that what is common is not a unity. If we suppose that this paragraph is intended to be read closely with the previous paragraph (as $^b19$–22 has indicated), then we can bring in here the thesis of that paragraph, that only unities are substances. It then follows that what is common is not a substance, i.e. that no universal is a substance.

This is not, however, the inference that Aristotle explicitly draws himself; rather, he infers that no universal exists separately from the particulars. At first sight, it appears that this conclusion may be drawn simply from the second premiss, that what is common exists in many places at once. For we have only to observe that what is universal is common, and that the 'many places' that such a thing exists in are evidently the places occupied by its particular instances, and it then follows that the universal exists where its particular instances do, and hence that it does not exist 'separately' or 'apart' from them. But, if we bear in mind the Platonic theory that Aristotle is attempting to combat, it could well seem that more is needed. For a Platonist might perhaps admit that there is a sense in which the universal may be said to exist *in* its many instances, but he would wish to add that it *also and in addition* has a separate existence. (That is why it does not depend for its existence on being participated in.) But we can rule out this suggestion too if we construe the argument differently, as relying on both of the two premisses explicitly stated and on a further premiss that is left unstated, namely that only a unity is capable of separate existence. For by the first two premisses no universal is a unity, and then by the third no universal does have separate existence. If this reconstruction is correct, then we can restate Aristotle's point without using the obscure notion of 'a unity'. In the vocabulary of Z8, 33^b21–2, and Z13, 39^a1–3, a universal must be thought of as *such a kind* of thing, and the claim is that what is such a kind of thing can only exist *in* the things of that kind. There is no other kind of existence that could apply to it, and so it cannot be regarded as 'separable'.

But we are evidently supposed to infer further that, since the universal is not separable, it cannot be a substance. For the present point is offered as a further argument to what has gone before, and so presumably it is supposed to lead to the same conclusion. Moreover, in the present passage it would seem that Aristotle is ready to claim that every substance must be separable (though elsewhere he is more cautious). At any rate, the next paragraph begins by saying that the Platonists were *right* to suppose that if forms are to be substances then they must have a separate existence. This, however, creates a problem. For $^b16$–24 has continued to suppose that a substance must belong to something other than itself, so leaving us no alternative but to suppose that only particular forms can be substances; yet particular forms surely are not separable, and so cannot satisfy $^b25$–7. The only conclusion to draw is that there is nothing that can count as the substance of a perceptible thing. The next paragraph does indeed suggest this, for at any rate it switches its attention away from *perceptible* substances altogether.

40^b27-41^a3

This final paragraph proceeds to a diagnosis of the basic error of 'those who believe in the forms'. By this Aristotle clearly means the Platonists, and no doubt Plato himself in particular, but it should be noted that, since the word used is *eidos* rather than *idea*, the 'forms' in question may be taken to include the things that Aristotle calls forms as well as the things that Plato calls forms.

On the one hand, he says, the Platonists were right to suppose that if forms are to be substances then they must be 'separate'. But, he goes on, it was a mistake on their part to suppose that 'the one over many' is a form. In fact Aristotle must hold that it was a mistake to speak at all of a *one* over many, for we have just been told that the universal that is 'over many' is something common, and for that reason is *not* actually 'one'. But what he says here is that it is wrong to count this universal as a form. Yet that does not seem to be in itself an error—it would, after all, be quite an ordinary use of the Greek word 'form'—and presumably Aristotle's thought must be that it becomes an error when combined with the other assumptions about forms that the Platonists make. In particular, they take forms to be substances—and indeed, substances that are indestructible, as the next sentence adds—and therefore separable. When all these views are put together we obtain what is clearly a mistake, in Aristotle's eyes, namely the consequence that a universal is a single thing with an existence that is independent of its instances. For, he supposes, this can only lead one to think of the universal as if it were a Platonic 'paradigm instance' of itself.

Aristotle is agreeing with the Platonist, then, that there are some indestructible substances, and that these exist independently of the destructible substances that we know. He is agreeing also that these substances are forms, though here one suspects that this is more an equivocation than an agreement. For what Aristotle has in mind is primarily the unmoved mover of the universe, which is not at all the same kind of thing as the Platonist was thinking of. The Platonist was thinking of 'perfect paradigms', such as 'man-itself' and 'horse-itself', which are the same in form as things we know. This comes about, says Aristotle, because he cannot see what *else* to say about these indestructible substances: once one has decided that such a thing must *both* be 'one over many' *and* have an independent existence, no other conception seems to be available.

Aristotle therefore continues by pointing us towards his own conception of the indestructible substances: consider the stars, he says. It is not entirely clear what moral he means us to draw from the suggestion that we might never have seen them. What he actually says is that they would still exist even if we had never seen them. That is no doubt true, but does not seem very relevant. Should we perhaps understand him as implying that we could still know that they existed even if we had never seen them? This is not impossible, for in *Physics* VIII and in Λ6–10

Aristotle does profess to deduce that there must be an eternal rotation that is the primary movement in the universe, though his argument would not determine whether it is a rotation of something perceptible or something imperceptible. But of course the main message of that argument is that there must also be an unmoved first mover of that rotation, which is wholly immaterial, and not in any way like the perceptible things we are familiar with. This is what Aristotle calls God, and he takes it to be pure 'activity', and hence pure form. (He also *does* claim to know something of its nature, for its 'activity' is contemplation.)

41^a3-5

This brief sentence concludes the discussion of the universal (and of the Platonic form) which began in *Z*13. If the words 'and that no substance whatever is composed of substances' are due to Aristotle and not to an editor (cf. *H*3, 44^a11-14 n.), then we may apparently infer that Aristotle intended his discussion of 'the commonly accepted substances' at 40^b5-16 to form part of this discussion, however odd that may seem.

Epilogue to *Z*13–16

From the programme outlined at the beginning of *Z*3 (28^b33-6) one expects these four chapters of book *Z* to be devoted to the questions 'Is a universal a substance?' and 'Is a genus a substance?' Taking into account the recapitulation of that programme at the beginning of *H*1 (42^a12-16), one is not surprised to find also some discussion of the Platonic theory. Indeed, Aristotle's position seems to be that to claim that a universal is a substance is automatically to commit oneself to the Platonic theory. At any rate, this is so if we insist upon the point that a substance must have an independent existence, which in this case can only be taken to mean that the universal exists independently of its particular instances. For Aristotle takes it that this must inevitably imply that the universal is itself a kind of particular (an 'abstract object', as we would say), and that all the problems with the Platonic theory spring from exactly this point. He builds rather more into the point than we would. He seems to suppose that, if one accepts it, then one cannot avoid thinking of the universal 'man' as itself a kind of man, and that one must equally accept that some universals are parts of others in a very literal way. But in his basic claim he seems to be right: the heart of the Platonic theory is indeed the thesis that universals have an independent existence.

The arguments that Aristotle here presents against the theory are disappointingly weak. In *Z*14 (and earlier in *Z*13, 39^a3-14) he attempts to refute the idea that some abstract objects are literally parts of others, but the argument is wholly ineffective. In *Z*15, 40^a8-27 he attempts to exploit the idea that the form of man is itself a man, but the reasoning that he offers is strangely inconclusive, and the (unexpressed) thought behind it is once more easily parried. Much better, on this score, is his reference to the well-known Third Man argument at Z13, 39^a1–3. But in any case we may reply that this feature of the Platonic theory is by no means essential to it. When we turn to what is essential, we find in effect three arguments. At Z13, 38^b15–16 he urges that a substance must be a subject and not a predicate, but to this the Platonist simply replies that he sees no reason to agree: there is no ground for supposing that a thing predicated depends for its existence on the things it is predicated of. At Z16, 40^b25–7 he urges that a substance cannot be in many places at once if it is to be 'a unity', and to this the Platonist replies that it does not touch the point at issue. For the abstract objects that he believes in are not supposed to be literally 'in' the particular things they are predicated of, and they do not strictly occupy a *place* at all. The third argument we get twice, at Z13, 38^b9–15 and at Z16, 40^b16–24, and it relies upon the principle that a substance must be the substance *of* something, coupled with the premiss that no two things can have the same substance. Here again the Platonist would do well to reject the principle, for a universal may exist independently without being 'the substance of' anything at all. (But he could also allow, harmlessly, that it may always be regarded as the substance of itself, and of nothing else.) In any case, one may very rationally dispute the premiss that no two things can have the same substance, for elsewhere Aristotle himself shows little tendency to accept it.

Setting aside the question of how good these arguments are, we may at least agree that they are all relevant to the stated topic, i.e. whether a universal is a substance. We may also agree that, once Aristotle had decided to argue for the strong claim that *no* universal is a substance, it is not surprising that he should pay little separate attention to the genus. In our present text, the claim of the genus to be substance is treated only in the mutilated second paragraph of Z13 (i.e. 38^b16–34). On the conjecture that I have offered (in the epilogue to Z13), this formed part of an early version of Z13 but was not intended to appear in the final version at all. I would now extend that conjecture by adding Z14 too to the supposed early version, for there is then a common theme that runs through it all: we get into trouble if we suppose that *both* the species *and* the genus each count as substances, for this must lead to one substance being part of another. But I do not take it to follow that Z14 was not intended to appear in the final version. On the contrary, just as the final version continued to include Z13, 39^a3–23 (*almost* unchanged), so I would suppose that it continued to include Z14, entirely unchanged. So even in the final version the genus does receive some attention, i.e. in Z14, but only under the hypothesis that it is a Platonic form. In any case, there can be no charge of irrelevance against any part of either Z13 or Z14. But what of Z15 and Z16?

Z15 argues that no particular can be defined. No doubt this is something that Aristotle has long believed, but why should he choose to expound the point here, at greater length than he does anywhere else, when his stated topic is universals? (Note that there is no connection between the arguments of the main part of the chapter and those of 40^a8–27, which concern Platonic forms. It was not necessary to include the one for the sake of the other.) Again, the first part of *Z*16 (i.e. 40^b5–16) argues that most of the perceptible particulars commonly counted as substances are not really substances. What is this argument doing in a discussion of the claims of the universal? Both of these passages are surely digressions from the main topic of *Z*13–16. But is there any reason why Aristotle might have chosen to locate them in this section of his discussion and not elsewhere?

Well, it is possible that it was not really a 'choice' on his part, but is mainly accidental. His original discussion of the universal and the genus may have occupied only *Z*13 and *Z*14, and then been followed at once by the summary at the beginning of *H*1. (*Perhaps* *Z*17 intervened, but I am inclined to think not; see the prologue to *Z*17.) At some later stage he determined to write out more fully his reasons for saying that no particular can be defined, and since there was nowhere else in the existing version of *Z* that specially called for this discussion, he simply added it at what was then the end of *Z*. (*Perhaps* the original addition was just the first half of our present *Z*15, i.e. 39^b20–40^a7; it then occurred to him that the point could be turned into an argument against Platonic forms, so the second half was added too.) The history of *Z*16, 40^b5–16 may be similar. At *Z*2, 28^b13–15 he had promised to consider which of the things commonly held to be substances were rightly so held, though his basic programme for book *Z* (i.e. *Z*3, 28^b33–6) contained no place for such a discussion, and so it was at first omitted. Later he recognized the omission, wrote the promised discussion, and again added it to what was then the end of *Z*. Then he saw how its point too could be put to use in the discussion of the universal, since we must distinguish between the claims that every substance must be a unity and that unity is itself a substance. So this led to the rest of *Z*16. There is some independent reason for supposing that neither *Z*15 nor *Z*16 was a part of the original draft. As we noted, *Z*15 refers to the doctrine of *Z*8 as preceding (39^b26–7), though it is quite probable that once upon a time *Z*8 did not precede (see the prologue to *Z*7–9). Further, *Z*16 argues that most of the things commonly held to be substances are not so (40^b5–16), whereas *H*1 refers to these things as 'agreed by all' to be substances (42^a6, $^a24$) with no hint that 'all' no longer includes Aristotle. This makes it quite difficult to believe that when *H*1 was written *Z*16 stood shortly before it.

Whatever merit there may be in this conjecture, I think that one can anyway detect a feature common to almost all of *Z*13–16 as they now stand, distinguishing them from most of the rest of books *Z* and *H*, and that is their uncompromising stance on what does *not* qualify as a substance. For example, it is claimed that *every* substance must be a subject and not a predicate (38^b15–16), a this and not such a kind of thing (38^b33–39^a3), without parts that are substances (39^a3–4, 41^a4–5), an actuality rather than a potentiality (40^b5–6, $^b14$), in a strong sense a unity (40^b8–9, $^b25$), and I think we may add that it must be separable (40^b26–9). Contrast here the attitude of *Z*3, which had put forward the proposal that a substance should be a subject and not a predicate, but had apparently *rejected* this proposal precisely because it allowed too little to qualify as a substance (in fact, it allowed only (prime) matter). Moreover, *Z*3 had gone on to add that we must allow for *some* substances to be separable and to be thises, but had not insisted that all must be (29^a27–8). Contrast again *Z*8, which had insisted that a form must be such a kind of thing and not a ('determinate') this (33^b19–22), but had shown no tendency to infer that a form is not a substance (cf. 32^b1–2, $^b14$). Or again we may contrast *Z*10, which is happy to say that a form is a substance, and that it is given by a formula which has parts that are prior to the whole. But perhaps the most significant contrast is with *H*1, 42^a26–31, which reaffirms that (prime) matter is a substance, though it is a potentiality, not actually a this, and (presumably) not separable either; and which reaffirms too that (universal) forms are substances, though they are not really separable (and it is hard to see how they could be always subject and *never* predicate).

Evidently there is no reconciling this more conciliatory attitude which we find in most of the rest of *Z* and *H* with the harsh claim of *Z*13 (in its final version), and of *Z*16, 40^b16–27, that *no* universal is a substance—not even a form or essence; or with the harsh claim of *Z*16, 40^b5–16 that *no* kind of matter can be a substance—neither simple stuffs nor parts of animals—since it will not qualify as a genuine unity, and exists only for the sake of the more developed things that can be made from it. Perhaps we may also see *Z*15, in its present context, as making an equally harsh claim. For when *Z*13 had noted that if a substance cannot be a universal then it cannot be defined, it had gone on to suggest a compromise: 'Perhaps in a way it can, while in a way it cannot.' But *Z*15 allows *no* way in which a particular can be defined.

Did Aristotle suppose that these harsh and uncompromising claims of *Z*13–16 left us with any substances at all? It is very difficult to see how they could. Only particular forms will satisfy the three requirements that a substance cannot be universal, and cannot be matter, but must be the substance of something other than itself, to which it belongs. But particular forms of perishable things will not satisfy the requirements of being definable and being separable. The final paragraph of *Z*16 may be taken as a hint that only an indestructible particular form, such as Aristotle believed God to be, could qualify on all counts. But the hint is very slight, and the truth is that Aristotle does not tell us, here or elsewhere, what he takes to be the moral of *Z*13–16.

CHAPTER 17

In this chapter Aristotle explicitly takes a new approach to the question of what substance is, based on the idea that substance is 'a principle and a cause'. The argument is independent of anything else in book *Z* (though the theme of its closing paragraphs is taken up once more in *H*3). But the answer reached is familiar: the substance of a thing is its form.

Prologue to *Z*17

*Z*17 seems to stand outside the programme of discussion introduced at the beginning of *Z*3, summarized at the beginning of *H*1, and apparently brought to its close at the end of *H*2. If it had been designed as part of that discussion, one might have expected it to be placed somewhere in the treatment of form and essence in *Z*4–11, for we noted that that treatment several times *assumes* that substance, form, and essence are all to be equated, but does not seem to contain any very direct *argument* for the point. *Z*17 provides such an argument. Its thought is perhaps most closely connected with that of *Z*7, for in *Z*7 too the emphasis was upon the causal role played by form. But *Z*7 was concerned with the causes of coming to be, and it gave us little by way of analysis of the notion of a cause. By contrast *Z*17 is concerned rather with the causes of being, and it does begin with some analysis of what it is to be a cause. But the more important contrast is that *Z*7, being written originally for a different context, does not really address itself to the question 'What is substance?' That is precisely what *Z*17 aims to do.

One difficulty about understanding *Z*17, especially in its present context, is that it appears to pay no attention whatever to the problems that *Z*13–16 have brought to the fore. It simply has nothing to say on whether the form that it finds substance to be is or is not to be counted as something universal. Nor does it say whether this form is something that is always subject and never predicate (38^b15–16), not such a kind of thing but a determinate this (39^a1–3), definable (39^a18–20), or separable (40^b27–9). Perhaps, when he was writing *Z*17, Aristotle took the answers to these questions to be so obvious that they did not need stating explicitly, but if so that was a misjudgement on his part; his readers have not found them obvious at all. So it may well seem more probable that the questions were not fresh in his mind at the time of writing. If so, this can only be because *Z*17 was not written for its present context. There would be two ways of accounting for this (which are not mutually exclusive). One is to suppose that when *Z*17 was written the context was different, i.e. that there was at that time an earlier version of *Z*13–16, which aimed to allow the species-form to be a substance, as I conjectured in my epilogue to *Z*13. In that case the nasty questions that are posed by our present version would not then arise. (Since *H*2 also reverts to the idea that substance is form, but again without paying any attention to these questions, one is tempted to say that that must be the explanation in this case.) The other is to suppose that *Z*17 (like *Z*12?) owes its present placing only to an editor. For as I have noted, *Z*17 stands outside the programme that governs *Z*3–*H*2, but it *is* closely connected with parts of *H*3, and it seems probable that all of *H*3–6 owes its present position to an editor. One might, therefore, prefer to place *Z*17 after *H*2 in any case.

41ᵃ6–10

Aristotle proposes to attack the question 'What is substance?' from a new angle, and he once more suggests that if we can answer this question for perceptible substances, this will be of assistance when we turn to consider substances that exist independently of what is perceptible. (Cf. *Z*3, 29ᵇ3–12 n.) The new angle begins from the idea that substance 'is a principle and a cause of some sort'. Aristotle frequently runs together the notions of 'principle' and 'cause'; sometimes the two are explicitly equated (e.g. *Γ*2, 1003ᵇ22–4; cf. *Δ*1, 1013ᵃ17), but more usually his position seems to be that a principle is always a cause, though not conversely, since the principles are the more important causes. But so far as the argument of this chapter is concerned, we may concentrate simply on the notion of a cause, and take the opening premiss to be that substance is a cause of some sort. As at once emerges, Aristotle thinks of a cause in much the same way as we think of an explanation, i.e. as the answer to a question 'why?' So his premiss is that substance is the answer to a why-question (or, as we would prefer to say, that it is the salient factor mentioned in answering a why-question). A problem in interpreting the chapter is whether Aristotle is wishing to maintain that *every* why-question has a substance as its answer, or that only some do. On the face of it, one would expect the latter, especially as the premiss is that substance is a cause *of some sort* (*aitia tis*). But it is not too easy to say where Aristotle specifies just *which* why-questions are the relevant ones.

41ᵃ10–27

When one asks 'why?' one is always asking for the explanation of some fact, a fact being something that can be stated in a whole sentence. Many sentences do indeed state 'that one thing belongs to another', but Aristotle is mistaken in supposing that it is *only* of statements of this sort that one can sensibly ask 'why?' He provides a counter-example himself later in this paragraph, when he says that one can sensibly ask why it thunders (ᵃ24–5). Despite his gloss, the statement 'It thunders'—or perhaps, 'It is thundering' (the Greek is ambiguous)—does not state that one thing belongs to another; it is better assimilated to the explicitly existential statement: 'There is thunder (now).' Of course one can ask for an explanation of what is stated by an existential statement, but this is not a question of Aristotle's preferred form. The argument (as I shall understand it) would need some considerable reformulation in order to overcome this objection, but since it is not the most relevant objection, let us waive it.

Aristotle claims, then, that all why-questions ask why one thing belongs to another. The alternative that he notices is that it might sometimes appear as though one is asking why a thing is itself, and his suggestion seems to be that this appearance is due to an ambiguity. Thus it *is* possible to ask why an artistic man is an artistic man, and this *looks* as if it is asking why a thing is itself, but it is not really doing this. For in fact it is asking why a man is artistic, which is a perfectly sensible question, since it does ask why one thing (artistry) belongs to another (a man). But if the question is not taken in this way, and the questioner does really mean to ask why a thing is itself, then his question can only be dismissed as pointless. Aristotle offers a very odd explanation of why such a question would be pointless, namely that before one can ask why something is the case one must already know that it is the case ($^a15$, repeated at $^a23$–4, and recalled at 41^b4–5). I conjecture that his thought is this: before one can ask anything at all about x, one must first know that x exists (cf. Z15, 39^b31–40^a7 n.), and if one does know that x exists, then one also automatically knows that $x = x$. Thus the information that $x = x$ is not extra information, and hence requires no further explanation. He adds a further point that is more straightforward: the explanation of why $x = x$ will be the same in all cases, and so will not tell us anything more about x in particular. Moreover, any explanation—he rather suggests—could only be a merely verbal explanation. If we may fill out this thought a little more, it is that the law of identity is so fundamental a law that it cannot usefully be deduced from anything more fundamental. In any case, we may reasonably accept Aristotle's claim that it is pointless to ask why a thing is itself, if this does indeed mean asking why it is the case that $x = x$. But does it?

Aristotle is right to see an ambiguity in the words 'to ask why an artistic man is an artistic man', but his diagnosis of this ambiguity is not quite right. We may take the construction in a *de dicto* fashion, in which case it envisages someone asking, 'Why is it the case that all artistic men are artistic men?' or possibly, 'Why is it the case that this artistic man is this artistic man?' In either case, this is to ask for an explanation of a tautology (either of the form 'All F are F', or of the form '$x = x$'). We may sympathize with the claim that such a question is pointless. But the alternative is to take the construction in a *de re* fashion, in which case it envisages someone asking, *of* an artistic man, why he is an artistic man. (He formulates his question in some such way as this: 'Why is *that* man an artistic man?') No doubt we can accept Aristotle's comment that this is a perfectly sensible question to ask, and that it can very naturally be construed as asking why one thing belongs to another, namely why artistry belongs to a man (in particular to that man). But we should not accept the implication of his discussion in this paragraph, that such an ambiguity arises *only* where the question employs a *complex* term such as 'artistic man'. It is clear from $^a17$–18 that this is the implication. For he there cites the case of asking why a man is a man, or why an artistic thing is artistic, as *unambiguous* cases of requesting an explanation of a tautology. So his thought is that since in these cases only a *simple* term is involved, there is no possibility of construing the question as asking why one thing belongs to *another*. But the fact is that the *de re* construal is equally available in these cases too, and we can perfectly well take the question to be asking why one thing (being a man, or artistry) belongs to another (this particular man).

Either Aristotle has not seen that these questions could be taken in this way, or—if he has seen it—he nevertheless thinks that the questions, even when taken in this way, still ask why a thing is *itself*. I am inclined to think that the latter is correct, and that the formulation in $^a22$ ('why one who is a man is a man') is intended as an explicitly *de re* formulation. But my reason must be postponed to 41^a32–$^b9$n.

(At $^a17$ 'explanation' translates '*logos*', which is elsewhere translated 'formula'. At $^a19$ 'explanation' is supplied by me, and corresponds to no Greek word. Aristotle has no word which is standardly rendered 'explanation'—except, of course, for his words '*aitia*' and '*aition*', which I always translate as 'cause'.)

41^a27–32

Since a why-question asks why one thing belongs to another, Aristotle infers that 'what is sought is the cause'. Our text then adds 'and this is the what-being-is, to speak logically'. Alexander proposed that these words be deleted, for they apparently say that *every* cause is a cause-as-essence, which does not appear to be correct Aristotelian doctrine. Jaeger's text follows Alexander. Ross, however, defends the words, claiming that Aristotle did really mean to say that *every* cause is a cause-as-essence. Frede & Patzig follow Ross. This question is crucial to the interpretation of the argument of the chapter as a whole.

Aristotle's standard doctrine of causes is that there are four distinct kinds of cause, namely the material, formal, efficient, and final causes, and it is the formal cause that he also calls the cause-as-essence. (The *locus classicus* is *Physics* II, 3; most of this is repeated in the *Metaphysics* at *Δ*2.) The paragraph at once proceeds to remind us that there are different kinds of cause; for example, there is the final cause (that for the sake of which) and the efficient cause (that which first began the change). But it could be said that the examples Aristotle has in mind are intended to be examples of final causes, and efficient causes, which are also, at the same time, formal causes. At any rate he often observes that the final cause and the formal cause may coincide, and presumably they do in the case of a house or a bed, which he mentions here. Thus if one defines a house as a shelter for people and property (*H*2, 43^a16), one is both giving its purpose and at the same time its essence, or form. The same is true if one defines a bed as something for sleeping on. As for the efficient cause, he does not give an example here, but it would be natural to think of the cause of thunder just mentioned. (Thus $^a30$ recalls $^a24-5$ as $^a29$ recalls $^a26-7$.) But Aristotle tells us elsewhere that the cause of thunder, which is that fire is being quenched in the clouds, ought to be incorporated into a proper *definition* of thunder (*An. Post* II, 93^b8, 94^a5). He says very much the same of the definition of an eclipse both there and at *H*4, 44^b9-15. So here too, to give the efficient cause is at the same time to state part of the essence, i.e. form. We may recall too that in *Z*7 Aristotle argued that the efficient cause of any created object—whether an artefact or one that exists by nature—is always its form, but 'in another'. It thus begins to seem quite probable that Aristotle might really be meaning to claim that the final cause, and the efficient cause, are always at least a part of the essence.

Accepting this for a moment, what of the material cause? One might take the view that Aristotle is here ignoring it, as he does apparently ignore it in the *Posterior Analytics*. (At II, 11, 94^a21-4, where we expect a mention of the material cause, we in fact find something different, namely the way in which two premisses may 'cause' the truth of a conclusion.) Otherwise, I think the best that one could say would be this. When one looks at the way the four causes are characterized in *Physics* II, 3, it is quite difficult to see what why-questions are supposed to be answered either by the material cause or by the formal cause, for no relevant examples are given. But Aristotle's answer might be that in II, 1 he has already claimed that the matter and the form of a natural object must between them constitute its 'nature' (*phusis*), and that this 'nature' will be the cause of all its natural behaviour. So this perhaps is the kind of why-question that he thinks relevant: it is one that asks why objects of a certain kind naturally behave in a certain way. For example, if one asks why a tree falls in air but floats on water, the answer will be that it has *matter* of a certain kind. The matter of a thing is thus allowed as contributing to its 'nature', though Aristotle wishes to insist that its form makes a more important contribution. Moreover, in this same chapter of the *Physics* the 'nature' of a thing is identified with its substance, i.e. its essence (193^a9-11). Hence, when what is sought is a material cause, we can once again say 'and this is the essence, to speak logically' (taking 'logically' here to mean, as Ross suggests, 'abstractly' or 'schematically' or 'very generally' or something of the sort).

If all this is admitted, then it will yield an explanation of Aristotle's strategy of argument in this chapter. For he began (at 41^a9-10) with the idea that substance is a cause of *some* sort, and he will conclude in the next paragraph (at 41^b7-9) that substance is in particular a cause *as form*. How does he move from one to the other? Ross's suggestion is that he does it in the present paragraph, with his claim that *all* causes are formal causes. Nevertheless, it is very difficult to accept this interpretation.

First, the explanation of how the material cause may also be seen as part of the formal cause cannot be accepted. It is true that in the opening chapter of *Physics* II Aristotle does allow that the matter of a thing contributes to its 'nature', and he also equates a thing's 'nature' with its substance, but he does not *there* go on to equate nature, and substance, with form. He does quite often do this *elsewhere*, and in particular he does it in this very chapter of Z (41^b7-9 and $^b30$); but when he is in this mood he *excludes* a thing's matter from its 'nature' (41^b30-3). Indeed, one would not know what to make of the contrast between matter and form if matter is itself to be counted as a *part* of form. To maintain the interpretation, then, we must suppose that the material cause is not here being counted as a cause, presumably because Aristotle no longer sees it as answering a why-question. But it is difficult to believe that such a change of doctrine could be being slipped into the argument without any explicit statement at all. (By contrast, the fact that the material cause is missing from the *Posterior Analytics* is unsurprising. For the matter/form contrast never appears in *any* of the Logical Works, presumably because they were written before Aristotle had thought of it. For an extended argument to this conclusion see Graham [1987].)

Second, although Aristotle does indeed say that formal, final, and efficient causes may coincide with one another, he never says that they *always* do, and there would be many exceptions to such a thesis. Thus, to take one of Aristotle's own examples from *Physics* II, 7, one may ask, 'Why did they go to war?' and the answer may give either the efficient cause ('because they were raided') or the final cause ('in order to conquer') (198^a19-20). But it would surely be absurd to suppose that either of these causes should be built into the definition of going to war (in general), or—if there is such a definition—of their going to war (on this occasion). These are causes that are no part of the essence of that which they cause, no matter how 'logically' we are speaking. To maintain Ross's view, then, one must suppose that Aristotle failed to notice a large number of counter-examples to his claim, though they do seem rather obvious.

Apart from these objections, there are also two indications that Aristotle does not mean to put forward, and to rely on, the strong claim that Ross credits him with. (*a*) I have already noted that the premiss to his argument in this chapter is that substance is a cause *of some sort*, which surely suggests that it will be a particular kind of cause; (*b*) his own description of the relevant kind of cause is that it is a form by which this or that matter constitutes what it does (41^b7-9), and this sounds far too specialized to cover all causes. Indeed, it would not naturally be taken to cover all the examples of causes mentioned in this chapter. For instance, to apply it to the cause of thunder one would have to say that this is a case of some matter, namely clouds, acquiring a form, namely having fire quenched in them, by which they come to constitute thundering clouds. But while one *could* describe the situation in this way (cf. *Z*3, prologue), it is much more natural to say that this matter/form model is not appropriate to such a case, which is just what Aristotle does say about the similar case of the eclipse at *H*4, 44^b9–15.

If we reject Ross's interpretation, then we need to explain how the premiss that substance is some kind of cause can be made to yield the conclusion that it is in particular a cause as described, i.e. a formal cause of something that is (in the other sense) *a* substance. The alternative interpretation that I shall propose sees the *next* paragraph as introducing the crucial limitation. It sees the present paragraph largely as an aside, not intended to make any point that is important for the argument, save in its opening claim that what is sought, when it is asked why one thing belongs to another, is the cause. It can remain neutral on whether or not to retain the words 'and this is the what-being-is, to speak logically', but if they are retained then they are to be regarded merely as a comment on the two preceding examples, i.e. the cause of thunder and the cause of a house. They do not introduce any general and sweeping doctrine about all causes. And the phrase 'to speak logically' we may take simply as meaning 'to speak in the abstract and topic-neutral way characteristic of logic, by which something such as thunder counts as having a what-being-is, just because it has a definition. But, as *Z*4 argued, this is not what-being-is, or definition, in the primary sense.'

41^a32–^b9

At 41^a10–27 Aristotle argued at length that a cause is the answer to a why-question, and that any sensible why-question will ask why one thing belongs to another. He also implied, by his examples, that such a question will therefore need two distinct terms for its formulation. He now observes that the question 'What is a man?' does not expressly contain two distinct terms, one predicated of the other, and—to our surprise—he infers that it is not correctly formulated. This is evidently because he supposes that it *is* a why-question, and he proceeds to reformulate it as such. But why should he think that it is a why-question?

In *Posterior Analytics* II, 1–2 we find the same claim, supported by some unexpected analogies. He tells us there that there are four kinds of things one can enquire into, namely (i) whether a subject has a certain attribute; and, if so, (ii) why it does; also (iii) whether a subject exists; and, if so, (iv) what it is (89^b23–35). He then tells us that both in case (i) and in case (iii) we are asking whether there is a 'middle term' (i.e. a cause or explanation), and that both in case (ii) and in case (iv) we are asking what that middle term is (89^b36–90^a1). What something is, and why it is, are—he says—always the same question (90^a14–15). He illustrates this thesis with the case of an eclipse: to ask what an eclipse is is the same as to ask why it occurs, i.e. why the moon is eclipsed, the answer in each case being that it is (or is due to) the light being cut off by the earth getting in the way (90^a15-18). He does not illustrate how the thesis would apply to the question what a man is (89^b35), but he continues to claim that it does (90^a31-2).

One may *speculate* that the line of thought is this. First, if to ask whether there are men is to ask whether there is a middle term, then perhaps the middle term that Aristotle is thinking of is a particular man (preferably available to perception, cf. 90^a24-30). This would be a middle term between 'man' and 'being', since we can say 'This is' and 'This [is a] man', from which it follows that 'Man is' (i.e. 'There are men'). The point is that this thought gives us a predication, 'This is a man', to parallel the predication 'The moon is eclipsed', and so allows us to offer a further elucidation. To ask what an eclipse is is to ask why eclipses occur, which in turn is to ask why *the moon* is eclipsed (90^a15-18). Similarly, to ask what a man is is to ask why there are men, which in turn is to ask why *this* is a man. So the general question 'What is a man?' is equated with the singular question 'Why is *this* a man?', as also happens in Z17. But although the questions are different in this way, nevertheless their answers will be the same, for in each case the answer will spell out what it is to be a man, i.e. the essence of a man, which this thing must possess if it is to be a man. However, the *Posterior Analytics* is so elusive on this topic that it would be rash to rely on it to interpret Z17. I therefore return to consider Z17 on its own merits, offering a slightly different train of thought to the same conclusion, but this time one that makes use of the confusion between the *de re* and the *de dicto* that we have already noted in 41^a10-27n.

One premiss to the reasoning is that substance is a cause of some sort, i.e. an answer to some why-question. The other premiss, which I now supply, is that substance is the answer to a what-is-*X* question. It is hardly surprising that this should be used as a premiss, for it is quite standard Aristotelian doctrine that the question 'What is *X*?' asks for the substance of *X*. Putting these two premisses together, we infer that the answer to a what-is-*X* question must also be the answer to a why-question, and hence that a what-is-*X* question must *be* a why-question. (This evidently illegitimate step is no doubt assisted by a recollection of the *Posterior Analytics*.) So we must now ask what why-question it is that is the same question as 'What is a man?', and I suggest that Aristotle's first thought now is that it is the question 'Why is a man a man?'. Understanding this latter as 'What is it about a man that makes him a man?', this is actually a perfectly sensible suggestion as to how to turn a 'What is *X*?' question into an equivalent why-question. But there appears to be this objection to it: the question 'Why is a man a man?' seems to be asking why a thing is itself, which is a silly question to ask. Because this point is important to his argument, Aristotle begins the chapter by devoting some space to it. Nevertheless he is drawn (subconsciously?) by the *de re* interpretation of what is being asked: it does seem to make sense to ask, *of* some man, why he is a man; at any rate, this does not ask for the explanation of a tautology. So he envisages someone asking: 'Why is that man a man?'—or better, to avoid even the appearance of a tautology, 'Why is that thing a man?'

On my speculation, we have now reached the same result as in the *Posterior Analytics*, but here Aristotle does not rest content with it. For he goes on to claim that the words 'that thing', in the question 'Why is that thing a man?' cannot actually refer to a man. His reason is that, if they did, then one would again be asking why a man is a man, i.e. why a thing is itself, and that is a silly question. The clause 'since the existence of the thing must already be given' at 41^b4-5 reminds us of this, for it reminds us that at 41^a15 and $^a23-4$ this was the reason for saying that such a question is a silly question. Accordingly, the words 'that thing' must refer not to a man but to something else, and the obvious suggestion for what else they might refer to is the matter of the man. So in the end the question is taken to be 'Why is that matter a man?', which genuinely does ask why one thing belongs to *another*. And the answer to the question, of course, is that the form of a man belongs to it. Hence the substance of a man is the form of a man, and generally substance is form.

41^b9-12

Aristotle has claimed that we can seek for a cause only where we have one thing predicated of another, for the question will be 'Why is it that *A* is *B*?', and the cause—if there is one—will be a middle term to be inserted between *A* and *B*, i.e. '*A* is *B* because *A* is *C* and *C* is *B*.' So it is possible that when he here mentions 'simple things' he has in mind propositions '*A* is *B*' which are 'immediate', i.e. have no middle term, and therefore no further explanation. If so, his account of how we gain knowledge of these is given in *An. Post* II, 19. But it seems more probable from his next sentence that he is thinking of simple and complex items, not of propositions. In that case his thought is that where we have a complex item, e.g. some matter *A* in a form *B*, then we can extract from it the predication '*A* is *B*' about which the question 'why?' can at least be raised. But if we consider a simple item, perhaps the form *B* by itself, then the question 'why?' cannot even be raised, because there is no suitable predication to ask for an explanation of. For Aristotle's rather mystifying account of our knowledge of these simple items, see $\Theta 10$, $1051^b17-1052^a4$.

The second sentence of this paragraph breaks off incomplete, as Aristotle develops, for all the rest of this chapter, the parenthesis begun at 41^b12.

41^b12-28

A compound which is not a mere heap will consist of certain components (or 'elements'), but should not be identified with those components.

There must also be what Aristotle throughout this paragraph just calls 'something else'. When he resumes this topic at *H*3, 43^b4, he begins by calling this 'something else' the 'composition' or the 'mixture' of the elements. I shall use the word 'arrangement', which seems better suited to what is actually being talked of. A compound such as a syllable, then, will consist of certain elements (the letters) *in* a certain arrangement. The arrangement cannot be ignored, since one can destroy the compound by destroying the arrangement, and without destroying the elements. (It may be noted in passing that the same applies to a compound that *is* a mere heap.)

$^b19$–25: Aristotle proceeds to argue that the arrangement of the elements is not itself a (further) element, or composed of elements. On the first point, he says that 'the same argument will apply again', and so we shall have an infinite regress. His thought appears to be that if we say that the syllable BA is put together from three elements, namely the letter B, the letter A, and the arrangement of the two, then we shall need yet a further arrangement to be the way in which the two letters and their arrangement are themselves arranged. But it is not clear how this could be shown by 'the same argument', i.e. by the argument that you can destroy the syllable simply by separating its elements and without destroying them. For if we separate the letter B from the letter A, then apparently we *have* destroyed the supposed third element, the original arrangement of the two, so there is no need to posit a further arrangement to be what is destroyed when our three elements are separated. In fact the argument required seems rather to be this: the notion of an element or component of something must be so understood that all the elements of a thing could be separated from one another without any being destroyed (cf. 41^b31–3). It then follows at once that the arrangement of the letters B and A in the syllable BA cannot be taken to be a third element of the syllable, and no regress argument is required.

Turning to the second point, Aristotle first claims that if the arrangement of the two letters is itself composed of elements, then it will be composed of more than one element, for otherwise it would be that one element. If this relies on the general principle that anything composed of one element must be that element, it appears to be mistaken. There is no obvious objection to the view that a bronze statue consists of just one element, its bronze, *in* a certain arrangement (i.e. shape), or that a threshold consists of just one element, a stone slab, *in* a certain arrangement (i.e. position), and this is a point that Aristotle himself will grant at *H*3, 43^b8–10. But perhaps the more interesting question is whether one could say that the arrangement of the two letters B and A, in the syllable BA, is itself composed of two elements, namely those same letters B and A again. Aristotle's response to this suggestion is that we shall apply the same argument once more, presumably to show that the original arrangement would then have to consist of those two letters in a further arrangement, which threatens a regress of arrangements. But it is not clear that a *further* arrangement would be required, for why could we not invoke the *same* arrangement all over again? This would have the consequence that the syllable is identified with the arrangement of its letters, since each consists of just the same elements in just the same arrangement, but it is not clear to me whether this consequence is absurd. (It *would* be absurd if an arrangement is something universal, so that the same arrangement is found in other syllables too, but Aristotle does not tell us whether the arrangements he is talking of are or are not supposed to be universals.)

$^b25$–7: So far in the paragraph Aristotle has simply been asking us to recognize that a syllable is 'something else', over and above its elements, and that this 'something else' is not an element or composed of elements. He now tells us that it is in fact the cause of the thing's being a syllable, and indeed 'the *primary* cause of its being'. So it is the substance of the syllable. No doubt we can accept that the arrangement of the letters is *a* cause of the syllable's being, for the syllable could not exist unless its letters were so arranged. But also, it could not exist unless its letters did, so apparently they too have a claim to be 'a cause of its being'. It is not clear from this paragraph why it is the arrangement, rather than the letters, that deserves to be called the *primary* cause. In so far as we have had an argument for this claim, it was in 41^a37–$^b9$, where the cause which answers the question, 'Why is this matter a so-and-so?' was assigned a priority as a 'cause of being'. But perhaps a further argument can be extracted from the final paragraph of this chapter.

41^b28–33

Aristotle here restricts substances to things that exist by nature. Such a restriction is hinted at elsewhere (*H*1, 42^a7–8; *H*2, 43^a5–6; *H*3, 43^b21–3; cf. *Λ*3, 1070^a18–19). But this is the only place in *Z* and *H* where he makes the claim quite directly. He offers nothing by way of argument for it. If we put this claim together with what is argued in *Z*16, 40^b5–16, the conclusion seems to be that Aristotle will allow *only* living things as perceptible substances. (This may indeed be the implication of the phrase 'things formed naturally' at $^b29$–30. See *H*3, 43^b14–23 n.)

If we accept this, it appears that we may offer a further reason for saying that it is their form rather than their matter that should be counted as 'the primary cause of their being'. For living things change their matter over time, as Aristotle knew (*GC* I, 5, 321^b24–8), and in the initial stages of growth this applies not only to the 'remote' but also to the 'proximate' matter. (For this distinction, see *Z*10, 35^b22–7 n.) It is also true, of course, that in the initial stages of growth (and sometimes at other stages too—e.g. puberty in humans) the 'shape' and 'arrangement' of the material parts changes as well. But what Aristotle means by the form of a living thing is not literally the arrangement of its elements, but its soul, and this is not to be regarded as subject to a similar flux. On the contrary, when Aristotle is thinking of the soul as a cause, then he takes it that it itself is the cause of all growth and development, and more generally the cause of every life-manifesting activity. It is no wonder, then, that he says that this, rather than a thing's matter, is 'the primary cause of its being'.

BOOK ETA

CHAPTER 1

Book *H* begins by promising to summarize what has been said so far (i.e. in book *Z*) and to draw the final conclusions. Accordingly, chapter 1 starts with the promised summary, and then turns to what is apparently intended as the final conclusion about matter. (It argues that matter must be a substance, because of its role in change.) Chapter 2 is apparently intended as the final discussion of form, and at the end of chapter 2 the enquiry is indeed brought to an end (at least for the time being).

42^a4–26

The distribution of emphasis in this 'summary' is surprising. After a brief sentence apparently intended to recall *Z*1 ($^a4$–6), there are then ten lines devoted to *Z*2 ($^a6$–12) and the programme outlined at the start of *Z*3 ($^a12$–16). The whole of the rest of *Z* is then assigned only five and a half lines ($^a17$–22), and thereafter the paragraph looks forward to what comes next. I comment on it piece by piece.

$^a4$–6: The summary begins with the statement that we have said that our aim is to find 'the causes, principles, and elements of substances'. This was not actually said in *Z*1, which instead promised to address the question 'What is substance?' Yet clearly Aristotle means to refer here to something said in *Z*1, since his next sentence at once goes on to summarize *Z*2.

One may speculate that he has confused the opening of his enquiry in *Z*1 with the earlier opening in *Γ*1 and *Γ*2. For on that occasion he had also begun with the point that being 'is spoken of in many ways', and that one kind of being is primary, namely substance (1003^a33–$^b10$). But there he had gone on to infer that the philosopher will need to know 'the principles and causes of substances' (1003^b17–19). (Or it may be that he is (also?) confusing *Z*1 with *Λ*1, which begins by saying that its task is to find 'the principles and causes of substances', 1069^a18–19.)

$^a6$–12: These lines summarize *Z*2, but with one discrepancy. *Z*2 had opened with the cautious statement 'Substance *seems* most clearly to belong to bodies', and had then continued with a list of such bodies which entirely matches the list given here (except that it did not say, as is said here, that all the bodies in question are ones that exist by nature). By contrast, our summary claims that these substances 'are agreed by all', which apparently commits Aristotle himself to agreeing to them. Thus *Z*2 is consistent with *Z*16, 40^b5–16, whereas our passage is not. On this point, see my epilogue to *Z*13–16.

^{a}12–16: These lines outline the programme introduced at the beginning of *Z*3, and in fact contain more information on that programme than is to be found in *Z* itself. (See *Z*3, 28^b33–6n.; *Z*13, prologue; *Z*14, introductory note.) They do not, however, allude in any way to the *results* obtained in the pursuit of that programme.

It may be remarked that an argument purporting to show that 'the universal is more a substance than the particulars' may actually be one that compares the more universal with the less universal (as would fit the conjectured early version of *Z*13). For Aristotle quite often uses 'particular' to mean 'less universal' rather than 'not universal' (e.g. *An. Post* II, 97^b28–31; *PA* I, 644^a30; *EN* VI, 1141^b14–21).

^{a}17–21: These lines are all that we have by way of summary of the discussion of form and essence, which in our text runs from *Z*4 to *Z*11 (and to which *Z*17 also contributes). The first sentence certainly refers to *Z*4, and perhaps is intended to include *Z*5, but it can hardly be seen as mentioning *Z*6. The second sentence certainly refers to *Z*10, but one may doubt whether *Z*11 was also meant to be included. Again, it is said only that certain topics were discussed, not what the results of those discussions were.

^{a}21–2: This is the one place where a result is given: 'Neither the universal nor the genus is substance.' Evidently it is the result of *Z*13. But the statement is so brief that one cannot be sure whether it means '*No* universal is a substance', or 'Not all universals are substances' (in the latter case because it is not true that what is more universal is more of a substance). On the face of it, the first interpretation is the more natural, since Aristotle surely does mean to say that *no* genus is a substance; but the second is not impossible.

^{a}22–6: The summary ends by again postponing a full consideration of Platonist views, presumably to books *M* and *N*, and proposing to consider the 'agreed' substances, i.e. the perceptible ones. It may be noted that there is no acknowledgement here that Plato's views on the forms—though not his views on the objects of mathematics—have already been subject to a sustained attack in *Z*14, *Z*15 (40^a8–27), and *Z*16 (40^b16–41^a5). (Objections were also raised earlier at *Z*6, 31^b15–18, and more importantly at *Z*8, 33^b19–34^a5.) But in view of the very economical nature of this summary as a whole, one perhaps should not expect anything more on this topic than has already been implied by ^{a}15–16.

One might mention the following parts of *Z* as important discussions which are in no way alluded to in this summary:

*Z*3: Substance cannot be identified with what ultimately underlies, for only prime matter fits this description,

*Z*6: Things 'spoken of in their own right' are identical with their essences, and hence eligible to be substances; other things are not.

Z7–9, and perhaps especially Z8: Forms neither come to be nor cease to be.

Z11: It has to be admitted that there are universal compounds as well as particular compounds.

Z12: How a definition can be a unity (at least, when it is a definition obtained by division).

Z15: No particular can be defined.

Z16 (40^b5–16): Most of the things commonly agreed to be substances are not so.

Z17: Substance is a cause, and in particular a cause as form (or essence).

It may be remarked that, with one exception, my notes on these passages have already canvassed some independent reasons for supposing that they did not form part of the 'first draft' of book Z. The exception is Z6, and there is surely no reason to suppose that it too was absent from the first draft. (For the coherence of Z6 with Z4–5, see my epilogue to those chapters; note also that Z6 is summarized at the end of Z11.) The exception shows, then, that not being mentioned in this summary at H1 cannot be held to be a *sufficient* condition for being absent from the first draft. But I would take it to be a necessary condition, since the summary itself seems to belong to the first draft, in view of the attention that it gives to the programme of the whole book.

42^a26–31

The previous paragraph has ended by promising further consideration of perceptible substances, and has remarked that they all have matter. The following paragraph will argue that matter must itself be accepted as a substance because it is what underlies. The present paragraph apparently wishes to introduce first a more general perspective. It returns to the claim first propounded in Z3 (29^a1–5), that what underlies is substance, but adds that all three of the favoured candidates for being substance do count as underlying—both matter, and form, and the compound of the two. It should be noted that, since Aristotle says that it is *only* the compound that can come to be and cease to be ($^a30$), the matter that he is talking of here should be prime matter, and the form should be the same form as was the topic of Z8. This was described as 'signifying such a kind of thing' (33^b21–2), and hence as a universal (Z13, 39^a1–3). The same conclusion might be inferred from its description here as something 'given by a formula' ($^a31$), or indeed as something that *is* a formula ($^a28$), for a formula is inherently general (as is emphasized in Z15, 40^a11–12, $^a38$–$^b1$).

In Z3 underlying was explained as being a subject of predication but never a predicate (28^b36–7), and we could not see why Aristotle should find it even initially plausible to claim that form satisfies this description

(28^{b}36–29^{a}10 n.). Moreover, he then argued that only (prime) matter does satisfy the description, and seemed there to be content with this result. In the present passage underlying is not explained, so we could suppose that he means here that forms are the subjects for other predicates, though they can also be predicated themselves (e.g. of matter). But we also have another avenue open to us, for in the next paragraph it will be urged about matter that *it* underlies by persisting through change. Perhaps, then, that is the kind of underlying that is also here attributed to the form and to the compound: at any rate, both of them will persist through many changes, namely all except 'substantial changes', and this was given as one of the marks of substance in the *Categories* (4^{a}10–22).

As well as underlying, two other criteria of substancehood are here mentioned (as at *Z*3, 29^{a}27–8), namely 'thisness' and 'separability'. Matter is said not to be a this 'in actuality', though it is a this 'potentially'. This is a loose and indeed indefensible use of the notion of potentiality (cf. *Z*16, 40^{b}5–16 n.). For if matter is *capable* of being a this, then the matter that constitutes (say) a living animal *is actually* a this when it does so. And if it is not so capable, then it is not true to say that it is a this 'potentially'. Aristotle's point could be remedied by inserting an 'in its own right' (as at *Anim* II, 1, 412^{a}7): matter is on occasion a this, but never in its own right (because that same matter may persist without being a this). But perhaps it would be better to refuse to say that matter ever *is* a this, and to insist that all that may be said is that it can, and sometimes does, *constitute* a this. Whichever we say, it is clear that the kind of 'this' that matter can either be or constitute must be the individual that is a compound of form in matter, though in fact our text does not characterize the individual either way in terms of thisness. Instead it insists only that the form is a 'this', a claim that is no easier to interpret now than it was before (*Z*3, 29^{a}27–8 n.). As for separability, it is clear that it is the individual that excels on this score, and whatever exactly is meant by the form's being 'separable in formula' (*Z*3, 29^{a}27–8 n.), this is a less satisfying kind of separability. (The exceptional forms that are genuinely separable are presumably the unmoved mover(s) of the universe.) Matter is not characterized either way in terms of separability, but one presumes that it is held not to be separable in *any* way.

^{a}28: The word translated 'actuality' here is *energeia*. Throughout *Z* it has been *entelekheia* (i.e. 34^{b}17, 36^{a}6, 38^{b}6, 39^{a}4–7, 14, 17, 40^{b}12). In *H* *entelekheia* is used only twice (44^{a}9, 48^{b}17), whereas there are many occurrences of *energeia* in *H*2, the first paragraph of *H*3, and *H*6. (It is clear that Aristotle is using 'actuality' as a synonym for 'form' in those places.) The two words have different etymologies, *energeia* suggesting work, function, or activity, and *entelekheia* presumably deriving from *to enteles ekhon* meaning 'completed' or 'perfected'. Nevertheless Aristotle often slips from one to the other, and apparently he sees no difference between them. (See Ross on *Θ*3, 1047^{a}30.)

42^a32-^b8

Aristotle's reason for saying that matter is substance is that in all changes there is something that underlies the change. So his premiss must be that whatever underlies a change is a substance (as at *Cat* 4^a10-22). One is at a loss to supply any rationale for this premiss. He proceeds to enumerate his four standard varieties of change (cf. *Z*7, 32^a12-15 n.), and to indicate what it is that underlies each case. Evidently in the first three cases we may suppose that what underlies is, say, a man, and presumably this is something which qualifies as a substance on other grounds too. Matter, in the proper sense, enters only with the last kind of change, where a substance either comes to be or ceases to be. It is mildly odd that Aristotle does not pause to emphasize this point. Nor does he emphasize that what *ultimately* persists through change, and so is genuinely eternal, is 'prime' matter, which has no properties in its own right. (Contrast *Z*3, 29^a20-6.)

It may be noted that at $^a32-3$ we find an assumption that Aristotle quite often makes, and which he argues for at *Phys* I, 5, 188^a26-^b36, that all change is 'between opposites'. As his own examples show, this is a mistake. (For example, two distinct places are not 'opposite' to one another, and similarly for the other cases.) The characterization of what underlies a change of substance at $^b1-3$ requires some correction. It is apparently said to be 'what is now coming into being and at another time perishing, and which now underlies as a this and at another time underlies by way of privation'. But when bricks are built up to form a house, or knocked down again, it is surely the house, and not the bricks, that is 'now coming into being and at another time perishing'. Yet Aristotle evidently means by this phrase to point to the matter of the change, i.e. the bricks, and not the house. Again his description seems to imply that it is when the house is being built that the bricks 'underlie as a this', and when it is being destroyed that they 'underlie by way of privation'. But it is surely more natural to take it the other way round, for an underlying (i.e. persisting) element is naturally characterized in terms of its state at the start of the change and not at the end of it. But evidently the bricks start 'as a this', i.e. as a house, when the house is being destroyed, and they end 'by way of privation', i.e. as *not* a house (or anyway, as not *that* house). One can only conclude that Aristotle's description is somewhat careless.

At $^b3-7$ Aristotle points to some relations between his various kinds of change. His claim that generation 'implies all the other changes' should presumably be taken as a rough generalization. For example, from the fact that a bronze statue may be generated it evidently does not follow that, once generated, it can change in size. Or again, from the fact that an island may be generated by volcanic action it evidently does not follow that, once generated, it can move from place to place. As for the converse, in Aristotle's view the heavenly bodies are things which move from place to place but cannot be generated or destroyed. He tells us at *Θ*8, 1050ᵇ16–18 that 'nothing prevents' an indestructible thing from being able to change, not only in place, but also in quality. It is not very clear, however, what example he may have had in mind. (Perhaps the moon, changing from being illuminated to not being illuminated, during an eclipse?)

The reference to 'the Physics' is no doubt to *Phys* V, 1, 255ᵃ12–20. It may also include *GC* I, 1–4, where the question is raised several times (and Aristotle's answer to it remains somewhat mysterious).

CHAPTER 2

As the previous chapter ended with a consideration of matter, so the present chapter considers form once more, though it prefers to describe the opposition between the two as that between potentiality and actuality. Form, or actuality, is identified with the differentia, and the chapter ends by recommending us to regard a definition as something that combines matter and differentia.

$42^b 9-11$

In the previous chapter matter, form, and the compound of the two were all said to underlie ($42^a 26-31$). The opening of the present chapter seems to imply that it is only matter that underlies, but perhaps the point is that it is only matter that is generally agreed to be a substance because of the way that it underlies. Matter is then characterized as 'that which is potentially' (cf. *H*1, $42^a 26-31$ n.), and Aristotle proposes to pass on to 'that which is the substance of perceptible things as actuality'. By this he evidently means 'form', as is explicit at $43^a 20$ later in the chapter. But he is apparently thinking of a thing's form as what makes it 'actual', and this leads to some difficult remarks at $42^b 25-31$. He at once appears to presuppose that this 'form' or 'actuality' may also be regarded as the thing's 'differentia'. This is presumably connected with his changed view on the ingredients of a definition.

$42^b 11-25$

The view here credited to Democritus is, of course, a view about how *atoms* and their combinations differ from one another. (It is given at greater length at *A*4, $985^b 4-20$ with the illustration that A and N differ in shape, AN and NA differ in arrangement, and N and Z differ in position.) In rebuttal of it, Aristotle recognizes no such limitation on the kinds of things whose differences are to be listed, and so naturally concludes that there are very many differentiae. He opens with a list of the several ways in which the material ingredients of a thing may be combined, which has something in common with the thought of *Z*17 that a thing's form is the way that its ingredients are arranged. But his further examples seem to be a rather miscellaneous lot.

There are, then, many differentiae. As we shall soon be told, these are 'the principles of being' ($42^b 32-3$). The next paragraph apparently aims to show why they merit this description.

$42^b 25-31$

The claim that 'is' is said in many ways is a rephrasing of the claim with which *Z*1 opened, that what is is spoken of in many ways. But whereas

*Z*1 went on to say (with a reference back to *Δ*7) that there were as many of these ways as there are categories (i.e. eight or ten), what Aristotle claims here is that there are as many as there are differentiae, i.e. a huge number. Unfortunately his very brief explanation of this point is ambiguous.

On the face of it, the first 'is' in 'a threshold is because it is situated so' means 'exists'. (There is no second 'is' in the Greek.) If so, then the 'being' that is said to signify 'its being situated so' should also mean 'existence', and Aristotle's thesis is that, for a threshold, to exist is to be situated below a door. If this implies that when one says, *of* a threshold, that it exists, then this is the same as to say, of the threshold, that it is below a door, then evidently the doctrine is mistaken. For if I do not know that the object I am pointing to is a threshold, then I might well claim (falsely) 'That is not below a door', without at all wishing to claim 'That does not exist.' But if we understand the doctrine so that it applies, not to saying *of*, but only to saying *that*, then perhaps it is true that 'That threshold exists' comes to much the same as 'That threshold is below a door.' If so, this is because everything that is a threshold must *both* exist *and* be below a door, so in describing a thing as a threshold one has already implied that it has both these properties. It does not follow that those properties are the same as one another, but one can see how Aristotle might have been led to suppose that they are, as Owen [1965*c*] has argued. But the difficulty with this line of interpretation becomes more apparent when we follow it through with the next example.

The Greek phrase '*to krustallon einai*' may be translated either as 'being ice' or as 'ice being' (i.e. 'there being ice') depending on whether the word 'ice' is taken as subject or complement to the verb 'to be'. If we are to preserve any kind of parallel with what has just been said about the threshold (on this interpretation), we must evidently take it in the second way, as making an existential claim. If the parallel is to be really close, then we should understand that some *particular* expanse of ice is being talked of, and the claim will again be that to say of this that it exists is the same as to say that it is solidified by cold. But I do not see that the Greek phrase could be taken to mean something tantamount to 'there being *this* ice'. If it represents an existential claim at all, it must surely represent the general claim 'There is ice', or 'Ice exists'. Thus Aristotle's claim will be that to say that ice exists is the same as to say that 'it' (i.e. ice) is solidified by cold, and a parallel claim for the threshold would be that to say that thresholds exist is the same as to say that thresholds are situated below doors. But this doctrine is even more clearly mistaken, for it equates a contingent existential truth with what is merely a matter of definition, and so not contingent at all. In each case, the mistake is one of confusing '*that X* is' (i.e. that *X* exists) with '*what X* is', and we have already observed that Aristotle is capable of this confusion (*Z*4, 30^a17–27 n., *Z*15, 39^b31–40^a7 n.). But where '*X*' is a general term, rather than a singular term, the confusion is particularly gross.

One might therefore be tempted to Owen's way of construing the claim about ice, which is this. To say that ice exists is the same as to say that *some* ice exists, which is the same as to say that 'it', i.e. *that* ice, is solidified by cold. Since this implies that some ice is solidified by cold, and hence that something is solidified by cold, it remains contingent after all (Owen [1965*c*], 86–8). But evidently this supplies a great deal more than is actually said, especially as the Greek does not contain the word 'it' at all. So this brings us to the alternative interpretation.

If we take *to krustallon einai* to mean 'being ice', rather than 'there being ice', then what Aristotle says about ice is that the predicate '. . . is ice' means the same as the predicate '. . . is solidified by cold'. To interpret the remarks about the threshold as making a parallel claim to this, we must supplement the text in this way: 'A threshold is [what it is, i.e. a threshold] because it is situated so, and [something's] being [a threshold] signifies its being situated so.' Again in the next sentence we must take the words 'The being of some things . . . is defined' to mean 'In the case of some things, being [them] . . . is defined.' Thus in each case the relevant 'is' becomes a predicative 'is'. This is certainly not the most natural way of taking the Greek, though I would not say that it is wholly impossible.

Apart from the linguistic awkwardness, there are two further objections to this way of taking the paragraph. (*a*) It is no longer clear how this shows that 'is' is said in many ways. This is evident in English, where the 'is' in 'is a threshold' or 'is ice' simply reappears in the suggested paraphrase 'is situated below a door' or 'is solidified by cold'. But it may be replied that the point is less clear in the Greek, where there is no 'is' in the paraphrase, since it is absorbed into the verb. So it is as if Aristotle had said: 'It is clear that "is" is said in many ways, for "is a threshold" means "lies so", and "is ice" means "congeals so".' Of course this would not really show that the two cases of 'is' have different meanings, but I suppose that Aristotle may have thought that it did. (*b*) The suggested paraphrases are clearly inadequate. Despite the implications of 43^a12–14 below, there is more to being ice than being frozen, since other things besides ice may be frozen too. Similarly with a threshold; for example, a hole that is situated below a door is not a threshold. Now apparently Aristotle recognizes this a little later at 43^a7–12, where he proposes to define a threshold as *wood* or *stone* that is situated so, and ice as *water* that is solidified so. *But* he does not seem to regard this as correcting what he has said here; he continues to regard only the 'differentia' as being 'the substance of things as actuality'. This is difficult to explain if what he means by the 'actuality' of a threshold, and the 'principle of its being' (42^b32–3), is the paraphrase defining 'is a threshold'. It is easier to accept if what he means by it is the paraphrase defining 'is' in 'a threshold is'.

For these reasons I am inclined to think that the first interpretation is correct, and that it is the 'is' of existence that Aristotle is claiming to have many different meanings. Its meaning in each case depends upon the definition of whatever it is that is being said to exist, as was suggested in account B of my prologue to *Z*1. But the present suggestion differs from that account of Aristotle's earlier doctrine in two ways. The earlier doctrine thought of a definition as combining genus and differentiae, and it regarded the genus as the part that explains the kind of being of the thing defined. But here in *H*2 a definition is characterized as combining matter and form (though the form is still called the differentia), and it is the form that gives the being of what is defined. Given Aristotle's general attitude to the matter/form contrast, it is not surprising that he should now regard the formal component of the definition as the more important one, and so, given also his earlier view that the definition explains the kind of being, we can understand why he should now come to think that it is form that does this. It would seem to be largely because form is in this way the 'principle' or 'cause' of being—i.e. the explanation of what being is in each case—that it is so constantly called 'actuality' here and elsewhere in *H*.

(At $^b28$–31 Aristotle apparently implies that a hand or a foot is to be defined, not by its function (as one might have expected), but by the way its ingredients are held together. Similarly at 43^a8–9 he at first suggests that a house should be defined by the arrangement of its materials, but then adds in parenthesis that the purpose should be considered too. No doubt this parenthesis applies equally to the hand and the foot.)

42^b31–43^a14

I take this long paragraph in three sections.

$^b31$–$^a4$: The first section is presented as if it were an argument, though it is difficult to understand it as such. It appears to run: (*a*) the differentiae are principles of being; moreover (*b*) the various differentiae fall into a limited number of kinds; and (*c*) the substance of a thing is a cause of its being; hence (*d*) the causes of the being of each of these things will be among these. The conclusion (*d*) apparently means: the causes of the being of each of the things just listed by way of example will be among the kinds into which the differentiae fall. The things just listed by way of example could be taken to be the various differentiae just mentioned (more and less, dense and rare, and so on), or the things differentiated by them. The latter seems to be the more probable. The 'argument', then, comes out like this: (*a*) the differentiae which differentiate x, y, z, w . . . from one another are principles (= causes) of the being of x, y, z, w . . . ; (*b*) these differentiae fall into kinds K_1, K_2, K_3 . . . ; hence (*d*) for any of x, y, z, w . . . , the cause of its being will be one of K_1, K_2, K_3. . . . So far as one can see, there is no role to be played in this argument by premiss (*c*), stating that the substance of a thing is a cause of its being, and indeed nothing will follow about substance if there can be more than one cause of a thing's being. On this last point, our 'argument' is scarcely consistent, since it says that if a differentia *D* is *a* cause of the being of *x*, and if *D* falls under *K*, then *K* is *the* cause of the being of *x* (from which it follows, taking the 'the' strictly, that $D = K$). It seems better not to try to discern any genuine argument here, but just to note the assumption that the differentia which is 'the cause of a thing's being' will also be its substance, and otherwise to see Aristotle as recommending an exhaustive classification of such differentiae. He is not seriously trying to *give* such a classification here, for several of the examples mentioned in 42^b11-25 are here omitted (namely position, time, place).

$^a4-7$: Aristotle adds by way of an aside that the examples of differentiae (i.e. forms) so far mentioned are not actually substances, no doubt because the concrete things differentiated by them (i.e. the compounds of that form in some particular matter) are not in the other sense substances. Presumably he will be relying here on one or both of the claims (*a*) that among perceptible things, only those that exist by nature are substances (*Z*17, 41^b28-30), and (*b*) that among these, only living things are substances (*Z*16, 40^b5-16). But since he does not explain, we cannot deduce any firm conclusion on whether either *Z*16 or *Z*17 already preceded this passage when it was written. It may be remarked that this aside applies not only to the examples that we have had so far, but also to those that are to come (not only in this chapter, but also in the rest of *H*). It seems that, for the purpose of the *Metaphysics*, Aristotle prefers to avoid the task of characterizing the form (i.e. soul) of a genuine substance, and to work with simpler examples throughout. (The main exception to this statement is *Z*11.)

$^a7-14$: The aside in $^a4-7$ has told us that in a definition actuality is predicated of matter—it is a genuine actuality where what is defined is a genuine substance, and 'what is closest to actuality' in other cases. This Aristotle proceeds to illustrate by giving some specimen definitions. He does not remark that in the terminology of *Z*10–11 the matter that figures in these definitions is matter 'taken universally', so that what is defined is a 'universal compound'. But he apparently does commit himself to the view that *every* definition will take this form. This clearly contradicts the earlier thesis that definition, essence, and form may all be identified, since definition is of the form alone. It also contradicts the thesis that in a definition we do *not* find one thing predicated of another (cf. *Z*12, epilogue).

At $^a12-14$ Aristotle proceeds to draw a very surprising consequence, that where the matter is different 'the actuality and formula is also different'. Now, no doubt, if the matter must be mentioned in the definition, then where the matter is different the formula (i.e. the whole definition) must also be different. But it evidently does not follow that the actuality (i.e. form) that is predicated of the matter must be different too. And one would suppose that in many cases it is not. For example, the definitions of a bronze circle and of a wooden circle presumably differ only in their matter, and not at all in their 'actuality'; similarly the definitions of a statue and a snowman, of limestone and sandstone, and many others. (The point is granted, in passing, at *H*4, 44^a29-32.) It is possible that Aristotle has been misled here into supposing that what holds of his *genuine* substances will hold also of the kinds of things that he is using as examples here. For we observed at *Z*11, 36^b21-32 n. that Aristotle does think that the form of a man determines the matter he is made of, and he would evidently extend this claim to all other animals and to all plants (cf. *Phys* II, 9). But even if the principle does apply to what he would count as genuine substances, it surely does not apply as widely as he here suggests.

43^a14-26

The direction of thought in this concluding paragraph would seem to be this. A proper definition should mention *both* the matter *and* the form (or 'actuality') that is predicated of it. The fact that both are needed explains the divergences among the definitions that people actually give, for some give only the one, and some give only the other, and in each case they have got hold of half, but only half, of the truth. But there are some, for example Archytas, who have seen the whole truth. One may note, incidentally, that those who combine both are said to give 'the third substance' ($^a18-19$), which implies not only that those who give only the form give a substance, but also that those who give only the matter give a substance. And if Aristotle is being precise here, this last substance is a specific kind of matter, taken universally, and not a particular chunk of matter. But presumably it is particular chunks of matter that qualify as substances by being underlying things in the sense of *H*1, 42^a32-^b8, i.e. by persisting through change.

43^a26-8

This final sentence signals the 'completion' of the enquiry that was promised at the beginning of *H*1. Matter, form, and the compound of the two are each in their own way substances. One presumes that by 'the compound' in this sentence Aristotle means *particular* compounds, such as particular animals and plants; and hence that by 'matter' he means particular chunks of matter. In view of the preceding paragraph one might suppose that he *also* means to include universal compounds, but it cannot be to the exclusion of particular compounds. They, after all, satisfy the criterion of separability better than any other candidate, as *H*1, 42^a29-31 has recently reminded us.

The 'completion' of the enquiry was only temporary; in fact we have more to come. The remaining chapters of book *H* are isolated discussions, not arranged into a continuous treatment, and may well be regarded as a series of notes and appendices. Some of them, notably *H*4 and *H*5, do not take us much further forward with the main problems, and there is no particular reason to suppose that they were written after *H*2. They might well be relatively early pieces, which Aristotle decided not to incorporate, but which are preserved for us by an early editor (cf. prologue to *Z*12). But *H*6 at any rate builds upon the doctrine of *H*2 in a significant way, and the same might be said of parts of *H*3.

CHAPTER 3

This chapter contains three quite unconnected parts.

The first paragraph elaborates upon a point made in *Z*10 (35ᵃ6–9) that the same word may signify sometimes the compound and sometimes the form alone. It is not related in any way to what precedes or follows it. (But it does constantly equate form and actuality, in the manner of *H*2.)

The third paragraph gives us our fullest statement of a point omitted from *Z*8, but hinted at in *Z*10 (35ᵃ28–30) and clearly stated in *Z*15 (39ᵇ24–7), that the fact that a form cannot come to be or cease to be does not imply that it is eternal. It is verbally connected with what precedes it, and could not stand on its own, but the connection is quite incongruous.

The second, fourth, and fifth paragraphs apparently contain a continuous discussion, which begins where *Z*17 left off. It uses the premiss that a syllable is not just its letters to draw conclusions about the structure of definitions, and goes on to compare definitions with numbers. (But if this analysis is correct, then the summarizing sentence with which the chapter ends is misleading.)

43ᵃ29–ᵇ4

At *Z*10, 35ᵃ6–9 Aristotle had claimed that the word 'statue' may be used either to mean a compound of form in matter or to mean the form alone. Later in *Z*10, with the example 'animal', he had more cautiously taken this to be merely a possibility (36ᵃ16–25). His attitude in the present note is the more cautious one. He says that it is not clear whether such words as 'house', 'line', and 'animal' do have both these meanings, and he leaves the question open.

In *Z*8 and in *Z*10 Aristotle firmly said that 'man' signifies a universal compound (33ᵇ24–6, 35ᵇ27–31). In *Z*11 he argued at some length that 'man' and 'animal' *must* be construed as signifying compounds, and cannot be taken to mean the form alone (36ᵇ21–32, 37ᵃ5–7). The same implication may also be obtained from *H*2, which tells us that any proper definition must predicate form of matter, and that those who offer a definition of 'house' that mentions only the form are mistaken (43ᵃ7–26). It is somewhat surprising, then, that here Aristotle does not commit himself, but says only that the word 'animal' *might* have both meanings. At once he goes on to indicate how such a double meaning—if it exists—could be explained, i.e. as a case of focal meaning. (Presumably the meaning 'soul in body' would be derivative from the meaning 'soul', and obtained by 'adding' something to it. Cf. *Z*4, 30ᵃ32–ᵇ1.) But then he apparently dismisses the question as unimportant for the present enquiry, *because* the essence belongs to the form. His sequence of thought would seem to be this. For the present enquiry we shall need to know what the essence of an animal is, and if 'animal' has a double meaning, then this question threatens to be ambiguous. But it turns out that the ambiguity does not matter. For in either sense of 'animal' the essence of an animal is just its form, i.e. soul. There is not *one* essence for the form alone, and *another* essence for the compound.

It may be noted that the equation between definition and essence, introduced in *Z*4 and apparently retained for *most* of *Z*4–10, is here explicitly abandoned.

43^b4–14

This paragraph falls neatly into two halves. In the first ($^b4$–10) the doctrine of *Z*17, 41^b12–33 is recalled, and applied to a prominent example of *H*2, the threshold. In the second ($^b10$–14) the doctrine is given a novel application, bearing upon the old problem of the unity of a definition.

$^b4$–10: *Z*17 had urged that the syllable BA was not just its two letters, B and A, but also 'something more'. It had gone on to claim that this 'something more' was the primary cause of its being, and its substance, but still without any other name for it than 'the something more'. In my commentary I called it the arrangement of the two letters; here Aristotle calls it their 'combination' (*sunthesis*) or alternatively their 'mixture'. *Z*17 had also urged that the arrangement or combination of the two letters was not itself a further component of the syllable, in addition to the two letters. This justifies the opening statement here, that the syllable is not composed of the letters *and* their combination. Unfortunately, our passage proceeds to offer its own justification, which appears to be a confused recollection of *Z*17. In *Z*17 the claim that the combination is not itself an element was argued at 41^b20–2, and then a different argument was given for the further point that the combination is not composed of elements (41^b22–5). Here in *H*3 the further point is cited as if it were a reason for the first point, which it evidently is not. Aristotle would appear to be forgetting the details of his earlier discussion.

In another way the present passage clearly improves on *Z*17, despite its awkward terminology. *Z*17 had claimed that what was composed of only one element would be that one element (41^b23), so that there could be no contrast in this case between the single element and 'something more'. One might have expected our passage to fall into the same error, since there would not seem to be such a thing as the 'combination' or 'mixture' of a single element. (But there is no similar bar to an 'arrangement' of one element.) Nevertheless, under the influence of *H*2 (42^b19–20, 26–7, 43^a7–8), our passage observes that a threshold may well be regarded as composed of one element, e.g. a stone slab, with 'something more', analogous to the combination of several elements. The threshold is the stone slab *in* a certain position; the stone slab is its only element, but nevertheless it is not to be identified with that element.

Unfortunately, Aristotle does not say *quite* the right thing about this example. What he should have said is this. Just as a syllable is several letters in a certain combination (arrangement), so the threshold is (say) a stone slab in a certain position (arrangement). And just as the combination of the letters is not itself composed of those letters, so equally the position of the slab is not itself composed *of the slab*. What he says instead is that the position is not composed *of the threshold*. No doubt the slip is not important, but without it he could not have gone on 'it would be better to say that the threshold is composed of it'. Perhaps there is a temptation to say that *the threshold* is 'composed of' the position, but there would be no temptation to say this of the slab. In any case, this temptation should certainly be resisted, if we are to remain consistent with what has been said already. For Aristotle has been at pains to say that if a thing is composed of certain elements in a certain arrangement, then the arrangement is *not* itself one of the elements, i.e. *not* something that the thing is *composed of*.

^{b}10–14: In these lines we get a curious application of the present thought to the old problem of the unity of a definition. Consider again the sample definition of a man as a two-footed animal, and the question 'Why does not this make man *both* animal *and* two-footed?' (*Z*12, 37^b10–14; *H*6, 45^a12–20). Well, Aristotle here says, suppose that it does. Suppose, that is, that animality and two-footedness are two elements that man is composed of, both acting as matter to the compound that is man. Then man will have to be those two elements *in* a certain arrangement, and it will be this arrangement, and not the elements, that is the substance of man. So on this hypothesis one who gives 'two-footed animal' as the definition of man will not have stated the substance of man at all. But that is obviously an absurd result.

It follows that we must reject the doctrine discussed in *Z*14 (and very probably in *Z*13, 39^a3–14), that 'animal' and 'two-footed' may be regarded as two 'parts' of equal status of which 'man' is composed. Whether Aristotle means to draw any more positive moral is unclear. It follows, of course, that if the definition is retained, then it cannot be construed as suggested, but that at most one of the two words (say 'animal'?) can be taken as introducing a quasi-material element, with the other specifying its 'arrangement'. But ever since we have been introduced to the idea that 'man' signifies a (universal) compound, i.e. such a kind of body with such a kind of soul, we have had reason to suppose that Aristotle means to reject the traditional kind of definition outright. See further *H*6, 45^a20–5 n.

(The text and interpretation that I have offered for ^{b}12–14 follows Ross, and it seems to me to make good sense. Jaeger has quite a different text, which makes no sense.)

43^b14–23

The opening words of this paragraph are 'this must be . . .', and the 'this', being in the feminine, evidently looks back to a recent mention of substance, or actuality, or possibly shape (meaning form). (Aristotle's other expressions for form or essence are not feminine but neuter.) With the paragraph placed as it is, the 'this' looks back to the final occurrence of 'substance' in the previous paragraph. But that is incongruous, for the 'substance' mentioned there is a non-existent substance—a form that one *would* have to posit if one held, absurdly, that man is composed of the two elements animality and two-footedness in just the way that the syllable BA is composed of the two elements B and A. But it is not this, wholly chimerical, substance that the present paragraph is concerned with. It has something serious to say about perfectly genuine Aristotelian forms. So one cannot believe that the paragraph was composed for its present context. I return at the end of this note to consider for what position it was composed.

One alternative for an Aristotelian form is that it is eternal; the other, as phrased here, is literally translated: 'It is perishable without being perishing, and has come to be without being coming to be.' What Aristotle means is that the *present* tense 'it is coming to be' or 'it is ceasing to be' is never applicable to it, though the *perfect* tense 'it has come to be' or 'it has ceased to be' is so applicable. Elsewhere he mentions contacts, points, and temporal instants as also meriting this description (e.g. *Cael* 280^b26; *B*5, 1002^a32–$^b11$; *H*5, 44^b21–2). In their case at least, his reason is quite clear: since they have no parts, their coming to be or ceasing to be cannot take time. From this he takes it to follow that the present tense 'it is coming to be' cannot be true of them, *even* at a single instant. For he assumes (*a*) that for anything that has come to be there is always a first instant at which it has come to be, and (*b*) that no instant can be both an instant at which a thing is coming to be and an instant at which it has come to be (*Phys* VI, 235^b30–$^a7$, and 234^b10–12). Given these assumptions, it follows just from the continuity of time that if anything is coming to be then it is doing so over the whole of some stretch of time.

Aristotle applies to forms the same doctrine as he also applies to such things as points and instants. We need not suppose that his reason is that forms too have *no* parts, for he refers us to his argument in *Z*8 which did not rely on any such claim. But one might say that the premiss of *Z*8 was that a form has no *material* parts, and hence that it is not itself a matter/form compound. Nevertheless, one may grant the premiss and still doubt the conclusion. We may observe first that Aristotle would presumably accept that a person may bring it about that a form *has* come to be. At any rate, he reaffirms here that the form of a house, or (say) a pendulum clock, cannot exist apart from the particular houses or clocks, and so he is committed to the view that if there ever was or will be a time when there are no houses or clocks, then that is a time when these forms do not exist. Consequently he who creates the first pendulum clock, or destroys the last, has brought it about that the form has come to be, or has ceased to be. More accurately, we should perhaps speak of him who first *conceives* a clock, and him who last *forgets* clocks, for *Z*7 speaks also of forms existing in the mind of the creator before creation (32^b1–14). But the main point is unaffected: apparently one may bring it about that a form has come into being, and it seems that Aristotle himself would accept this. However, making the first pendulum clock is clearly a process that takes time, and the same must also be true of the mental activity of inventing one. But if there is a process which ends in a form existing, when it did not before, is there really any reason to deny that while this process is going on the form is coming into existence?

At the end of this paragraph Aristotle tentatively suggests that we should not count the form of a house, or an implement, as substances, but only the forms of things that exist by nature. (Cf. *Z*17, 41^b28–30, which is definite and not tentative on this point.) No doubt he means in particular the forms of living things, i.e. souls. (Cf. *Z*16, 40^b5–16; also *Λ*3, 1070^a13–20, with Jaeger's text.) But the reason that he suggests is puzzling, namely that the form of a house, or an implement, cannot exist in separation from the particular houses or implements. While that is true, the same also applies to the soul of a horse or a tree, so no relevant distinction has been drawn. In fact the only aspect of the soul that Aristotle ever seriously suggests might be 'separable' is the intellect, and this of course is found only in humans (and in God). But presumably Aristotle does not wish to suggest that the only genuine perceptible substances are human beings. The relevant contrast between houses and implements on the one hand, and the species of living things on the other, is that (in Aristotle's view) the form of a species exists always while the form of an artefact does not. This is exactly the contrast suggested by what has gone before. Being separable is *one* way of enjoying eternal existence, but it is not the only way, and not the way that is relevant here.

Finally, it may be noted that this stray paragraph in *H*3 seems to envisage a *future* treatment of the question of which parts of the soul (if any) can exist separated from the body. (Cf. $^b19$: 'Nothing is *yet* clear.') The same applies to a rather similar passage in the second half of *Λ*3, i.e. 1070^a13–26 (cf. $^a24$). Both passages, apparently, look *forward* to the discussion of this topic in the *De Anima*. By contrast, when *Z*10 introduces the idea that the form of a living thing is its soul (35^b14–16), it is evidently *presupposing* the doctrine of the *De Anima*. This suggests that our paragraph in *H*3 belongs with *Z*7–9, which was not originally written for the *Metaphysics* at all (cf. prologue to *Z*7–9). The suggestion is strengthened by the way in which *Λ*3 combines the two. Its first half, i.e. 1069^b35–1070^a13, is a résumé of many of the themes more fully developed in *Z*7 and *Z*8; its second half includes the thought of our passage, and of *Z*16, 40^b5–16; and as a coda it returns to a further theme of *Z*8 at 1070^a26–30. But on the other hand, our paragraph in *H*3 refers to the doctrine of *Z*8 as 'elsewhere' ($^b16$), which shows that the suggestion cannot after all be right. I am therefore at a loss for a conjecture as to where our paragraph was originally written for. As I observed at the beginning of this note, it surely cannot have been written for thc context in which we now find it.

$43^b23–32$

This paragraph begins 'Consequently' (*hōste*). Evidently, the point that it wishes to make is not in any way a consequence of what was said in the previous paragraph, but it may perhaps look back to the paragraph before. At any rate, this paragraph is clearly concerned with the possibility of definition, and that one too had ended with a point about definition. Our paragraph first mentions a problem raised by 'the followers of Antisthenes', which they took to show that definition was impossible altogether. But then Aristotle apparently resumes in his own person at $^b28$, and agrees that definition is only possible in *some* cases, namely where what is to be defined is composite.

$^b23–8$: The only hint we are given as to *why* the Antistheneans supposed that definition was altogether impossible is in the words 'since a definition is a long formula'. It is possible that even this hint is to be discounted, since the phrase 'a long formula' (*makros logos*) can be taken just to mean 'a long story' in a pejorative sense, i.e. one that evades the point at issue. (Cf. Ross, ad *N*3, 1091^a7.) But if we take the hint seriously, the source of Antisthenes' problem must be that a definition is supposed to contain several words. Here it is relevant to recall that in *Δ*29 Antisthenes is described as holding the view that 'nothing can be spoken of except by its own formula, one to one' ($1024^b32–3$). If we understand this as intended to imply that nothing can be spoken of except by means of its own *name*, then we may perhaps elucidate the thought in this way. The definition of man as a two-footed animal does not actually mention man at all; instead it mentions two different things, animality and two-footedness, neither of which is man. And every definition is bound to do the same, since a definition is required to be a 'long formula', i.e. something longer than a single name. So the consequence is that definition is impossible, for a definition is supposed to mention just one thing, and yet we require it to mention more than one. If this is indeed the right account of Antisthenes' puzzle, then one can see why Aristotle should say that it 'has some point here', for Aristotle too has just said that if you construe this specimen definition in a certain way, then it simply fails to mention what it is supposed to be giving an account of, i.e. the substance of man. (For that would have to be the 'arrangement' of the two 'elements' animality and two-footedness.)

ᵇ28–32: Whatever exactly the puzzle of the Antistheneans was, Aristotle does not pause to explain just what is wrong with it. Instead he draws a moral, apparently both from this puzzle and from his own puzzle about man being two-footed *and* animal (43ᵇ10–14), that a definition will always predicate one thing (form) of another (matter). So it is only a compound of form in matter that can be defined. A form itself cannot, nor can matter itself (i.e. prime matter, presumably). This is a conclusion entirely in accordance with what was claimed in *H*2, but quite at odds with the bulk of *Z*10, with *Z*6 as summarized at *Z*11, 37ᵃ33–ᵇ7, and with *Z*4, 30ᵃ7–14. For it was claimed there that it is only the form that is defined, and that the compound is not.

Aristotle adds that his claim holds both for perceptible and for 'intelligible' compounds. On the latter, see *H*6, 45ᵃ33–5 n.

43ᵇ32–44ᵃ11

The overall structure of this chapter (from 43ᵇ4, and omitting ᵇ14–23) appears to be this. The syllable consists of certain elements *in* a certain arrangement, where the arrangement is not itself one of those elements (ᵇ4–10); from this it is clear (*a*) that man is not animal *and* two-footed, for a definition must give the form (or arrangement) as well as the matter (the elements) (ᵇ10–14, 23–32); it is *also* clear (*b*) in what way substances, i.e. definitions, are numbers (ᵇ32 ff.).

Aristotle denies that a substance is—as some say—'a number of units' ([*arithmos*] *monadōn*); nevertheless he affirms that a definition is 'a sort of number' (*arithmos tis*). Now elsewhere he often distinguishes between 'pure' or 'abstract' numbers (as studied in arithmetic) and 'applied' numbers, which are groups of some definite sort, such as ten horses, or ten men. When he is drawing this distinction at *Phys* IV, 219ᵇ5–8, he uses the phrase 'a sort of number' for the latter. If that is his point here too, then he is saying that a substance (or definition) is not a number of *abstract* units—i.e. those units that the mathematician calls 'ones', each exactly like one another in all respects—but it is a number in the other sense. This is difficult to accept. For example, if we say that a syllable is 'a sort of number', namely a number of letters, we seem to have left out the crucial fact that the letters must be *arranged* in a certain way in order to form the syllable. So the thesis that Aristotle needs is apparently more like this: a substance, or its definition, is 'an arranged number' of certain elements. It is not altogether clear whether his phrase 'a sort of number' could be regarded as including this idea. In any event, the arguments that follow do not seem to have any tendency to show that a definition *is* a number (of this or any other sort); for they merely point to four ways in which definitions *resemble* numbers (i.e. ᵇ35–6, ᵇ36–ᵃ2, ᵃ2–9, ᵃ9–11).

ᵇ35–ᵃ2: The first two points seem straightforward, but not very exciting. Both a definition and a number are divisible into units that are not further divisible, and will not survive the loss of any unit, or the addition of an extra one. It seems probable that the 'units' of a definition are 'indivisible' in the sense that they are themselves indefinable. The 'units' of an abstract number are held to be not in any way divisible (*Δ*6, 1016^b24–6); the 'units' of a concrete number, such as ten horses, are no doubt divisible in various concrete ways, but the division would destroy them.

$^a2$–9: By far the most difficult comparison is the claim that a number is a unity, that a definition is a unity, and that the explanation is in each case the same; a substance is a unity because it is 'an actuality and a certain nature'. No doubt 'actuality' here indicates form, as it did in *H*2 (though the word used here is *entelekheia*, as at *Z*13, 38^b6; see *H*1, 42^a26–31 n.). Presumably 'a certain nature' also indicates form, since the form of a natural object was identified with its 'nature' at *Z*17, 41^b28–30. A substance, then, is a unity because it consists of certain materials *with* a certain form. In the case of a genuine substance, this form is its soul, which is responsible for the material body *acting* 'as a unity' (*Z*16, 40^b5–16); in the case of the simpler examples that Aristotle often invokes, e.g. the syllable, the form is merely the arrangement of the material components, which, however, is still enough to prevent the syllable being regarded as 'a mere heap' (*Z*17, 41^b11–12). What is it, then, that is supposed to provide in a similar way for the unity of a number, and to distinguish it from a mere heap?

One suggestion would be that Aristotle does actually think of a number as fairly literally an arrangement, structure, or pattern of units. For example, three is literally a triangular number, four is literally a square number, and so on. (This view is usually credited to the Pythagoreans, see, e.g., Heath [1921] i. 76–84.) If we tone down this suggestion a bit, but still without losing its basic idea, we may perhaps think of Aristotle as holding that we have three horses only where the three form a *group*, not necessarily in any particular pattern, but at least so situated that they are all close to one another. For this too is an arrangement of a kind, though not such a specific kind as suggested previously. Of course, such a view is mistaken, for three horses remain three however they may be scattered, but it would not be too surprising if Aristotle had failed to grasp this point.

There is, however, a way of generalizing this idea which is not obviously mistaken, and which goes like this. To say that there are three horses, is—so far—to say something incomplete and needing a completion. The completion *may* be, and often is, one which implies a measure of togetherness, as with: 'There are three horses *in this field*.' But it may also be one that has no spatial implications, as with: 'There are three horses *owned by me*.' In any case, the thesis is that the basic form of a 'statement of number' will always be: 'There are *n* so-and-so's which are such-and-such.' In this schema the general term 'so-and-so' specifies the 'unit' for the number being asserted, or in Aristotle's language 'what sort of number' is in question, e.g. a number of horses, or of rivers, or of cities, or whatever it is. But in addition there must also be the further clause 'which are such-and-such', which will often locate the *n* so-and-so's in question, though it need not. What it will always do is specify a property which these *n* so-and-so's share, and which distinguishes them from other so-and-so's (if any). So it may always be taken as providing the 'form', or 'principle of unity', that metaphorically 'holds together' these *n* so-and-so's, and allows us to apply a particular number to them. And such a 'principle of unity' must be supplied, if the statement is to be even grammatical.

In the form in which I put it here, this thesis is (perhaps unnecessarily?) controversial, but I shall not pause to consider objections, replies, and possible reformulations. At any rate, there is clearly *something* right about it, and it illustrates how Aristotle could plausibly have held that in any application of numbers to concrete objects there will always be an appropriate 'principle of unity' for that case. The point I wish to make is that one would *expect* him to seek for this desired 'principle of unity' in the concrete applications, for on his view these are basic. Numbers as conceived by the mathematicians are merely abstractions from these. And this is why he thinks that on this question of 'the unity of a number' he can score a point over his Platonist opponents (cf. *A*9, 992^a1-2). For the Platonists are committed to there being just one thing which is *the* number two, and prior to all other twos, and yet at the same time they suppose that, like other twos, it consists of a pair of units. But then we can ask: what is it that makes this pair of abstract units a unity? Clearly it is not that they are 'next to' one another in any literal way (*M*7, 1082^a20-2). And in fact the only thing that the Platonist can say to distinguish these units from any other pair of units is that they are the ones that make up *the* number two. (I take it that this is the thought behind *M*6, 1080^a23-30.) But this reply is evidently circular, and the truth is that if there were such abstract units then none of them could be distinguished from any others (1082^b1-9, 1083^a1-17), so there could be no saying what it is that 'unifies' or 'holds together' those particular units that are supposed to constitute the number two, i.e. what it is that distinguishes them from other units.

In sum, there is an important question about numbers which the Platonist cannot answer, and this because he has a mistaken view about what sort of thing a number is. (The mistake in this case arises because he puts abstractions first, and concrete applications second, which gets things backwards.) Similarly, the Platonist cannot say what it is that makes a definition a unity ($^a6$), because again he has a mistaken conception of what a definition is. In particular, he does not realize that a definition must always specify certain elements *in* a certain form. (See *H*6, 45^a20-5.)

$^a9-11$: The last sentence of this paragraph appears to be something of an afterthought; at any rate, Aristotle draws no particular moral from it.

The claim that no number 'admits of being more or less' may be interpreted as meaning that no number is more a *number* than any other, or as meaning that (e.g.) no ten is more *a ten* than any other, i.e. ten men and ten horses are each equally ten. The latter is perhaps more probable, as it provides a better parallel with substance. At any rate, when Aristotle claims at *Categories* 3^b33-4 that substance does not admit of being more or less, he hastens to add that he does *not* mean that no substance is more *a substance* than any other; he means that (e.g.) no man is more *a man* than any other. But here he appears to qualify that claim: it holds of the substance 'taken as form' (or more literally 'the substance in accordance with form'), but perhaps does not hold of the substance 'with matter'. Presumably his thought is that one might reasonably say that *x* is more a man than *y* if, for example, *x* is an adult and *y* an infant, or more generally if *x* is living to the full the life that is specified in the definition of man, whereas *y*'s life falls short of this in one way or another. This, he implies, will be due to some shortcoming in *y*'s matter. But if we consider just the form alone, then if *x* and *y* are both men, they will be indiscernible in this respect (cf. *Z*8, 34^a5-8).

It may be noted that in this paragraph substance, definition, and essence are at first all equated ($^b33-4$, $^a1-2$), though we have just been told that a definition must mention both form and matter (43^b30-2). But at $^a9$ substance is once more equated with the form alone, and in this final sentence we return to the familiar contrast between substance as form alone and substance as a compound of form in matter. Presumably this latter contrast is primarily concerned with the *particular* compound (as, e.g., at *Z*11, 37^a24-30), whereas the definition, which we now find is also compound, will define a *universal* compound.

44^a11-14

If the interpretation of this chapter that I have offered is on the right lines, then the summarizing sentence that concludes it must be regarded with some suspicion. Reasonably, this summary omits the miscellaneous note with which the chapter began in its first paragraph. Somewhat less reasonably, it mentions first the digression in the third paragraph, treating it as an explanation of how a substance such as a house can come into being (i.e. considered as a compound) and of how it cannot (i.e. considered as a form). But quite unreasonably it then jumps to the final paragraph, which it characterizes as a discussion of 'the reduction of substances to numbers'. Such a reduction was briefly discussed at *Z*11, 36^b12-32, but all that has been said about it in this chapter is that it clearly cannot be done: 'if substances are in some way numbers . . . it is not as numbers of [abstract] units' ($^b33-4$). The positive comparisons that were drawn did not in any way suggest a *reduction* of substances to numbers. The summarizing sentence, then, appears to mistake the purpose of the last paragraph, and to omit altogether the main theme of the chapter, which is to show how the considerations of *Z*17 lead us to a true view of the structure and unity of a definition. For these reasons one may well suspect that it is not the work of Aristotle himself, but was added by a somewhat careless editor.

Chapters 4 and 5 might both be headed 'Miscellaneous Observations on Matter'. But in chapter 4 what starts as an observation on matter is then generalized to a point about all of the four causes, namely that one should in each case seek for the 'nearest' causes.

44^a15–25

(In the translation of this paragraph, occurrences of the word 'stuff' correspond to no Greek expression, and are supplied by me; occurrences of the word 'matter' or 'material' translate Aristotle's corresponding words. But I have used the two different words, 'stuff' and 'matter,' only to mark where the word is or is not my own supplement. No difference in sense is intended.)

The phrase 'primary matter'—or, more literally, 'first matter' ($^a16$, $^a23$)—is comparatively rare in Aristotle. On several occasions it is clear that what he means by the 'primary matter' of a thing is what commentators call its 'proximate matter', i.e. the most specific kind of matter from which it is made (as bronze is the matter of bronze things). (See, e.g., *Phys* II, 1, 193^a29 (cf. $^a9$–12); *GA* I, 20, 729^a32; *Δ*4, 1014^b32.) But he does also distinguish between matter that is 'primary in relation to the given thing' (i.e. its proximate matter), and matter that is 'primary in general' (*Δ*4, 1015^a7–10; cf. *Δ*6, 1016^a19–20), where the latter appears to mean 'ultimate matter'. At any rate, it is clearly 'ultimate matter' rather than 'proximate matter' that he calls 'primary matter' at *Θ*7, 1049^a24–7. The same applies to the present passage, where the proximate matter of a thing is called 'the matter appropriate to it', and this is contrasted with a primary matter, or perhaps several primary matters (e.g. earth, water, air, and fire), from which *everything* is made. I have claimed in the prologue to *Z*3 that Aristotle's own belief is that there is just one genuinely ultimate kind of matter (which the commentators call 'prime matter'), which functions as a 'principle' for all things that come to be. ('Principle' is here used in a sense which includes 'element', as at *Λ*4, 1070^b16–26, not in a sense which contrasts with it, as at *Z*17, 41^b31–3.) In the present passage he does not commit himself to this, but leaves open the possibility of there being several such ultimate kinds of matter. In any case, he mentions the point only to set it aside. His concern here is to stress the different point that there are many specific kinds of matter, and different kinds of thing will have different specific kinds of matter 'appropriate' to them.

It may be noted that his examples, phlegm and bile, are themselves specific kinds of matter, so the proximate matter of each is the next less specific kind of matter that they can be said to be 'from'. But the word 'from' is ambiguous in this context, as Aristotle notes at $^a23$–5, since it covers both what a thing is made *from* in our sense and what a thing is made *of*, which need not be the same. So his suggestion here is that phlegm may perhaps be made from and made of fatty stuff, and this in turn may be made from and made of sweet stuff, whereas bile is made from and made of bitter stuff. Phlegm may also perhaps be made *from* bile, but it is not made *of* bile. Rather, it comes from bile 'by the resolution of the bile into its primary [i.e. ultimate] matter'. For the bile does not persist in the phlegm that is made from it, nor does the bitter stuff that is the proximate matter of the bile, but only some more ultimate matter.

44^a25–32

The previous paragraph had begun with the claim that there is a different [proximate] matter 'appropriate' to each different [kind of] thing. The present paragraph notes exceptions to that claim. It is possible for different articles to be made of the same [proximate] matter, as, e.g., a box and a bed are both made of wood ($^a25$–7); and it is possible for the same article to be made of different [proximate] matters, as presumably a bed may be made of either wood or metal ($^a29$–32). This comes about, Aristotle says, because in the first case a different efficient cause is applied to the same matter, and in the second case the same efficient cause is applied to a different matter, the efficient cause being in each case a skill (*tekhnē*, $^a31$). One is tempted to object that it is the same skill, carpentry, that can produce both wooden boxes and wooden beds, whereas a different skill, metal-working, is required to produce metal beds. No doubt Aristotle's response would be that he is using 'the skill' here to mean the form of the finished product that exists beforehand in the mind of the craftsman, for it is really this that is the efficient cause (cf. *Z*7, 32^a32–$^b1$, $^b13$–14). This seems to leave out of account rather a lot of what we would wish to include in the efficient cause.

Between making these points Aristotle notes that in *some* cases the nature of the finished product dictates the kind of matter that it must have. The saw is one of his favourite examples to illustrate this point: if it is to fulfil its function, and hence *be* a saw, then it must be made of metal. (See, e.g., *Phys* II, 9, 200^a10–13.) Both in *Phys* II, 9 and in *PA* I, 1 he claims that, in the case of things that exist *by nature*, the form or function of the object will always necessitate the specific kind of matter that it is made of.

44^a32–$^b3$

At this point the interest of the chapter shifts from matter in particular to the four kinds of cause more generally. The connection is evidently that matter is one of these four causes. Aristotle has pointed out that (with some exceptions, as just admitted) different kinds of thing are made of different specific kinds of matter, and the moral that he draws is that when one is stating the material cause one should state the specific kind of matter in question. This is the 'nearest' material cause. But the same moral applies to the other kinds of cause too, for in *each* case one should state the 'nearest' cause. However, the point is not at once illustrated with other kinds of cause, for the discussion gets side-tracked to a different point. Aristotle gives here a case where all four kinds of cause are applicable, but then in the next two paragraphs he digresses to note that in some other cases some of the causes do not apply.

The question 'What is the cause of a man?' seems to be understood here as asking for a 'cause of coming to be' rather than a 'cause of being' (*Z*17, 41^a31-2). That is why there is an efficient cause to be cited, and why Aristotle can give as the material cause the matter that a man is made *from*, not the matter that an adult man is made *of*. (For his theory of sexual reproduction, see *Z*7, 32^a15-19 n.; *Z*9, 34^a33-^b4 n. For the equation between essence and purpose—the idea that what a man *is* is the same as what a man is *for*—cf. *Z*10, 35^b16-18 n.) One may note the assumption that the matter that a man comes from is 'peculiar' to man; it cannot, for example, be fertilized by the seed of any other animal to give rise to something that is not a man. (Contrast the mule, *Z*9, 34^a33-^b4.)

44^b3-8

The heavenly bodies are substances that exist by nature and are eternal. Since they are eternal, there is of course no matter *from* which they are made (and no efficient cause of their generation). But Aristotle supposes that there is a matter *of* which they are made, and that this is necessary to explain their capacity to be now in one place and now in another (cf. *H*1, 42^b3-6). In view of what he says in the next paragraph, it would seem that he need not have posited any matter for them to be made of. For if it is correct to say that a phenomenon such as an eclipse has no matter, since *instead* there is a substance (namely the moon) that undergoes this change, then it is not clear why one should not say exactly the same of the moon's movement: it has no matter, since the moon itself is what moves. But perhaps Aristotle would reply that the moon would not move if it were not made of a suitable matter, in fact a matter whose nature is to move not upwards nor downwards but in circles.

44^b8-15

The very accommodating expression 'things which are by nature but are not substances' seems intended here to be a way of referring to *changes* that occur by nature. At any rate, that is what the example illustrates. Aristotle's general doctrine is that for any change there is always an 'underlying thing' which is first in one state and then in another (*Phys* I, 7). Using the term 'matter' in a broad sense, this underlying and persisting thing can always be called the matter of the change (cf. *Z*3, prologue). But here Aristotle resists the broader usage, and says that when the underlying thing is itself a substance, then it should not be called 'matter'. Such a change, then, has no material cause, properly speaking, but only an analogue to what in other cases is the material cause. The particular example chosen, i.e. an eclipse of the moon, also illustrates a change that (probably) has no final cause either. But it does have an efficient cause, here specified first simply as 'the earth', but later filled out as 'the earth being in between' (i.e. in between the sun and the moon). It also has a formal cause, which is the definition of what an eclipse is. Aristotle recommends us to build into this definition a specification of the efficient cause (cf. *Z*17, 41^a27–32 n.). He says that unless we do this the definition will not be 'clear', but that does not seem to be right: the original definition was perfectly 'clear'. What he has in mind, one presumes, is that the expanded definition will give a more informative answer to the question: 'What is an eclipse?'

From our point of view the extra information is of course contingent; the moon's light *might* fail for quite different reasons. Even if Aristotle would claim that no other cause is in his sense 'possible', still he would surely admit that other causes are *imaginable*. But if a definition is allowed to include information that may be imagined otherwise, while still being a proper definition, then his claim that even eternal particulars cannot be defined must surely be rejected (cf. *Z*15, 40^a27–$^b4$ n.).

44^b15–20

The final paragraph is introduced abruptly, without any clear connection to what has preceded. But the explanation, I think, is that Aristotle has now recalled the point that he had in mind at 44^a32–$^b3$, that one should seek the 'nearest' causes for all four kinds of cause (where all are applicable). He is here illustrating this claim by pointing out what is involved in the attempt to give the 'nearest' causes of sleep, and revealing that the question is not simple. It requires us to say what part of the animal is first affected, what exactly it is that happens to it, and what brings this about. (A full account would also include the purpose of sleep.)

In the *De Somno* Aristotle describes sleep as an affection of the primary seat of all perception, which is the heart (455^a20–$^b2$, 456^a2–6). It is brought about when hot matter, absorbed into the blood from food, rises to the brain, is cooled there, and then recoils to settle round the heart (457^a33–458^a10; cf. *PA* 653^a10–20). Its purpose is relaxation, which is necessary for all animals (455^b16–25).

CHAPTER 5

The first paragraph of this brief chapter claims that only things which change have matter. It is very loosely connected to the rest of the chapter by the fact that opposites are given as an example of things that do not change, and the next paragraph professes to introduce a problem about the relation of matter to opposites. But in fact this problem has no special connection with opposites, for it concerns the relation between matter and potentiality.

44^b21–9

For things that 'are or are not without coming to be or ceasing to be', see *H*3, 43^b14–23n. This paragraph claims that none of such things have matter, and apparently it offers as an argument that (as *Z*8 has shown) whatever comes to be does have matter. Of course it does not actually follow from this that what does not come to be does not have matter, and the heavenly bodies would provide a counter-example. Whether Aristotle is right to say that points do not have matter is a curious question, but I set it aside. At any rate he seems to be on safe ground when he claims that the attributes (or 'forms') of being pale and being dark do not have matter.

At $^b24$–6 Aristotle apparently contradicts himself, saying first that *not* all opposites come to be from one another, evidently because the attribute of being pale does *not* come from the attribute of being dark, but then going on to say that the attributes *do* come from one another, but not in the same way as a pale man comes from a dark man. Clearly, if the attributes do come from one another, it is not in the same way. There is in this case no persisting, underlying thing which is first the one attribute and then the other, and (Aristotle has claimed) there is no time during which the one is coming to be and the other is ceasing to be. So at best they *succeed* one another, apparently in the sense that at one time the one exists but not the other, and at another time the other exists but not the one. But how should we understand this?

If the attributes in question are *universal* attributes, then such a change will happen only if at one time there are dark things but no pale things, and at another time there are pale things but no dark things. But it is impossible to believe that Aristotle was envisaging such an extraordinary, world-wide transformation when he made this casual remark. He was surely thinking of the quite ordinary change whereby one particular man changes from being dark to being pale. But then, if that is to bring about a succession of opposite attributes, as described, the attributes in question must be '*particular* attributes', capable of existing only in that one particular man and not elsewhere. (And it is implied that such a 'particular attribute' does *not* have matter; contrast *Z*15,

39^b24–25 n.) But I do not think we need press the remark so far. The suggestion that opposite attributes do come from one another 'in a way' need only mean that it comes about that one exists *where* the other once did, e.g. in Socrates, not that one exists and the other no longer exists at all.

(The scepticism about points, suggested by 'if they exist' at $^b22$, is surprising. Aristotle was familiar with such scepticism—see, e.g., *A*9, 992^a20–2, with Ross's note—but he certainly does not share it.)

44^b29–34

Matter has the potentiality for opposite states, or—more generally—just for different states. It is not clear why Aristotle should here hesitate to say that the same matter, the body, is potentially both healthy and sick, and that the same matter, some liquid, is potentially both wine and vinegar. But apparently he overcomes this hesitation, accepting that the same matter is potentially both, while nevertheless wishing to mark a distinction in a different way. It is the matter of the one, he suggests, 'in virtue of its state and form', but of the other 'in virtue of the privation of that state'. What 'state and form' does he mean?

It appears that he should mean the state and form *of the matter*, i.e. of the body in one case, and of the liquid in the other. Moreover, we can make some sense of this in the first case, for the form of a living body is its soul, i.e. its life, and this also is what it is for. If so, then it is natural enough to add that the kind of life that the body is for will be a healthy life rather than a sick life, so the healthy life will be in accordance with its nature, and the sick life contrary to its nature. This distinguishes between the two potentialities in just the way that Aristotle describes. But we would find it absurd to distinguish in this way between wine and vinegar. If we do wish to assign any purpose, 'in accordance with its own nature', to the liquid which exists first in the form of grape-juice, then in the form of wine, and then in the form of vinegar, then we shall probably say that what that liquid is for is to be grape-juice. That, after all, is its 'natural' form, and it is in that form that it has a role to play in what we think of as 'nature'. From this perspective, both wine and vinegar are equally 'unnatural' forms of that liquid.

Nor does it mend matters to suppose that Aristotle means to refer, not to the 'state and form' of the liquid (the matter), but to the 'state and form' of the wine, and of the vinegar. For here again the position is surely symmetrical. When the liquid is wine, then no doubt that is because it has the 'state and form' of wine, but equally, when it is vinegar, that is because it has the 'state and form' of vinegar. We may add that when it is in either form it lacks the other, and so suffers the 'privation' of the other. Evidently Aristotle is allowing himself to be influenced by the fact that he values wine more highly than he values vinegar, but it was a mistake on his part to suppose that this evaluation is in some way justified by the 'nature' of the items concerned.

44^b34–45^a6

Wine is not the matter of vinegar because although vinegar comes *from* wine, it is not made *of* wine; similarly, a corpse is not made *of* the living animal that it comes *from*. (Cf. *H*4, 44^a23–5.) But our understanding of this point does not seem to be improved by the suggestion that 'the decay is coincidental'. (Indeed, one wonders in what sense death is 'a coincidence'.) Nor does the comparison with night and day at first seem helpful, though it makes more sense when we recall that in Aristotle's view there is a persisting matter for this change, namely the air, in which light and darkness each inhere (*Λ*4, 1070^b21). So the night comes *from* the day, but is not made *of* the day; rather, it is 'made *of*' the same matter as the day was 'made *of*'.

The case of day and night is evidently a case of reciprocal change. Generalizing on this case, Aristotle adds that whenever *A* comes from *B* and *B* from *A* then neither is the matter of the other, though all that he seems entitled to is that it cannot be the case that *each* is the matter of the other (i.e. is made of the other). For example, we may say that a house was made from certain bricks (despite *Z*7, 33^a19–22), and then later, when the house is knocked down, that those bricks came from the house. This should not prevent us saying that the house was made of those same bricks that it was made from. To illustrate his point about reciprocal changes Aristotle does not change his examples (as I have just done), but speaks of a living thing coming from a corpse, and wine coming from vinegar. He uses explicitly temporal terminology in a way which is perhaps incautious. His words suggest that if wine is to come from vinegar, then *first* the vinegar 'reverts to its matter' and becomes water, so that there is an intermediate stage in which we have just water, and *then* that water becomes wine. Presumably this is an implication he did not intend. There is no more need for an intermediate stage here than there was in the change from wine to vinegar. All that needs to be insisted upon is that neither is made of the other, though there is a common matter that both are made of.

A curious question that arises is this. It seems very probable that Aristotle did believe that animals, such as maggots, may come from corpses. Did he also believe that wine may come from vinegar?

CHAPTER 6

This chapter is a further attack on the problem of the unity of a definition. As I read it, it brings to bear on that problem the new conception of a definition, developed in *H*2 and in *H*3, and it claims that with this understanding the old problem disappears.

47^a7–8

The question of the unity of a definition was linked with the question of the unity of a number at *H*3, 44^a2–9, but numbers are not mentioned again in the present chapter.

45^a8–20

Aristotle opens his discussion with the general principle that whenever a thing has parts, but is not to be identified with the sum of those parts, then there is always a cause of its unity. (As at *Z*16, 40^b9, and at *Z*17, 41^b12, a heap is given as an instance of something that *is* just the sum of its parts.) Then he briefly illustrates how this principle applies to bodies, before stating the main problem at $^a12$ ff. (For the suggestion at $^a13$ that the *Iliad* is a unity by being bound together, see *Z*4, 30^b9–10 n.)

As before, Aristotle states his problem in this way: a definition is a unity because what it is a definition *of* is a unity, but the problem is to explain how the thing defined *could* be a unity. As I said at *Z*12, 37^b8–14 n., the source of the problem seems to be that the definition has parts, and so it must appear that the thing defined has corresponding parts. If this is admitted, then to conform to the general principle with which we began, we must either say that the thing defined is simply the sum of those parts, or we must supply an appropriate cause of unity for it. But in the light of *H*3, 43^b10–14, the second alternative now appears to be impossible. For if there is a cause of unity, then it is the substance of the thing defined, and so should certainly have been included in the definition. Yet, if it had been, then the words which specify it would simply have formed another part of the definition, and so by hypothesis would correspond to another *part* of the thing defined. We should then still be at a loss for the cause of the unity of all those parts. The moral is that *if* the parts of the definition do each correspond to parts of the thing defined, then the thing defined can only be the sum of those parts, as it were the 'mere heap' of them.

It seems to be just this consequence that Aristotle proceeds to elaborate. Suppose, for example, that man is defined as a two-footed animal. What is defined is of course the universal 'man', not this or that particular man, so the suggestion is that this universal be construed simply as a 'heap' of two others. Now one can see why, from his own philosophical perspective, Aristotle should find this suggestion intolerable. But why does he think that the Platonist too would be bound to reject it? I think it is because he is pressing very hard on the idea that absolutely *no* 'cause of unity' is supplied by the suggested definition. Consequently, what is defined is not *any* kind of unity, which means that it is not 'one thing' at all. But that is simply a way of saying that it does not exist. So on this proposal there is actually no such thing as being a man; there are *only* the different universals in terms of which man is defined. Aristotle is confident that even a Platonist could not accept this.

Is this inference fair? Well, if we continue to think in terms of his own metaphor, it seems not to be. After all, heaps do exist, and a heap is one thing (one heap) even if there is not much to hold it together. In fact heaps do have a 'cause of unity' in Aristotle's sense, namely the arrangement of the items that they are heaps of. So let us drop the metaphor. Then we may say that even when one property is explicitly defined as the conjunction of two others, still it is *one* property that is defined, and not two. This again is because the definition does after all specify a suitable 'cause of unity', i.e. a way in which the two 'constituent' properties must be 'arranged' in order to form the property defined, namely that they must be 'arranged' *by conjunction*. (Clearly the *disjunction* of those same constituents would define quite a different property.) A definition which really did not supply *any* 'cause of unity' would simply be a list, and a phrase such as 'a two-footed animal' is not a list. But Aristotle's argument, I think, overlooks this point.

45^a20–33

A more literal rendering of the first sentence of this paragraph is: 'So it is clear that, for those who proceed in this way, as they are accustomed to define and to say (*legein*), it is not possible to . . . solve the problem.' The Greek word '*legein*' has a wide range of meanings, and it is not clear what kind of 'saying' is in question here. I have adopted the translation 'to explain' because that suits equally well the two interpretations of this sentence that seem worth pursuing. On the one interpretation, the point is that definitions are themselves explanations, so 'to define and explain' just means 'to define'. Aristotle is saying, then, that the problem cannot be resolved if we retain the traditional way of defining man, e.g. as a two-footed animal. On the other interpretation, the Platonist is taken to be adopting a certain explanation *of definitions*, so 'to define and to explain' is short for 'to define and to explain that definition'. On this account Aristotle is not objecting to the definition itself, but is saying that the Platonists have misunderstood it. In particular, they think that the two parts of the definition correspond to two parts of the universal defined, but that is a mistake. This second interpretation seems to me an unnatural way of taking the Greek, yet it seems to the vast majority of commentators to be what the argument requires at this point. So it can fairly be called the orthodox interpretation. (Among its adherents are Ross; Balme [1962]; Grene [1974]; Rorty [1974]; Lloyd [1981], 32–6; Burnyeat *et al.* [1984]; Scaltsas [1985]; Furth [1988], 246; Irwin [1988], 568; Gill [1989], 139–44.) Let us pursue this suggestion first.

On this account the problem is to show how the universal 'man', still defined as 'two-footed animal', can be a unity. It is perfectly clear from what follows that Aristotle is claiming that his notions of matter and form provide the solution. There then seems to be only one possible explanation of how they could do so: the phrase 'two-footed animal' does not mention two co-ordinate parts of the universal defined, for one word gives its matter and the other its form. Taking a hint from *Z*12, 38^a6–8, it will be the genus 'animal' that gives the matter of 'man', and the differentia 'two-footed' that gives its form. So the universal 'man' is a compound of a sort, but not one whose 'cause of unity' is still to seek. For Aristotle goes on to argue in the rest of this paragraph, and again in the final paragraph (from 45^b10), that it is ridiculous to ask for any further explanation of how matter and form can together make a unity.

There are three objections to this line of interpretation. One I have already mentioned, namely that it requires us to understand the opening sentence at $^a20$–2 in an unnatural way. The second is its reliance on the thesis that the genus is matter. Since this thesis is by no means a standing feature of Aristotle's thought (cf. *Z*12, 38^a5–9 n.), one would certainly expect him to *state* the thesis somewhere in his discussion if he is in fact relying on it. But he never does. The interpretation must, then, depend upon the point that one of the very few occurrences of this thesis is in *Z*12, where again the topic is the unity of a definition. Perhaps the suggestion comes readily to Aristotle's mind when he is thinking of this problem, though very seldom in other contexts? But this raises the question of the relation between *Z*12 and *H*6. If *H*6 was written first, it is then puzzling (on this interpretation) that in *Z*12 Aristotle puts no great weight on the idea that the genus is matter, but casually disjoins that suggestion with another (i.e. that the genus does not exist apart from the species), as if it makes little difference which we say. But anyway it is much more probable that *Z*12 was written first, for I have argued in my epilogue to that chapter that it was a relatively early attempt, whereas *H*6 evidently presupposes the doctrine that form is actuality, as introduced in *H*2. (The doctrine was anticipated at *Z*13, 38^b6; it is also prominent in book II of the *De Anima*.) On this hypothesis, however, it is puzzling that *H*6 makes not the slightest mention of the question that occupied much of *Z*12: how does a series of several different differentiae form a unity? It would appear that *H*6 no longer regards this as a relevant problem, though one cannot see why, if it is still retaining the traditional style of definition discussed in *Z*12.

Finally, one must ask how Aristotle supposes that his problem will disappear if the genus is dubbed 'matter'. It is no doubt fair to say that if the two parts of the definition may be distinguished as matter and form, then this *could* help to prevent us from supposing that each corresponds to an independent part of the item defined. But Aristotle's own illustration signally fails to bring home this point. He introduces the definition 'a round [piece of] bronze' as one that clearly combines matter and form, and says that it is obvious that this defines a unity. But on the contrary, in the terms in which this problem is usually seen, it is obvious that it does *not* define a unity. Being round is one property, being bronze is another, quite independent property, and the conjunction of the two is an entirely accidental compound, with no more unity than the property of being a pale man. *Z*12 said (at 37^b14-18) that 'pale' and 'man' will form a unity when the one belongs to the other, i.e. when some particular man is pale, but it went on to argue that that model will *not* explain the required unity of the universal 'two-footed animal'. On the present interpretation, *H*6 appears to say exactly the opposite. At any rate, it must be particular round pieces of bronze that Aristotle is thinking of when he says that there is no cause, other than the efficient cause, of what is potential being actual ($^a31$, repeated $^b21-2$). For efficient causes apply only to particulars. So his thought appears to be: (i) a particular round piece of bronze is a unity; therefore (ii) the universal 'round bronze' is a unity; and so by analogy (iii) the universal 'two-footed animal' is a unity. But on this interpretation the step from (i) to (ii) is wholly illegitimate, and we may add that the step from (ii) to (iii), founded only on an unpersuasive analogy, is anyway left entirely to our imagination. Our text simply does not assert (iii).

These are serious problems for the orthodox interpretation of *H*6. So I now turn to a different interpretation, which begins from the different reading of $^a20-2$. On this reading, Aristotle's opening remark is that we cannot solve the problem if we still retain the traditional style of definition, such as 'man is a two-footed animal'. But what does he think is wrong with such a definition? Well, he says that it does not show how what is defined is a unity, and so far we have supposed that what is defined is the universal 'man'. But we can also say that the definition defines *a man*, and we can certainly take $^a14-15$ as asking 'What is it, then, that makes *a man* a unity rather than a plurality?' When the question is taken in this way, Aristotle's answer to it is obvious: what makes a man a unity is his form, or in other words his soul. Accordingly, a definition of man should take the form 'such-and-such a formula in such-and-such a matter taken as universal' (*Z*10, 35^b27-30), for 'it is clear that the soul is the primary substance, that the body is matter, and that man or animal is the compound of the two taken universally' (*Z*11, 37^a5-7). What is wrong with the traditional kind of definition is that it simply ignores the soul, yet it is the soul that *is* the desired cause of unity.

We may generalize this interpretation. In *Z*17 (esp. from 41^b11) Aristotle argued that the cause of unity of each thing is always its form. In *H*2 he argued that *all* proper definitions will predicate form of matter (43^a5-7), and the examples show that 'matter' is there meant in its ordinary sense. There is no particular reason to suppose that this doctrine of *H*2 was influenced by the discussion of form in *Z*17, but the doctrine is repeated in *H*3, at 43^b30–2, in a context which very clearly does depend both on *Z*17 and on *H*2. Aristotle views this as a new conception of definition, for when he is thinking of a definition as combining genus and differentiae, he says that the differentia is *not* predicated of the genus (*Z*4, 30^a10–14; *Z*12, 37^b18–21; and see *Z*12, epilogue); but when he is thinking of a definition as combining matter and form, he says that the form *is* predicated of the matter. What he is proposing here in *H*6 is that the traditional style of definition be abandoned, and the new style adopted in its place. Then, he thinks, the problem he has stated will disappear, for the new style of definition always does specify the cause of unity, since it specifies the form, and the form is the cause of unity.

Of the three objections that I raised to the orthodox interpretation, the first is straightforwardly met by this revised interpretation, and the second does not arise. As for the relationship between *Z*12 and *H*6, we may suppose that *H*6 was written long after *Z*12, and that it ignores the problem of many differentiae because the new conception of definition has rendered it irrelevant. In any case, on this revised interpretation there is really nothing in common between the problem tackled in *Z*12 and the problem resolved in *H*6. This defence, of course, does admit that a revised form of the third objection may fairly be raised. We could put it by saying that, on the present interpretation, *H*6 is guilty of *ignoratio elenchi*: it professes to be answering the problem of 'the unity of a definition', but is actually doing no such thing, for the 'real' unity problem concerns the unity of the universal 'man', not the unity of *a man*. It seems best to admit this charge, but to add that it applies not only to *H*6 but also to *H*3, 44^a2–9. There too Aristotle claims that a definition is a unity, and that the Platonists cannot explain this, whereas he can ($^a5$–6). But when he comes to state his explanation it is that 'substances are one in this way . . . because each is an actuality and a certain nature' ($^a7$–9). This again seems to provide the answer to the wrong question, i.e. to the question 'What makes *a man* a unity?'

I conclude that although there are objections to this revised interpretation, they are much less serious than the objections to the orthodox interpretation. It ought, therefore, to be accepted. (See further 45^b7–23 n.).

In *Z*12 Aristotle had taken it to be obvious that a particular pale man may be counted as one thing (37^b14–18). Here too he takes it to be obvious that a particular lump of matter, say bronze, and a form such as circularity, may together constitute one thing. But he also offers to *explain* this unity by relying on his assimilation of matter to potentiality and of form to actuality. This explanation is entirely bogus.

There is no genuine connection between form and actuality, and it only causes confusion to speak as though matter and potentiality were the same (cf. *Z*16, 40^b5–16 n.). Thus Aristotle says here that matter and form should be distinguished, 'and the one is potentially while the other is actually' ($^a24$), as if that explained the distinction between them. As we learn from 45^b17–19, what he means is that 'the one is potentially *what* the other is actually', but this is nonsense. It implies that when we have a round piece of bronze, then the matter, i.e. the bronze, is *potentially* round, whereas the form, i.e. the shape, is *actually* round. But (*a*) when the bronze is round, then of course it is actually round, and not just potentially round, whereas (*b*) it is the bronze which is round, and the shape itself is not round at all. (This is a category-mistake on a par with Plato's mistake of supposing that the form of largeness is a large thing.) Or again, consider his statement at $^a30$–2 that when what is potentially a sphere is actually a sphere, 'this is precisely what being is for each of them'. If this means that it is the essence, both of the potential sphere and of the actual sphere, to be a sphere, then apparently it is false. For the phrase 'the potential sphere' presumably refers to the bronze, and it is *not* part of the essence of the bronze that it should be a sphere. If, on the other hand, it means that it is the essence of the potential sphere to be potentially a sphere, while it is the essence of the actual sphere to be actually a sphere, then in a sense it can be accepted. But if we do accept it, then of course we must say that the potential sphere (i.e. the bronze) and the actual sphere (i.e. the sphere) are different things, since they have different essences (and hence different life-histories). This hardly supports the claim that a round piece of bronze is *one* thing.

Evidently Aristotle should not have attempted this explanation of how, when we have some matter in a certain form, we have one thing. For, even if we discount the awkward remarks I have just noted, potentiality anyway explains nothing. (If one is puzzled over how x could be F, one is not helped by the assurance that x has the potentiality of being F.) He should simply have said that it is obvious that a round piece of bronze can be regarded as one thing, and left it at that.

45^a33–$^b7$

$^a33$–5: *Intelligible matter.* Aristotle has just been talking of defining a circular (or spherical) piece of bronze. This reminds him that one can also define a circle (or a sphere), and at first glance such a definition does not mention any kind of matter. But he wishes to maintain that it does, since 'there is intelligible matter as well as perceptible matter'. In *Z*10 'intelligible matter' was evidently the matter of such geometrical entities as circles and spheres (see 35^b31–36^a12 n.), so the simplest hypothesis is that the same explanation applies here too. The example 'a circle is a plane figure' is intended to indicate that the ('intelligible') plane is the *matter* of which an ('intelligible') circle is made. Different circles differ from one another by being 'made of' different parts of the plane.

In this example what one might naturally regard as the *genus* of a circle, namely 'plane figure', is construed as mentioning the matter of the circle. This might be thought to be a point in favour of the orthodox interpretation of *H*6, according to which 'man is a two-footed animal' is still permitted as a proper definition, but the genus 'animal' is construed as mentioning matter. If so, then to preserve the analogy with an 'intelligible' circle, the genus 'animal' should be construed as mentioning the *perceptible* matter of which an ordinary perceptible animal is made, i.e. flesh and bones in the case of a man, but something rather different in the case of an oyster. (This view is adopted by Rorty [1974], 76.) But while I agree that Aristotle thinks that a definition should mention such perceptible matter, it is odd to suppose that he thought that the word 'animal' already did this. Accordingly, the usual version of the orthodox interpretation (following Ross) supposes that the genus 'animal' is itself an example of 'intelligible matter', i.e. the matter of which the ('intelligible') species 'man' is made. This implies that the phrase 'intelligible matter' does not mean the same here in *H*6 as it meant in *Z*10, which is a further count against this interpretation.

$^a36–^b7$: If a definition must always mention matter, then evidently what has no matter cannot be defined. Aristotle appears to infer that what has no matter must be simple, and for that reason must automatically be a unity. On Ross's account, what Aristotle is thinking of as simple are the *summa genera* that are the titles of the categories, i.e. substance, quality, quantity, and the rest. So the words 'a this, a quality, a quantity' at $^b1–2$ should be understood as 'being a this, being a quality, being a quantity'; they introduce three examples of things which have no matter. On the orthodox account, these 'have no matter' because they have no genus; they are themselves ultimate genera and hence 'ultimate matters'. While this is a possible view, it is nevertheless odd. One would more naturally expect what has no matter to be itself pure form rather than pure matter. In that case one might prefer to take the parenthetical words 'a this, a quality, a quantity' simply as a list of headings; they suggest merely that there will be simple and indefinable items *in* each of the various categories. But, as at *H*3, $43^b28–32$, we are left to speculate upon what Aristotle may have been thinking of as examples.

At $^b3–4$ Aristotle adds that an essence is also something that is 'at once' both a unity and a being. If he is retaining the view of *Z*4–6, which equates essence and definition, the explanation of this claim is that a definition defines a unity because it predicates form of matter, as the previous paragraph has explained. If he is retaining the view of *Z*7–10, which equates essence and form, then we could say (in conformity with Ross's account) that at $^b1–2$ Aristotle observes that what is (from a logical point of view) 'pure matter' itself has no matter, and here at $^b3–4$ he makes the corresponding point about 'pure form'. Alternatively, if we suppose that Aristotle has been thinking of forms throughout, then we may say that he adds a separate mention of essences because it is not at all clear that all essences do fall under one or other of the traditional categories. One could offer yet further speculations.

The remaining claims made in this paragraph are (i) that being and unity do not occur in definitions ($^b2-3$); (ii) that being and unity are not genera ($^b6$); and (iii) that they do not exist separately from particulars ($^b7$). It appears that (ii) is the reason for (i); at any rate, that is the way that Aristotle usually connects these two claims (e.g. *An. Post* II, 92^b13-14). It also appears that Aristotle has some motive for introducing (ii), namely to guard against a possible misunderstanding. For he has said of things without matter that each is 'just what is some unity' and 'just what is some being', and this is a form of words that might be taken to mean that each has unity and being as its genus. (The phrase '*estin hoper X*' is often used in this way in the Logical Works. See Barnes [1975], 168.) So it is natural for him to add an explicit disclaimer. For both of these reasons, one is strongly tempted to rearrange our text, so that $^b2-3$ comes after $^b6$. Certainly the text as we have it, with its several repetitions, runs very awkwardly.

Finally, it should be observed that Aristotle is surely exaggerating when he claims that *everything* without matter is a unity. For suppose that *X* and *Y* are each things without matter. Then it would appear that what is indicated by such phrases as '*X* and *Y*' and '*X* or *Y*' is equally without matter, but that hardly seems a good ground for saying that what is indicated must 'at once' be a unity.

45^b7-23

At *A*6, 987^b7-14 Aristotle tells us that Plato was led to talk of participation (where the Pythagoreans had talked of imitation) in an attempt to say how particulars were related to the forms after which they were called. But he could not explain what this participation was. So one might naturally suppose that when Lycophron talked of communion, and others of composition or of tying together, it was this relation of predication that they too were trying to describe. On the other hand, some evidently attempted to use the notion of participation to describe the relation between genus and differentia, as Aristotle shows us when he twice argues that this will not do (*Z*12, 37^b18-24; *Z*14, 39^b2-6). He also adds, on the second occasion, that one might try saying that genus and differentia 'are placed together and in contact, or intermixed', but comments that 'all this is absurd'. Perhaps, then, it was for this purpose that Lycophron talked of communion, and others invented other expressions. But 'the tying together of soul with body', though it may be meant as a definition of life, is surely not a definition through genus and differentia. Moreover, it would seem somewhat circular to propose 'the communion of knowing and the soul' as any kind of definition of knowledge. In fact, as Aristotle proceeds to elaborate his point further with examples such as 'the bronze being a triangle', it becomes clear that it is just ordinary predication that he is talking of. (Lycophron's concern with the 'is' of predication is also mentioned at *Phys* I, 2, 185^b27-8.)

The point, then, appears just to be this: people have invented all kinds of expressions for describing predication, but have not been able to explain that vocabulary in any useful way.

I postpone to the epilogue a speculation on why Aristotle might have thought that his own terminology of matter and form, potentiality and actuality, was superior. What needs to be considered here is why he should suppose that these remarks on predication are at all relevant to his topic in this chapter, the problem of the unity of a definition. The answer can only be that he is presuming that the unity of the proposition 'the bronze is round' carries with it the unity of the item referred to by 'the round bronze', and that this in turn carries with it the unity of the proposed definition 'a round bronze' (offered, we imagine, as the definition of some single word such as 'cloak'). The phrase 'a round bronze' is regarded as itself a phrase in which a form (signified by 'round') is predicated of matter (signified by 'bronze'). So we may generalize and say that any definition which predicates form of matter in this way will define a unity. On the orthodox interpretation of this chapter, *all* definitions may be so regarded, including the definition of a man as 'a wingless two-footed animal'. On the interpretation that I prefer, only some proposed definitions will qualify. In particular, the traditional definition of a man should be rejected, and replaced by something along the lines of 'such-and-such a body living such-and-such a kind of life'. But in either case the solution accepted here is just the same solution as was rejected at *Z*12, 37^b14–24. We must suppose that in the gap between these two treatments Aristotle has come to a radically different view of what the problem itself is supposed to be.

Final Epilogue: Unity and Definition

In *Z*4–11 there is little stress on the notion of unity. In fact unity is mentioned only once (at *Z*4, 30^b7–13), and the more prominent idea is that a substance, or form, ought to be something 'primary', which is twice explained as meaning non-compound (*Z*4, 30^a10–11; *Z*11, 37^b3–4). If we may discount *Z*12, unity does not begin to play an important role until *Z*16, 40^b5–16, where it is argued that many of the things commonly held to be substances do not merit that title, since they are not sufficiently 'unified'. Indeed, if we put this passage together with some others (notably *Z*17, 41^b28–31), it appears that Aristotle will accept only living plants and animals as proper examples of perceptible substances, and the main factor that is influencing him seems to be their well-developed 'unity'. In particular he is impressed by the fact that the activities of the parts can only be understood as contributions to the activity, i.e. life, of the whole. So it is not surprising that when *Z*17 introduces a new line of thought by considering substance as a 'cause' (i.e. explanation), it should describe the required cause not only as a 'cause of being' (41^a32, $^b28$) but also as a 'cause of unity' ($^b11$–12). In each case it is the form, i.e.

soul, that merits this description, and this is a thought that is carried further in book *H*.

The thought is combined with another new development, which we first find in *H*2, namely a revised view of the nature of definitions. During much of *Z*7–10 Aristotle had claimed that only form can be defined. In *Z*11 this doctrine is certainly modified, as he admits that *some* things have to be defined as compounds of form in matter, i.e. as 'one thing in another, or certain things in a certain state' (36^b23–4). But in the general context of *Z*7–11 it is natural to look upon such definitions as second-rate; what they define is a compound and not a pure form, and accordingly what they define should not be counted as a substance (*Z*10, 35^b27–31). But in *H*2 it is asserted that *every* definition defines such a compound, since *every* definition should combine both form and matter. The same claim recurs at *H*3, 43^b30–2, and I have argued that it is also required at *H*6, 45^a20–9, if we are to make sense of that passage. So on this view, if we are concerned with a pure form, something simple and not composite (*H*3, 43^b28–30), something which itself has no matter (*H*6, 45^a36–$^b1$), then we must say that it has no definition at all. (Presumably it may still be known, but in another way, and not via a definition. Cf. *Z*17, 41^b9–11). This is a very notable volte-face, and I can see no satisfying explanation of it. No doubt Aristotle was wrong in the first place both when he supposed that all forms can be defined and when he supposed that only forms can be defined. But he seems to be equally wrong in his second view that definition applies, not to forms themselves, but only to compounds of form in matter. So the change of view is not clearly an improvement, but it certainly is a change.

On the new view of definition it is not the whole of a definition that counts as a 'cause of being', but only the part which is form. This Aristotle somewhat oddly calls the 'differentia' (42^b32–3, 43^a2–4) as if any differences in the specified matter are of no significance (cf. 43^a12–14n.). In *H*2 he does not seem to be thinking of this cause as specially a cause of unity. At any rate, unity is not explicitly mentioned, and while several of the differentiae that he lists do indicate how a thing 'holds together', still many do not. But in *H*3, we find both the emphasis on unity from *Z*17 (43^b10–13) and the new view of definition from *H*2 (43^b30–2). This leads Aristotle to think once more of the problem that he used to call 'the unity of a definition', which he therefore brings in at *H*3, 44^a2–9, and which occupies him throughout *H*6. But though he now professes to have a solution to it, that is only because of his changed perception of what the problem is. For he now thinks that it is adequately answered so long as the definition says why the objects falling under it are unities, and that is exactly what the new style of definition does. For it says how the matter of the object is arranged, organized, and structured by the form.

In the course of further elaborating this reply, Aristotle's perception of the problem seems to change yet again, as he comes to see the unity of matter and form as somehow providing a solution to the much wider problem of the unity of predication. At any rate, he criticizes the attempts of others to explain this *latter* unity at 45ᵇ7–16, and he goes on to claim that we have only to see things in terms of matter and form, potentiality and actuality, and that problem too will disappear. If this suggestion is to apply to more than a very restricted range of predications, we must here understand 'matter' and 'form' in their wider sense (cf. *Z*3, prologue). So 'the bronze is round' is a satisfactory predication, and 'the round bronze' designates a single item, because bronze is related to roundness as matter to form. And similarly too, 'the man is pale' is a satisfactory predication, and 'the pale man' designates a single item, because again the man is related to pallor as matter to form. In the first of these cases one could plausibly say that it is the form, i.e. the shape, that ensures that the bronze in question does constitute one thing, say a coin. But in the second case the analogous claim would be absurd, for the man does not in any way owe his unity to his pale colour. Thus, when 'matter' and 'form' are understood in their wider sense, we can no longer suppose that it is form in particular that is the 'cause' of the unity. The significant point can only be that the two terms are *related* to one another as matter to form. But how is that supposed to help us understand how a 'unity' can result from them?

Aristotle himself seems to have thought that the equation between form and actuality, and between matter and potentiality, would continue to hold even when 'form' and 'matter' are understood in their wider sense, and would continue to remove any puzzle. But this suggestion is of no value, and I pursue it no further. There is, however, a different feature of the matter/form relationship which may have something to offer. Let us begin with a reflection upon the kind of view that Aristotle is rejecting. The terminology of 'communion', 'composition', and 'tying together' goes wrong because it suggests a symmetrical relationship; it treats the two entities in question as equal partners. This point applies with less force to 'participation' (and to 'imitation'), but one may still object that these idioms suggest a relationship between two entities which exist independently of one another. But Aristotle would say that the relation between matter and form is not like this. Though he does indeed speak of a compound of the two, still the 'ingredients' of this compound are not on an equal footing. It is definitely a mistake to suppose that the form (the 'arrangement') is as much an *element* of the compound as is the matter of which it is the form (the stuff 'arranged'). On the contrary, the two are quite different types of thing, and neither can exist without the other. The form, that is, exists only as the 'arrangement' of some matter, and equally matter exists only in some 'arrangement' or other. Moreover, this point, which was developed in *Z*17 and *H*3 with substantial form in mind, will also generalize perfectly nicely to all those other cases where Aristotle is ready to see an underlying thing which can be called 'matter', and a property which it acquires or loses which can be called 'form'. For the basic thought is simply this. Subject and predicate 'fit together' without the need of anything further to effect the combination, just because they are entities of different types. By contrast, two entities of the same type can be put together to make one only by adding some extra thing to link the one to the other.

SELECT BIBLIOGRAPHY

ABBREVIATIONS

AGP	
	Ancient Philosophy
CQ	*Classical Quarterly*
CR	*Classical Review*
JHI	*Journal of the History of Ideas*
JHP	*Journal of the History of Philosophy*
JP	*Journal of Philosophy*
OSAP	*Oxford Studies in Ancient Philosophy*
PAS	*Proceedings of the Aristotelian Society*
PBA	*Proceedings of the British Academy*
Phr	*Phronesis*
PPR	*Philosophy and Phenomenological Research*
PR	*Philosophical Review*
PS	*Philosophical Studies*
RM	*Review of Metaphysics*
BSS	*Barnes, Schofield, and Sorabji [1975–9]*

Ackrill, J. L. [1963], Aristotle's Categories and De Interpretatione (tr. and comm.), Clarendon Aristotle Series, Oxford.

—— [1981], *Aristotle the Philosopher*, Oxford.

Albritton, R. G. [1957], 'Forms of Particular Substances in Aristotle's *Metaphysics*', *JP 54*, 699–708.

Allen, R. E. [1969], 'Individual Properties in Aristotle's *Categories*', *Phr 14*, 31–9.

Annas, J. [1976], *Aristotle's Metaphysics, Books M and N* (tr. and comm.), Clarendon Aristotle Series, Oxford.

Balme, D. M. [1962], '*ΓΕΝΟΣ* and *ΕΙΔΟΣ* in Aristotle's Biology', *CQ 12*, 81–98.

—— [1972], *Aristotle's De Partibus Animalium I and De Generatione Animalium I* (tr. and comm.), Clarendon Aristotle Series, Oxford.

—— [1980], 'Aristotle's Biology was Not Essentialist', *AGP 62*, 1–12. (Reprinted in Gotthelf and Lennox [1987], 291–302.)

—— [1984], 'The Snub', *AP 4*, 1–8. (Reprinted in Gotthelf and Lennox [1987], 306–12.)

—— [1987], 'Note on the *aporia* in *Metaphysics Z*', in Gotthelf and Lennox [1987], 302–6.

Barnes, J. [1975], *Aristotle's Posterior Analytics* (tr. and comm.), Clarendon Aristotle Series, Oxford.

—— Schofield, M., and Sorabji, R. (eds.), *Articles on Aristotle*, 4 vols. (London, 1975–9). (= *BSS*)

Barnes, K. T. [1977], 'Aristotle on Identity and its Problems', *Phr 22*, 48–62.

Bonitz, H. [1848], *Aristotelis Metaphysica*, 2 vols., Bonn.

Brunschwig, J. [1979], 'La Forme, prédicat de la matière?', in P. Aubenque (ed.), *Études sur la métaphysique d'Aristote* (Paris, 1979), 131–58.

Burnyeat, M., *et al.* [1979], *Notes on Book Zeta of Aristotle's Metaphysics*, Oxford.

—— *et al.* [1984], *Notes on Books Eta and Theta of Aristotle's Metaphysics*, Oxford.

Charlton, W. [1970], *Aristotle's Physics, Books I and II* (tr. and comm.), Clarendon Aristotle Series, Oxford.

Code, A. [1976], 'The Persistence of Aristotelian Matter', *PS 29*, 357–67.

—— [1978], 'No Universal is a Substance', *Paideia*, Special Aristotle Issue, 65–74.

—— [1984], 'The Aporematic Approach to Primary Being in *Metaphysics Z*', *Canadian Journal of Philosophy*, supp. vol. 10, 1–20.

Cohen, S. [1984*a*], 'Aristotle's Doctrine of the Material Substrate', *PR 93*, 171–94.

—— [1984*b*], 'Aristotle and Individuation', *Canadian Journal of Philosophy*, supp. vol. 10, 41–65.

Duerlinger, J. [1970], 'Predication and Inherence in Aristotle's *Categories*', *Phr 15*, 179–203.

Ferejohn, M. [1980], 'Aristotle on Focal Meaning and the Unity of Science', *Phr* 25, 117–28.

Fine, G. [1984], 'Separation', *OSAP* 2, 31–87.

Frede, M. [1978], 'Individuals in Aristotle', translated from the German in Frede [1987*b*], 49–71.

—— [1981], 'Categories in Aristotle', in D. J. O'Meara (ed.), *Studies in Aristotle* (Washington, DC, 1981), 1–24. (Reprinted in Frede [1987*b*], 29–48.)

—— [1985], 'Substance in Aristotle's *Metaphysics*', in A. Gotthelf (ed.), *Aristotle on Nature and Living Things* (Pittsburgh, 1985), 17–26. (Reprinted in Frede [1987*b*], 72–80.)

—— [1987*a*], 'The Unity of Special and General Metaphysics', in Frede [1987*b*], 81–95.

—— [1987*b*], *Essays in Ancient Philosophy*, Oxford, 1987.

—— and Patzig, G. *Aristoteles, Metaphysik Z*, 2 vols. (Munich, 1988).

Furth, M. [1985], *Aristotle, Metaphysics VII–X* (tr.), Indianapolis.

—— [1988], *Substance, Form and Psyche: An Aristotelean Metaphysics*, Cambridge.

Gill, M. L. [1989], *Aristotle on Substance*, Princeton, NJ.

Gotthelf, A., and Lennox, J. G. (eds.) [1987], *Philosophical Issues in Aristotle's Biology*, Cambridge.

Graham, D. W. [1987], 'The Paradox of Prime Matter', *JHP* 25, 475–90.

—— [1987], *Aristotle's Two Systems*, Oxford.

Grene, M. [1974], 'Is Genus to Species as Matter to Form?', *Synthese 28*, 51–69.

Hare, J. E. [1979], 'Aristotle and the Definition of Natural Things' *Phr 24*, 168–79.
Harter, E. D. [1975], 'Aristotle on Primary *OUΣIA*', *AGP* 57, 1–20.
Heath, T. L. [1921], *A History of Greek Mathematics*, Oxford.
Heinaman, R. [1979], 'Aristotle's Tenth Aporia', *AGP 61*, 249–70.
—— [1980], 'An Argument in *Metaphysics* Z13', *CQ 30*, 72–85.
—— [1981], 'Non-Substantial Individuals in the *Categories*', *Phr 26*, 295–307.
Hughes, G. J. [1979], 'Universals as Potential Substances: The Interpretation of *Metaphysics* Z13', in Burnyeat *et al.* [1979], 107–26.
Irwin, T. H. [1982], 'Aristotle's Concept of Signification', in M. Schofield and M. Nussbaum (eds.), *Language and Logos* (Cambridge, 1982), 241–66.
—— [1988], *Aristotle's First Principles*, Oxford.
Jaeger, W., *Aristotelis Metaphysica*, Oxford Classical Texts (Oxford, 1957).
Jones, B. [1974], 'Aristotle's Introduction of Matter', *PR 83*, 474–500.
King, H. R. [1956], 'Aristotle without *Materia prima*', *JHI 17*, 370–87.
Kirwan, C. A. [1971], *Aristotle's Metaphysics, books ΓΔE* (tr. and comm.), Clarendon Aristotle Series, Oxford.
Kung, J. [1978], 'Can Substance be Predicated of Matter?', *AGP 60*, 140–59.
Lear, J. [1988], *Aristotle: The Desire to Understand*, Cambridge.
Lesher, J. [1971], 'Substance, Form and Universal: A Dilemma', *Phr 16*, 169–78.
Lewis, F. A. [1982], 'Accidental Sameness in Aristotle', *PS 42*, 1–36.
—— [1991], *Substance and Predication in Aristotle*, Cambridge.
Lloyd, A. C. [1981], *Form and Universal in Aristotle*, Liverpool.
Loux, M. J. [1971], 'Aristotle on the Transcendentals', *Phr 18*, 225–39.
—— [1979], 'Form, Species and Predication in *Metaphysics ZHΘ*', *Mind 88*, 1–23.
Matthews, G. B. [1982], 'Accidental Unities', in M. Schofield and M. Nussbaum (eds.), *Language and Logos* (Cambridge, 1982), 223–40.
—— [1990], 'Aristotelian Essentialism', *PPR 50 Suppl.*, 251–62.
—— and Cohen, S. M. [1967/8], 'The One and the Many', *RM 21*, 630–55.
Modrak, D. K. [1979], 'Forms, Types, and Tokens in Aristotle's *Metaphysics*, *JHP 17*, 371–81.
Morrison, D. R. [1985], 'Separation in Aristotle's Metaphysics', *OSAP 3*, 125–57.
Mueller, I. [1970], 'Aristotle on Geometrical Objects', *AGP* 52, 156–71.
Owen, G. E. L. [1960], 'Logic and Metaphysics in Some Earlier Works of Aristotle', in I. Düring and G. E. L. Owen (eds.), *Aristotle and Plato in the Mid-Fourth Century* (Göteborg, 1960), 163–90. (Reprinted in *BSS*, iii. 13–32; and in Owen [1986], 180–99.)
—— [1965*a*], 'The Platonism of Aristotle', *PBA 51*, 125–50. (Reprinted in *BSS*, i. 14–34; and in Owen [1986], 200–20.)

Owen, G. E. L. [1965*b*] 'Inherence', *Phr 10*, 97–105. (Reprinted in Owen [1986], 252–8.)

—— [1965*c*] 'Aristotle on the Snares of Ontology', in R. Bambrough (ed.), *New Essays on Plato and Aristotle* (London, 1965), 69–95. (Reprinted in Owen [1986], 259–78.)

—— [1978/9], 'Particular and General', *PAS 79*, 1–21. (Reprinted in Owen [1986], 279–94.)

—— [1986] *Logic, Science, and Dialectic*, London.

Owens, J. [1951], *The Doctrine of Being in the Aristotelian Metaphysics* (3rd edn., 1978), Toronto.

Patzig, G. [1960], 'Theology and Ontology in Aristotle's *Metaphysics*', *Kant-Studien* 52, 185–205; translated in *BSS*, iii. 33–49.

—— [1979], 'Logical Aspects of Some Arguments in Aristotle's *Metaphysics*', in P. Aubenque (ed.), *Études sur la Métaphysique d'Aristote* (Paris, 1979), 37–46.

Robinson, H. M. [1974], 'Prime Matter in Aristotle', *Phr 19*, 168–88.

Rorty, R. M. [1974], 'Matter as Goo: Comments on Grene's Paper', *Synthese*, *28*, 71–7.

Ross, W. D., *Aristotle: Metaphysics*, 2 vols. (London, 1924); corrected 1953.

—— [1928], *The Works of Aristotle, viii. Metaphysica*, Oxford.

—— [1957], 'The Development of Aristotle's Thought', *PBA 43*, 63–78. (Reprinted in *BSS*, i. 1–13.)

Scaltsas, T. [1985], 'Substratum, Subject, and Substance', *AP 5*, 215–40.

Schofield, M. [1972], '*Metaphysics* Z3: Some Suggestions', *Phr 17*, 97–101.

Sellars, W. S. [1957], 'Substance and Form in Aristotle', *JP 54*, 688–99.

Smith, J. A. [1921], '*Tode ti* in Aristotle', *CR 35*, 19.

Solmsen, F. [1958], 'Aristotle and Prime Matter', *JHI 19*, 243–52.

Stahl, D. [1981], 'Stripped Away', *Phr 26*, 177–80.

Sykes, R. D. [1975], 'Form in Aristotle', *Philosophy 50*, 311–31.

White, N. P. [1971], 'Aristotle on Sameness and Oneness', *PR 80*, 177–97.

Williams, C. J. F. [1982], *Aristotle: De Generatione et Corruptione* (tr. and comm.), Clarendon Aristotle series, Oxford.

Woods, M. J. [1967], 'Problems in *Metaphysics* Z13', in J. M. E. Moravcsik (ed.), *Aristotle* (Garden City, NY), 215–38.

—— [1974/5], 'Substance and Essence in Aristotle', *PAS 75*, 167–80.

—— [1991], 'Universals and Particular Forms in Aristotle's *Metaphysics*', *OSAP Supp. Vol.*, 41–56.

GLOSSARY

αἰτία, αἴτιον	cause
ἀντικείμενον	opposite
ἀόριστος	indeterminate
ἁπλῶς	without qualification, simply
ἀρχή	principle; *also* origin, beginning, starting-point
γένος	genus
διαφορά	differentia
δύναμις	capacity, potentiality
δυνάμει	potentially
εἶδος	form
ἐναντίον	opposite
ἐνέργεια	actuality
ἐνεργείᾳ	actually
ἐντελέχεια	actuality
ἐντελεχείᾳ	actually
ἰδέα	Form (i.e. Platonic form)
καθ' αὑτό	in its own right
καθ' ἕκαστον	particular
καθόλου	universal, universally
κατὰ συμβεβηκός	coincidentally
λόγος	*usually* formula (*but the word has other uses too*)
μορφή	shape
ὁρισμός	definition
οὐσία	substance
πάθος	attribute; *also* affection
σημαίνειν	signify
στέρησις	privation
στοιχεῖον	element, letter
συνειλημμένον	(whole) taken together
σύνολον	combined whole
σχῆμα	shape, figure
τί ἐστι	what (a thing) is, a what-it-is
τί ἦν εἶναι	what being is (for a thing), a what-being-is
τόδε τι	a this
ὕλη	matter
ὑποκείμενον	underlying thing
χωριστός	separable
ψυχή	soul
ὡρισμένος	determinate

GENERAL INDEX

This index is principally an index to the text. Since the commentary contains the page and line numbers of the text, it can be used also as a subject-index to the commentary. There are a few extra entries in square brackets which refer directly to the commentary. (These concern words not occurring in the text, comments not straightforwardly indexed to the text, or something similar.)

INDEX OF PERSONS

This index lists the authors referred to in the commentary.

INDEX OF PASSAGES

This index lists the writings of Aristotle referred to in the commentary, excluding *Metaphysics Z* and *H*.

(a) In the Metaphysics (by book and chapter)

(b) Elsewhere (by work and book)

Printed in the United Kingdom
by Lightning Source UK Ltd.
103899UKS00001B/86

9 780198 239475